the Unofficial Guide™ to Buying or Leasing a Car

Donna Howell

Macmillan • USA

Macmillan General Reference
A Simon & Schuster Macmillan Company
1633 Broadway
New York, New York 10019-6785

ISBN: 0-02-862524-2

Manufactured in the United States of America

10 9 8 7 6 5 4 3 2 1

First edition

For Dad

…and with special thanks to Jennifer Farthing and Matthew X. Kiernan at Macmillan, for their great help.

Contents

The *Unofficial Guide* Reader's Bill of Rights

We Give You More Than the Official Line

Welcome to the *Unofficial Guide* series of Lifestyles titles—books that deliver critical, unbiased information that other books can't or won't reveal—*the inside scoop*. Our goal is to provide you with the *most accessible, useful* information and advice possible. The recommendations we offer in these pages are not influenced by the corporate line of any organization or industry; we give you the hard facts, whether those institutions like them or not. If something is ill-advised or will cause a loss of time and/or money, we'll give you ample warning. And if it is a worthwhile option, we'll let you know that, too.

Armed and Ready

Our hand-picked authors confidently and critically report on a wide range of topics that matter to smart readers like you. Our authors are passionate about their subjects, but have distanced themselves enough from them to help you be armed and protected, and help you make educated decisions as you go through your process. It is our intent that, from having read this book, you will avoid the pitfalls everyone else falls into and get it right the first time.

Don't be fooled by cheap imitations; this is the genuine article *Unofficial Guide* series from Macmillan Publishing. You may be familiar with our proven track record of the travel *Unofficial Guides*, which have more than three million copies in print. Each year, thousands of travelers—new and old— are armed with a brand new, fully updated edition of the flagship *Unofficial Guide to Walt Disney World*, by Bob Sehlinger. It is our intention here to provide you with the same level of objective authority that Mr. Sehlinger does in his brainchild.

The Unofficial Panel of Experts

Every work in the Lifestyle *Unofficial Guides* is intensively inspected by a team of three top professionals in their fields. These experts review the manuscript for factual accuracy, comprehensiveness, and an insider's determination as to whether the manuscript fulfills the credo in this Reader's Bill of Rights. In other words, our Panel ensures that you are, in fact, getting "the inside scoop."

Our Pledge

The authors, the editorial staff, and the Unofficial Panel of Experts assembled for *Unofficial Guides* are determined to lay out the most valuable alternatives available for our readers. This dictum means that our writers must be explicit, prescriptive, and above all, direct. We strive to be thorough and complete, but our goal is not necessarily to have the "most" or "all" of the information on a topic; this is not, after all, an encyclopedia. Our objective is to help you narrow down your options to the best of what is available, unbiased by affiliation with any industry or organization.

In each *Unofficial Guide* we give you:

- Comprehensive coverage of necessary and vital information

- Authoritative, rigidly fact-checked data

- The most up-to-date insights into trends

- Savvy, sophisticated writing that's also readable

- Sensible, applicable facts and secrets that only an insider knows

Special Features

Every book in our series offers the following six special sidebars in the margins that are devised to help you get things done cheaply, efficiently, and smartly.

1. "Timesaver"—tips and shortcuts that save you time.

2. "Moneysaver"—tips and shortcuts that save you money.

3. "Watch Out!"—more serious cautions and warnings.

4. "Bright Idea"—general tips and shortcuts to help you find an easier or smarter way to do something.

5. "Quote"—statements from real people that are intended to be prescriptive and valuable to you.

6. "Unofficially..."—an insider's fact or anecdote.

We also recognize your need to have quick information at your fingertips, and have thus provided the following comprehensive sections at the back of the book:

1. **Glossary:** Definitions of complicated terminology and jargon.

2. **Resource Guide:** Lists of relevant agenices, associations, institutions, Web sites, etc.

3. **Recommended Reading List:** Suggested titles that can help you get more in-depth information on related topics.

4. **Important Documents:** "Official" pieces of information you need to refer to, such as government forms.

5. **Important Statistics:** Facts and numbers presented at-a-glance for easy reference.

6. **Index.**

Letters, Comments, and Questions from Readers

We strive to continually improve the *Unofficial* series, and input from our readers is a valuable way for us to do that.

Many of those who have used the *Unofficial Guide* travel books write to the authors to ask questions, make comments, or share their own discoveries and lessons. For Lifestyle *Unofficial Guides*, we would also appreciate all such correspondence, both positive and critical, and we will make best efforts to incorporate readers' feedback and comments in revised editions of this work.

How to write to us:

Unofficial Guides
Macmillan Lifestyle Guides
Macmillan Publishing
1633 Broadway
New York, NY 10019
Attention: Readers' Comments

The *Unofficial Guide* Panel of Experts

The *Unofficial Guide* editorial team recognizes that you've purchased this book with the expectation of getting the most authoritative, carefully inspected information currently available. Toward that end, on each and every title in this series, we have selected a minimum of three "official" experts comprising the "Unofficial Panel" who painstakingly review the manuscripts to ensure: factual accuracy of all data; inclusion of the most up-to-date and relevant information; and that, from an insider's perspective, the authors have armed you with all the necessary facts you need—but the institutions don't want you to know.

For *The Unofficial Guide to Buying or Leasing a Car,* we are proud to introduce the following panel of experts:

> **Scott Landsman** Scott Landsman's automotive career started in 1948 when he was hired as a sales trainee in a Packard dealership in New York City. In his 50-year career in the retail auto industry, he has owned three new Hudson

Pacemaker agencies, two automobile leasing companies, and a school bus manufacturing and sales company.

Jonathan Banks and **Brian Jensen** are Senior Editors at *Automotive Lease Guide* (ALG) in Santa Barbara, California. ALG is generally regarded as the leading provider of residual values and lease-related analysis for the automotive industry.

Introduction

Welcome to your own private love affair with the automobile. They say it's an American thing, but it really stretches through borders to wherever there are drivers and lengths of open road, or simply commuters glad to be safely ensconced in their own air-conditioned vessels for the ride home from work.

Perhaps a fresh start beckons. You see shiny new cars everywhere and daydream of driving something different, something better. Or, you're shopping out of necessity. Whatever the reason, you're about to become one of the millions of Americans who will buy a vehicle this year. Or maybe you'll lease. And maybe a sport utility instead of a car. So many choices!

Don't apologize for being uncertain, even wary. Those feelings are clear, reasonable symptoms of new car fever and they go right along with that giddy anticipatory tingle. Everyone looks forward to getting a new set of wheels, yet no one wants to be taken for a ride.

The growing number of auto makers and models means competition for buyers' eyes has never been stronger. As if the choice wasn't hard enough, recently a major annual auto show saw the introduction of more than 60 new cars. With the average price of a new car having broken the psychological $20,000 mark, buying an automobile is a high-stakes choice. Add technological mystery and fear of hardcore negotiating to that, and it's no wonder seven of ten people surveyed consider the car buying process overwhelming.

But driving away in your dream car won't be a nightmare if you employ a little planning and knowledge. Part I of this book will help you through automotive adolescence. This is where you can prepare to shop effectively, by first getting a handle on the best vehicle for your needs and price range. We want to stress that the bottom line is not only financial. You may not be cut out for leasing, or for buying used, for instance, depending on some points about how you choose to live your life (or how you habitually live your life, anyway). In Part I we'll look not only at the money aspect but also the psychological impact buying and leasing has.

Your decision to get a new set of wheels probably started off simply—"I need a new car," or "I want a new red convertible!" We think after you've considered all the pertinent points, evaluated different models, and so on, you'll want to narrow down your search by re-asking one simple question: "Why do I want a new car, again?" It's easy to get lost in the car-shopping maze, so stay focused on your real reasons for starting all this in the first place. Cut a picture out of a magazine and tack it to a mirror if that's what it takes.

Once you have in mind why it is you most want a new vehicle, we'll help you sort out the differences between necessities, expectations, preferences, and extras. In our illustration just mentioned, for instance, the first guy needs a dependable set of wheels, period. The second car-shopper sounds like she has "sports car" pretty high on the list of necessities. Different necessities for different people, no matter how nonbasic they sound.

Also, if you're so caught up in new car fever that you hadn't thought of talking over your decision with your spouse, another family member, or significant other, we hope to change your mind. A car is often right behind a house as the largest purchase a person may make in his or her lifetime, so the automobile has a lot to do with family finances.

By the way, how much were you planning to spend on that car? Statistics suggest that on average Americans spend 7% of their incomes on transportation. But that's an average, and even double that is acceptable to some consumer credit counselors. We'll help you sort out what easily-calculated percentage is right for you. Remember that the cost of a new car isn't just the price you pay for it. The cost of financing, taxes, and extras can easily add even $10,000 to a typical vehicle.

That's one of the reasons so many people are turning to leasing now—the cost of new car ownership is getting out of reach for more and more

Americans. Leasing lets you drive more car for lower payments than buying. So what's the deal with leasing? If you find a good "deal" on both, the cost of leasing a new car can actually equal out to about the same cost as buying it, based on the presumption that you're going to sell it when you're finished with financing. So it makes all sorts of sense to lease, doesn't it?

If you're always a new car driver, it indeed may. But one top point about leasing—that you're paying just for the vehicle's depreciation and not the vehicle—is also a huge drawback. You're paying the depreciation just when the depreciation is phenomenally large. A used car buyer faces a less steep depreciation slope. Don't worry, we'll run you through a series of questions to determine where both your heart and finances are with the trilemma of buy new, buy used, or lease.

While you're doing a qualitative review of the models out there that you might want to drive, you'll (we hope) be considering safety, among a number of other important factors. Did you ever think about crash tests, and how well the vehicle you want would perform? Safety is an easy thing to dismiss—obviously no normal driver wants to have an accident, that's why they're called that—but safety can seem very important at two junctures: if you are indeed involved in (or nearly involved in) an accident, and when you price insurance on your new car. We'll show you, among other things, how crash testing is done. Did you know that a good crash-test score only compares vehicles of about the same weight? It's a big deal. Your life is at stake. Do whatever you want, but think about it first.

Generally speaking, the heavier and bigger the vehicle, the safer experts say it is likely to be. But there's also this story from a rental car agent: A young woman came in to rent a car after having been in an accident with a bus. Though her insurance would pay $20 or $25 per day toward a vehicle, she decided to rent a model that went for more than double the cost. The only model she would rent was the same kind she had been in when she had the accident, suffering minor injuries. And it wasn't the largest car the rental agency had—it was among the smallest. She was convinced that the model's sturdy frame construction had saved her life, and couldn't be swayed from that opinion.

The moral of the story is that either a) some rental car customers have odd requests or b) size and weight aren't everything, though they help. We hear announcements frequently about how carmakers are striving for that light, easy-on-the-fuel-intake vehicle, and worry a bit. Are crumple zones everything they're cracked up to be? Are the airbags really getting safer? Kudos to every automotive engineer doing his or her best to make an economical, stylish car without sacrificing (or better, while improving) safety. Yet we'll also say a good consumer relies on good, common sense and takes everything with a grain of salt (at a discount).

In Chapter 2 you'll get a handle on what constitutes safety, as well as some other seemingly amorphous terms like "reliability" (what is it?!) and "performance" (yes, want that). Reliability is important to all but aficionados of the most temperamental racing vehicles, who doubtless have a fallback vehicle when the super sportster is out of commission. But reliability to one consumer may mean never having to take the car in for service, an indication of a new car purchase or lease candidate. Another may be willing to tolerate a few trips to the mechanic, if it doesn't become a habit, in exchange for sizable savings. And guess what? You don't have to guess how reliable a vehicle's likely to be—we'll show you where to find long-term reliability rankings on the car you're interested in.

As you're narrowing in on the car you want, you're at a distinct advantage if you're comfortable using the Internet. The availability of truly helpful data has improved immensely over the past couple of years—and you can take advantage of the resources from scanning for cars of interest through investigating different models, to pricing them, buying them, and handling aftersell items like insurance.

Part II of this book deals specifically with shopping for your new car—how you can start from your armchair with a good car price annual and move right along to investigating dealers in your area and then making dealership visits. You have a lot more choices than even five years ago. Did you know there are now dealers where you don't have to haggle over the price of a car? Saturn, for instance, has "one-price" dealers, and dealerships representing other manufacturers are catching on that consumers appreciate direct, fair dealing.

You can find new car lots with many makes and models under the same sign, high-volume dealerships with every conceivable variation on a single make, and now you can also find a lot of variety in used car sales. Used car megadealerships have arisen where everything from flat pricing to warranties are featured. The proliferation of lease cars coming in at the end of their terms gives consumers a healthy crop of late-model used cars to choose from. Some of these are now "certified" in top condition and even have extended manufacturer warranties. It's a far cry from used car sales of years past. Though for the deepest discounts, used car shopping from private parties may be your best bet outside of an auction. Yes, we'll discuss those, too—but they're only for the hardiest car shoppers!

Part III is a numbers game—pricing and financing, two hefty topics you can't afford to be uninformed about. We'll take an Unofficial look at those official-looking sticker prices. What are they? More than you should pay! Did you know even "dealer cost" includes a profit? By the end of Part III you should know the bottom line on vehicle pricing and just how low a bottom dollar most dealers will take. New car pricing isn't the only type that's confusing, either. Used car pricing can be either trade-in (wholesale) or retail, and even those numbers aren't set in stone. If you've heard someone speak of the "Blue Book price," you may have wondered what it is and how it's calculated. You'll find out in Chapter 6.

And those who've leased before know new and used car purchase prices are kindergarten stuff compared to the intricate and clandestine windings of lease pricing. We'll tell you what those little lease pieces are and how they fit together, as well as guide you through a worksheet to compare leasing to buying.

Chapter 7 deals with the second-biggest expense in your car deal—the financing. You can start improving your odds of a great rate far in advance of actually purchasing or leasing a car, by the way—

by taking a look at your consumer credit report. Depending on where you shop and what your credit rating is, the annual percentage rate a shopper is offered could vary even 10 percentage points—a frighteningly wide swing. We'll show you how to get a hold of your credit report and tell you what to do about it when you see it.

It's a good idea to get preapproval on a bank loan when you're in the homestretch of car shopping—that way you'll have a ready comparison to a dealer's offered rate. And while having some cash for a down payment is advisable, paying for your entire purchase in cash may not be. We'll explain why.

One thing to watch out for, incidentally, is a type of dealer financing that's done "according to the rule of 78s." It's a method of calculating interest charges that favors the lender because most of the interest in a loan is paid off before most of the principal is paid off. What does this mean in real world terms? Say you buy a car, finance it with the dealer and a year down the road the economy's changed, interest rates have dropped, your credit file is looking a heck of a lot brighter and you decide, "I'll refinance!" (to save some money). When you check out your financing papers and do some figuring, you find out you haven't really scratched the surface of paying off the actual car—so refinancing wouldn't save you. A simple interest loan from a bank (even a variable rate loan) in this case could potentially have saved you some money.

Part IV of *The Unofficial Guide to Buying or Leasing a Car* is dedicated just to those who are thinking about buying a used car. When is it to your advantage? How can you get a great deal from a private party, what if you're itching to try getting a bottom-dollar deal at auction? You'll be thoroughly briefed on the topics in Chapter 8.

Buying used means you've got more variables to deal with when it comes to the specific model you want. Is it low mileage? How do you know if it's in good shape? Chapter 9 explains how to inspect a used car and what to ask the seller, as well as when to call out the mechanic to really check it out.

In Part V, those leaning toward leasing can learn if they really are candidates, and for the skittish we've included a section on how to know when it's really a bad idea. Though you're not exactly married to your car when you lease, when you own your car you at least don't have to have it in by curfew. Leasing is best cut out for those who don't rack up miles on their cars, and who don't mind a few restrictions in exchange for being able to drive a nice, new car at a much lower monthly payment rate than the purchasing customer.

Leasing has its own lexicon—if you don't know what a money factor is, you will, and we'll explain why one of the first things you should look for in a car to lease is a great resale value. Yes, really, that's one of the first things you should look for. Chapter 10 can tell you why. The government has tried to make leasing a little safer for consumers with the Consumer Leasing Act, which spells out plain-language disclosures dealers must make about leasing typical cars. If you've ever taken a close look at a lease ad in the newspaper, you know that plain-language disclosures are desperately necessary. Follow the rule of "if it sounds too good to be true, it probably is" when looking at car ads of any type, by the way. One legitimate thing you can turn to a car ad for, however, is foreknowledge of incentives such as rebates or promotional financing.

In Part VI, we'll get to the nitty-gritty negotiating, walk you through a typical visit to the dealership, and also give you some tips on negotiating with a private party when you're buying used. And unless you trade in your old car to a dealer, you could soon become one of those private party sellers. You might make more money disposing of your old car that way, but you could save on taxes by trading it in at a dealership. We'll help you sort out that decision.

Dealing with salesmen isn't fun and games for most people, but some can be genuinely helpful. Yet watch your wallet—as the consumer, you're the one who has to protect yourself from being overcharged. How do you negotiate with a sales expert who polishes his routine day in and day out? Answer a question of his, "So if I can knock $200 off the price, you'll buy today?" with one of your own, "Can you knock off $400?" It's also important to come across as a serious buyer, but not as an easy close. You want the salesman to pay attention to you, answer your questions and arrange test-drives, but not assume you'll pay top dollar because you're an eager buyer. More tips are in Chapter 12.

After that all-important test-drive (for which we'll give you a checklist to complete), and after you've decided what car you want and from whom you want it, it's time to make the deal. Part VII is devoted to doing that right, from deciding how much to pay to watching out for the after-sell, which is where dealers make some of their biggest profits (after you thought their selling was over). What about rust protection? Is that necessary? And what if the dealer tries to sell you insurance?

We'll tell you what to expect at signing time, and follow up on some of those dangling questions that only seem to occur once you're actually in the middle of a situation—"What about insurance, can I drive my new car home?"; "When do I get my license plate?"; "What do I do with the title?"

Once you've made your best deal, you still have to officially take delivery of the car—we'll show you how to check everything over and make sure it's in great shape before you sign. Don't sign for delivery with any dealer promises left unfulfilled or if the car is not up to your expectations.

This guide will also clue you in to some warranty talk, scheduled maintenance basics, and extras like buying good insurance cheaply. We'll also address that heaven-forbid scenario of "What do I do if I just bought a lemon?!" with the skinny on lemon laws and other legal recourse, as well as recalls and how to take advantage of so-called "secret warranties" (they could save you a bundle on repairs but you have to be inquisitive and persistent).

Why should you take the time and effort to complete worksheets throughout this book, check tables, and absorb definitions? Because making a deal on a car—new or used, lease or purchase—can have huge implications. Calling a dealer for a quote on a typical luxury-level car can elicit initial price variances of more than $10,000. With lower-priced car models, the variance might still be a couple thousand dollars. Figure how long you work to make that sum of money, and consider how much you could be saving.

The information you find in this book is designed to be helpful to you before and during your deal making—we have included a wealth of worksheets to help you figure important price points, tables that let you gauge, for instance, one financing deal against another, and figures to show you what things actually look like—a lease contract, for example. So please grab that pencil and use this *Unofficial Guide* as your personal workbook to a great deal on your next set of wheels!

So You're Thinking About New Wheels

PART I

GET THE SCOOP ON...
The kind of vehicle that's right for you ▪
How much car you can really afford ▪
What other people buy and what they spend ▪
Points you should talk over with your
closest companions ▪ What you'll need before
you go car shopping

Why Do You Want to Buy a Car?

Chapter 1

One hundred years ago, the word "automobile" was used to describe the horseless carriages many inventors were building. Brothers Frank and Charles Duryea were the first to produce more than one at a time. Their factory in Springfield, Massachusetts cranked out 13 vehicles in 1896, and thus began the automobile industry in this country.

Since Henry Ford's first Model T rolled off the line 90 years ago, more than 637 million vehicles have been sold in the United States, and consumers have spent $5 trillion to buy them. Cars serve our transportation needs, rank among our biggest-ticket purchases, and sometimes express who we are.

Shopper, know thyself. The first step to buying or leasing the right car is to fully understand why you're thinking about getting a new car. What are your real motivations? We'll analyze concrete needs, wants, and what you can afford in this chapter, but take a moment to remember whatever it was that first prompted you to think, "I want a new car."

If you've just been awarded a promotion and that bonus is burning a hole in your pocket, you're a different kind of car buyer from the person whose old auto is on its last legs. And both are different from the couple who is expecting a baby and needs a minivan. Be true to yourself. Are you buying simply to commute and get around town in a mild climate? Four-wheel drive might not be so necessary. And if a new car means a new image to you, admit it, and look for what fits the bill.

Individual considerations

Logically, you should buy or lease the car that best suits your requirements, desires, and lifestyle for the lowest price. So spell out those factors before you shop, then shop confidently.

We'll start with general questions and then identify three categories—your needs, your expectations, and what you'd like in an automobile. Then we'll do some prioritizing. At the end of the process, you'll have a road map to keep you on track amid all those car-shopping possibilities.

Questions to ask yourself

No matter what your price range, there's room to think about your own aesthetic preferences, and whether you esteem great engineering and innovative features, or simply want a good basic car without a lot of gadgetry.

How do you think of yourself? As a rugged individualist with a terrain-worthy vehicle that can go anywhere? Or as stylish and understated, in need of fluid design lines and an elegant interior; no faux-Navajo print in sight? There's a car marketed with you in mind, no matter where you fall in the spectrum. It's a question of taste and practicality to get what pleases you—you'll probably be in your car almost daily, and spending a prominent chunk of your income on it into the 21st century.

If you have your eye on a model that you like, that intuitive preference might be so strong you don't want to consider another. But verify that it's right for your lifestyle rather than just a passing attraction. Ask yourself the following general questions (note where you have *no* preference—you may be able to save some money):

- Is your ideal vehicle specifically a car, sport utility vehicle, or light truck?

- Will you be hauling sports equipment or other bulky materials, or towing anything?

- How many passengers will you usually have? How many must you be able to accommodate occasionally?

- Do you prefer a two-door coupe or a four-door sedan? A hatchback? A convertible?

- Automatic or manual transmission?

- Do you want or need four-wheel drive? Are there snowstorms where you live? Is there rough terrain?

- How much power do you need? Will you be doing mostly city driving or longer highway stretches? What about steep hills or mountain roads?

- Do you want a large car, a midsize model, or a compact?

- Do you prefer sports car styling or something more conservative? A luxury model or a basic commuter vehicle?

Watch Out!
Profit margins can be high on luxury models and sport utility vehicles. Make sure there's substance behind the price tag rather than cheap parts that look fancy. Before you buy, also consider a well-outfitted basic model with all your favorite options.

- Is the "big and tall" men's store a frequent stop on your shopping rounds? Will you have over-sized passengers?

- What about age and mobility? Will elderly or handicapped passengers need easy access?

- Is this a car you're buying because of kids? What about safety locks, accessibility for child seats, and other features?

- How many miles per year will you likely drive? How important is fuel economy to you?

- Do you prefer an American-made car, an Asian import, or a European car?

- How old or new a car do you prefer?

- What options do you need or want—air-conditioning, a sunroof, leather seating? Something else?

- Over how many years do you prefer to pay for the car?

If this is a car you'll be *sharing* with your spouse, go over the possibilities again for his or her input.

Criteria to discuss with your spouse or significant other

Some things should be discussed with your spouse or significant other, regardless of whether he'll be sharing the driver's seat. The best advice is to get his feedback on the previous questions and to talk candidly along these lines in a comfortable setting:

- Am I being an idiot?

- What have I overlooked that will matter later?

- Is this auto something you'll be comfortable with me/us having?

- Whose name is this car going to be in? Who is paying for it?

Timesaver
What do you love or hate about the car you have? You cared enough to buy or lease it once, and it speaks volumes about your needs and preferences. Write down the pros and cons—it's a quick way to get a handle on what or what not to get next time.

- Is this an appropriate price range? Can we afford it?

- What other costs in our lives might affect this purchase?

- Babies? Beach vacations? The ballet? Four-wheeling with the guys? Let's talk lifestyle.

Remember that when couples argue, it's most often about money. Evaluating a car purchase with your closest companion isn't only respectful, it can help to thwart future retorts of "I told you so."

Deciding what you want in a car

Armed with the lifestyle and cost points just considered, you can now narrow down the most important. Nitty-gritty needs are where to begin. Later, we'll look at your general expectations and a range of wants, preferences, and options.

What's a necessity, what's just a nicety?

It's bottom line time. Rank what you really must have in your new car in order of importance (1,2,3...). Don't list yet those things you're less certain about, or those you would like but don't have to have.

Checklist 1.1   Car Purchase Necessities

____ Specific price range (from $_____ to $_____)

____ Monthly payments (no more than $_____ over _____ years)

____ Type of vehicle (car, sport utility vehicle, light truck)

____ Room to haul sports equipment or other big items

____ Room for at least ____ passengers

____ Number of doors (sedan, coupe, hatchback)

___   Automatic transmission

___   Four-wheel drive

___   Strong power train (six-cylinder or higher engine, and other factors)

___   Specific car size (large, midsize, compact)

___   Styling (sporty, conservative, luxury, basic)

___   Favorite color

___   Sports car performance

___   Roomy interior and adequate headroom

___   Easy accessibility for handicapped or elderly passengers

___   Accessibility and safety features for children and infants

___   Very good fuel economy

___   High safety ratings

___   Import or domestic (circle one)

___   Specific make or model

___   New or used (circle one)

___   Certain options: Air? Sunroof? Leather seating? Premium sound system? What else?

_____

___   Other _____

Now that you've got the real necessities down on paper, you're better prepared to consider different makes and models, and to reach a rational, comfortable buying decision. Think about your top three must-haves.

If you found, for instance, that you don't absolutely have to have a sport utility vehicle but do need some cargo room, you might take a look at some of the newer station wagons, larger hatchbacks, or vans on the market. Although they may not be what you want, over the past few years designers have been devoting their attention to the needs of people like you. You might be surprised to find that those vehicles have changed significantly, and many makers are offering different versions.

Be realistic as well. If the extra room you need is only for an annual family trip, consider the possibility of renting a larger vehicle for that week or two. Getting a smaller car might not only cost thousands less, but also might fit your everyday needs better.

Expectations

Necessities can be clear-cut, but expectations are your beliefs about what defines a good car. They're very solidly in the realm of opinion. What are yours? You probably expect a certain level of reliability, safety, and performance. And whether you've thought consciously of it or not, you have some expectation of how long you'll be keeping your new car and of its cost to you over the long run.

We'll go into the details of what constitutes reliability, safety and performance in the next chapter, and introduce you to the relevant industry rankings as you start to research different models.

Consider your own views on reliability, safety, performance and handling, length of ownership, and cost. If necessary, revise your list of "must haves."

1. Reliability

Reliability is wanted and expected, but we all have a different idea about what it means. Is your definition of reliability that your car is never in the shop and needs only minimal required maintenance during the entire time you own it? If that's the case, and you feel very strongly about it, you'll probably be

Moneysaver
Someone else's lease car could be your bargain buy. Many more lease returns have been popping up on dealers' lots than used to, due to the popularity of leasing. You may be particularly in luck if you're thinking of a small car or a large sport utility vehicle. And a continuing supply of lease returns should help keep all used car prices down.

Timesaver
Remembering what's really motivating you to look for a new set of wheels can be a handy shopping tool later on—an acid test when deciding between fine points of vehicles.

Unofficially...
Today, 198 million vehicles are in operation, according to the National Automobile Dealers Association. And you thought the freeway looked crowded before you heard this?

happiest leasing or buying new with a full warranty if you can afford it.

No one wants a clunker, but if you can tolerate an occasional trip to the repair shop, buying a used car in nice condition with low mileage can save you money over a new car. It also allows you to get into a better category of car—perhaps a more comfortable luxury model; one with more power, better performance, or styling that more adequately appeals to your tastes. You'll have to weigh your car's reliability reputation against the other things important to you—zippy performance, price, or outright obsession with a particular make and model.

2. Safety

You should also take a hard look at your safety expectations before you buy. If you've known someone involved in a serious accident or if you're getting a car to accommodate a new baby, you might naturally give safety a higher priority. Airbags and other advancements are improving safety, but they're certainly not without controversy. Lighter design materials coupled with specifically engineered *crumple zones* mean that the accident equation is very different from the age when cars were heavy hunks of steel. As you consider which car to get, ask about safety records and ratings. Insurance carriers can help you, too—knowing how safe one car is versus another is vital to the survival of their business.

Moneysaver
If you're afraid of used car repair bills, take heart. Manufacturers and dealers are increasingly offering good and lengthy warrantees on the preowned cars they sell. Many are lease returns with low mileage.

3. Performance and handling

A rule of thumb is that you probably want performance from your new car to be as good as your current car's performance. If you have an older, larger car now and you're thinking economy and a four-cylinder vehicle, you could be in for a rude performance surprise. Likewise, if you have an older, small-engine vehicle, you may be impressed by engineering modifications that have improved performance on newer versions.

The performance and handling you need is that which you feel most comfortable with. Can you pass another car, or enter a freeway safely and easily? Do the brakes respond gracefully but firmly? How will the car respond in the rain or on ice? Is steering the car difficult for you? Does the vehicle feel balanced, or is the center of gravity so high that you're personally uncomfortable maneuvering it? Sport utility vehicles, pickups, and vans have to be driven differently than cars. Make sure you're really at ease behind the wheel.

4. Length of ownership

How long do you expect to keep the car you'll buy or lease? Look back at the cars you've bought before—how old they were when you got them, how long you've kept them, and how long you've been happy with them. If you're the sort who only wants to drive a new car and you're fine with the idea that you'll always be making car payments, leasing instead of buying may work out more economically for you in the long run. You'll find out how to evaluate that issue later in this book, but do take time to think about your general preference now.

Reliability reputation becomes more and more important the longer you'll be driving the vehicle, and repair costs for certain imports can far outpace average repair costs on other cars (something to keep in mind when you're considering buying a used car). Another reason to know how long you expect to keep a car has to do with financing terms

Bright Idea
You need adequate power. If you have any questions about your own preference, this is the time to test-drive friends' cars. And when renting a car, try out something similar to what you're considering buying.

and *trade-in value.* If you expect to keep a car for three years but are paying for it over five, beware owing more on your car than it's worth when you try to trade it in. If the dealership's made a big profit on you, you could wind up "buried" or "upside down" on your payments, in industry terms. We'll of course address ways to avoid that, and discuss ways to get a really good deal, in chapters to come.

> **"**
> When I recently went shopping, it was for a used car that looked the same as the current model year. Even though it's used, I didn't want it to look that way.
> —Rick
> **"**

What if you're looking for a good, reliable used car and you plan to keep it for as long as you reasonably can? If current styling is at all important to you, consider an established model that has stayed largely the same since your preferred year, and for which no major alterations are planned. Some vehicle models start looking old quickly, and some look quite respectable for a very long time—a point that matters if you don't want to be stuck in the automotive equivalent of a bell-bottom leisure suit.

5. Cost

The real cost of a car is not just the purchase price. Financing expenses, depreciation, maintenance, unexpected repairs, and insurance premiums figure into the picture—sometimes dramatically. From your present budget, work out how much you can reasonably afford per month for a car—payments, gasoline, insurance, and servicing.

If you have a model already in mind, call your insurance company and inquire how much more your policy would cost with a vehicle of that model and year. It could be a substantially higher figure, especially for sports cars or if you're moving up in price ranges.

You may be allowed to pay off a new car over six years. If you're getting a used car, be aware you may have to finance it over a shorter period—three or four years—and that financing rates tend to be higher on used vehicles.

Preferences and extras

You've decided what your necessities are, the things you won't do without, and you've evaluated your expectations. Now, what are the next most important things—your wants and preferences, the extras you'd like to have?

Use the questions you answered in Checklist 1.1 to construct your own top ten list. If your car-buying decision will involve a spouse or someone else with whom you'll be sharing the vehicle, do this together, of course.

Moneysaver
The value of a new car plummets as soon as you drive it off the dealer's lot. Let someone else pay the *depreciation* by vowing to buy a late-model used car with low mileage and plenty of warranty time left.

CHART 1.1   NEEDS VS. WANTS

List your necessities, preferences, and what you're very flexible about.

My basic reason for getting a car is _____.

Necessities	Preferences/Wants	Don't Care
1.	1.	1.
2.	2.	2.
3.	3.	3.
4.	4.	4.
5.	5.	5.
6.	6.	6.
7.	7.	7.
8.	8.	8.
9.	9.	9.
10.	10.	10.

More than 10 necessities? Write them in, but consider whether some belong in your Preferences/Wants category instead.

You ranked necessities from the list of general questions earlier in this chapter. Go back and rank your preferences and wants on that page, either by using a different color pen or noting them as "P1, P2, P3..." Then transcribe them here.

What you want vs. what you can afford

Now let's find out if your reality check will bounce. If you're already hearing strains of "You Can't Always Get What You Want," have patience. You'll get what you need, and we're going to try to include as many of those preferences as possible, too.

Setting your goals

You may see a clear pattern emerging from the exercises you've completed—the kind of car you want may now be obvious. But what do you do if your list looks like a creature not found in nature—an all-wheel-drive blue convertible sports car with child seats that fits 12? Maybe you're really thinking about two cars for your family, a blue convertible sports car for you and a minivan for hauling the kids. Buying used or leasing could make it feasible. Or consider not trading in your current car.

If all of your *must haves* and your top *preferences* aren't found in a single vehicle, try to visualize the two or three types of cars you could live with. Your goal might be *either* an entry-level European sedan, a relatively inexpensive, sporty Japanese model, or perhaps a preowned but respectable American sport utility vehicle. Though it sounds like a simple question, all the while ask yourself *why* you're looking for a new set of wheels, and try to answer with your choices.

See if you can come up with a general mission statement... "My goals for buying or leasing a car are _____, _____, and _____." It can be as simple as "My goals for buying or leasing a car are to get something reasonably decent to drive, to keep it for about three years, and to pay no more than $12,000."

Setting your budget

How on earth do you figure out how much you can prudently spend for a new set of wheels? Here, safe at home, with pencil and calculator, let's figure out how much you can afford.

By some estimates, Americans are said to spend roughly 7% of their income for transportation. But when compared to baby boomers, younger and older people may pay a larger percentage of their incomes on cars. The sad truth is that many Americans can't afford to buy new, and the market for preowned cars has been growing in response.

Using the 7% figure as a very conservative guideline, someone who makes $50,000 a year could buy a new car that is priced no more than $13,000. Monthly payments would be just over $200, assuming 5% dealer financing for five years and $3,000 down. There would be just $55 left over each month to pay for gas and oil, maintenance, insurance, and repairs.

Some consumer credit counselors simply recommend spending no more than 15% of your income on auto-related expenses, which certainly gives more breathing room than does the average transportation costs figure. Using this 15% as a guideline, a $50,000 annual salary breaks down to $625 as a monthly max. But remember, that payment has to include insurance, fuel, maintenance, repairs, and any fuzzy dice you feel compelled to adorn your new set of wheels with. So what's the ballpark amount you should consider spending on an automobile? You can find out by filling in a couple of simple worksheets.

Bright Idea
Fire up your budgeting software. Some popular programs include loan calculators. You can easily play with different purchase prices, interest rates, loan terms, monthly payments, and trade-in values to see what works for you.

WORKSHEET 1.1   HOW MUCH CAR CAN I AFFORD?

To get the Prudent Cash Price you should pay for a car, use your income and current car expenses as guidelines. First, figure your yearly Fuel & Upkeep Costs.

   $____ Fuel, Maintenance, Repairs, Insurance (per month)

× 12

= $____ Yearly Fuel & Upkeep

Make adjustments if the car you expect to get will have much better fuel economy or lower upkeep costs.

Now decide what portion of your income you will base your car purchase on (seven to 15% is suggested), and subtract Yearly Fuel & Upkeep from that figure to arrive at your Prudent Cash Price.

$____ Annual Income

× .07

= ____

– $____ Yearly Fuel & Upkeep

– $____ Any Additional Amount Insurance Will Cost You

= $____ Subtotal Prudent Cash Price

And perform a little calculation to cover the cost of sales tax and incidentals at purchase.

$____ Your state sales tax percentage plus 1% (6% sales tax would be stated as ".07")

× $____ Subtotal Prudent Cash Price

= $____ Sales Tax & Incidentals Allowance

One more step and you're done.

$____ Subtotal Prudent Cash Price

– $____ Sales Tax & Incidentals Allowance

= $____ Prudent Cash Price

Unofficially...
The homely little car that became a movie star named Herbie in the 1969 Disney movie *The Love Bug* is at it again. Volkswagen has restyled and rereleased the Beetle. The new version goes for upwards of $15,000, and VW expects to sell 50,000 in its first production year. Among its standard equipment features is a dashboard bud vase for those still into "flower power."

The "How Much Car Can I Afford?" worksheet shows how much you can spend on a new auto if you pay cash and want to stick between the 7% of income that the average American spends on transportation (remember that's just an average—many people spend more) and the 15% cap some consumer credit counselors suggest. Because you're probably not paying cash and you'd doubtless like to unload that old set of wheels, we've got to do more figuring.

WORKSHEET 1.2   I HAVEN'T GOT CASH, HOW MUCH CAR CAN I AFFORD?

From the Prudent Cash Price you just determined, subtract both the expected value of your trade-in and any down payment you expect to make.

$____ Prudent Cash Price

– $____ Value of Trade-In

– $____ Down Payment

= $____ Amount to be Financed

Now use the Financing Cost Scale (Table 1.1) to see how much interest you'll have to pay on a typical four-year loan.

$____ Prudent Cash Price

– $____ Financing Cost (from table)

= ____

+ $____ Value of Trade-In

= $____

× ____ Your State's Sales Tax (.05,.07, etc.)

= $____ Your Affordable Car Price

Your Affordable Car Price takes financing, sales tax, and insurance costs into account, but remember that it's just a rule of thumb.

The initial costs of automobile ownership add up. Consider that 3% of the total revenue of all states is the result of sales tax generated by the sale of new cars and trucks. That's not even the full story—your state may have a personal property tax on vehicles as well. Be sure to check on those insurance rates because changing the model or year of the car you drive can alter how much you owe by a substantial amount.

What about monthly payments? Generally, paying off a car loan over three years is very prudent and five years is the max for a new car. Although six years is not unheard of, the amount of interest you would pay and other factors could make it a bad choice.

You'll learn a lot more about budgeting and financing in the next few chapters of this book. It can't be said too early, though, that you shouldn't ever let a sales person do your budget figuring or advise you on how much you should spend.

Watch Out!
Don't forget to factor in what you'll have to pay in sales tax and personal property tax. Consumers pay $60 billion annually in motor vehicle-related taxes.
(Source: National Automobile Dealers Association)

If you're thinking of buying new from a dealer who may offer promotional financing, try using a 4% loan rate. If you're buying used and your credit is good, try the 10 or 12% column. (Just find the place where it meets with your Amount to be Financed.) But always check prevailing interest rates in your area before you deal. Interest rates change—keep current!

TABLE 1.1   FINANCING COST SCALE

How much will you spend on interest over the life of your loan? This table gives you a good idea of the real cost hidden inside an extra percentage point or two.

Amount to be Financed/Loan Rate (4-year)

	2%	4%	6%	8%	10%	12%	14%	16%
$5,000	200	400	650	850	1,100	1,300	1,550	1,800
$10,000	400	850	1,250	1,700	2,150	2,650	3,100	3,600
$15,000	600	1,250	1,900	2,600	3,250	3,950	4,700	5,400
$20,000	850	1,700	2,550	3,450	4,350	5,300	6,250	7,200
$25,000	1,050	2,100	3,200	4,300	5,450	6,600	7,800	9,000
$30,000	1,250	2,500	3,800	5,150	6,500	7,900	9,350	10,800
$35,000	1,450	2,950	4,450	6,000	7,600	9,250	10,900	12,600
$40,000	1,650	3,350	5,100	6,850	8,700	10,550	12,450	14,400
$50,000	2,050	4,200	6,350	8,600	10,850	13,200	15,600	18,000

(Amounts are rounded to the nearest $50.)

Watch Out!
Sales lines such as "How much would you like to spend every month on payments?" can get you into trouble. In coming chapters, you'll learn how to figure what the dealer paid for the car and negotiate from that number.

There are many different pricing labels for automobiles, from the *Manufacturer's Suggested Retail Price* or *MSRP* (which may or may not mean the *sticker price*), to the *Dealer Invoice Price,* and wholesale or retail Blue Book rates. Leasing offers its own variations. For now, just compare Your Affordable Car Price to whatever advertised number you see.

Determining what is feasible

After all that figuring, take a break and browse. You've probably got some car models in mind, so check the Sunday newspaper classifieds and display ads for vehicles that sound like what you want, in your ballpark price range. Look for both new and used autos, but bear in mind that you could end up spending a lot more than what many new car ads seem to suggest, once your desired options and other things are added in. Or pick up one of the many full-color annual car pricing guides available and browse car-buying sites on the Internet (check Appendix C for a list of resources) to familiarize yourself with what's out there.

What can you get for your money?

The following table shows what cars Americans bought most frequently during 1997. The most popular model is Toyota's Camry—almost 400,000 of them rolled out of dealerships during the year.

TABLE 1.2   BEST-SELLING CARS BY PRICE RANGE

These models came out tops in car sales for 1997. They're sorted here by price range rather than rank.

Under $13,000	Honda Civic
	Chevrolet Cavalier
	Ford Escort
	Saturn
$13,000–$18,000	Toyota Camry
	Honda Accord
	Chevrolet Lumina
	Toyota Corolla
	Pontiac Grand Am
$18,000–$25,000	Ford Taurus

(Source: Ward's Automotive Reports)

The top-selling vehicle isn't actually a car at all. For the past many years, the Ford pickup has outsold its car and light-truck competition. Next up is Chevrolet's C/K pickup, and the Ford Explorer sport utility still outranks Taurus.

Top Twenty Vehicles in 1997 Sales

1. Ford pickup
2. Chevrolet pickup
3. Toyota Camry
4. Honda Accord
5. Ford Explorer
6. Ford Taurus

Moneysaver
Financing over 60 months instead of 48 or 36 will make your monthly payments lower, but in the end you could wind up spending quite a bit more on interest. Go for the shortest term you can handle unless your interest rate is very, very low. And remember, that interest rate can be negotiated.

Ranges reflect 1998 list prices.

7. Dodge Ram pickup   14. Saturn (GM)

8. Honda Civic   15. Ford Expedition

9. Chevrolet Cavalier   16. Chevrolet Lumina

10. Ford Ranger   17. Chevrolet Blazer

11. Dodge Caravan   18. Toyota Corolla

12. Ford Escort   19. Ford Windstar

13. Jeep Grand   20. Pontiac Grand Am
    Cherokee

(Source: Ward's Automotive Reports)

If you're thinking of going with the consumer trend toward sport utilities, be prepared to pay more than you might for a car. Prices for the most popular models run thousands of dollars more by category than entry prices for the most inexpensive popular automobiles.

TABLE 1.3   MOST POPULAR CONSUMER LIGHT TRUCK MODELS

Ranges reflect 1998 list prices.

These models were the top-selling light trucks in America for 1997.

Under $13,000	$13,000– $17,999	$18,000– $25,000	Over– $25,000
Ford Ranger pickup	Ford F-series pickup	Dodge C/K Caravan	Ford C/K Explorer
	Chevrolet C/K pickup	Chevrolet C/K Blazer	Jeep Grand C/K Cherokee
	Dodge Ram pickup		
	Ford C/K Windstar van		Ford Expedition

(Source: Ward's Automotive Reports)

The sales success of sport utilities and other light trucks has led to the introduction of new, economical model lines, though they're not yet represented among the hottest sellers. You can easily rack up options and spend several hundred to thousands of dollars more than the price of a base model on both trucks and cars.

Let's be realistic

You've figured out your needs and wants, and your thumbnail budget. You've also reviewed the best-selling cars. But what if you're still stuck? What if the only car that seems to fit your needs isn't in production yet and will cost twice your annual salary if it's ever offered for public consumption? What should you do?

Take a deep breath and start doodling in the fine art of compromise. If you don't think you'll be able to afford what you want, take another look at why you're buying a car in the first place, then start looking at *different* options that might satisfy you.

- A used sports car instead of a new budget car
- Leasing instead of buying
- A full-powered American car instead of a certain prestigious European
- Getting that Euro make you want, but without extras
- A used car to keep while you save for what you really want
- Keeping and upgrading the car you have

One in three new cars are leased rather than bought, and used car sales have been on the rise. Like you, many people want to drive a late-model car but are feeling a money crunch.

What do you want to avoid?

Since you've thoroughly thought out what you want in a car, you're ahead of the game. But what should you look out for as you research cars, shop, and

> 66
> Since it is Reason which shapes and regulates all other things, it ought not itself to be left in disorder.
> —Greek philosopher Epictetus (ca. A.D. 70)
> 99

finally make a deal? You don't need to swim in data, so follow a methodical approach and avoid anxiety.

Things you don't want to do:

- Pay too much
- Be talked into buying extras you don't need
- Get a car that's not right for you
- Buy a car with a body style about to change
- Or buy a car with bad resale prospects
- Or buy a car that has been damaged (with a *salvage title*)
- Let a salesman tell you how much you can afford
- Stress unnecessarily

Anticipating the overall experience: Ready, set...

Many people consider the car-buying process intimidating. But there's reason to take heart—the word is out that buying a new car or truck is getting easier. More than half of consumers agree that buying a car or truck is now easier than it was in the past, according to the National Automobile Dealers Association.

How long should shopping for and buying a car take?

The more time you have to wait and watch, the better your chance of getting the car you want at a very good price. Sometimes it seems like luck. A woman who followed ads in two states over a few months wound up serendipitously finding exactly the model she wanted on the way to work, at a dealership willing to offer a real bargain. The car had been accepted as a trade-in to clinch a sale, but hadn't attracted interest among the specialized dealer's usual clientele.

If you can take a few months, do, while checking ads and simply keeping your eyes open. Buying a specific used car or a very high-demand, out-of-stock new car can take the most time. There's also seasonality to consider—later in this book we'll go over the best times of the year for a bargain.

One month is a reasonable measure of time to adequately do your research, line up a loan, and find a new car you'll like, if you're diligent about it and not horribly choosy.

What am I going to need?

Popular automotive and consumer magazines put out annual chronicles filled with reviews of the year's new cars. I recommend picking up the one or two you're most comfortable with—and your selections should have plenty of pictures. If you think a used car is a possibility, spend a couple of dollars on the best local used car ad paper that has photos with its listings.

What else? Here's a short camping list of what you'll need:

- **Time:** As you move forward in the car-buying process, you'll need some spare time to research different automobiles, and then to shop and test-drive.

- **Ready cash:** If you've got plenty of time before you need to make a buying decision, take advantage of it. Keep your credit in good shape and accumulate as much available cash as you can. Dealers advertise cars for sale with 0% down, but the voice of conservatism says you should generally plan to at least be prepared to make a down payment of 20% (whether you decide to

Timesaver
If you have less than a month, seriously consider using a discount buying service for a new car or getting your used car from a reputable dealership (though you'll spend a bit more than you would buying from a private owner).

Bright Idea
The Internet can be a terrific resource for the used and new car buyer alike, so access to a computer is a plus.

or not). When buying a used car and going through a bank, you may be required to put 10% or more down in order to get the loan at all.

- **A trusted mechanic:** To look over a used car you might buy.
- **Clear title on your trade-in vehicle:** A necessity for selling it (so that a new owner can properly reregister the car with your state's motor vehicle department).

In the next chapter, we'll focus on your priorities in a car and evaluate concepts like safety, reliability, performance, and value. We'll also sort through that smorgasbord of available options. You're already on your way to a new set of wheels. Enjoy the trip.

Just the facts

- Thoroughly understand the difference between your underlying motivations for getting a car, your needs, expectations, and wants.

Moneysaver
Save now so you'll be able to pay 10%–20% or more in cash toward your new car. However, low manufacturer and dealer financing rates could make it smart to put as much of the purchase price as possible on credit. And you're more likely to hear about such financing options if the dealer doesn't think you have ready cash.

- Decide how much of your income to devote to transportation. One estimated average is 7% and some consumer credit counselors suggest a 15% cap, but talk to other people in your income bracket and with your lifestyle—many people pay a lot more than the average and manage well.

- Don't forget to figure in financing, tax, and insurance, which can be the biggest expenses in car ownership beyond sticker price.

- If the car you want is more than you can afford, consider buying used or leasing.

- Discuss car-buying plans with your spouse and ask for input, particularly on cost issues.

GET THE SCOOP ON...
Criteria to compare models ▪ Why safety is much
more important now ▪ Crunching numbers for
value, reliability, and performance ▪ Options
that pay for themselves

Getting to the Perfect Car

Chapter 2

So many new cars vie for your attention and dollars. How do you narrow down all those choices to an ideal few and then to the perfect one?

In the last chapter, you outlined what you want and need in a car. Now you need to find the cars that offer those features at the right price. In this chapter, we'll scout candidate cars and screen them, using some solid evaluative criteria.

Finding cars that meet your requirements

Homing in on new or used cars that meet your standards can be relatively easy—if you know what to look for. An abundance of information is aimed at you in dealer ad literature, and auto magazines make a big production out of annual buyers' guides. If you're an Internet fan, you're in an excellent position to make comparisons (and get that computer to help pay for itself).

Bright Idea
Springing for a well-illustrated magazine annual of new car models, prices, and basic features is worth the money. You can do this research entirely by phone or on the Internet, but having a good annual to flip through will cut frustration.

Timesaver
Even if you're leaning toward leasing, new car buyers' guides will do fine for the moment. One objective when you're lease shopping is to figure the real buying price out of all those lease numbers—so it's actually better to start shopping as if you're a buyer.

How to start screening

Begin with the type of car you're looking for (a mid-size sedan, for instance), a price range (under $20,000), along with your thoughts on whether you're leaning toward new or used (let's say new for now). You'll need some visual resources with basic statistics. Most rankings sort cars either by size and basic type (sports car versus economy car), or price.

You'll be able to compare the cars you like best (and can afford) against criteria for performance and reliability, safety, and value that will be described in this chapter. We'll also talk about styling and all the options available.

Where to look

If you think that there's a plethora of car models out there, wait until you see the number of new car annuals on the shelves. Some are stacked with stats on newsprint. A better idea at this point is to go for the visually appealing ones that you'll actually want to look through, with color pictures of many different car and truck models.

These guides exist for used car buyers as well. Although libraries often carry copies of auto annuals (ask the reference librarian), it's much easier having your own. Five minutes at a decent newsstand and you'll find your own favorite.

Most guides tend toward consumer or automotive specialty journalism. The first kind (such as the very good Kiplinger's annual *Buyer's Guide to New Cars & Trucks*) typically offers rankings in compact format and with money-relevant statistics such as insurance cost, resale value, etc. Auto aficionados set on getting from zero to sixty in the shortest amount of time will want to make a beeline for the other kind, often put out by auto specialty magazines, which may offer more extensive test-drive editorials and performance data.

The Internet is, of course, an invaluable resource for information—more so than ever before. Many of the new car buyers are using the Internet. Crash-test data and other comparison material is on the Web, and those databases are often searchable. More about actual buying services can be found in upcoming chapters—for now, the emphasis is on research.

We'll identify Web sites that provide specific data as we discuss each type of criterion that you may use in your car evaluation. Table 2.1 is a preliminary list of some useful major car sites. The breadth and scope of what's available may surprise even jaded Internet users.

TABLE 2.1   CAR CRITERIA ON THE INTERNET

National Highway Traffic Safety Administration
www.nhtsa.dot.gov

NHTSA Auto Safety Hot Line:
(800) 424-9393

Insurance Institute for Highway Safety
www.highwaysafety.org
(703) 247-1500

Microsoft CarPoint
www.carpoint.com

Bank Rate Monitor (for auto loan rates)
www.bankrate.com

Edmunds
www.edmunds.com

IntelliChoice
www.intellichoice.com

Kelley Blue Book
www.kbb.com

National Automobile Dealers Association
www.nada.com

You may find CD-ROMs put together by car manufacturers appealing, too, as you try to decide

Moneysaver
If you have only one or two cars in mind, consider getting promotional materials and performance statistics directly from a car manufacturer (toll-free phone numbers and Web sites are listed in Appendix C) or by stopping in at a dealer.

Some auto sites good for research offer links to making a purchase. (More about Internet car buying services can be found in Chapters 4 and 5.) There are a number of great sites out there—check current major links from your favorite search engine.

which car to go with. There are two advantages to taking the trouble to get them. Short videos can give you a better look at a model than anything except a test-drive, and many CDs feature visuals and information about a manufacturer's entire line of cars. Best for the graphics-hungry.

Your priorities

You identified your car-buying priorities in Chapter 1. Probably price was among the important factors. But how do you figure the idea of value into the price? What is value, anyway? Safety and reliability are aspects that can't be ignored, either.

Here, we'll take a look at how those concepts are quantified, and dig a bit deeper into the issue of style and that pile of options you'll be considering.

At the end of this process, you should be more comfortable comparing one car to another and formulating opinions based on relevant criteria.

Price

Price, of course, determines what you can drive. Who wouldn't be in something higher-end if they could afford to? But the purchase price of a car isn't at all the end of the money trail.

It is a mistake to assume that you can really afford any car under $30,000 (or $15,000, or whatever amount your economic situation dictates). Without good value in a car, the long-term cost can be much higher.

Price is a beginning point, and what that figure is depends on who and what you ask. A couple of quick clarifications are needed here, although you'll learn the full details of pricing in Chapter 6:

▪ **Manufacturer's Suggested Retail Price (MSRP):** just that—what the manufacturer thinks dealers should reasonably charge. But the dealer's not

> 66
> Price is a big factor for me. There may be a car I want to own on the top of my list, but if the car second on my list is half the price, I'm going to buy that car.
> —Lisa
> 99

bound to adhere to that price. (MSRP usually includes destination and delivery charges.)

- **Dealer cost (or invoice price):** what it costs a dealer to acquire a car, usually including transportation to get it to the car lot.

Part of the dealer cost figure often includes the "holdback," a manufacturer discount paid to dealers. In Chapter 6, we'll show you the formula for figuring what holdback is and deducting it from the stated dealer cost to get the real dealer cost. Then you can figure in a reasonable profit and negotiate your way up. Remember, dealers have their own costs for maintaining a business and keeping cars on their lots. Holdback helps defray those expenses. But you have a right to know what's what, and that "dealer cost" isn't really the lowest figure relevant to your car shopping experience.

Used cars have two basic prices you need to know, wholesale and retail:

- **Wholesale price (or trade-in value):** what a reputable dealer might offer for your used car or the lowest you can usually expect to pay if you buy from a private party.

- **Retail price:** the price of a used car when costs of refurbishment, detailing, and any needed repairs are factored in, plus dealer carrying costs and some profit. If you're buying from a private party, this is the highest you should consider paying—and you can probably do better.

Wholesale and retail prices usually refer to figures derived from the Kelley Blue Book, the NADA. Official Used Car Guide, or a similar statistical list of prices.

Moneysaver
Take your price guide with you to the lot. *Watch out for artificially inflated and weasel-worded stickers.* Look for official Manufacturer's Suggested Retail Prices rather than a potentially higher Dealer's Suggested Retail Price.

Moneysaver
Real-world pricing can vary from Blue Book pricing by region, season, supply, and demand. A glut of used red convertibles can make sellers more eager to settle for what they can get. Used cars may hold their value better in dry, hot places where rust is not a problem. And economically depressed areas sometimes have lower used car prices.

Watch Out!
A car will have
cost you more to
own and operate
by the fifth
anniversary of its
purchase than
what you origi-
nally paid for it.
So look for one
with reasonable
ownership costs.
(Source:
IntelliChoice
Inc., Campbell,
CA)

Value

Value is how much a car is worth in terms of quality, features, your own satisfaction, upkeep expense, and resale value—and that's weighed against the initial cost of buying. It's a harder concept to evaluate than simply price, but you can.

Good value is:

- More bang for the buck versus other car choices
- A vehicle that is economical to own and operate
- One that fits your needs and expectations without costing too much.

So how much will it cost to own and operate? That's a question worth considering. Comparably priced cars can differ by thousands of dollars in operational costs over a few years. A company called IntelliChoice lists purchase prices along with expected five-year costs of ownership and operation. Cars that ranked as the best values in their class are in Table 2.2.

The costs of car
ownership
reflected in the
study include
everything from
depreciation to
financing, insur-
ance, state fees,
fuel costs, main-
tenance, and
repairs.

TABLE 2.2   BEST CAR VALUES (OVER FIVE YEARS)

Best Car Value Under $20,000:	Honda Accord DX 4-Cylinder Sedan
Best Car Value Over $20,000:	Mercedes Benz C280 Sedan
Best Truck Value Under $18,000:	Toyota Tacoma Xtracab 2WD
Best Truck Value Over $18,000:	GMC Sierra K1500 Club Coupe 4WD
Best SUV Value Under $25,000:	Jeep Wrangler SE
Best SUV Value Over $25,000:	Toyota 4Runner SR5 4WD

(Source: 1998 The Complete Car Cost Guide™, IntelliChoice®, Inc., Campbell, CA)

Net users can
search for and
compare car val-
ues for recent
models at www.
intellichoice.com.

Here's what to look for to ensure that you'll have decent value over the life of your vehicle:

- Competitive purchase price

- High resale value

- Good fuel efficiency rating—it saves every day

- Repair and maintenance costs that aren't out the window (watch those exotic imports)

- Modest insurance premiums (check—costs vary widely by model)

- Low purchase price: The lower the purchase price of the car, the less you're likely to have to pay in personal property tax and state sales tax

Resale value

What about resale value, the worth of a car two to four years after you've driven it off the dealer's lot? Resale value, expressed in dollar values in used car guides, may also be expressed as a percentage of the suggested retail price in consumer publications when projecting the future worth of a vehicle. It shows how well a certain car "holds its value." Resale value indicates how quickly a car depreciates.

You want a car with a good resale value. Think about it—a high resale-value percentage means that many people are willing to pay good money to buy that model of car used, which implies its long-term reliability and desirability—it's unlikely to be a clunker.

But there's an arguably even more practical reason than reliability to go for a car with a high estimated resale value. A car with a poor resale value percentage may depreciate faster than it's financed and leave you "upside down" on payments. If you resell that car in two years, the money you get won't pay off the principal on your loan. You'll have to continue making payments for some time after the car is being driven around by its new owner.

Timesaver
Want a car that won't cost an arm and a leg to drive? Higher-priced vehicles tend to have higher ownership costs than lower-priced vehicles, so act accordingly (but remember, it's the relationship between ownership cost and purchase price that determines whether a vehicle is a good value).
(Source: IntelliChoice, Inc., Campbell, CA)

Moneysaver
Consider buying used to get good value for your money. Used cars may hold their value better than new cars because the greatest slope of depreciation typically occurs in the first year of new car ownership—drivers pay for the privilege of driving a virgin vehicle off the lot.

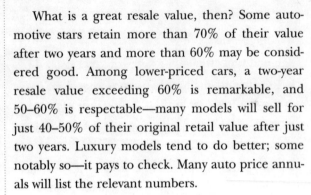

Bright Idea
Insurers sell "gap coverage" to make up the difference between what a car's worth and what's owed on it. Gap coverage is routine when leasing, and it's a very good idea when buying.

What is a great resale value, then? Some automotive stars retain more than 70% of their value after two years and more than 60% may be considered good. Among lower-priced cars, a two-year resale value exceeding 60% is remarkable, and 50–60% is respectable—many models will sell for just 40–50% of their original retail value after just two years. Luxury models tend to do better; some notably so—it pays to check. Many auto price annuals will list the relevant numbers.

Some rules of thumb for seeking out autos that are likely to resell well include these:

- The latest, greatest thing may not be—standard models and makers with reputations for quality are a safer bet.

- Pause before you buy a model with imminent major style changes ahead (although a dramatic increase in the price of a new model can potentially boost the value of used models as shoppers seek relief from sticker shock).

- Go for the middle of the road in options—not everything, but at least the basics.

- Avoid buying a vehicle that is notorious for needing repairs as it ages—or a pricey major maintenance.

- Use your eyes—is a car's styling going to seem current (perhaps classic) or very dated in a couple of years?

Safety

Car safety—what a good idea, who's not for that? But wait a moment. Automobile safety is a slippery concept backed by statistics that are little understood.

We've all seen car crashes, many of us have had them, and everyone wants to avoid one. The most important advice we can give you is to think about what you've seen and what happened to those cars—that's invaluable real-world criteria. And then crunch some numbers on car safety for yourself.

Driving was different twenty to thirty years ago, in the age of the gas-guzzling steel behemoth. Has safety improved, what with crash testing, airbags, antilock brakes? Yes and no. Three factors make it much more important today to really seek out safety in the next car you get:

- **Basic ballistics.** Many more cars crowd freeways and highways and that very simply increases the chance of collision.

- **Weight matters.** Lighter materials are being used to build autos, for fuel and other savings. Despite design enhancements, they may not respond like steel in a crash.

- **Size matters.** In relation to their numbers on the road, small cars have more than twice as many occupant deaths each year as large cars.

The recent American love affair with the big sport utility puts drivers of cars—especially small, lightweight ones—at increased risk. Crash fatalities by type of vehicle are shown in the figure on the next page, and they're worth reviewing.

What constitutes safety, then? The Insurance Institute for Highway Safety concludes that the most important safety features are those that reduce the risk of death or serious injury when a crash occurs—a concept appropriately called "crashworthiness."

There are really two components to safety—factors that minimize the risk of injury in a collision,

Timesaver
Want to find a reasonable lease? Check out cars with a high resale-value percentage first. Leasing is really just paying mainly for the depreciation on the car during the lease term (and, of course, profit). The higher the resale value percentage of the model you want, the less a lease should cost.

Watch Out!
One injury factor in collisions between automobiles and trucks is the typical higher wheel base of the latter. It's not just that one vehicle's larger, but that its chassis is pitted against the other vehicle's more vulnerable passenger compartment.

DEATHS PER MILLION LATE-MODEL PASSENGER VEHICLES (1-3 YEARS OLD) IN 1996

	0	150	300

Small Cars — wheelbase < 95"
95-99"

Midsize Cars — 100-104"
105-109"

Large Cars — 110-114"
>114"

Small Pickups — weight < 3,500 lbs.

Large Pickups — > 3,500 lbs.

Small Utility Vehicles — wheelbase < 100"

Midsized Utility Vehicles — 100-120"

Large Utility Vehicles — > 120"

Cargo & Large Passenger Vans

(Source: Insurance Institute for Highway Safety)

and features that help drivers avoid getting into crashes in the first place.

Crashworthiness Factors include:

- Vehicle structural design
- Vehicle size and weight
- Seat belts, airbags, and other "occupant-protection devices"

Crash Avoidance Features include:

- Antilock brakes
- Traction control systems
- Lighting features—headlamp illumination distance and scope, daytime running lights

We have some statistics to help sort out the safest cars, thanks to crash test dummies and the people who put them through so much. Every new car has to meet federal minimum safety levels. Models are compared for driver and front-seat passenger protection in collision tests conducted by the National Highway Traffic Safety Administration. The figures on the following page show what those rankings look like.

Unofficially...
Checking safety rankings of cars you're interested in is a good idea. Testers find pretty large gaps in safety response between models in the same weight category.

Crash testing can be confusing, though. It doesn't mimic every scenario, although crash tests are conducted at different speeds and angles, by more than one testing group. In the real world, severe frontal crashes are more than twice as common as severe side crashes, although a lot of attention and some advertising has gone toward preventing the latter.

NATIONAL HIGHWAY TRAFFIC SAFETY ADMINISTRATION NEW CAR ASSESSMENT PROGRAM CRASH TESTING

STAR RATING:

★ ★ ★ ★ ★	=	10% or less chance of serious injury
★ ★ ★ ★	=	11% to 20% chance of serious injury
★ ★ ★	=	21% to 35% chance of serious injury
★ ★	=	36% to 45% chance of serious injury
★	=	46% or greater chance of serious injury

A serious injury is considered to be one requiring immediate hospitalization and may be life threatening.

Most injuries happen in front- or side-impact crashes. NHTSA ranks the risks for drivers and front seat passengers in both types of crashes. A five-star ranking system applies to both frontal and side crashes.

1997 COMPACT PASSENGER CARS (2500 - 2999 lbs. CURB WEIGHT)								
MAKE & MODEL		FRONTAL CRASH RATINGS		SIDE CRASH RATING		BELTS & AIR BAG	BELTS	SIDE AIR BAG
		DRIVER	PASSENGER	DRIVER	REAR PASSENGER			
OLDSMOBILE ACHIEVA 2DR	2935 lbs.	★ ★ ★ ★	★ ★ ★ ★ ★	NOT TESTED	NOT TESTED	D/P		
OLDSMOBILE ACHIEVA 4DR	2983 lbs.	★ ★ ★ ★ ★	★ ★ ★ ★	★	★ ★ ★	D/P		
PLYMOUTH NEON 4DR	2547 lbs.	★ ★ ★ ★	★ ★ ★ ★	NOT TESTED	NOT TESTED	D/P		
PONTIAC GRAND AM 2DR	2935 lbs.	★ ★ ★ ★	★ ★ ★ ★ ★	NOT TESTED	NOT TESTED	D/P		
PONTIAC GRAND AM 4DR	2983 lbs.	★ ★ ★ ★ ★	★ ★ ★ ★	★	★ ★ ★	D/P		
PONTIAC SUNFIRE 2DR	2650 lbs.	★ ★ ★ ★	★ ★ ★ ★	★	★ ★	D/P		
PONTIAC SUNFIRE 4DR	2734 lbs.	★ ★ ★ ★	★ ★ ★	NOT TESTED	NOT TESTED	D/P		
SUBARU IMPREZA 4DR	2769 lbs.	★ ★ ★ ★	★ ★ ★ ★	NOT TESTED	NOT TESTED	D/P		
SUBARU LEGACY 4DR	2654 lbs.	★ ★ ★ ★	★ ★ ★ ★	NOT TESTED	NOT TESTED	D/P		
TOYOTA COROLLA 4DR	2553 lbs.	★ ★ ★ ★	★ ★ ★ ★	★ ★ ★	★ ★ ★	D/P		
VOLKSWAGEN GOLF 4DR	2725 lbs.	★ ★ ★	★ ★ ★	NOT TESTED	NOT TESTED	D/P		
VOLKSWAGEN JETTA III 4DR	2725 lbs.	★ ★ ★	★ ★ ★	NOT TESTED	NOT TESTED	D/P		

(Source: National Highway Traffic Safety Administration New Car Assessment Program)

NHTSA frontal tests mimic collisions between cars of the same weight class. Frontal impact rankings illustrate head-on crashes where both vehicles are traveling at 35 mph. Side impact testing simulates a typical intersection collision—technically, when a moving deformable barrier is impacted at an angle into the side of the car at 38.5 mph.

Chest and head data for frontal crashes, and chest data for side crashes, best represent life-threatening injury. Although pelvic and thigh injuries are rarely life-threatening, they are measured because they can be disabling.

Timesaver
Get detailed crash test results for your vehicle model and year at the National Highway Traffic Safety Administration's Web site at www.nhtsa.dot.gov or by calling their Auto Safety Hot Line at (800) 424-9393.

Bright Idea
You've heard it over and over, but wear your seat belts! A respectable four out of five star rating in crash tests still indicates up to a 20% chance of serious injury in a typical collision. Bear in mind that all of a vehicle's occupant safety protection equipment is being used while the test is under way—seat belts included.

The NHTSA stresses that results for frontal impact tests are meaningful only for comparing relative injury risk in collisions between vehicles of similar weights. An excellent ranking on a small car does not mean that it would fare that well in a collision with a large sport utility vehicle (which isn't only bigger, but also may weigh half a ton more).

Since 1995, the Insurance Institute for Highway Safety has been conducting 40-mph crash tests. In these tests, only part of a vehicle's front end hits a deformable barrier that simulates the front of another vehicle. Called the frontal offset test, it's a good indicator of how well the vehicle's crush zones and safety cage manage the energy forces of impact and keep them away from occupants. Table 2.3 shows the top IIHS rankings (of cars reviewed) in popular classes, based primarily on those tests.

TABLE 2.3   MOST CRASHWORTHY VEHICLES BY CLASS

Small Four-Door Cars	
Good:	Volkswagen New Beetle (1998)
Average:	Honda Civic (1996–98)
	Toyota Corolla/Chevrolet Prizm (1998)
	Ford Escort/Mercury Tracer (1997–98)
	Hyundai Elantra (1996–98)
	Saturn SL (1995–98)
	Mazda Protege (1995–98)
	Nissan Sentra (1998)
Midsize Four-Door Cars	
Good:	Ford Taurus/Mercury Sable (1992–98)
	Chevrolet Lumina (1995–98)
	Toyota Camry (1997–98)
	Volkswagen Passat (1998)
	Volvo 850/S70 (1995–98)

Large Luxury Cars

Good:	BMW 5 Series (1997–98)
	Lexus LS 400 (1995–98)

Midsize Utility Vehicles

Average:	Toyota 4Runner (1996–98)
	Land Rover Discovery (1994–98)
	Mitsubishi Montero (1996–98)
	Ford Explorer Mercury Mountaineer (1995–98)

Passenger Vans:

Good:	Ford Windstar (1995–98)
	Toyota Sienna (1998)

(Source: Insurance Institute for Highway Safety)

Agencies that conduct crash testing are among the first to admit the tests can't tell us everything. One problem area that's being looked at is the risk of rollover crashes. In 1996, 30% of all passenger vehicle occupant deaths occurred in crashes in which a vehicle rolled over, according to the Insurance Institute for Highway Safety. But light trucks are involved in fatal rollover crashes at a much higher rate, with sport utilities faring worst. In these types of crashes, a big danger is ejection through doors or windows. Another problem is roof crush. The National Highway Traffic Safety Administration is looking at whether roof or seat construction standards should be modified to better prevent problems.

What should you look for in a car, beyond a good crashworthiness rating? Remember that the bigger and heavier the vehicle—other things being equal—the safer it's likely to be. Here are a few more factors to search out:

■ **Lap and shoulder belts:** choose a car whose belts fit you comfortably. Many new cars are

Get complete crash test data and descriptions on the Insurance Institute for Highway Safety's Web site, www.highwaysafety.org, or by calling (703) 247-1500.

Among 1991–95 model vehicles during the calendar period of 1992–96, the vehicle groups with the lowest driver death rates were large and midsize station wagons and passenger vans, large and midsize luxury cars, and large utility vehicles. Highest rates were found with small and midsize sports cars, small two- and four-door cars, small pickups, and small utility vehicles. (Source: Insurance Institute for Highway Safety)

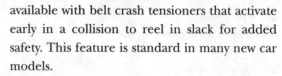

available with belt crash tensioners that activate early in a collision to reel in slack for added safety. This feature is standard in many new car models.

■ **Airbags:** risk assessors say these features double the protection against serious head injuries (versus using just a lap and shoulder belt), but they have also been blamed for injuries. For instance, risk occurs if you're on top of or very close to an airbag when it begins to inflate, and much has been said about the dangers to children or infants in child safety seats. Safety experts say drivers should always use belts and sit with the center of the chest at least 10 inches away from the center of the steering wheel. Passengers, of course, should always wear seat belts and sit as far back as possible.

Airbag injury risk is considered lower in many new car models because of the less-powerful inflators that carmakers are now using in most of their airbags. Some also have dual deployment thresholds or offer on/off switches that give drivers a choice of when and when not to have airbag protection.

NHTSA advises that children age 12 and under should ride in the back seat. There are instances when children must sit in the front because the vehicle has no rear seat, there are too many children for all to ride in back, or a child has a medical condition that requires monitoring. If children must sit in the front seat, they should use the seat belts and/or child restraints appropriate for their weight or size, and sit against the back of the vehicle seat. The vehicle seat should be moved as far back from the airbag as is practical. Make sure that the child's shoulder belt stays on. If adult seat belts do not fit properly,

Watch Out!
Safety experts warn you should never place a rear-facing infant seat in the front seat if the airbag is turned on—it puts an infant's head too close to the passenger airbag. Always secure a rear-facing car seat in the back seat.

use a booster seat. Also, children must never ride on the laps of others.

- **Side impact airbags:** serious side impacts are more likely than frontal collisions to involve some intrusion into the passenger compartment—crash forces can drive doors into a car's occupants. Some automakers are finally addressing this with side impact airbags (as well as a car's interior padding), and BMW offers an innovative head protection system on some cars.

- **Head restraints:** what are those? You've probably called them headrests before. They're a requirement in the front seat of all new passenger vehicles, and as you might guess, they're designed to keep your head from snapping back in a rear-end crash, when many neck injuries occur. In order to work, however, a head restraint has to be directly behind and close to the back of your head (not just your neck). If the restraints are adjustable, they should lock. Otherwise, they can be pushed down in a crash. Automakers are beginning to introduce head restraints with enhanced safety designs now, as well.

- **Built-in child restraints:** using them can avoid the hassles of fitting a portable child restraint into the car or worrying about whether you've done so properly.

- **Roll cage–style enhancement:** available on sport utility vehicles (and some autos), it's designed to provide some safety during rollovers.

Crash-avoidance features can make driving your car safer, but some drivers have difficulty with them,

Bright Idea
In some crashes, rib fractures and other injuries can result from the forces of the shoulder belt on the upper body. But airbags offer additional protection, so carmakers can now modify their shoulder belts with a force-limiting design.

Bright Idea
When you consider safety factors of the car you want, don't forget how performance figures in. A car with enough power and agility to maneuver in fast-moving traffic (or out of the way of an obstruction) may be a safer car for drivers who are comfortable and adept with that level of performance.

and the positive effect can be negated if they're not used properly:

- **Antilock brakes:** these are a case in point. Widely available on new car models, they're designed to prevent wheels from locking and skidding when a driver brakes hard. Antilocks pump your brakes automatically, many times a second, and let you retain steering control. But many drivers, in a pinch, apparently forget about their antilocks and pump the brakes themselves as a reflex—negating the extra protection that antilocks may offer.

- **Daytime running lights:** these are standard on many new cars. These reduced-intensity headlamp lights are designed to increase the contrast between vehicles and backgrounds. Perhaps particularly useful on darker days.

- **Headlamps:** there is some variation in the rate at which illumination drops off at a certain headlamp distance, intentionally—with traditionally different styles between American and European makes. The best advice is to make sure you test-drive a car you're serious about at night before you decide to buy it.

- **Stability control systems:** this is a new addition to the safety repertoire, adding traction-control capabilities to antilock braking, and can be found increasingly on luxury models.

A new category of safety feature doesn't fit into crash avoidance or injury deterrence descriptions—smart-car systems. Among the benefits these may offer are tracking signals relayed to an emergency service center if an accident occurs, roadside assistance and remote door locking and unlocking.

Smart car systems are being offered on some new car models.

Although new safety features are being added to cars every year, nothing replaces common sense, both when shopping for and driving a car. You know that heavier, larger vehicles tend to be safer than their smaller counterparts (though less likely to offer fuel economy). Some small sport utilities and pickups are prone to rolling over. High-performance vehicles typically have higher-than-average death rates for obvious reasons, too.

Use your head. If you do a lot of high-speed freeway travel or live in an area where drivers seem particularly crazy, give extra thought to safety and to getting a vehicle that can protect you best under those conditions. Cutting corners on safety to save a few dollars or even a few hundred probably won't seem wise if you look at it in retrospect from a hospital bed.

And use your vehicle responsibly. Sport utilities are logically safer for drivers who understand they can't be driven like a car—no careening around corners allowed. If you can't help yourself, get something else. Likewise, if you've gotten a ticket every time you've been behind the wheel of a high-performance car, perhaps you're best suited to one in which 70 mph doesn't feel like only 35.

Reliability

Is reliability not owning an outright lemon, or is it never having to take your car to the mechanic? Reliability means different things to different people and isn't easily quantifiable.

There are some common sense ways to gear your search toward the most reliable vehicles:

Watch Out! Don't be misled by safety advertising. Enhancements such as "crumple zones" that absorb the shock of impact in a crash may not make up for cheaper, lightweight materials used in the construction of a car. Go for quality, and check safety rankings before you buy.

- Choose from among the most widely sold types of automobiles (some are identified in Chapter 1).

- Tried-and-true models are a better-known commodity than a brand new model or style.

- Seek out cars with a high resale value, which implies their reliability.

Many cars go through design changes every three to five years, and one rule of thumb is to avoid the first-year that major design modifications are introduced, before thousands of consumers road test them.

Microsoft's CarPoint Web site (carpoint.com) includes reliability ratings based on hundreds of thousands of incident reports. It's a reasonable assumption that low and infrequent repair bills translate as reliability.

Performance

Performance is, simply, how well a car does and how good it feels on the road. It's partly the oomph of the power train, the responsiveness of the brakes and steering, and the synergy of all those factors with myriad other points of the car's engineering. Putting together a fine automobile is an art as well as a science, and while power and other rankings are helpful, none in the world take the place of trying the car out for yourself.

How much "performance" do you need? Some subjective rules of thumb are:

- Enough power to safely (and quickly) get onto a freeway from a low speed on the entrance ramp, and then keep up with other cars (but not so much power that you feel like you're driving a bullet)

Unofficially...
Early attempts at car-building fall far shy of the power today's cars sport. An Ohio man built a gasoline-driven car in 1890—with a single cylinder.

- Enough power to accelerate 10 mph faster to pass the guy in front of you without undue strain

- Enough power for comfortable performance when fully loaded and with the air conditioning on high when it's hot out

- Agility to avoid obstacles suddenly appearing in your path (and the stability to let you keep control of the vehicle)

- Agility to maneuver into a tight parking space

- Brakes that work with you—not too grabby, not too dull—to smoothly and quickly decelerate the vehicle in a straight line

- Ease of starting in the coldest weather you're likely to encounter

- A ride both smooth enough and tight enough for your tastes

- Whether automatic or manual, a transmission that shifts smoothly and responsively enough not to annoy you

- Engine torque enough to climb a hill without resorting to a very low gear (even with the air on)—if you live on a steep street or travel in the mountains this will matter a lot (and you should consider a well-powered vehicle)

The American automobile legacy is one of big engines, eight cylinders, and resultant muscle. Unfortunately, those cars guzzled fossil fuel like the dickens. So cost and environment-conscious engine design arose, autos got smaller and lighter, and their power needs diminished, arguably anyway.

Refinements blur the basic assumptions a bit more now—the basic assumptions being that the

Watch Out!
Even if you can't test-drive a car under every condition, keep minimum performance rules of thumb in mind—you'll know soon enough if you've bought a car that doesn't have "good enough" performance, and you won't like it.

bigger the engine and the more cylinders, the more powerful the car. A very well-designed four-cylinder auto will perform much better than the four-cylinder model of ten or even five years ago.

What goes into performance, anyway? Basic evaluative factors for power (that you can look at before test-driving) include:

- **Engine size (liters):** bigger can indicate more power (compare the 1.6-liter engine of a small economy car to the 5.7-liter engine of an American muscle car), but it's not the best way to gauge power

- **Number of cylinders:** more cylinders generally equal more power (the range for most cars is three to twelve, with four, six, and eight being most common)

- **Horsepower:** obviously, the higher the horsepower rating, the more power (compare a very modestly powered economy edition at 55 with a higher-end sports car that has 450)

- **Torque:** the better the torque rating, the more turning or twisting force in the drive train—an important factor, particularly for starting and negotiating anything other than flat terrain (one popular small Japanese roadster has a torque of 114 lb-ft at 5500 rpm, while another exotic foreign sports car weighs in with a torque rating of 295 lb-ft at 4250 rpm)

Engine size, cylinders, and horsepower ratings tend to go up together for most passenger vehicles. Remember that when you're making comparisons, it's fairest to do so within a vehicle's own class—don't expect an economy car to do the work of a bona fide sports car.

Other factors that have to do with performance are:

■ **Steering:** power steering offers much greater ease in this department—steering should be fluid but not loose, and you should still be able to sense the road (the car should continue going straight when you gently relax your grip on the wheel)

■ **Suspension:** sports cars typically have stiffer suspension (and hold together tightly on fast curves or over bumps), and luxury cars have a more comfortable ride

■ **Brakes:** Antilock brakes are standard on many cars now and are supposed to help you keep control of the car when braking—what you're looking for in brakes is the ability to come comfortably and quickly to a controlled stop

The best ways to gauge a vehicle's performance:

1. Drive it yourself

2. Check out articles on road tests

3. Compare basic performance factors on paper

You can find statistics on engine size, horsepower, and other factors anywhere: from manufacturer literature to automotive buyers' annuals to the Internet—and some annuals (and Net sites) offer road test comparisons.

Styling

For the most part, automotive styling refers to the subjective look of the car and, to some extent, its ergonomics. Sport styling does not equal sport performance. But, it may suffice for the driver seeking a sleek look without the horsepower that may lead to traffic tickets.

Timesaver
Annuals and Web sites of car enthusiast magazines offer the most extensive performance critiques and data; consumer-oriented ones tend to be short and sweet. Pick the ones that best suit your research style.

The best advice is to consider car class when you're shopping (economy, midsize, sport, luxury...), but to realize that the labels are just that—labels. You can find good economy in a midsize car and good performance in a luxury car.

Options

Even if you've narrowed down your car possibilities to a favorite, deciding how to equip it lies ahead. Option choices can affect your purchase price by thousands of dollars; change the vehicle's potential resale value; and alter the personality, performance, and feel of the vehicle.

What options are available? More car manufacturers are moving toward equipment packages rather than just individual add-ons—a sport package, a luxury package, or just the basics. Your best guide to available options is the manufacturer's literature—brochures and spec sheets that lay it out with glorious color pictures.

Popular equipment packages can add a few thousand dollars to the base price of an automobile. A typical basic popular equipment package might include automatic transmission, air, power steering, and power brakes. A one-higher package can add power windows and doors, a tilt or telescoping steering wheel, and cruise control. And the all-out package may include leather seats, a premium sound system, and the moon—at least a moonroof.

Deciding which options you want can be part preference and part foresight—some options may enhance the resale value of a car, such as those in the following list. Other options aren't always as well-appreciated by a second owner when they're considering price.

Bright Idea
Buying used? Once you decide on the models you like, get dealer literature on the current year's version and read up. Some aspects of the car will probably remain the same and you'll be better informed about the line.

- Automatic transmission (except on some sports cars and occasionally on specialty-sport utilities, particularly those used for "off-roading")
- Power steering
- Power brakes
- Air conditioning
- Power windows and locks
- Alloy wheels
- Four-wheel drive (particularly on sport utilities)
- Sunroof or moonroof
- Car alarms and remote entry systems
- Cruise control

Many other options may be desirable to the next owner of a car, but few used car shoppers are willing to pay extra to get loads of incidental options. Basics like an automatic transmission are more likely to help pay for themselves at resale time.

Whether an option will add to the resale value depends, of course, on what kind of car it is. Don't get a stripped-down luxury car and expect to be able to resell it easily. Likewise, a small economy car with all the trimmings probably won't go for what you'd like to ask.

Some options may actually detract from the future value of your car, among them:

- Automated seat belts
- Automatic transmissions on certain sports cars

Among the other options often available are:

- Rear window defroster (the larger the vehicle, the better an idea this is)
- Power mirrors (you can consider this a safety factor)

Moneysaver
Though the base price of a "luxury" car may be higher than a lesser model, the luxury one may have more features as standard equipment. That other car might seem inexpensive only until you add on an automatic transmission, power steering, air-conditioning, or other simple options.

Timesaver
Some cars tattle-tale the options they're carrying via the model number emblazoned on their bodies. An "S" may indicate sport package; an "L" limited edition. Get to know the manufacturer's private lingo once you're serious about that make.

Moneysaver
Options are a big profit center for dealers and manufacturers. Don't get stung with a big price tag for things you don't need.

- Remote entry systems

- Adjustable steering

- Power seats (helpful, again, for different drivers or drivers with limited mobility)

- Traction control (great for rough weather)

- Premium sound systems (although getting a great stereo on your own can be less expensive and it will probably only return a small fraction of its purchase price on resale)

- Leather seating (expensive, but durable)

- Heated seats (only if you really want them and live in a cold climate)

- Seats with adjustable lumbar support (a godsend for those with bad backs)

Important car criteria checklist

Here's where you can put all the data together in a manner that means something to your automotive search. You can compare the vehicles you're considering by using Worksheet 2.1 (filling in as few or as many of these categories as you like).

Rankings are available from many different sources. Stick with the same source for comparisons on a set of criteria.

WORKSHEET 2.1   IMPORTANT CAR CRITERIA*

Compare the cars you're seriously considering according to their price and value, safety, reliability, and performance ratings.

	Car 1	Car 2	Car 3	Car 4	Car 5	Car 6
Make/Model/ Year						
Order of Preference (1 to 5)						
Best Points of Each						

*First fill in the options section on page 51

Price & Value

Suggested Base
Retail Price

Base Retail
Price Plus
Cost of Desired
Options*

Resale Value
Percentage
(2 Year)

Insurance
Cost

Cost of
Ownership
Index

Fuel Efficiency
(MPG City/Hwy)

Data sources:

1. Good car annuals and Web sites

2. For options cost: dealer literature or Web sites,
   exhaustive annuals

3. For cost of ownership: IntelliChoice, among
   others (www.intellichoice.com)

4. For insurance cost: Edmund's Car Guides and
   Web site, among others (www.edmunds.com)

Start with a good car annual or comprehensive auto Web site— a lot of the information's likely to be found in one place. See Appendix C for additional recommendations.

Safety

Crash Test
Ranking
(number of
stars: driver/
passenger
protection)

Crash
Avoidance
Equipment

Data sources:

1. Microsoft CarPoint, among others—carpoint.com

2. Insurance Institute for Highway Safety for crash tests—www.highwaysafety.org, or (703) 247-1500

3. Some car annuals, commercial Web sites, and manufacturers' literature

Reliability

Reliability
Ranking

Data sources:

1. Microsoft CarPoint, among others (uses reliability ratings by Automotive Information Systems)—carpoint.msn.com

Performance

Engine Size
(in liters)

Number of
Cylinders

Horsepower

Torque
Rating

Power
Steering?

Power Brakes?
Antilock Brakes?

Data sources:

1. Most car annuals, comprehensive consumer auto Web sites, manufacturers' literature

2. For most extensive data (and things like torque ratings) head for auto enthusiast magazine sites and annuals

---

Styling & Options

Car class
(sports car,
economy,
midsize, etc.)

What "options"
are standard on
the base model?
(Power steering?
Power Brakes?
Automatic
Transmission...)

Options you
would need to
order "on top"
with this car

Data sources:

1. Manufacturers' literature, the most comprehensive auto annuals, and Web sites

The money-related criteria that you looked at in this chapter will come in handy for worksheets in the next chapter, in which you can figure insurance and other costs of car ownership into a workable budget. Consider the comparisons among the cars you've evaluated so far—is one looking like a really good bet for the money?

Just the facts

- Start screening for cars that meet your requirements with a well-illustrated magazine car-buying annual and on the Internet if you use it—both are great sources for hard numbers.

- Consider cars that do well in crash tests and models that are equipped with the most comprehensive safety features: side-impact airbags, antilock brakes, and traction control.

- Remember that the costs of car ownership outweigh the initial price, so check resale value, insurance costs, and long-term maintenance and repair likelihood.

- Don't skimp on good performance and adequate power (particularly if you do long-distance driving, or travel in hilly or mountainous areas).

- Options cost extra—don't rule out cars with a higher base price but more standard features.

GET THE SCOOP ON...
Whether you should buy new or used, or
lease ▪ How you're going to pay for the car ▪
Auto budget planning basics ▪ The joys and
drawbacks of laying out cash

Matching Your Practical and Emotional Needs to Your Budget

Chapter 3

You're looking for the best car for your needs, wants, and money—but if the latter was no object, would your choices be different? Getting what will make you happy and not bust your budget is an art.

You identified some very basic budget parameters back in Chapter 1. Here, we'll take a much closer look at what you can and can't afford. And we'll see how much icing on the cake you may be able to get without breaking the bank. There are three practical financial elements to be sorted out in a preliminary way before you shop, and two of them are how you'll pay for the car:

1. Will you use cash, get a loan, or look for automotive financing?

2. How will you actually pay for it (within your budget)?

The other element is:

3. Should you buy new or used, or should you lease?

There are some dramatic cost differences to think about.

How will you pay for the car?

Among cash, loans, or automotive financing, cash seems like the most forthright alternative, and if you have money in the bank saved for purchasing an auto, you can consider it—but also consider the drawbacks.

Cash

Watch Out!
"Cash" here refers to an official form of payment such as a bank cashier's check, not rolls of dollar bills. To have a good payment receipt and for other reasons, don't consider handing over real twenties, hundreds, ones, or any other denomination.

The advantages of paying cash up front are that you will own the car outright, you won't incur hefty interest charges (or have to deal with financing paperwork and costs), and—especially with used cars—you may be able to get a better deal by offering on-the-spot payment. But offering to pay cash at a new car dealership may work against you.

Dealers profit from the financing they arrange. If they can't make money there, you may not be able to negotiate as low a buying price as you would otherwise. A dealer who marks up his financing 1–2% over cost may make more than $1,000 financing a midrange new car buyer.

There's something called "opportunity cost" to consider—what else you could be doing with all that money instead of using it to pay for a car, when many good and readily available auto-financing options are available.

Paying $15,000 cash for a car means that money won't be available if you need it for emergencies, and it won't be earning interest. Suppose that these are your banking and investment options:

- Bank checking account interest of 2%

- Bank savings account interest of 3%

- Money market fund interest of 4.75%

- Three-year bank CD interest of 5.75%

- Stocks or a mutual fund with expected returns of 20%

Socking away $15,000 for just one of the three years you might finance a car would mean an extra $300 earned on a bank checking account, $450 on a savings account, $713 with a discount brokerage's basic money market fund (similar to a checking account), an extra $863 on the first year of a three-year bank certificate of deposit or, if the stock market doesn't falter, perhaps $3,000 extra dollars.

Each additional year, those figures would more than double, meaning that if you can get cheap auto financing, it's wise to consider using it and putting your cash to work elsewhere. But don't overextend yourself with a mortgage, auto financing, and credit card bills—being prudent pays off with less stress and in myriad other ways.

Loans

What about getting a loan? Many banks can pre-arrange an auto loan for you shortly before you intend to buy, and can tell you roughly what rates you would pay, even if you're casually shopping. They're particularly necessary to look at when you're buying a used car and have to get your own financing.

The procedure goes something like this: call your bank and ask to speak to the auto loan department. Some banks will take your credit application by phone and have a loan approver call you back; otherwise, you can make an appointment to go in and fill out the application in person.

Moneysaver
Rather than paying cash for a new car, consider getting the best on-the-spot financing possible (ideally, when the manufacturer is offering discounts). Then go look for a great interest rate on the cash you have in the bank. It's smart money management, and you'll cut stress by hunting in less haggle-happy waters.

Unofficially...
Dealerships have seen success in the service and parts departments over the last decade. But sales there were projected to be flat for 1998, due to better-built vehicles that need fewer repairs and require less scheduled maintenance, according to the National Automobile Dealers Association.

Moneysaver
Check auto loans
at credit unions
in your area.
They may be
worth joining for
the discounted
rate you can get
versus bank
rates.

You'll be asked basic information about your income, outstanding debt, and auto purchase plans. Then the loan officer will tell you how much the bank is willing to lend and at what interest rate. You'll also be told what finance and other charges apply, what down payment you'll need to come up with, and—most importantly—what your monthly payment will be if you buy a car in the range you expect to.

If the payment is too expensive to comfortably handle, you can ask the loan officer about lending money over a longer time span—say, four years instead of three. New car loans seldom go over five years, and used car loans may be restricted to three—the older the car, the shorter the allowable loan term.

Prequalifying yourself for a car loan has some advantages, among them peace of mind and fewer haggle points to go over with car dealers. You know they won't make the bulk of their profit with financing because they're not the ones financing the car, which will instead be owned by your bank until you finally pay it off. But consider carefully before you mention loan preapproval during negotiations. In some situations, you may benefit from avoiding the topic until late in the game.

Unofficially...
If you've got rot-
ten credit and
can't get a bank
loan, there are
still secondary
financing institu-
tions (finance
companies, credit
unions, and deal-
ers) that may
lend you money.
Such high risk
loans have much
higher interest
rates—15% to
well over 20%.
Use them as a
last resort, and
only for an inex-
pensive car you
absolutely need.

Financing

What about dealer-arranged financing? Although promotions in this department can mean savings, dealers can sometimes make a ton of profits and unsuspecting buyers are frequently confused.

The F&I (financing and insurance) department is where you come to terms with financing terms at a dealership. Look for manufacturer-backed low interest rates. If the rest of the financing language is fair, you can save. Shopping around for good interest rates is more important than many people realize, for the rates can vary several percentage points, depending on where you shop, what type of loan you're after, and how good your credit is. You'll get the lowdown on comparing loans and a worksheet to figure your own in Chapter 7.

Budget planning

An auto is the second biggest expense most families have, ceding only to a home. For many others, a car is the single biggest expense. Carefully budgeting for it makes sense and really can save money—not to mention hassle.

Elements of a successful car budget

The major car cost areas to take into consideration when budgeting include:

- A *down payment* or, if you're leasing, *up-front costs* (if you're making a trade-in, figure its estimated value into the down payment)

- What your *monthly car payments* will be and over how long a term (two years, three years, four, or five?)

- Your *insurance premiums* on the car

- *Personal property taxes* based on the vehicle value

- Any *change in maintenance, repair,* or *fuel costs* likely to be incurred versus your old set of wheels

Only you (and to some extent, your creditors) can decide how much of your income to devote to your vehicle. Consider your lifestyle and look for a vehicle economical enough to allow you to continue living in the manner to which you've become accustomed.

Timesaver
Loan calculators in money management software can give you a quick look at the way different interest rates compare over the life of the loan. And some automaker Web sites include calculators for comparing their financing alternatives. Check the Web sites of the manufacturers of cars you're interested in by accessing the Web addresses listed in Appendix C.

The timetable

No matter when you're planning to get your car, you're already well within the time frame for planning the money aspects. If you have a few months or longer, start setting aside savings to accumulate 20% of the planned purchase price of your car for a down payment if you can.

It's a good idea to get a copy of your credit report, if you have some time as well, and report any errors or contest untrue adverse credit information. Your bank may be able to help you get a copy.

You can also call your bank months in advance of a planned car purchase to go over ballpark loan figures with them. The interest rates will change, but probably not that much, and you'll be better prepared.

It's not too early to start keeping tabs on manufacturer rebates and promotional financing, too. More about that, and the best months for buying cars, are in Chapter 4. If you know the model you want and the manufacturer starts offering $1,500 off for a limited time, it's probably worth jump-starting your purchase plans to take advantage of the deal. And, by the way, when there's a high incentive available, it may mean that the vehicle isn't meeting volume expectations or that shoppers consider it overpriced. So be persistent about seeking out a good deal (close to or below invoice), particularly on cars with nice incentives attached.

Think, too, as soon as possible, about the monthly payment that you'll be making and prepare yourself for the altered cash flow.

In the month prior to serious shopping, prequalify a loan with your bank (or another lender you've found with even better rates) and review

Bright Idea
Even if you think your credit is healthy, remember that every point, or fraction thereof, that you shave off an interest rate adds up quickly, especially on a big-ticket item like a car. Keep your credit in good shape—it's more important now than ever.

manufacturer financing options if you've narrowed down your potential choices (Web sites and phone numbers are in Appendix C).

Most dealer-arranged financing issues can be handled on the day of purchase or very shortly thereafter.

Your buying preparations then, may look like this timetable:

- Months ahead: save for a down payment, check your credit report, make initial loan inquiries, watch for specials, prepare for a change in your cash flow

- Up to one month before purchase: prequalify for a bank loan

- Day of purchase: any dealer-arranged financing will be handled and the bank loan is finalized

Then, of course, there are post-purchase budgeting considerations to keep in mind. For instance, if you have a four-year bank loan and interest rates drop, you may save by refinancing at the lower rate. If your income improves dramatically during the term of the loan, consider paying off the balance at an accelerated rate to save on any high interest charges.

Planning and budgeting techniques

How do you figure auto expenses into your life? You estimated the price of a car that you could prudently purchase in Chapter 1. You found out that people spend an average of 7% of their income on transportation expenses (but some spend a lot more) and that some consumer credit consultants advise a 15% cap. Another oft-stated rule of thumb is to never spend more than one week's net income on each monthly car payment.

Unofficially...
Auto icon Henry Ford used to say money is like an arm or a leg— use it or lose it.

66

Remember that time is money.
—Benjamin Franklin

99

If a person making $50,000 annually pays 30% of that money in taxes, he or she nets about $673 per week. Spending that much monthly on transportation expenses is a far cry from the $292 that would reflect the average 7%-of-income expenditure (many people would be uncomfortable squeezing their payroll checks that tightly for a set of wheels). But it's not that far from consumer credit consultants' 15%-of-salary suggestion, which amounts to $625 per month for car and other transportation expenses, based on a $50,000 salary. You can consider "household income" in place of salary if the car you're shopping for is for the family.

How much should you spend? Only your budget knows for sure—and your car payments have to balance out with the other things in your life. Based on these disparate rules of thumb, it seems prudent to consider that many car shoppers can spend up to around half a week's net income per month on car costs at the low end and one week's net income only at the very top end. To get a bit firmer fix on your finances, use Worksheet 3.1.

WORKSHEET 3.1   APPROXIMATE MONTHLY CAR PAYMENT AFFORDABILITY RANGE

$_____ (1/2 Weekly Net Income) to $_____ (Weekly Net Income)

Multiply each number by 48 to find acceptable purchase-price and finance-cost figures (assuming four year financing)

$_____ to $_____

Then to estimate acceptable purchase prices, refer to Table 1.1 in Chapter 1 and pick out a likely interest rate. Subtract from each amount the figure from Table 1.1 best representing the total expected cost of interest:

$_____ to $_____ is the range of purchase prices you should not exceed.

Deciding on new or used, or maybe a lease?

This year, Americans are expected to buy about 14.6 million new cars, according to the National Automobile Dealers Association, but by some estimates more than double that number of used cars will be sold. Certainly, more people are being priced out of the new car market, but there are also fewer somber factors for the popularity of the used car market.

Perhaps most significant is the coattail effect of leasing, which is how as many as a third of new vehicles have been leaving dealerships. A plethora of lease returns in good condition with low mileage means that consumers can increasingly find used cars that aren't beaters.

Because dealers are more confident about these lightly-used lease returns, they're beginning to offer extended warranties on the cars they resell, and that further attracts used car buyers into what looks like a no-lose proposition. And because more people are buying used, you could conjecture that any stigma associated with it is evaporating and instead used car buyers are being lauded as good money managers. But what about you? Let's look.

New cars

You're an ideal new car buyer if you meet the criteria in Checklist 3.1—the optimal new car buyer is someone who's rich, busy, and picky.

The advantages of buying new are numerous. Among them:

- **Reliability:** that's a big appeal about new cars— the idea that yours won't spend half its life in the shop, and if something does go wrong, there's a warranty. Your car payments may be high but your repair bills won't be.

66

Never invest money in anything that eats or needs painting.
— theatrical producer Billy Rose

99

- **Time savings:** it's not just avoiding lengthy repair times—shopping for a new car can be done quickly if needed, rather than hunting for the perfect used car over hill and dale and months.

- **Condition:** no gum balls under the seat, no body dents, no unhooked hoses flapping in the breeze (see Chapter 17 for lemon laws).

- **Safety advances:** face it—the latest gadgets are on new cars and you won't find a side-impact airbag on a '92 model (see Chapter 2).

- **Rock bottom financing:** it won't make buying a new car cheaper than buying the same one used, but no bank can beat 0% new car financing promotions. Carmakers are sometimes more willing than banks to lend credit to a higher-risk individual. The car can be repossessed and resold; selling cars is, after all, the business that carmakers and dealers are in.

- **Variety:** more models are being produced to accommodate diverse individual tastes. And if you want a red one, you can usually get it.

- **Prestige:** new cars are pricey, and people know it. If owning one will elevate your status among your peers, so be it (but are you sure you want that peer group?).

- **The "feel good" factor:** it's a new toy, it's all yours, and you may feel like a million dollars behind the wheel (until you realize you'll be spending 20, 30, or 40 grand paying for it).

The drawbacks of buying new have mostly to do with price. You could wind up "upside down" on payments and owe more than the car is actually worth if you sell it before the loan term is up. And there is

Watch Out!
New car financing promotions offering 0% or 1.9% financing are just that—promotions. Costs can be and are reshuffled to other areas of the price you pay. Always examine the fine print carefully and crunch the numbers yourself.

the opportunity cost of the money you're spending on the car.

CHECKLIST 3.1   ARE YOU CUT OUT FOR NEW CARS?

___ You have adequate income to pay top dollar for a car.

___ You don't have time for extensive shopping or repairs.

___ You hate the idea of—egads!—owning a car someone else has been driving around.

Another factor is your credit. Ambitious new car financing plans may make it easier for you to buy a new car than a used one when your credit isn't sterling (see Chapter 7).

Used cars

The rising costs of new cars have priced many Americans out of the market for new car purchases entirely. When consumers buy used, they spend an average of roughly $12,000 per vehicle. Just about every benefit of buying used stems from the fact that a used car is cheaper—on average, somewhat over half of what shoppers spend on new ones.

Buyers can get a higher-end model with more desirable features for the same money. The big depreciation downdraft has been covered by the original owner. Used cars are likely to cost less in taxes because they're worth less than new cars. And insurance can be cheaper too, although new car safety gizmos sometimes get insurance discounts for their owners.

There are of course disadvantages to buying used—the price you pay for saving huge chunks of money:

- **Car condition:** it obviously varies from vehicle to vehicle (have your mechanic check it out).

> **"**
> I passionately believe that modern cars are a waste of money and that '60s American cars are the coolest... massively cheap to buy, cheap to insure and register, cheap to maintain... lots of power. Big and heavy, which makes them safer, so long as they have seat belts. Much simpler than modern cars.
> —Ken, who owns a '67 Buick Skylark, found over the Internet
> **"**

Watch Out!
Every state has a new car lemon law, which requires manufacturers to repair, replace, or buy back chronically defective new cars. But only a handful of states have similar protection for those buying used cars. For a list of which states have the best used car lemon law coverage, see Chapter 17.

- **Haggling:** you may have to for the right price. Only about one out of ten used car dealers surveyed present themselves as "one-price" or "no-haggle" lots, and only about three out of ten even posted prices on all cars at the lot, according to the Consumer Federation of America.

- **Warranty coverage:** not automatic, and it can be problematic (see Chapter 17).

- **Dealer profit:** new cars are expensive, but, based on purchase price, dealers make more money on used cars. The average dealer gross on a trade-in runs close to $1,500, according to the National Automobile Dealers Association.

Is a used car a better choice for you? Check the criteria in the checklist below.

CHECKLIST 3.2   ARE YOU AN IDEAL USED CAR BUYER?

___ You want or need to save money.

___ You're willing to tolerate some variables.

___ You have adequate income or cash reserves to pay for repairs and maintenance, as needed.

___ You can find a reliable mechanic and don't mind occasionally having your vehicle in for service.

___ You tend to keep your cars as long as possible.

The leasing option

Moneysaver
Don't buy a used car for just a few months and then sell it for something else. You'll pay dearly—$700 on a $10,000 car if your state sales tax is 7%.

Leasing seems counterintuitive to the penny-pincher. You make a down payment, shell out monthly checks, then you have to give the car back in a couple of years and wind up with nothing to show for your expense.

But a bellwether change in American attitudes to leasing has made it an increasingly popular way of getting a new car today. Along with that has come an impressive consumer-friendly change in the way leases are constructed.

What happens when a penny-pincher looks a little further and considers a good lease deal versus buying a new car? Lease proponents remind us that cars depreciate. If you buy a new car, you pay all that initial depreciation, at which point you'll effectively have a used car and pay that off. With a lease, all you're doing—if you get a good deal—is paying for depreciation (and its financing), plus dealer profit. You can decide at the end of the lease deal whether to buy your lease car.

However, the unfamiliar territory of leasing can lead shoppers to cede more in profit to a dealer in a lease than they would if they were buying, so it's important to run your numbers and specifically seek out a good deal.

Some who have leased in recent years actually got a break on costs in one way—lessors eager to seal deals were too optimistic about what vehicles would be worth at resale, and wrote contracts noting residual values above what guidebooks recommended. As it turned out, their faith in the future strength of the used car market was unfounded. Many lessors were hit with losses in the thousands on a per-car basis, after lease return.

Good points of leasing include:

- The ability to drive a newer, better model car with more options than you can afford to buy

- No surprise repair bills—your monthly expenses for the car are a known commodity (in cases where the warranty period covers the lease term)

> **"**
> I got a newer model of the same thing I had last time. Get a car just like the car that's been good to you for a long time.
> —Rick
> **"**

- Manufacturer and dealer incentives abound for leases—good deals are out there
- Tax benefits for business use

And the drawbacks of leasing:

Moneysaver
Closed-end leases that let you buy the car at the end of the term for a specific amount put risk on the dealer, not you. If the lease-end price is $12,000 but market value has plummeted to $8,000, it's not your problem. But if it's worth more than expected, you can buy and save, in a way.

- No real equity. Say you need a car three years from now and lease one for 36 months today. You spend $2,000 up front and $300 per month. At the end of three years, you'll have had a nice ride and spent $12,800, but you will have no car (remember that the average price of a used car is not far from that).

- The car's not really yours (granted that until you've paid off any car, it technically belongs to the financing bank). Leasing a car is like having a leash. Required scheduled maintenance, keeping the car in great shape, not driving it too many miles, worrying what to do about the lease return if you move across the country next year, and knowing that you'll be severely penalized unless you keep the car exactly the length of the lease term.

Timesaver
Remember that an attractive price in a lease ad may be a lot lower than what you'll wind up paying, once all the variables are considered. Do some research on your own.

- Cost. Payments may be much lower than with buying a new car, but if you're not committed to always driving new, continually paying for "just the depreciation on a new car" by leasing may start to seem like folly.

- Paperwork and fine print can make leasing a frightening proposition. If you decide to lease, know what you're getting into and learn the terms—this is a different world from buying.

Part V of this book is dedicated to prospective lessees because leasing has become such a popular method of driving away in a new car. This section goes into the nitty-gritty of lease deals. But maybe you're wondering now whether you're a leasing candidate? Let's start with when you're not:

- If you drive a lot (more than 12,000–15,000 miles per year)

- If you're hard on cars and this one is likely to get dinged.

- If you need for any reason to return a car before a lease term's up

- If you're moving out of the area

- If your economic situation will be tight soon (if you won't have any money at the end of the lease term with which to buy or lease another car, you're a much better candidate for buying used now)

If you make the cut and aren't affected by the lease-deterring situations just listed, stay on the fence for now, but consider factors that could screen you in. You're a good lease candidate if you meet the criteria in Checklist 3.3.

CHECKLIST 3.3   ARE YOU A LEASE CANDIDATE?

___ You have a strong preference for a new car.

___ You typically put cars to relatively light use, with little wear and tear (and no more than 15,000 miles per year).

___ You typically don't keep a car more than about three years anyway.

___ You can afford or almost afford to buy new.

Leasing can be a good option, although you may want to wait until you have all the numbers in front of you before you decide whether to go for it. The next chapter will, among other things, show you where to look for current manufacturer leasing promotions.

Bright Idea
Look at your psychological make-up when considering leasing. If you hated sharing toys as a child (or would be anxious about something happening to a car that must be returned in good condition), shy away. Likewise, if you really, truly hate complicated contracts and feel uneasy about leasing (even after you've read through Part V, where we'll talk about how leasing's often simpler than it used to be).

Bright Idea
Look for so-
called "closed
end" lease deals,
where a manufac-
turer will guaran-
tee that the car
will be worth a
certain figure
when you turn
it in. They're the
kind typically
offered.

Just the facts

- Don't assume that paying cash is the best alternative—weigh opportunity, cost, and other financing options.

- Consider leasing if you strongly prefer to drive a new car and seldom keep yours longer than two to three years.

- Leasing may not be a good idea if you typically drive more than 12,000–15,000 miles per year, are hard on your cars, your income will be reduced in two or three years, or you will be moving out of the area.

- On average, people spend about $12,000 for a used car versus a little over $22,000 (according to the National Automobile Dealers Association) for a new car, and more than twice as many buy preowned as buy new.

Going Shopping

PART II

GET THE SCOOP ON...
The best ways to armchair shop ▪ Useful
resources for auto pricing ▪ When to get the
best car deals ▪ Finding promotions, rebates,
and other money-saving incentives ▪ How to
take a test-drive without selling your soul

Scouting Your Finalists

Your short list of makes, models, and years

You have perhaps four models (or at most half a dozen) in mind, and now you need to decide between them. Part of the criteria is price—you may go with one model if the rate is right and another is not. So you're ready for some serious shopping.

This chapter will show you where to get the best price data available, give you information on current lease rates and rebates, and tell you when to shop for the best prices. Taking an exploratory, no-commitment test-drive is also covered.

If you haven't already squeezed your list of favorite candidates down to four or fewer, do it now. Worksheet 4.1 can be used throughout your shopping process.

WORKSHEET 4.1   CARS TO CONSIDER

Favorite Makes and Models	Best Points of Each	Suggested Retail Price
1.		$
2.		$
3.		$
4.		$

Chapter 4

Armchair shopping

Before you get out on the road and run from one dealer to another—heavens, instead of doing that—find out the skinny from the comfort of home. Price information you get through the sources described here will be used in a car comparison worksheet later in this chapter.

Read it in the Sunday papers

Newspapers are a ready source of price information, but watch for misleading ads. Used car shoppers can check the classifieds without much worry, but the amount of fine print on an average "low low rates!" new car dealer display ad is daunting.

Checking the paper isn't a necessity, but one's usually close at hand. Get a magic marker and flag the deals you see associated with the cars you're most interested in. You can use the following worksheet to note what dealers say they're offering.

Check the fine print for information about up-front lease costs.

In particular, jot down any specials where a "manufacturer" incentive is advertised. That's a flag to a legitimate sale.

WORKSHEET 4.2   NEWSPAPER SALE ADS

Dealer-ship	Sale Price Quoted	Promo Interest Rate	Lease (Monthly Term, Up Front)	Model & Options Included	Incentive Type & Amount
Car 1:_____					
Car 2:_____					

Car 3:_____

Car 4:_____

Magazines

Magazine auto annuals consolidate a lot of good pricing information in one place, and they're an excellent resource. Look for one or two that include this type of basic information for the vehicles you're considering:

- Manufacturer's Suggested Retail Price (on the version you're most interested in—4dr. versus 2dr.; V6 versus V8)

- Dealer cost

- Resale value (after two or four years)

- Insurance cost or cost of ownership rankings

- Options price list

Check your best local newsstand for the annuals, usually under $5.00, that fit your needs. For specific data on manufacturer incentives, you can turn to *Automotive News* (a trade publication) or *CarDeals* (from the Center for the Study of Services, 800-475-7283).

Netcruising for deals

The state of car information on the Internet today gives anyone with basic access an edge in finding the best car pricing. Along with accurate basic price

> **"**
> Beware of little expenses; a small leak will sink a great ship.
> —Benjamin Franklin
> **"**

data (plus extras such as insurance and ownership cost), two of the most useful pieces of car shopping information on the Internet are:

- Current manufacturer incentives
- Current competitive lease rankings

Some useful sites for price information are in Table 4.1. Each site is a little different; a quick browse through these (or a look-see for other sites with your favorite search engine) should produce one well-suited to your needs.

Kelley Blue Book and NADA Official Used Car Guide are among the standard sources for used car pricing.

TABLE 4.1   AUTO PRICING WEB SITES

AutoSite www.autosite.com
Microsoft CarPoint www.carpoint.com
Edmund's www.edmunds.com
IntelliChoice www.intellichoice.com
Kelley Blue Book www.kbb.com

Knowing the best deals going on leases can save you lots of money. The following table shows a sample page of IntelliChoice listings.

These are examples—not deals that are necessarily being offered right now. Check the IntelliChoice Web site for current lease deals.

TABLE 4.2   INTERNET LISTINGS OF COMPETITIVE LEASE RATES

Model	Total Net Interest Rate	Ad Rate (month)	Term	Upfront Costs
1998 Saab 900 5-door S	0.60%	$278	39	$1,827
1998 Saab 900 SE	1.63%	$339	39	$2,138
1998 Cadillac Eldorado	4.10%	$499	36	$3,349

1998 Cadillac DeVille	4.27%	$499	36	$3,349
1998 Acura 2.5TL	5.60%	$339	36	$2,138
1998 Acura 3.2TL	5.66%	$369	36	$2,193
1998 Cadillac Catera	5.73%	$399	36	$2,749
1998 Saturn SL	6.17%	$129	36	$1,424
1998 Volkswagen Jetta GL	6.44%	$189	36	$1,538
1998 BMW 740i	6.71%	$699	30	$6,399
1998 Volkswagen Golf GL	6.87%	$179	36	$1,528
1998 BMW Z3 Roadster 1.9	7.39%	$299	27	$3,099

Model	Expiration Date	Availability
1998 Saab 900 5-door S	4/30/98	National
1998 Saab 900 SE	4/30/98	National
1998 Cadillac Eldorado	3/31/98	National
1998 Cadillac DeVille	3/31/98	National
1998 Acura 2.5TL	4/30/98	National
1998 Acura 3.2TL	4/30/98	National
1998 Cadillac Catera	3/31/98	National
1998 Saturn SL	4/30/98	National
1998 Volkswagen Jetta GL	3/31/98	National (ex. CA, HI, MA & NY)
1998 Volkswagen Jetta GL	3/31/98	Calif., Mass. & New York
1998 BMW 740i	4/30/98	Tri-State (CT, NJ, & NY)
1998 Volkswagen Golf GL	3/31/98	Calif., Mass. & New York

Model	Expiration Date	Availability
1998 Volkswagen Golf GL	3/31/98	National (ex. CA, HI, MA & NY)
1998 BMW Z3 Roadster 1.9	4/30/98	Bay Area (San Francisco Bay Area)/Tri-State regions (CT, NJ, & NY)

(Source: IntelliChoice, Inc., Campbell, CA)

Rebates and other manufacturer incentives can potentially save you thousands off the cost of a new set of wheels, but only if you know they're out there. How to find out? Edmund's turned out to be a great source for hot incentives around the nation, like the example shown in the following Table 4.3.

TABLE 4.3   MANUFACTURER INCENTIVES (SAMPLE LISTING)

CUSTOMER REBATES:

Chrysler Corporation (Effective through: 4/6/98)

1998 Models:

Chrysler Cirrus	$1,000
Chrysler Sebring Coupe	$1,000
Chrysler Town & Country SWB	$750
Chrysler Town & Country LWB	$1,000

1997 Models:

Chrysler Cirrus	$2,000
Chrysler Concorde LX	$1,500
Chrysler Concorde LXi	$2,000
Chrysler Sebring	$1,500
Chrysler Sebring Conv.	$2,000
Chrysler Town & Country SWB	$750
Chrysler Town & Country LWB	$1,000

(Source: Edmund's)

Some sites offer to link you with web pages of dealers in your area or offer to send e-mail, and the dealerships will call you back. Depending on the

Moneysaver
AutoSite, as well as Edmund's, lists current manufacturer incentives. Edmund's also lists dealer hold-back rates, which you'll hear more about in Chapter 6.

These are examples that aren't necessarily still being offered—check Edmund's Web site for current listings.

outlet, you might try making first contact this way, soliciting basic information or setting up an appointment for a test-drive.

Dealer and manufacturer phone calls (and the fax)

With a short list of models under consideration, can you cut to the chase and simply call a dealer or even a manufacturer? Dealers should be more than happy to tell you the current direct manufacturer incentives, but it's not necessarily in their best interest to be straight with you about their own costs for a car.

In the case of one-price dealers (as described in Chapter 5), you should be quoted the firm purchase price, if not the dealer cost. An independent source of information, however, is always good to have.

What do you say anyway? Opinions are divided on whether to soft-pedal your approach or lay it on the line. Your results will vary, according to the person with whom you're dealing. During an initial call, you can ask for the sales manager and get his name or you may choose to just deal with a salesman. Either way, tell him why you're calling—you're perhaps a week away from buying a vehicle and you're calling dealers in your area to inquire about prices on specific models and arrange test-drives. And you'll buy from whoever has the lowest price. Describe the vehicle you're looking for and ask him for his best price on it. If you have a fax machine, you can ask him to fax the information (you want it in writing whenever possible). And mention that you'd like to know what, if any, incentives are going into that price. Some dealership personnel are open to this approach; some are not. By asking directly for pricing information in this manner, you're really doing an informal bid solicitation, as some

Timesaver
Download a listing of local dealerships and phone numbers while you're surfing car sites, for later use.

Timesaver
See Appendix C for a list of manufacturer phone numbers, and call them directly to inquire about specials. While you're at it, have them send you literature and descriptions of the financing plans they offer.

Watch Out!
Phone manners
can be indicative
of what your
in-person experi-
ence with a deal-
er can be. If your
phone inquiry
isn't greeted
courteously and
with care, con-
sider moving on
to a different
dealer.

consumer buying services will do for you—but at a price.

Handling the first dealer contact this way lets you find out which dealerships are most comfortable to do business with and which may be the least expensive place to buy from. It takes only a few minutes of your time—if time really were money, you'd be getting a lot of bang for your buck.

Taking a closer look

Sounds like you're heading out of the armchair and behind the wheel soon. You'll want to speed up the process, particularly if your request for great prices gets promising leads, and more so if any of those leads include promotions that have the clock ticking.

The no-commitment test-drive

As you get to know your local dealerships, remember one thing: they're intent on making sales. If you come off to the salesman as a casual browser who may never buy, you're unlikely to get premium attention. If you are ready to buy and followed the script, terrific. You now have salesmen assigned to you from whom you can request a no-commitment test-drive.

If you aren't ready to buy, calling using the same guidelines but explaining that at the moment you're only a potential buyer should work. The key is to let dealers know that you will be serious at some point in the near future.

Then follow Checklist 4.1 for a useful no-commitment test-drive.

CHECKLIST 4.1   TEST-DRIVE CHECKLIST

___ Call first to arrange an appointment.

___ Arrive at the lot during off-peak hours and ask specifically to see the salesman you've already spoken with.

___ Pick up dealer literature on the car and give your driver's license to the salesman, who will make a photocopy of it for security, then return it.

___ Ensure that you get your driver's license back before you go back onto the lot.

___ Refresh the salesman's memory as to what car you have in mind and why. With his help, choose a car on the lot closest to what you're really looking for.

___ Ask the salesman to briefly describe the differences between the version you're about to drive and those with other power or options packages.

___ Remind him you want to drive the car, not just be driven in it (!).

___ Let the salesman drive the car off the lot (for insurance reasons).

___ At the earliest convenience, switch seats (not in traffic—it's illegal).

___ Turn off the ignition, start up the car (make sure you know where all the controls are before you begin driving), and drive slowly.

___ Put most of your focus on the car, not the salesman. Note your performance criteria from Chapter 2—How does it handle over bumps and smooth surfaces, at low speeds and while shifting, or with the air on.

___ Think about the interior of the car as well as its performance—how does everything "fit," including the seat belts.

___ Ask to try the car out on a freeway for at least a short distance.

___ Once you're back at the dealership, pull over in a safe place, and let the salesman drive onto the lot and repark the car.

___ Handle any follow-up questions you've thought of, thank the salesman, and tell him when you'll be getting in touch with him.

Bright Idea
When you're calling and not ready to buy, ask when the slowest times on the lot are. The salesman should appreciate your consideration in not wasting time that he could spend with immediate buyers, and you're more likely to get his full attention once you are on the lot.

Bright Idea
Once you've finished the test–drive (preferably right afterwards), make some notes to yourself of features, what you liked, what you didn't, and anything you'll need to ask next time. Worksheet 4.3 is where your top picks should end up.

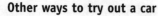

Bright Idea
Auto rental agencies, particularly in cities or vacation spots, can sometimes lend you—for a price—a do-it-yourself test-drive.

Other ways to try out a car

You may feel that it takes more than one test-drive to accurately gauge how well you like a car. Asking for a second test-drive isn't a bad idea, but only if you're serious about the car and the dealership.

Depending on the vehicle you're enamored with and where you live, there's another alternative to dealer drives, but not a cheap one. Inquire of local car rental agencies whether they carry your make and model, then arrange to rent one for a weekend day when rates are likely to be lowest. Plan a pleasant excursion and have some fun in the name of car shopping.

A cheaper form of extended test-drive is to ask a friend or relative with a car similar to one you're considering. Put the word out that you're looking, but expect to owe a favor.

Getting serious

Getting off the fence and becoming serious about what you'll be spending money on is hard for some. But treat this car-buying enterprise like a task to be finished without procrastination.

Moneysaver
Don't pay too much for power. If a car you're test driving is overpowered, move to the next smaller engine size. If it's still very acceptable for your needs, you've just avoided a potentially needless cost.

Arrange for dealer test-drives of all the cars on your short list. If necessary, take comparison test-drives of slightly more or less powerful editions of the same model, (or stick shift versus automatic, or a new model versus the last year's). Then put it all together.

Car comparison worksheet

After you've test-driven the vehicles you're most serious about, rank them again, using Worksheet 4.3.

WORKSHEET 4.3   CAR COMPARISONS

Favorite to Least Favorite:	Best Points:	Worst Points:
1.		
2.		
3.		
4.		

Bright Idea
Try test driving under different conditions: after it snows or after dark.

Does each model fit your basic reason for wanting to buy a car?

1.

2.

3.

4.

Using your "most important car criteria" from Chapter 1, note how well each vehicle does and any specifics:

Priority (list)	Car 1	Car 2	Car 3	Car 4
A				
B				
C				
D				
E				
F				
G				

Finally, compare prices using resources from earlier in this chapter and the price criteria you looked into in Chapter 2, as well as any serious offers you've solicited from a dealership.

	Car 1	Car 2	Car 3	Car 4
Suggested Retail Price (base)				
Dealer Cost (base)				
Cost of Desired Options				
Incentives in Effect				
Quote from Dealer 1				
Quote from Dealer 2				
Quote from Dealer 3				

Revise your worksheet—and your prices—if a test-drive has changed your mind on the engine size or options package you want.

Hunting for a great price

Serious dealer haggling is handled in Chapter 6. But vigilance on your part and some inquiries and time to shop can pay off. Don't accept a price above what you think you should pay (as outlined in Chapter 6). And keep an eye out for promotions.

When to shop to get the best deal

Great deals are found any time. Traditionally, the beginning of the year has been called a fortunate time to buy, largely because of winter doldrums and the holidays. The rationale goes that people are less likely to venture out in inclement weather to dealerships that may be snowed over when they can just as easily wait a couple of months. Add to that the crimp that holiday spending puts in most wallets, and you have valid reasons for making a New Year's resolution to buy soon.

The advantages of shopping during this season:

- Otherwise bored sales staff gives you their full attention.

- Hungry salesmen may concede to your dickering more easily.

- If winter has made sales sluggish, the selection on the lot can be better.

- It's a great time to test-drive a car for handling in less-than-ideal conditions (particularly if you're shopping for a four-wheel-drive).

Watch Out!
There's a downside to shopping when other people aren't. Eagerness to deal may be there, but so is a salesman's predisposition to extract the most out of every scarce customer he sees to make up for the low volume of cars moving off the lot. You'll have to prove your case to get the goods cheap.

One drawback is that it's a rotten time to try to sell your old car, for the same reasons that make shopping in the first two months of the year ideal.

According to some in the industry, a better time to sell your old car is during the spring, or late summer, when it's also a good time to buy because carmakers are doing everything they can to get rid of the current year's models—the new model year traditionally begins in October.

Minor (as well as major) holidays are times when you can expect to see sales running—Presidents' Day, for example. To some extent, the best time to buy a car depends on what you're shopping for. Convertibles sell briskly in the summer, four-wheel-drives better in the winter, so going against the grain may benefit you. Table 4.4 takes a look at the seasonality of sales.

TABLE 4.4   BEST MONTHS FOR CAR BUYING

January–February: Winter doldrums and holiday bills keep shoppers away.

June–July: Conventional wisdom says that people are more concerned with vacationing; there's a sales lag waiting for the new models to arrive.

August–September: Old model clearances make way for next year's editions; there are aggressive efforts to move the most popular cars (to gain "best-seller" status in industry rankings).

November: Efforts to get rid of old models before winter sales sluggishness.

December: Year-end holiday clearances; Christmas slump. Some auto industry insiders consider this the best time for consumers to shop.

Sales are going on constantly, so if you need a car now, don't be dissuaded into waiting needlessly. Good research will still save you a bundle.

No matter what season you shop, the end of the month can be a good time to buy—when salespeople and indeed the dealership may be eager to meet quota deadlines. Likewise, the latter part of the week and day are good times, but not right before closing time!

Beyond these rules of thumb, the best times to shop are whenever business is slow, such as during economic slumps, and, of course, when the models you're interested in are subject to discounts and rebates.

Unofficially...
Carmakers have
the liberty of
selling a certain
year's model line
365 days before
that year actually
starts. Before
you deal on a
"new" 1998 car,
find out if 1999's
edition is out
yet!

Cars on sale: Promotions and rebates

Isn't there always some car promotion in the works? Every Sunday newspaper seems rife with ads encouraging you to "buy now!". Rebates and incentives are special deals offered by the manufacturers to speed sales of slow-selling models or trim excess inventories. As you saw in Table 4.2, much more consumer information is out for you to easily track where and when promotional pricing is available—and how good it really is.

The most beneficial and plainly written kinds of promotions to look for are manufacturer incentives:

- Rebates can knock more than $1,000 off the MSRP in the form of a cash-back allowance
- Low or 0% manufacturer financing
- Lease subsidies

Some of these programs go directly from manufacturer to consumer, but others are dealer incentives, and it's up to the dealer whether he wants to pass that incentive savings along. Ask if the program is what's called a "graduated" one, in which the incentive relies on the number of cars that a dealer moves (he may or may not tell you, but it's worth a shot). If that's the case, try to buy after the dealer has met quotas and moved up a notch to a heftier incentive category.

Moneysaver
What's better:
money back or
lowball financ-
ing? The more
modestly priced
the car to begin
with, the more
likely you should
go for cold, hard
cash.

Dealers run their own specials, but take ads with a grain of salt. Often, rock-bottom promotions apply to only one or a few cars on the lot, and for a very limited time. If you can snag one of their deals, you probably won't have much choice between models or options.

Just the facts

- You may not be able to get as great a deal as a newspaper display ad seems to indicate, once everything's factored in. Use a good research source for basic price and incentive information.

- Shopping when legitimate incentives are underway can shave hundreds off your car-buying bill—check out the industry's current promotions at Edmund's (www.edmunds.com) or in *Automotive News*.

- Lease rates can vary dramatically, but you can check for the lowest ones by checking IntelliChoice (www.intellichoice.com) or other services.

- Shop during midwinter and late summer, when deals may be more favorable.

All About Dealerships

Chapter 5

Anyone who has set foot on a car lot, new or used, knows what it's like to feel as if they're prey. Buying a car is among many people's least-enjoyed shopping tasks. One of the reasons is the pervasive feeling that someone's out to get your money, a lot of it.

But while aggressive tactics are still around, a lot has changed in car-buying lately. It's safer and easier for the informed consumer to deal with a dealership.

In this chapter, you'll find out all about old dogs and new tricks, so you can be that informed consumer. You should be able to handle interactions with a dealership comfortably, and there are ways to avoid a dealership altogether if you know that you'd just crumple at the first whiff of negotiation pressure.

Traditional dealerships and some new kinds

Once upon a time, you went out to the edge of town to the local Pontiac, Dodge, or Lincoln-Mercury dealership. Life was simple. Then, through a series of acquisitions and consolidations, your local dealer of one brand became the dealer for several brands. Nowadays, megadealerships have sprung up in the biggest car-selling locales—virtual cities selling numerous makes of cars all on one giant lot. Too many cars for any person to see in a single visit!

So what could possibly be new in this wonderland of cars for sale? Plenty, as it turns out. Traditional dealers remain alive and well, but, in response to customer chagrin over the haggling process, one-price dealers now promise to stick with the sticker price and not gouge customers with hidden charges.

Megacar stores now exist, not only for nearly all varieties of new cars under a single proverbial roof, but also for used cars (often adhering to no-negotiation pricing policies). And finally, there's direct purchase—no dealership visit involved. Car-buying services offer to get a discount price without effort on your part, and manufacturers are now starting to offer cars for sale directly as well (which leads one to ask, "What about the testdrive?!").

The typical type

Traditional new-car dealerships offer one or a few brands for sale, and they're characterized by their representative out front—the salesman. You come to the lot and are escorted around the autos of your choice (or the salesman's persuasion), take a test-drive, and then engage in deal-making negotiations in which a number of tactics are used by a number of players.

If it's a well-run and reasonably upstanding dealership, you may leave with a car you paid too much (but not exorbitantly) for, you may have been offered too little on your trade-in and may have

Unofficially...
Dealers are constantly looking for new ways to keep customers shopping—at least one even has a diner on the premises!

Timesaver
Check your Sunday classifieds. Many carry a display page listing all the local dealerships with their phone numbers and addresses.

spent too much on financing charges. But you have what feels like a good personal relationship with the dealership, and a ready place to turn to for warranty work and maintenance.

Some of the challenges that dealers face in their day-to-day business can clue you in to potential savings. For instance, manufacturers may allot only a certain number of hot sellers to a dealership, based on how well it sells less desirable models. What this means is that if you're intent on getting a model of car that the dealer can barely get his hands on, and in a specific color with a specific options package, you shouldn't expect much leeway at negotiation time. But if you know you'll be helping a dealer move a much less popular car off the lot (perhaps you just like that model, even if not many other people seem to!), you're in a great position to deal on wheels.

What about the size of the dealership? Bigger dealers logically have better selections (usually) and cost efficiencies. But certain small dealers, particularly those that strive to be "boutiques" offering the best cars, can give more personalized service and attention. There's a difference between the small dealer that's short on quantity and the small dealer that's long on quality—you'll notice the difference as soon as you're on the lot. Choice new vehicles, trade-ins in very good condition, above-average sales personnel, lots of "quality award" plaques on the wall, and a soft-selling approach may be hints.

One-price dealers

Whether or not you have an interest in touring that much-touted Saturn plant in Spring Hill, Tennessee, or attending their annual car-owners' picnic, you have to admit one thing about the

Watch Out!
Caveat emptor (buyer beware): There are wide variations in the quality of service centers at dealerships, and in their willingness to handle warranty repairs without a hassle. Make sure that there's some emphasis on customer service before you establish a buyer-dealer relationship. Your local Better Business Bureau may be able to give you a heads-up on that (check your local phone directory, or get links to your local BBB's home page at www.bbb.org).

Saturn brand: it has done things differently. This General Motors subsidiary was a pioneer in the concept of the one-price dealership.

The idea of a one-price dealer relies on the premise of straightforwardness over salesmanship, a low-pressure approach.

But is there truly a one-price dealership? Even if each has such a policy, the flat rate you're offered may differ between dealers.

Dealerships associated with other car manufacturers advertise that they are also one-price dealers. Should you take them at their word? Never go to any dealership without knowing the difference between MSRP and dealer cost on the car you're considering (more on that in Chapter 6). But as more car sellers tune in to what customers are asking for, the number of one-price dealerships is likely to expand, and yes, if there's a one-price dealer near you, it's a worthy alternative to consider (but make sure, despite the "flat" price of the car, that you aren't stung on the "back end").

Megacar stores

There are essentially three types of car megastores:

1. Multiple-brand megastores owned by the same dealer group
2. A high-volume dealer of a single brand
3. Used car superstores

A cluster of different dealerships that are adjacent and advertise together may look like a megacar store, but they're not really in that category.

The first type of superstore, those vast car lots featuring nearly every brand of car from Audi to Volvo under one roof, are another trend that consumers are showing interest in. These stores are a particularly good option for car shoppers who want

Moneysaver
A good rule is to consider a one-price dealer the best way to shop only after you've compared its pricing (sticker price, financing, and the rest) to other area dealers and your own pricing reference.

Timesaver
Is it a multiple-make mega-store? Just look for the same dealer name attached to each brand.

to compare brands, and volume selling creates efficiencies that can be passed along to the consumer. The different makes have their own sales staffs and are largely separate entities, but there's a lot of cooperation between them.

The second type of megastore, the high-volume dealer of a single brand, often can't be touched by anyone in terms of selection. These lots may sell the most and get the largest inventories from their manufacturers. Volume sales means you should be able to strike a reasonable bargain. One risk is getting lost on the lot—such as at a dealer spanning eight acres and perhaps carrying $8 million in inventory.

The third type of outsized auto store is the used car ranch (you find out more about used car megastores in Chapter 8). Briefly, these outlets—with names like AutoNation USA, CarMax, and Driver's Mart—are trying to standardize used car sales and provide more selection at one location. Used car megastores can offer flat rate no-haggle pricing, the assurance that a vehicle has been through a thorough mechanical check, and warranties on the cars they sell. Hundreds of dollars worth of bodywork and repair may go into a car before it's put up for sale, but the stores seek to keep retail prices low through volume sales.

Dealing with no dealer at all

A sea change is underway in how people buy cars. Increasingly consumers are looking for alternatives to just arriving at the local dealership. Better-informed shoppers intent on convenience and price comparison are choosing the armchair approach, thanks in large part to the Internet.

Online selling began in a trickle, but it is now a booming business, with analysts expecting further

Unofficially...
There are nearly 22,700 dealerships nationwide, and they employ more than a million people, according to the National Automobile Dealers Association.

explosive growth. Direct sellers of products such as computers themselves (Gateway, for instance) rely on the Internet for orders (although people certainly still shop for computers in conventional stores).

It looks as if the car industry is heading in the direction of home shopping. According to the National Automobile Dealers Association, more than half of the new-car dealership franchises in the U.S. have a Web site, and more than a quarter allow customers to set up sales appointments online and fill out electronic finance applications. Nearly a quarter even accommodate new- and used- vehicle orders online.

Car-buying services

Car-buying services don't exactly eliminate the middleman—they know him well and get a low price without requisite haggling. Although car-buying services can be enormously helpful for those who really hate negotiation, will they really get you the best prices? The economics behind the method say yes.

Two popular Internet-based buying services are listed in the following table.

TABLE 5.1   BUYING SERVICES ON THE INTERNET

Auto-By-Tel	Web site: www.autobytel.com
AutoVantage	Web site: www.autovantage.com

Buying services based on the Internet have enjoyed growing popularity recently. One of the biggest is Auto-By-Tel. Fill out a no-obligation (free) purchase request at its Web site, request low-price quotes on new and used cars from its network of 2,700 dealers, and then apply for competitive financing and insurance quotes—all online.

Unofficially ...
New car and truck dealer franchises with Web sites credit their Internet presence with an average of five new vehicle sales monthly, according to the National Automobile Dealers Association.

Auto-By-Tel says it seeks to provide consumers with all the information and data they need to make savvy car purchasing decisions, through a "quick, efficient, low-cost, and hassle-free process for purchasing, financing, leasing, and insuring vehicles"— in a phrase, the company says it believes that the informed consumer is the empowered consumer.

Why would a dealer offer preferred pricing to a buying service?

1. Cars are cheaper to sell online
2. Volume, volume, volume

Dealerships can spend less marketing vehicles online than via traditional advertising. The more cars a dealership sells that way, the bigger the efficiencies get, and some of the savings are passed on to customers.

Not all buying services are primarily Internet-based. Even at a fee of $165, car-buying assistance is sought from CarBargains, (800) 475-7283, run by the Center for the Study of Services. The nonprofit group promises it will contact at least five dealerships and have them bid competitively for your business, and also operates a sister service called LeaseWise. Is it worth the money? "In a March 1998 independent test by *Money Magazine,* CarBargains beat Internet services 9 out of 10 times on prices even with our fee," says Robert Ellis, operations director for the Center for the Study of Services.

Car brokers

Car brokers come as close as it gets to dealing without the dealer. A broker may promise to help you find any make and model at the lowest price. They may charge several dollars for a quote and refund it if you buy a car through them.

Auto brokers often work as a sort of franchisee, placing factory orders through a buying company that arranges delivery through a local dealer. The problem with auto brokering is that "middleman" fees may be worked in along the way.

Some disadvantages of going through auto brokers can include:

- Not being able to make a trade-in and having to sell your old car yourself

- Factory-ordering your vehicle limits your ability to inspect it (and you have to go elsewhere for test-drives on the model)

- You're limited in local representation after having bought the car—the broker made the arrangement and the dealer may have delivered the car, but the factory is where you really got the car and they aren't set up to deal primarily with individual buyers

Picking and choosing between dealers

Consumers in this country aren't used to buying the way car dealers ask them to. When you go to a fast food franchise for a burger, you expect it to have a price equivalent at another franchise in the same city, and the local newspaper costs the same— perhaps $.35—at every vending machine that dispenses it.

Because Chevrolet dealers sell Chevrolets, it doesn't easily sink in that dealers are stores that are independent from one another—we're so used to flat pricing. The dealer model exists (with appliances, for example), but it's not our most recognized way of doing business.

Thus, there can be differences of thousands of dollars between prices for the same car at different dealerships, and the consumer who realizes it can benefit.

Look for a dealer with both reasonable pricing and good customer focus. A salesman shouldn't be just an obstacle to overcome in your hunt for the right vehicle. He should be interested enough in your needs to show you the types of cars that fit your requirements, point out their benefits, and be somewhat candid about where another model may offer a better alternative.

Some things that can clue you in to a customer-focused dealership with reasonable pricing:

- Ads with clearly stated terms that shy away from shouting and patronizing

- Taglines in the yellow pages (or ads), affirming their customer orientation

- Window stickers and advertised prices are the MSRP or less; not more

- A good reputation with the local Better Business Bureau.

A customer-focused dealership is important because owner-dealer interaction doesn't end when a car is driven off the lot. Warranties mean that maintenance and repair are dealer issues, and those items are usually handled at the dealer from which the vehicle is bought. Customer focus is extremely critical with leases because you're tied to a specific dealer for as long as four years.

A few words to the wise are in order about where you buy or lease your car—not from whom, but where. If a dealer with reasonable pricing and good customer service is available close to you, that's your preferred dealer. For scheduled maintenance and (heaven forbid) warranty repair, the easier and quicker the trip to the dealer, the better.

Watch Out!
Be careful! Auto sales and service problems top consumer complaint lists year after year, and auto-related complaints consistently top the charts in surveys conducted by the National Association of Attorneys General. (Source: Consumer Federation of America)

Bright Idea
Ask a dealer if they provide courtesy transportation when your car's in for service. Some do, and it's a welcome convenience.

Watch out!
Thinking of buy-
ing from a dealer
you don't like but
who has a rock-
bottom price?
Think twice! That
rock-bottom price
might turn out to
be very expen-
sive. And what-
ever you do,
make sure you
have a good rela-
tionship with
whoever you con-
sider leasing
from.

What about iffy dealerships? When should you simply leave, go somewhere else, vamoose, hide? There are plenty of clues to let you know that a dealership's one to stay away from:

- Extremely misleading advertisements
- Bad attitudes at the dealership (apathetic, uninformed or patronizing salespeople; visibly irritable management; angry customers who arrive during your visit; or absent customer support staff
- Salesmen who tell outright lies to you or are clearly saying only what you want to hear
- Signs of failure such as a very poor inventory of cars, incompetent staff, or little upkeep of the dealership

You'd do well to trust your gut and avoid a dealership that just doesn't feel right. There are plenty of others to choose from.

Understanding how a dealership works

Successful car dealerships can be phenomenal money producers. It's not unusual for a top salesman to gross over $100,000 annually. Where do all those profits come from?

Bright Idea
If buying a car
comes down to a
matter of a cou-
ple hundred dol-
lars between one
dealership (a
great one) and
another (an iffy
one), in the long
run you'll proba-
bly be far happi-
er if you choose
the former. It's
not wrong to pay
a premium for
good service,
just to pay too
much of one.

A dealership makes money anywhere it can—the sale of the car, options, financing, extras, delivery charges, servicing, and maintenance—you name it. As much as two-thirds of a dealer's profit comes not via the basic auto package you buy up front, but through financing and additions (like rustproofing) that are tagged on to your purchase at the "back end." *Back end* is anything that's sold to you other than the vehicle itself, and it pays to cover yours. You'll learn all about the back end in Part VII.

The salesman isn't the only one making money or trying to get yours. Who's who at a dealership and what roles do they take in selling a car to you? The cast list includes:

- The salesman
- The sales manager
- A finance (or business) manager
- Sometimes the general manager
- Sometimes other salesmen
- The leasing manager

The first person you're likely to encounter is, of course, the salesman, who sells maybe a car a day. He will show you different cars, take you for a test-drive, discuss pricing, and bring you in for negotiations in his office. Once you're there and price discussions begin, other figures from the dealership, with potentially deceptive roles to play, may make an appearance. At some point in the negotiations, the sales manager is likely to be called in by the salesman, perhaps to clarify a point, say hello, and perhaps engage in a little good guy/bad guy role-playing with the salesman. After the initial introduction, you're likely to see little of the sales manager. He'll be in another room, and for every negotiating concession you request, the salesman may have to run to his office to seek his approval.

The salesman may "try to see what he can do" about your request for a lower price, and the sales manager may say "we just can't," but offer a counterproposal. This can continue either until you give in to what sounds like a good deal, or they decide to fold on your request and leave most of the profit-seeking to the next dealer representative you'll meet—the financing manager. On the way there, you may even be introduced to the dealership's general manager, who often plays a courteous parental role.

Once a car price is agreed upon, and sometimes before, you'll likely be introduced to the finance (or business) manager. By this time, many car buyers are relaxing and feeling as if their work is largely done, but not so. This could be farther from the truth. One of the real goals of the financing manager is to get ahold of perhaps more than half of the profit a dealership makes on a customer, at what is called the "back end" of the buying deal.

In addition to handling financing arrangements, the finance manager may also:

- Push extended warranties

- Try to sell you high-profit extras like rustproofing or alarm systems

- Handle the act of actually getting the car to you

Sometimes, the leasing manager is a different person from the financing manager, which increases the opportunities to sell to you and delay your exit from the dealership.

Who really has the power? The salesman is the one whose bread and butter depends on selling you a car, and he's the foot soldier of the battle. Salespeople typically earn commissions based on the number of vehicles sold, dealer profitability, or a combination of the two. Incentives and bonus systems are frequently at work, though, encouraging the sales staff to sell quickly or push a certain model.

Salesmen are seldom in a position to make decisions on their own, however. The sales manager is usually the person with the power and, in cases of serious negotiating concessions, the general manager himself may sign off on a deal. Significant power is also in the hands of the financing manager, though the customer may regard him as an incidental figure.

The remaining significant cast member in dealership negotiations is the customer. The dealer's most profitable customer is likely to be any of these:

Watch Out!
The number of different strategies in use at the average dealership can amaze the uninitiated.

- A consumer ready and willing to pay retail and agree to every addition (a dream customer with no idea how the car-buying process really works)

- The customer with a big ego who can be given one or two concessions and think he's walking away with a great deal (when in fact he's being gouged at the back end)

- A busy person without time or interest in comparing pricing at different dealerships (though it may cost her thousands)

- The person who buys on emotional impulse and without a good grasp of figures

- Anyone who walks in saying "I only want to spend this amount per month" (he or she will spend that, but into eternity)

- The desperate customer without reliable transportation who must get a car as soon as possible.

- The customer who is unsure of what she wants and is easily steered toward whatever slow-seller the dealership has left on the lot

The kind of customer you want to be:

- Visibly courteous, knowledgeable, conservative, on a schedule, and serious about buying

- Reasonable enough to allow some selling tactics (this is, after all, what a salesman does), but firm about not giving in

- Logical and well-prepared, with figures that back up your claims about how reasonably they can sell you a car and still make money (though this shouldn't be a main topic of conversation)

- A shopper who takes time to compare and seek out a very good deal

- A thorough reader of all fine print

- One who's aware of where dealers profit and how to avoid being taken in

- True to yourself about how much negotiating you can handle, or whether a one-price dealer or a buying service might be the best route

Bright Idea
Let a salesman know up front that you know how much you can afford and have been researching cars. If you're ready to buy at the right price, tell them, you'll have their full attention.

The amount of money that dealerships make supports the idea that not all that many customers are well-prepared going into negotiations. You will be, but keep your cards close to your chest. Be human and personable, as well as a smart consumer. You want the salesman to like you and feel alright about giving you a deal better than the next customer might get. That means not being overblown or obstinate, and not throwing down a paper with a price on it that you demand the dealership meet. Be straightforward and on your best behavior.

Just the facts

- Dealerships are leaning more toward consumer demands for fair or even flat pricing, but the old heavy-negotiating model still exists.

- Car-buying services sell cars at modest prices directly, even over the Internet, without a dealer visit involved.

- Dealerships make up to two-thirds of their profit selling you anything but the car—financing and hidden charges known as the "back end."

- The sales manager (and sometimes the financing manager) has the real negotiating power at a dealership, not the salesman.
- Dealers aren't bound to sticker a car at the Manufacturer's Suggested Retail Price. Even so-called one-price dealers may deviate.

Money—Nitty Gritty Price and Financing Numbers

PART III

Understanding Pricing

Domestic auto manufacturers alone are posting record profits topping $16 billion a year. A lot of money is pouring into profit margins, and this year some of it may be yours. The objective is to pay a fair price—in this case, fair should be as little as humanly possible. The car industry is doing quite well, thank you, and you don't need to subsidize it.

One way you can pay a relatively measly amount for an automobile—if you're buying new—is to help out the dealer and the manufacturer. They've got a hot new model out that buyers are lining up for, ready to pay more than they should. You can take a slow mover off their hands (provided, of course, that it suits your tastes). Manufacturers will let you know when their inventory numbers aren't balancing and they need to clear the decks—they'll put cars on sale, using rebates and other incentives—legitimate ways to say, "Hey you, move this car!"

In this chapter, we'll rein in numbers run amok. What's an MSRP? What's a dealer sticker price? Why

Chapter 6

Unofficially...
The annual pay-roll for all dealer-ships is over $35 billion, and over $5 billion is spent each year by franchised dealers on advertising. (Source: National Automobile Dealers Association)

Bright Idea
How do some people find their best price? New car shopper Barney explains his technique, "I called from another dealer, where I was get-ting ready to sign on the dot-ted line. Dealer invoice $19,800; my price $19,300."

a delivery charge? How much did Joe Dealer pay the manufacturer in the first place, and how much should you let him take from you? Yes, used cars are different. And your trade-in's different still. Then, we'll get to leasing...

New car pricing

The way new cars are priced, it could almost seem as if you're in a land of rug bazaars being run by accountants. Lots of numbers. It all appears official. Prices look as if they're set in stone and seem unar-guable. But you, politely of course, can and should question them—not outright, but by ignoring post-ed prices altogether and doing research like a good consumer.

Dissecting the Manufacturer's Suggested Retail Price

It's usually the sticker price, and you'll be having it stuck to you if you pay that much. Manufacturer's Suggested Retail Price (or MSRP) is that thing usu-ally plastered on the window of a new car (amid other numbers). Here's what that label usually lists:

- The car's year, manufacturer, and model
- The base MSRP price (and what equipment comes "standard" in that base price)
- The options package on the car and its overall price
- Any individual options on the car and their prices
- Engine and transmission specifications
- Fuel economy ratings (city/highway)
- The MSRP, once all the options are added in
- Where the vehicle was built

What's the "real" price you need to know?

The Manufacturer's Suggested Retail Price is usually 6–18% higher than the "dealer invoice price" (what a car actually cost the dealership to acquire).

The dealer invoice price, also known as dealer cost, is almost but not quite the "real" price you need to know. It turns out that some income is usually assured for the dealer at an even earlier stage of the car-selling process. Dealer invoice is what the dealer paid for the car, but when he sells it, the manufacturer typically gives him something known as "holdback," an amount usually 2–3% of the MSRP.

This is a built-in cushion for the dealer, who, after all, has bills to pay. If you've ever seen an ad proclaiming that a dealer is clearing out cars at cost, now you know how he can be such a nice guy and still stay in business. Even selling cars at "cost" (meaning dealer cost with no add-ons), he'll make a few hundred dollars on the average new car because of holdback.

If you assume that the holdback covers the costs of doing business, ignore it and just figure in 3–5% above dealer invoice to allow for a reasonable profit—there you have a good target buy price, as a rule of thumb (see Worksheet 6.1).

WORKSHEET 6.1   TARGET BUY PRICE (RULE OF THUMB)

$_____ Dealer Invoice Price + 5% – $_____ Any Dealer Rebate Amount = $_____ Target Buy Price

Dealer rebates are incentives that a manufacturer offers to the dealer, not directly to the customer. They can amount to thousands of dollars and you might not be told about them. How to find out? Look them up yourself! Table 6.1 shows a sample list of dealer rebates.

Timesaver
The final selling price of a new car is usually at the lower end of the markup over dealer cost because of rebates and other incentives.

Bright Idea
Webheads will find Edmund's a great spot to get into the issue of dealer holdback (www.edmunds. com), with a lift of current percentages for different car makes and models.

You can check dealer rebates at Edmund's Web site, www. edmunds.com.

Remember,
these are just
examples, not
what's offered
currently—check
the Edmund's
Web site or other
sources for the
deals going now.

TABLE 6.1   DEALER INCENTIVES (SAMPLE)

BMW

(Effective through: 4/30/98)
1998 Models:

BMW 318i	$1,000
BMW 328i	$1,500

Chrysler Corporation

(Effective through: 4/6/98)
1998 Models:

Chrysler Town & Country SWB	$250–$1,500
Chrysler Town & Country LWB	$250–$1,500
Dodge Caravan	$250–$1,500
Dodge Grand Caravan	$250–$1,500
Dodge Dakota	$500–$1,000 (excluding 4-cylinder models)
Dodge Ram Pickup	$500
Jeep Cherokee	$500
Jeep Grand Cherokee	$500–$750
Plymouth Voyager	$250–$1,500
Plymouth Grand Voyager	$250–$1,500

(Source: Edmund's)

Still want to know what the dealer really paid for that vehicle? Worksheet 6.2 shows you how to find out. Remember, destination charges, which you'll see on window stickers, are not used in figuring real dealer cost as a percentage of MSRP. You can use Table 6.2, a list of dealer holdback rates by manufacturer, in your figuring.

WORKSHEET 6.2   WHAT DID THE DEALER REALLY PAY FOR THIS CAR?

First, figure the amount of the dealer's built-in cushion in dollar terms:

$_____ Manufacturer's Suggested Retail Price (less any destination charges if included in MSRP)

× ._____ Dealer Holdback Percentage (usually 2–3% of MSRP—expressed as .02 or .03)

= $_____ Dealer Holdback Amount in Dollars

Now use that figure to compute the real cost of a car to the dealer—it's less than what's commonly called "dealer cost":

$_____ Dealer Cost

− $_____ Dealer Holdback Amount in Dollars

= $_____

+ $_____ Vehicle Delivery Charges

− $_____ Any Dealer Rebate Amount

= $_____ REAL DEALER COST

Most carmakers use holdbacks, but not all. Table 6.2 sorts it out (dealer holdback rates may change—check the Edmund's Web site for the most current list).

TABLE 6.2—DEALER HOLDBACK RATES BY MANUFACTURER

Make	Holdback
Acura	2% of the Base MSRP
Audi	No Holdback
BMW	2% of the Base MSRP
Buick	3% of the Total MSRP
Cadillac	3% of the Total MSRP
Chevrolet	3% of the Total MSRP
Chrysler	3% of the Total MSRP
Dodge	3% of the Total MSRP
Eagle	3% of the Total MSRP
Ford	3% of the Total MSRP
GMC	3% of the Total MSRP
Honda	2% of the Base MSRP (except Prelude, which has no Holdback.)
Hyundai	2% of the Total Invoice
Infiniti	1% of the Total MSRP + 1% of the Total Invoice
Isuzu	3% of the Total MSRP
Jaguar	2% of the Base Invoice
Jeep	3% of the Total MSRP
Kia	No Holdback

Where to get the numbers: the Manufacturer's Suggested Retail Price (MSRP) and often the Dealer Invoice Price can be obtained from dealers, manufacturers, magazine ads. But independent sources abound and are recommended—car-buying annuals or any number of Internet sites. (Be sure to ask a dealer or review your source for any amount in destination charges included as a portion of MSRP.)

As a rule of thumb, the hold-back amount varies from 2% for many imports to 3% for most domestic cars, based on the MSRP of the car with desired options. But import car hold-backs may be calculated as a percentage of base MSRP or base Dealer Invoice instead. (Sources: *Kelley Blue Book*)

Land Rover	No Holdback
Lexus	No Holdback
Lincoln	3% of the Total MSRP
Mazda	2% of the Base MSRP
Mercedes-Benz	3% of the Total MSRP
Mercury	3% of the Total MSRP
Mitsubishi	2% of the Total MSRP
Nissan	2% of the Total Invoice + 1.5% (floor-planning allowance)
Oldsmobile	3% of the Total MSRP
Plymouth	3% of the Total MSRP
Pontiac	3% of the Total MSRP
Porsche	No Holdback
Saab	3% of the Base MSRP
Saturn	One-price sales; customer pays MSRP
Subaru	2% of the Total MSRP
Suzuki	2% of the Base MSRP
Toyota	2% of the Base Invoice (Amount may differ in Southeastern U.S.)
Volkswagen	2% of the Total MSRP
Volvo	$300 Flat Amount

Source: Edmund's (1998 percentages)

Understanding the terms

New car pricing terminology is reviewed in Table 6.3, as the definitions relate to each other.

TABLE 6.3   NEW CAR PRICING TERMS

Pricing Term	Also Known As	Means	To Calculate
Manufacturer's Suggested Retail Price	MSRP (sometimes known as "sticker price")	What a manufacturer thinks deal-ers should sell their cars for	Usually 6–18% above Dealer Invoice Price
Dealer Invoice Price	Dealer Cost	What a dealer paid to acquire a car from the manufacturer	

Holdback	A "hidden" amount that the manufacturer pays the dealer upon selling the car (not reflected in Dealer Invoice Price)	Usually 2–3% of MSRP

With this basic vocabulary, you should be able to find your way around the basics of new car pricing. In a sentence, the way to find a good price on a new car is this:

Find the Dealer Invoice Price, deduct 2–3% of the MSRP from it as holdback, add delivery charges (and sometimes advertising charges, as we'll explain later on), subtract any rebate amount, add in the profit you want to allow the dealer (a few percentage points), and voilà!

Used car pricing

Price labels on preowned autos bear little similarity to new car terms. That in itself can be a reason to consider buying used! The one consistent thing you can say about used car prices is that they're lower than new car prices. Here's how they work.

The used car price bazaar

There are many different ways to buy used cars—from a new car dealership (where you're getting lease returns or trade-ins), a used car lot, a private party, an auction, or even a rental car company.

The price you pay for a car from these different sources varies. In the case of a new car lot, you're often paying not only for the car but for some refurbishment that the dealer has done to bring it up to snuff. At the opposite end of the spectrum, there's the used car auction, where you and a mechanic may have a few hours to inspect a car, but what you

Watch Out!
Don't buy a new car without establishing its model year. Check the Vehicle Identification Number (VIN), usually seen on the dashboard of the driver's side. The tenth character in the 17-character VIN refers to the model year:
1981....B
1982....C
1983....D
1984....E
1985....F
1986....G
1987....H
1988....J
1989....K
1990....L
1991....M
1992....N
1993....P
1994....R
1995....S
1997....T
1998....W
1999....X
2000....Y

Unofficially...
Of the over 50
million used
vehicles sold
annually, half are
individual-to-
individual sales.
(Source:
Progressive
Basics)

see is what you get. These cars may be repossessions from people who couldn't pay their financing (see the next chapter to ensure that you don't wind up in the same situation), or they may come from a host of other sources.

Underneath it all, there are three vital pricing terms to know, as we'll describe next.

Kelley Blue Book and other price guides

A number of guides are used in the automotive industry to determine appropriate pricing, and it's worth the time to educate yourself about them. You've probably heard the term "Blue Book," but there are also guides known colloquially in the auto industry as the Black Book, the NADA book (N.A.D.A. Official Used Car Guide), the Red Book, the AMR, and others. If you're terribly curious, you can inquire at a few dealers in your area about which company's data they use—there can be regional variations in preference.

Kelley Blue Book has its competitors, but the popular term "Blue Book" (that is, as it's used in the auto industry) originated with Kelley, the company says. It all started back in 1918 in California. Les Kelley, an Arkansas preacher's son, parked three Model T Fords in an open lot, put $450 in the till, and thus began a used car lot known as the Kelley Kar Company. Four years later, Kelley started putting together used car price lists; in 1926, he published the first *Blue Book of Motor Car Values*.

Unofficially...
The *Kelley Blue
Book* was called
"Blue Book" after
the Social
Register, imply-
ing that you'd
find valuable
information
inside.
Coincidentally,
around the same
time as the car
price reference,
Emily Post pub-
lished *Etiquette:
The Blue Book of
Social Usage.*

Kelley's books were used primarily by dealers until 1993, when the first consumer edition was published. They feature 15 years of used car values on over 10,000 models of vehicles.

Two vital prices listed for every used car are the "wholesale" price and the "retail" price:

- **Wholesale:** what your old car is worth to a dealer if you're trading it in with the reconditioning factored in

- **Retail:** the price the dealer is listing it for when you drive by next week

The retail figure adds in not only the cost of making the vehicle ready for sale—reconditioning and repairs, but also advertising, the cost of keeping the vehicle on the lot, and some profit. Although you're most likely to see this figure at dealerships, many private parties try to sell their used cars at or near "retail." Some, however, settle for closer to wholesale or lower, and that's often where you can get a great deal.

What does a Blue Book listing look like? The figure on the next page shows a sample page. In addition to "wholesale" or "retail," you need to determine what condition the car is in and how many miles it has.

The real value of a used car isn't set in stone. There are differences between what one price service thinks a car is worth and what another does. There are also differences between pricing in the *Kelley Blue Book,* designed for the auto industry, and Kelley's Web site (www.kbb.com), meant for consumers. The company explains it this way:

"The trade publications are intended for use by the wholesale industry and represent vehicles that have been thoroughly reconditioned to manufacturer specifications, completely safety checked, and warranted by the dealer. The value contained in the trade publications is widely used by dealers as a starting point to estimate a vehicle's value, depending on its condition."

Timesaver
To save yourself a trip to your local library's reference desk, check *Kelley Blue Book* prices on the Web at www.kbb.com. The pricing information is geared more toward consumers there, too.

1996 JAGUAR

Body Type	VIN	Wt.	List	Whls.	Sug. Ret.
XJR—6-Cyl. Supercharged—Equipment Schedule 1					
W.B. 113.0"; 4.0 Liter.					
Sedan 4D	PX114	4215	66850		
XJS—6-Cyl.—Equipment Schedule 2					
W.B. 102.0"; 4.0 Liter.					
2+2 Convertible 2D	NX274	4022	62150	**37200**	**44200**
XJ12—V12—Equipment Schedule 1					
W.B. 117.9"; 6.0 Liter.					
Sedan 4D	MX634	4440	79950		

1997 JAGUAR — SAJ(HX124)-V-#

Body Type	VIN	Wt.	List	Whls.	Sug. Ret.
XJ6—6-Cyl.—Equipment Schedule 1					
W.B. 113.0", 117.9" (L & Vanden Plas); 4.0 Liter.					
Sedan 4D	HX124	4080	54980		
L Sedan 4D	HX624	4110	59980		
Vanden Plas Sedan 4D	KX624	4130	64380		
XJR—6-Cyl. Supercharged—Equipment Schedule 1					
W.B. 113.0"; 4.0 Liter.					
Sedan 4D	PX114	4125	67980		
XK8—V8—Equipment Schedule 2					
W.B. 101.9", 109.9" (Conv); 4.0 Liter.					
Coupe 2D	GX574	3673	65480		
Convertible 2D	GX274	3867	70480		

1998 JAGUAR — SAJ(HX124)-W-#

Body Type	VIN	Wt.	List	Whls.	Sug. Ret.
XJ8—V8—Equipment Schedule 1					
W.B. 113.0", 117.9" (L & Vanden Plas); 4.0 Liter.					
Sedan 4D	HX124	3996	55330		
L Sedan 4D	HX624	4044	60330		
Vanden Plas Sedan 4D	KX624	4048	64380		
XJR—V8 Supercharged—Equipment Schedule 1					
W.B. 113.0"; 4.0 Liter.					
Sedan 4D	PX184	4075	67980		
XK8—V8—Equipment Schedule 2					
W.B. 101.9"; 4.0 Liter.					
Coupe 2D	GX524	3673	65480		
Convertible 2D	GX224	3867	70480		

KIA

1994 KIA — KNA(FA121)-R-#

Body Type	VIN	Wt.	List	Whls.	Sug. Ret.
SEPHIA—4-Cyl.—Equipment Schedule 6					
W.B. 98.4"; 1.6 Liter.					
RS Sedan 4D	FA121	2339	10130	**5025**	**7425**
LS Sedan 4D	FA121	2383	10674	**5475**	**7975**

96   DEDUCT FOR RECONDITIONING   0198A

If you're figuring the value of a used car that you want to trade in (or buy from a private party), look at the wholesale figure and work your way down, depending on the car's condition. If it's in excellent shape, will it take under a hundred bucks in detailing to bring it up toward the "wholesale" standard? Or does it really need a few hundred dollars in repairs to get in the ballpark?

The Kelley Web site is geared more directly toward the consumer. Rather than simply stating a "wholesale" price, it asks you to ascertain the condition of a vehicle in order to determine the "trade-in" value, a figure that, unlike "wholesale," doesn't factor in dealer refurbishing costs.

How do you determine what the car's condition is? A few basics:

- **Excellent:** the car looks terrific, is mechanically excellent, doesn't need anything done to it, and would readily pass smog inspection. Even the tires should look nearly new.

- **Good:** free of major defects and mechanical problems. Cosmetically, only minor blemishes, if any, and a bunch of tread left on the tires.

- **Fair:** a vehicle in safe running condition, but with some mechanical and cosmetic defects (such as rust damage), and probably in need of new tires.

- **Poor:** it takes a pro to accurately gauge the value of a car in this shape—which can mean anything from a damaged frame, to title and odometer uncertainties, to rust. This is an excellent category not to concern yourself with!

What's the difference between the trade-in and retail price on a used car? Table 6.4 shows an example.

TABLE 6.4 TRADE-IN VS. RETAIL VALUE

1996 Toyota Camry DX (four-door sedan)
12,000 miles
"Good" condition
Typically equipped
Trade-in Value: $13,045
Retail Value: $17,125

(Source: *Kelley Blue Book* Consumer Wev site www.kbb.com)

As you can see, hunting for a price closer to trade-in can save you thousands.

Watch Out!
Avoid cars with "salvage titles," which means they've been in serious accidents or other disasters. The industry standard for pricing these vehicles, according to Kelley's, uses a rule of thumb to deduct 50% of the value, sometimes more.

Moneysaver
Although a consumer with common sense may be able to guesstimate a vehicle's condition, it's good advice to get a trusted mechanic's opinion because major mechanical (and other) problems aren't always apparent.

Moneysaver
There are services
on the Web that
will sell you a
detailed report of
a car's history
based on its VIN
(try plugging
"VIN number"
into your favorite
search engine to
find them).

Determining the real price of your target car

Used car pricing is a more variable game than new car sales—the underlying commodity is less known. With new cars, every vehicle is in the same shape and specific values are placed on all the options that can be ordered.

With used cars, the right price is an estimate that is based on myriad factors. As an estimation, a great price is one that comes within a couple to a few hundred dollars above the trade-in price when buying from a private party. When buying from a dealer, assume that a car (that may have come in as a trade, for instance) was acquired for slightly less than wholesale value, or for wholesale value at most. Most of the amount quoted above is dealer profit, and you should expect the dealer to have figured in several hundred dollars profit from the outset.

The used car industry, however, has been undergoing both a boom time and some difficulties. There are lots of lease returns and many consumers are buying used, but the profits that can be squeezed out of each car are diminishing.

Unofficially...
Very few con-
sumer transac-
tions are as
deceptively sim-
ple as entering
into a new car
lease, but this
seemingly simple
transaction is
fraught with con-
sumer risk.
(Source: Center
for the Study of
Services/
LeaseWise)

The strange world of lease pricing

As if new and used car pricing weren't complicated enough, along comes the concept of leasing, with its own peculiar brand of gee-whiz figuring. A third of new vehicle "sales" are actually leases, so it's clearly an area that consumers might as well get friendly with.

With a lease, you don't own the car, but you get to drive it for awhile—two to five years, depending on the lease you choose. You pay an amount up front, and for the term of the lease you also dish out monthly checks just as if you were buying a car. The payments are usually lower, however, which is why people have grown fond of leasing.

It's totally different

Buying is much closer to a straightforward transaction, and aside from renting homes, consumers are most familiar with this purchase process in their daily lives. Although leasing may have benefits, a certain amount of fear and bewilderment has accompanied the whole idea for many people.

Leasing's intricate and inscrutable nature has led many a car shopper down the primrose path to paying way too much, a testament to the difficulty of understanding the terminology and concepts involved. But as the public has sought out lower payment rates, leasing has cozied up.

After years of vagueness, new federal rules make dealers give shoppers more information about their prospective leases (such as comparisons to purchase prices). And the automotive industry itself recognizes the appeal of an understandable lease that won't ward off dollar-conscious consumers.

What determines a great lease price?

The main concept of lease pricing is this: when you're leasing, you're paying for the depreciation on a new car and not for the car itself. So rather than locating the cheapest car you can, you want to look for the one that holds its value best over time—and that's where your best deal will be hidden.

Simply: you're paying for depreciation, so that's what you should economize on; the better the car, the lower the likely depreciation.

The difference between a $20,000 car that retains 60% of its value over two years and a similarly priced car that depreciates 50% is a whopping

Watch Out!
Be on the lookout for leasing traps like ads that tell you a car is $500 down and $199 a month. In actuality, your up-front charges could be double the alleged down payment because there are all sorts of "up front" charges besides the down payment.

66
Treat a lease in the beginning as if you're going to buy a car...if you find a car of quality, you're going to get a high residual and that's just basically the bottom line: the higher the residual, the lower your payment.
—Jonathan Banks, Editor, *Automotive Lease Guide*
99

$2,000. That's two thousand dollars you won't have to pay if you get the better-faring auto.

So that's cost number one, the big one: the amount of depreciation. Cost number two is the amount of interest you're being charged. The closest analogy to a purchase interest rate is, in leasing, a net interest rate (which you'll find out more about in the next few paragraphs).

The third cost factor is dealer profit. A dealer can make money a number of ways on a lease, from padding traditional fees associated with leasing; to simply calculating the lease from a higher starting point (more toward MSRP than "dealer cost"); and of course, from financing and aftersell.

The three things, then, determining a great lease rate are:

1. **Depreciation:** how well a car holds its value.

2. **Interest rate:** how low is the effective interest rate you're being offered on the lease.

3. **Dealer profit:** how little profit the dealer is willing to make on up-front (and other) charges.

Now, on to some important definitions.

How lease pricing works

We've stated that the price of a lease is determined most fundamentally from the difference between a car's original cost (plus markup, interest, and incidentals) and what it is expected to be worth at the end of the lease term, two or even five years down the road.

To defeat the many misleading avenues that you can fall victim to in lease negotiations, you need to know how to get out of lease-land and talk about the car as if it were a purchase.

The closest thing to the real price of leasing a vehicle is something called "capitalized cost," which is the price the dealer actually gets for the lease. And just as if you were going to purchase a car, you'll be asked to put something down on the vehicle. In leasing, that's called a "capitalized cost reduction." The more capitalized cost reduction you pay, the less your monthly payments should be (just as they would be less if you made a down payment when buying a car).

After you've made that down payment of sorts, and after any rebates or other incentives are offered, the remaining amount of the capitalized cost becomes known as "net capitalized cost." That's what is distributed over a certain number of years to come up with your monthly payment figure. And from that is derived the important "net interest rate," the closest thing leasing offers to a comparable figure against interest rates you might get when financing the purchase of a car.

Among the fees you'll find tucked into lease paperwork are miscellaneous fees such as the "acquisition fee," a charge to process the lease; and a "disposition fee," a charge you pay to fund the dealer's expense to refurbish the vehicle for sale when you turn it in at the end of the lease. You'll also pay a (usually refundable) security deposit at the inception of a lease (as if you aren't paying enough toward the vehicle anyway!). Be aware that other fees may apply if you turn in the vehicle with more mileage than allowed, or with more than normal wear and tear. See Part V, "The Lease Option," for specifics.

Moneysaver
As a quick rule of thumb, the better the resale value percentage of a car and the lower the net interest rate on the lease, the less you'll pay.

How new government rules help

New mandates should make it less confusing to lease. As of 1998, dealers are required to give shoppers a written disclosure of the lease's major terms separately before they sign the contract, when the lease has a total cost up to $25,000.

Among those disclosures is a handy item called "total inception cost," which may disuade a seller's temptation to rave in ads about some low amount down and then hide other up-front charges in the fine print.

Other required disclosures go like this:

- **Amount due at lease signing:** includes capitalized cost reduction ("leasespeak" for the down payment), bank or acquisition fee, first monthly payment, security deposit, and title and registration fees

- **Monthly payments:** due dates for payments and total over the lease term

- **Other charges:** mileage, for instance (see Chapter 10 for an explanation of the various kinds of charges you may encounter in a lease)

- **Total of payments:** everything you're paying, in one fat number

- **Calculation of monthly payment:** how the dealer arrived at that installment figure

- **Early termination fees:** a warning that you could be out hundreds or even thousands if you try to end the lease early

- **Excessive wear and use:** a warning if you're rough on the car or drive it too many miles, you'll pay (generally between a dime and a quarter per excess mile)

▪ **Purchase option:** tells you whether you have the right to buy the car at the end of the lease and at what price

The alchemy of distilling "buy" prices from "lease" prices

You'll learn how to crunch numbers and solidly compare a buy versus a lease in Chapter 11, and we'll go over some of the older, more confusing terminology there.

The shortcut for comparing a lease price to a buy price is to not look in the details but at the overall figures. What are you being offered for the lease (net capitalized cost and net interest rate); what are you being offered for the purchase (your total purchase price and financing interest rate)?

It's important to negotiate the price of a car with a dealer as if you intend to purchase it. Follow the same steps as you would for finding a target price on a new car, and let your lease decision be based on that and the competitiveness of financing offered. Don't focus on the monthly payment as your basis for getting the vehicle or you'll risk paying too much.

Just the facts

▪ The MSRP (Manufacturer's Suggested Retail Price) of a car runs 6–18% higher than "dealer invoice price."

▪ In most cases, a dealer really pays 2–3% of the MSRP less than the dealer invoice price on a vehicle.

▪ Used car pricing is divided between trade-in, wholesale, and higher retail figures.

Timesaver
Worksheet 7.2 in the next chapter lets you compare leasing against buying and financing a car (or paying cash for it).

Unofficially...
Three percent of the total revenue of all states is the result of sales taxes generated by the sales of new cars and trucks, and consumers spend $60 billion annually on motor vehicle-related taxes.
(Source: National Automobile Dealers Association)

- New leasing disclosure regulations make it easier to compare purchases and leases—net capitalized cost and net interest rate are terms to be familiar with.

- A good price on a lease relies on a high resale value percentage and a competitive net interest rate.

GET THE SCOOP ON...
Arranging financing before you shop for an auto ▪
When dealer financing may be your best bet ▪ Typical
new and used car loan rates ▪ What's a good rate
and how to get it ▪ How your credit rating figures
into the rate you get ▪ Understanding financing lingo

Financing Ins and Outs

Chapter 7

D ebt. Leverage. Hock. OPM (Other People's Money). Borrowing power. Whatever you call it, owing money has become a phenomenally popular thing in America. Did the guy down the street really go out and drop $40,000 cash for that new Mercedes he's zipping around in? We don't think so...

Americans are spending almost one-fifth of their take-home pay wrestling with debt, and critics say that their ability to meet financial obligations is precariously dependent on brisk economic times.

Which brings us to the topic of financing your new car, your used car, or your lease car. If lenders are pushing credit, should you bite? And how big a bite? We'll address those questions over the next several pages, but we start with one stern piece of advice: Don't let easy credit or even a terrific rate tempt you into a car you really can't afford.

What's a good rate?

New car loan rates have been averaging just under 9%, and used car rates just under 10% (Bank Rate

Monitor, March, 1998). But great financing rates vary, and what's good at any particular time depends on many things, such as:

- Prevailing interest rates
- What region of the country you live in
- Demand for loan money
- Your credit rating
- Whether you're buying new or used
- Efficiencies created by the self-interest of the lender (as with dealer and manufacturer financing)

What matters is that you get a rate you can afford, and that it's competitive with other rates in the marketplace.

A recent marketplace sampling yielded the national average rates shown in Table 7.1, although it's important to remember that rates vary constantly and you should seek out current figures. You can find them in the business section of your local newspaper at least once a week, or check sources noted elsewhere in this book (also scan bank display ads throughout the paper, and don't overlook that once-a-week automotive section in the sports pages).

TABLE 7.1   SAMPLE AUTO LOAN RATES

	Lowest	Average	Highest
New Car	6.9%	8.89%	16.38%
Used Car	6.95%	9.99%	16.63%

(Source: Bank Rate Monitor, March 31, 1998)

The whopping nearly 10 percentage point difference between lowest and highest available rates noted here illustrates how important it is to shop around and maintain the best credit file you can! Where your financing falls between those figures is determined by a number of things...

What determines the rate you get?

To go in depth on this—how good your credit is, where you live, where you shop, and what length and type of loan you want—determine the financing rate you'll end up with. Table 7.2 gives a quick look at how it works.

TABLE 7.2 WHAT DETERMINES YOUR RATE?

Credit Rating	A great credit rating comes from having borrowed before and paid back like a good consumer, but not having too much outstanding debt, too many credit cards, or too many recent checks of your credit.
Location	Rates vary from city to city and region to region, depending on economic, competitive, and other factors.
Lender	The better a financial institution is at doing its job of investing other people's money, the better rate it can offer you, generally speaking. (Credit unions, for instance, keep costs down with their spartan ways and try to turn those savings into low borrowing rates.)
Loan Type and Length	New car loans traditionally have lower interest rates than used car loans, and shorter loans have lower rates than longer ones. Whether you choose a fixed or variable rate loan will affect how much you pay, as well.

Where you live in the country can affect rates one or two percentage points or more. Economic conditions change and thus so do rates by area, but Table 7.3 gives a look at how recent car loan offerings varied by region—as much as 2.19%—New Mexico having the highest average rate and Florida the lowest.

TABLE 7.3 AVERAGE NEW CAR LOAN RATES BY REGION

West:	
California	9.78%
Colorado	9.30%
Oregon	8.96%

Rates noted are for a $16,000 loan amount over 48 months.

Bright Idea
Be sure to look for rate incentives on used cars as well as new ones. Some manufacturers offer low rates on their preowned vehicles to promote sales.

Northeast:	
New York	8.67%
Massachusetts	8.58%
Maine	9.08%
Southwest	
Arizona	9.73%
New Mexico	10.56%
Texas	9.09%
North Central	
Ohio	8.63%
Indiana	8.75%
Missouri	8.68%
Southeast:	
Florida	8.37%
Louisiana	9.20%
North Carolina	8,85%

(Source: Bank Rate Monitor, June 19, 1998 bank rates)

It also matters whether you're buying new or used, and how old that used car might be. Taking a look at even recent model used cars, Table 7.4 shows that the newer the car, the more willing lenders are to finance at low rates.

TABLE 7.4   THE NEWER THE CAR, THE LOWER THE RATE

	New	Used
National Average	8.84%	9.95%

(Source: Bank Rate Monitor, June 19, 1998 bank rates. Auto loan criteria, New: 48 mos., $16,000; Used: 36 mos., $10,000)

When you've done everything you can to ensure a pristine credit rating and shopped at various lenders for competitive rates, the type and length of loan you choose is the most pronounced variable you'll have to deal with. Later in this chapter, we'll give you a worksheet to compare the lengths and types of loans that you may be offered.

Here are some rules of thumb you can use when considering how to get the lowest interest rate possible:

- The older the car being financed, the higher your interest rate is likely to be (although, of course, a lower car price may make it more than worthwhile).

- New car loan rates may be a percentage point or two lower than used car loan rates.

- The shorter the term of the loan, the better the rate you'll usually be offered.

How your credit rating figures in

Your credit rating is the variable most under your control, and it's one that makes a huge difference. Just as those people who have bad driving records wind up paying more than others for car insurance, consumers who crash their credit cards (or other loans) pay through the nose to get future credit, if they can get it at all.

Finding out how good or bad your credit is

Whenever you use or abuse credit, the information is funneled through various channels and ends up at one or more of three major credit bureaus (see Table 7.5) in a credit file similar to the example on the next page. The credit bureaus are called *consumer reporting agencies* (CRAs, in government lingo).

Bad marks can typically stay on your report no more than seven years after an account becomes delinquent, but bankruptcies may remain for a decade.

Moneysaver
Moving soon? Check financing rates in your current place of residence (as well as tax implications!) against rates in your new state and city, and buy your car wherever is cheapest.

CREDIT REPORT

THE FOLLOWING IS YOUR CONSUMER IDENTIFICATION NUMBER. PLEASE REFER TO THIS NUMBER WHEN YOU CALL OR WRITE US. ID# 1234567890

JANE LORRAINE CONSUMER
1234 PLEASANT STREET
LOVELY, RI 12345

AN ENCLOSURE WITH THIS REPORT EXPLAINS YOUR CREDIT RIGHTS. IF IT IS MISSING OR YOU HAVE QUESTIONS, PLEASE CONTACT THE OFFICE LISTED ON THE LAST PAGE OF YOUR REPORT. AS PART OF OUR FRAUD-PREVENTION PROGRAM, ACCOUNT NUMBERS MAY NOT FULLY DISPLAY ON THIS REPORT.

YOUR CREDIT HISTORY:
THIS INFORMATION IS FROM PUBLIC RECORDS OR ORGANIZATIONS THAT HAVE GRANTED CREDIT TO YOU. AN ASTERISK INDICATES AN ITEM MAY REQUIRE FURTHER REVIEW BY PROSPECTIVE CREDITORS WHEN REVIEWING YOUR CREDIT HISTORY. IF YOU BELIEVE ANY INFORMATION TO BE INCORRECT, PLEASE LET US KNOW. INSTRUCTIONS FOR REINVESTIGATION ARE INCLUDED ON THE LAST PAGE.

1 ACCOUNTDESCRIPTION1*US BKPT CT RI
1234 FIRST STREET. CREDIT CITY RI 12345
DOCKET #1223456 VOLUNTARY BANKRUPTCY CH. 13 DISCHARGED 05/23/94. PETITION ON 06/01/95. RCRD ASSETS: $5,000, LIAB.: $5,000. YOU ARE SOLELY RESPONSIBLE FOR THIS PUBLIC RECORD ITEM.

2 THEBANK
P O BOX 1234 EASY STREET CA 12345
BANKING ACCT #12345678XXXX THIS CREDIT CARD ACCOUNT WAS OPENED 06/01/92 AND HAS REVOLVING REPAYMENT TERMS. YOU HAVE CONTRACTUAL RESPONSIBILITY FOR THIS ACCOUNT AND ARE PRIMARILY RESPONSIBLE FOR ITS PAYMENT. CREDIT LIMIT: $10,000, HIGH BALANCE $9.569. AS OF 06/01/98, THIS OPEN ACCOUNT IS 120 DAYS 2+ TIMES PAST DUE. BAL. $1,987 ON 06/01/98. SCHED. MONTHLY PMT IS $82. NO. TIMES LATE: 30 DAYS=5, 60 DAYS=4, 90+ DAYS=10, DEROG=19.

THE FOLLOWING INQUIRIES ARE REPORTED TO THOSE WHO ASK TO REVIEW YOUR CREDIT HISTORY. INQUIRYDESCRIPTION: BIGM MOTORS AUTO 05/20/98

YOUR NAME: JANE LORRAINE CONSUMER SOCIAL SECURITY #:123456789 ADDRESS:1234 PLEASANT STREET LOVELY, RI 12345 YEAR OF BIRTH:1970

* * * END OF THE REPORT * * *
BIG CREDIT P.O. Box 1234, NEW YORK, NY 12345.
For prompt service, please call us at 1.800.123.4567
Monday- Friday 8:30 a.m. - 8:00 p.m. Eastern Standard Time.

Call agencies before writing to determine the specific criteria you need to include when requesting your credit report from them.

TABLE 7.5   CREDIT REPORTING BUREAUS

Equifax
P.O. Box 105783
Atlanta, GA 30348
(800) 685-1111
www.equifax.com

Experian (formerly TRW)
P.O. Box 2104
Allen, TX 75013-2104
(888) 397-3742
www.experian.com

TransUnion Corp.
P.O. Box 390
Springfield, PA 19064-0390
(312) 408-1400
www.transunion.com

Even if you've toed the line payback-wise, there may be incorrect information in your files that can count against you, such as:

- An incorrect or old address

- An account you closed that may still be listed as open

- Information from a relative or unrelated individual with similar name (and shady credit history!)

- Missing information, such as a loan you successfully paid off

It's worthwhile to take a little time well in advance of buying a car to correct anything that needs correcting on your credit report.

How do you do it? Make your inquiries to all three credit reporting agencies, not just one. Under the Fair Credit Reporting Act guidelines described in Checklist 7.1, you can't be charged for a copy of your credit report if you ask for it in writing soon after being denied a loan or another form of credit. Otherwise, checking it will cost you several dollars per agency. You'll get a walk-through of the procedures to get copies of your reports when you call the agency.

Depending on the agency, you may be able to pay by credit card and use the agency's automated phone system, or make your requests in writing and use a check or credit card, or request a copy of your credit report directly from the agency's Web site, charging any costs to your credit card. If you choose to make your requests in writing, use these guidelines:

Bright Idea
If you're truly over your head with credit problems, contact a personal credit counseling organization. But beware of scams from firms promising to repair your bad credit instantly.

Moneysaver
If you've been denied credit, insurance, or employment recently (generally within 60 days), you may be entitled to a free copy of your report. Save any "loan denied" or similar paperwork that comes your way, and call the numbers in Table 7.5 to see if you qualify for the freebie.

1. Keep copies.

2. If you want extra assurance, send your letters by certified mail with return receipt requested (although this will cost several dollars).

3. Include your entire name, current address, former addresses (for the past two years at least), Social Security number, birth date, phone number, spouse's name and social security number (if joint), current place of employment, and sign the request.

4. Include your Social Security number on your check.

You can use the following sample letter as a guideline.

Sample Credit Report Request Letter.

Jane Consumer
1234 Pleasant Street
Lovely, RI 12345
(123) 456-7890

Equifax
P.O. Box 105783
Atlanta, GA 30348

July 1, 1998

Dear Equifax:

Please send me a copy of my credit report on file with your agency. I am including a check for $8 made out to Equifax, and pertinent information is as follows:

Name: Jane Lorraine Consumer
Social Security Number: 123-45-6789
Date of Birth: 1/1/70
Current Address: 1234 Pleasant Street; Lovely, RI 12345
Current Phone: (123) 456-7890
Previous Addresses (last 2 years): 12 Sunny Lane; Near Lovely, RI 12345
Current Employer: Jane Lorraine Interiors

Thank you. I'll expect this report, sent to my address on the letterhead, in a timely fashion as required by law.

Sincerely,

Jane Lorraine Consumer

When you receive your credit report, check carefully for mistakes, and write another letter to the credit agency noting them, with supporting evidence for your claim photocopied and attached. Send this by certified mail with return receipt requested. According to the law, the credit bureau usually has a month to respond.

What's "supporting evidence"? The most official documentation you can readily find to verify your statements. For instance, if your address is listed incorrectly on a credit report, consider providing a photocopy of a utility bill bearing your correct address. For incorrect balances, "supporting evidence" may be as simple as a photocopy of your last installment bill (showing the right balance) or as elaborate as a clarification letter that you've solicited from the company you're incorrectly said to owe.

And if you disagree with its findings, the credit reporting agency may be required to insert your statement into your credit report without a charge. That way, any lender who requests your credit report is assured of getting to hear your side of the story.

You have more rights under the Fair Credit Reporting Act (FCRA), summarized in Checklist 7.1.

CHECKLIST 7.1 YOUR CREDIT REPORTING RIGHTS

__ 1. You must be told if information in your file has been used against you.

__ 2. You can find out what is in your file.

__ 3. You can dispute inaccuracies with the CRA.

__ 4. Inaccurate information must be corrected or deleted.

__ 5. You can dispute inaccurate items.

__ 6. Outdated information may not be reported.

__ 7. Access to your file is limited.

Moneysaver
Some states require credit reporting agencies to provide free annual disclosures of your credit.

More about the Fair Credit Reporting Act can be found by accessing the Federal Trade Commission's Web site at www.ftc.gov, calling (202) 326-3128, or writing to: Consumer Response Center, Federal Trade Commission, 6th Street & Pennsylvania Ave. NW, Washington, DC 20580.

___ 8. Your consent is required for reports that are provided to employers or reports that contain medical information.

___ 9. You may choose to exclude your name from CRA lists for unsolicited credit and insurance offers.

___10. You may seek damages from violators.

Here's how the information in Checklist 7.1 may apply to you (source: Federal Trade Commission):

1. **You must be told if information in your file has been used against you.** Anyone who uses information from a CRA to take action against you—such as denying an application for credit, insurance, or employment—must tell you; and give you the name, address, and phone number of the CRA that provided the consumer report.

2. **You can find out what is in your file.** At your request, a CRA must give you the information in your file and a list of everyone who has requested it recently. There is no charge for the report, if a person has taken action against you because of information supplied by the CRA, if you request the report within 60 days of receiving notice of the action. You also are entitled to one free report every twelve months if you certify that (1) you are unemployed and plan to seek employment within 60 days, (2) you are on welfare, or (3) your report is inaccurate due to fraud. Otherwise, a CRA can charge you up to eight dollars.

3. **You can dispute inaccurate information with the CRA.** If you tell a CRA that your file contains inaccurate information, the CRA must investigate the items (usually within 30 days) by presenting to its information source all relevant evidence that you submit, unless your dispute is

frivolous. The source must review your evidence and report its finding to the CRA. (The source also must advise national CRAs to which it has provided data of any error.) The CRA must give you a written report of the investigation and a copy of your report if the investigation results in any change. If the CRA's investigation does not resolve the dispute, you can add a brief statement to your file. The CRA must normally include a summary of your statement in future reports. If an item is deleted or a dispute statement is filed, you may ask that anyone who has recently received your report be notified of the change.

4. **Inaccurate information must be corrected or deleted.** A CRA must remove or correct inaccurate or unverified information for its files, usually within 30 days after you dispute it. However, the CRA is not required to remove accurate data from your file unless it is outdated (as described below) or cannot be verified. If your dispute results in any change to your report, the CRA cannot reinsert a disputed item into your file unless the information source verifies its accuracy and completeness. In addition, the CRA must give you a written notice telling you that it has reinserted the item. The notice must include the name, address, and phone number of the information source.

5. **You can dispute inaccurate items with the source of the information.** If you tell anyone— such as a creditor who reports to a CRA—that you dispute an item, they may not then report the information to a CRA without including a notice of your dispute. In addition, once you've

notified the source of the error in writing, it cannot continue to report the information if it is, in fact, an error.

6. **Outdated information cannot be reported.** In most cases, a CRA cannot report negative information that is more than seven years old; ten years is the limit for bankruptcies.

7. **Access to your file is limited.** A CRA may provide information about you only to people with a need recognized by the FCRA—usually to consider an application with a creditor, insurer, employer, landlord, or other business.

8. **Your consent is required for reports that are provided to employers or for reports that contain medical information.** A CRA cannot give out information about you to an employer or prospective employer without your written consent. A CRA cannot report medical information about you to creditors, insurers, or employers without your permission.

9. **You can exclude your name from CRA lists for unsolicited credit and insurance offers.** Creditors and insurers may use file information as the basis for sending you unsolicited offers of credit or insurance. Such offers must include a toll-free phone number for you to call if you want your name and address removed from future lists. If you call, you must be kept off the lists for two years. If you request, complete, and return the CRA form provided for this purpose, you must be taken off the lists indefinitely.

10. **You can seek damages from violators.** If a CRA, a user, or (in some cases) a provider of CRA data violates the FCRA, you can sue them in state or federal court.

What's great credit, then?

Lenders want in you the same thing you would want in a friend or relative to whom you're willing to lend a little cash. But they haven't known you since you were six, and have to rely on data about you rather than personal contact.

If you're determined to be the straight-A, squeaky clean type, here's how to maximize the status of your credit standing:

1. Make as much money as possible.

2. Have at least two major credit cards (in consumer folklore, American Express has sometimes been favored as a "harder to get," more prestigious affiliation). One is adequate for those just beginning to establish credit ratings, but two are preferred.

3. Don't have too many credit cards (although one CRA recommends having several). We suggest keeping the upper limit to perhaps six (and certainly not running unpaid monthly balances on them—for your own financial well-being).

4. Pay off your cards monthly and on time. Don't carry much of a balance; definitely not more than about a third of your monthly income.

5. Don't exceed your stated credit limits.

6. Successfully pay off other kinds of installment loans (a prior car, a big appliance, college loans), or have good mortgage payment records.

7. Make sure that the information on your credit report is correct.

8. Don't switch cards, banks, jobs, or living locations frequently (no one wants a flight risk).

Moneysaver
Just starting out? If you're having difficulty establishing initial credit, look into getting one or two store or gasoline credit cards, and pay off the charges promptly. And check into getting a secured Visa or Master-Card from your bank that's backed by the amount in your account.

9. Don't apply for more than one new credit card at a time.

10. Limit the number of inquiries made about your credit record (don't apply for every offer that comes down the pike, for instance). Anyone with a legitimate business purpose can get access to your credit history; and potential employers, insurers, landlords, and credit grantors may all make inquiries in the course of their business with you. Those inquiries show up on your credit record.

11. Be cautious about joint accounts.

12. Don't declare bankruptcy.

When a prospective lender reviews your credit report, it ranks certain aspects of your credit habits with a numerical value. These numbers are then weighed to come up with an overall "risk score" or "credit score," which the lender uses to decide whether to give you credit, how much, and at what rate. Different lenders have different formulas for determining all this, of course, making the situation more complicated. The dozen rules of thumb we've discussed cover the basics.

How do lenders figure out what to assign? Loads and loads of statistics. To develop risk-score computer programs, analysts review hundreds of thousands of credit reports for a couple of years or longer, and see which criteria are the best projections of future credit performance—current balances, timely payments, etc. At its most basic, risk scoring amounts to an officious game of "pin the tail on the deadbeat," and you should be out to prove you're no such thing.

As an aside to those dozen things you can do to keep your credit clean and healthy, the behaviors in

Checklist 7.2 are ways to maximize your risk score by increasing the "good" elements of your credit report and decreasing the "bad" ones.

CHECKLIST 7.2   GETTING A GOOD CREDIT RISK SCORE

Avoid This	Do This
(These behaviors are virtually certain to worsen your risk score)	(These behaviors are likely to improve your risk score)
Consistently paying your bills late	Consistently paying your bills on time
Owing a large amount of non-mortgage debt	Keeping your overall debt at a reasonable level, relative to your income
Carrying a large number of credit cards	Actively and responsibly using a limited number of credit cards
Applying for multiple credit cards or loans within a recent period of time	
Declaring bankruptcy	

Although some lenders may tell you your credit score if you ask, they're not required to by law. Because different scoring methods are used, finding out your actual risk number may be of little use. And because they must give you the reasons for denying credit, that's an easier place to look and these reasons give you more qualitative information that you can use.

By the way, whenever you're dealing with a loan officer, it may earn you extra kudos to provide a package of recent credit report copies and other details supporting or explaining your financial situation (in essence, a high-end, non-pandering plea-for-money letter).

Loan officers are human, too, and where they have discretion, your summary could be persuasive.

Bright Idea
Whenever possible and appropriate, speak directly to loan officers or meet them in person, so they can size you up—your being more than just a number may weigh into their decision.

For instance, a loan request might include a page noting that you moved twice recently due to job promotions and you closed one credit account because your sterling record led another lender to offer you a much better deal.

If you don't score well enough in your risk rating (or impress the lender otherwise), you may be turned down, offered a higher interest rate, or be asked to come up with a cosigner, someone who is liable for payment if you don't meet your obligations.

Sources of financing

You want a car or need one, as the case may be, and by golly you're going to have one. What now? Cash. Scratch. Green. Paper. A loan from Sharky.

It's all rather simple. Either you have the money and decide to pay for your car entirely up front or that old saying comes into play: "It's who you know."

Assuming that you're not a complete louse, lenders are scrambling to offer you the chance to become their indentured servant. Your priority is to find the kindest taskmaster among them. Let's take a look, then, at all the options.

The most conventional non-cash ways to pay for a vehicle are dealer financing, and bank or credit union auto loans. Although you can also turn to an outside finance company, consider a home equity loan, or borrow against investments you own; conventional financing methods are usually a much better bet.

The old cashola

You're considering paying cash for a car. Perhaps you're a penny-pincher (you hate it when they say "tightwad") and don't like the whole idea of debt.

Well, what borrower does? Many lenders and other financing authorities recommend making a 20% cash down payment on the vehicle you intend to get. But paying more than that in cash isn't always in your best interest.

When paying cash may be a good idea:

- When the opportunity cost (see Chapter 3) of using that cash elsewhere is low, such as if you have more-than-adequate savings but can't find a decent investment interest rate (although we would ask, why not?), and have high taxes

- When you have more-than-adequate savings but a truly bad credit rating (for which you would be assigned an exorbitant financing rate)

- When you have a more-than-adequate cash flow but a large amount of outstanding debt already, and don't want to jeopardize your credit rating by taking on a loan that will wind up listed in your credit report

And some occasions when cash isn't necessarily a good idea:

- When you don't have an emergency stash to see you through a few months with no income

- When you'll need a significant part of your savings for something expected during the next few years—buying a home, going to school, having a baby, moving, a big vacation you're determined to take

- When you can let the dealer "make a little money on the financing" to keep the negotiated price of the car itself lower

- When your financing expenses are tax deductible, such as when you sometimes use the car for business purposes

The underlying reason that financing a car makes sense over paying cash in many instances is this: Automobile loans are designed to be paid off over a few years, but other forms of consumer credit aren't so accommodating. Remember, a car is identifiable as collateral and typically insured, so it's a safer risk for a lender than simply handing out a plastic credit card. Car financing is also the norm, it's accepted, and that gives it cachet.

Say you paid $10,000 in cash toward a car and a year later you need $10,000 for another expense. You could try to use a credit card to pay for that surprise expenditure, but is your credit good enough that you have a card with at least a $10,000 limit? Even so, its interest rate would very probably be higher than the car loan rate. Bear in mind the average credit card rate in 1996 was more than 17%! And there's one other thing—whoever views your credit file could be a tad more worried—"Egads, this person has run up a $10,000 credit card bill!"

They wouldn't necessarily notice you had just paid $10,000 cash the year before for a car or that you have been a good citizen. They might think you're someone who's joined the hordes of spend-happy debtors and consider you a high risk. All because you tried to do the right thing and not go into debt in the first place.

When you really want to pay for a car in cash but feel that you're going to get a better deal from the salesman by financing, you might consider checking out the terms of the arrangement—if the prepayment penalty isn't prohibitive, finance the car. Then pay off the loan with your cash within a few months. You can also plan to pay cash for part of the deal and finance a portion to appease the dealer.

Bright Idea
True cash aficionados may be interested in the prepaid lease. It works this way: You pay an amount up front to lease a car for a set time and the dealer guarantees a price you can pay at the end of that lease to buy it. The advantage? No monthly payments. But weigh the pros and cons before you jump.

Yes there's no way around the simplicity of cash and the knowledge that financing incurs costs. A $20,000 car paid for in cash costs $20,000 (leaving taxes and the like aside). A $20,000 car paid for with 9% financing over four years costs almost $24,000.

Banking on it

At the risk of oversimplification, banks are a good place to seek auto loans because they have money. Your money, your neighbor's money, your boss's money (that you made for him). And it's the bank's job to put that money to work making more of it.

One way is with auto loans. The bank wants an assurance that money loaned out is coming back in spades. And who better to trust than you, their faithful customer these five or ten years, whose financial records they already have.

Bank loans are the first place people may think to look when buying a used car from an individual. And you can consider them for new car loans (leasing arrangements can be easier than purchasing arrangements, as well). Some pros and cons of beating a path to the bank are listed in Table 7.6.

Moneysaver
Apply for a bank loan in the same month that you intend to buy a car because you can prequalify. You may wind up going with dealer financing instead, but at least you'll have the option.

TABLE 7.6 BANK AUTO LOANS

Pros	Cons
You can prequalify for a bank loan before you've found your car and then compare it to any dealer financing you're offered.	Rates may not beat promotional dealer financing.
Your bank may offer a competitive rate based on your relationship (beating other banks' offers by more than a percentage point).	Some extra footwork is involved for you versus dealer financing.

Remember if you've prequalified for a bank auto loan and later a dealer orders your credit report, your bank's inquiry to your credit file may appear, tipping him off that you've applied for a loan recently. So, even if you've been evasive to this point about your credit options, don't be surprised if a salesman notices that you've been loan-shopping.

Pros	Cons
Features such as automatic withdrawal from your account to pay installments, eliminating paperwork and missed payments. Some banks offer loans of about ¼ percentage point less if customers choose this option.	Dealers may offer better financing options to those who aren't the best credit risk.

Where should you shop for a loan first? The logical place to turn is your own bank. Call and ask for the automotive loan department, armed with the questions noted in Checklist 7.3. Check ads in the local paper for your own bank's rates, rates of competing banks and financing concerns in the area, and consider trying the Internet as well.

CHECKLIST 7.3   INQUIRING ABOUT A BANK CAR LOAN

_____ Call and ask for the auto loan department.

_____ Ask what annual rates the bank generally offers on auto loans.

_____ Tell them if you are a customer of their bank.

_____ Ask whether any specials are in effect and for how long.

_____ Mention that you would like a vehicle loan of up to four years and can make up to a 20% down payment (if you can), including the equity in your trade-in.

_____ Tell the representative how much you can comfortably spend on each monthly installment.

_____ If you know the year or model car you'd like to get, tell the representative that, and how soon you intend to buy the car.

_____ If you're planning to buy used, ask whether buying a slightly older or newer car would affect the rate or term.

_____ Ask what additional fees apply.

_____ Ask whether the loan quoted is a fixed or variable rate, and, if variable, what the caps are.

_____ Ask whether it's a simple interest loan or a "rule of 78" loan (where interest and principal are not paid off at the same rates throughout the life of the loan).

_____ Ask for a written quote or to complete a by-phone application, if desired.

Once you've preapplied for a bank loan, whether in person, by phone, letter, or the Internet, you'll be sent a loan description like that shown below.

The Bank

The Bank NT & SA
P.O. Box 1234
Easy Street, CA 12345

July 1, 1998

Dear   JOE CARBUYER ,

Congratulations! Your AUTOMOBILE LOAN   has been approved with the following terms: USED/$15K/60MOS/10.750/AUTOPAY/10% DOWN   . These terms are subject to receipt and verification of the information listed on the following page.

Please give us a call at   1-800-123-4567   to complete the details and make arrangements for the funding of your loan. We look forward to providing you fast, convenient service through a The Bank branch of your choice.

This offer will be available to you through   July 30, 1998 . If we do not hear from you by this date, we will assume that you do not wish to proceed and will consider this offer canceled.

Thank you for selecting The Bank for your financing needs.

Sincerely,

JANE BANKWOMAN, RELATIONSHIP OFFICER
800-123-4567   EXTENSION 1234

Note: The above terms are based on several factors, including information we obtained from the following consumer credit reporting agency(ies). A copy of your credit file may be obtained by contacting them at:

Concerning: JOE CARBUYER
TRW INFO SERVICES NCAC, 701 TRW PARKWAY, P.O. BOX 949, ALLEN, TX 75013, 800-682-7654

If you choose not to accept the above terms, questions you may have about the specific reasons your loan was approved at the above terms should be made in writing to the Bank address above within 60 days. You will receive a written response within 30 days. Please note that on the reverse side of this letter we have included information that explains your rights under the Equal Credit Opportunity Act.

The following information is needed to complete your request:

- COPY OF PURCHASE AGREEMENT SIGNED BY BUYER(S) AND SELLER
- COPY OF SIGNED BILL OF SALE FOR PRIVATE PARTY TRANSACTIONS
- PROVIDE LICENSE PLATE NUMBER/VEHICLE IDENTIFICATION NUMBER
- COPY OF CURRENT STATE'S SMOG CERTIFICATION/SAFETY CHECK
- LIENHOLDER'S NAME/ADDRESS/ACCT#/PHONE# FOR PAYOFF WITH LOAN

Reference No. 000123-98-000-11234567

In this example, the prospective car buyer has been preap-proved for a $15,000 used car loan. The term is 60 months (five years) at a 10.75% annual interest rate. He must make a 10% down pay-ment and must find a vehicle by month's end. "Autopay" indi-cates that monthly install-ments will be direct-debited from his account.

See the section in this chapter on loan types for important dis-tinctions between differ-ent bank loans—they can affect how much you'll end up paying.

Your letter will have an expiration date, so remember that while you can preapply while you're still shopping, don't call the bank too early in the game. You may have only a month or so to shop until that offer expires (though you can reapply when it does).

Dealer and manufacturer financing

First, the good news. If you're out to buy a car, your chances of getting financing are probably best at the source—the dealership. And rates can be competitive. Here's why dealer financing is something to consider:

- **Easy credit.** Dealers make a lot of money on financing and they're eager to sell you a vehicle.

- **Convenience.** No outside effort is required on the part of the buyer because a dealer can set up financing arrangements at the same time that you're buying your car.

- **Leverage.** You may be able to negotiate a better buying price if you indicate that you're interested in dealer financing. Any lending institution stands to make money on a loan. By allowing the dealer instead of an outside bank to make that money (a conservative amount, please), you're reducing the profit he needs to make on the car itself.

But, as we've talked about in previous chapters, dealer financing has a dark side. It's at financing time that some of the more surreptitious sales tactics come out. Among the drawbacks to one-stop-shopping:

- It's an opportunity for the dealer to dazzle buyers with numbers and make back the money lost to a customer's good negotiation tactics.

- Rather than being restricted in the length of loan you can get (by a bank that wants to make sure it's a safe investment), a dealer may try to persuade you to max out your term to spend more but keep payments lower.

It's easy for even an astute consumer to trip up in a financing pitfall like agreeing to long loan terms to minimize down payment. If the buyer decides to trade the car early on, he may find out that he owes more on the car than it's worth because it has been depreciating faster than he is paying it off. The depreciation rate, however, slows after the first year of ownership, allowing him more chances to catch up the longer he keeps the car.

Let's make some distinctions between the types of financing you can get at the dealer.

- **Dealer Manufacturer Financing.** Your loan is handled by the dealer, who goes through the manufacturer of the car you're buying or leasing. The manufacturer's financing division has the efficiencies generated by a large business dedicated primarily to doing one thing—funding that line of cars. Specifically, they're captive finance companies that buy completed contracts from dealerships.

- **Dealer Bank Financing.** Your dealer actually has an arrangement with a bank, which will become the owner of the car during the time you're paying it off.

- **Dealer Finance Company Financing.** Your dealer has an arrangement with a financing company that is not affiliated with a particular make of car.

Moneysaver
Consider manufacturer financing with the same maker you've successfully bought from before—your credit profile may be better than with other forms of financing—those that rely more on your general consumer credit profile, which may not be up to snuff.

■ **Dealer Independent Financing.** The dealer is funding the financing arrangement himself. Be careful and watch the fine print, especially when this is the case. Most dealers don't finance independently, and when they do, sometimes it's specifically to fund high-risk individuals at a high interest rate with strict terms.

All types of financing done through the dealer may look like the same thing to the consumer. It's a seamless affair, handled through the F & I (Financing & Insurance) department, where, as described in Chapter 14, a lot of negotiation takes place and a lot of opportunity for dealer profit is hidden.

Dealerships may have special finance departments that advertise to and serve those with poor credit, but for a hefty take. If your credit is truly bad, you may be faced with this alternative. But never accept "special financing" without first seeing what your bank might be able to do for you in the way of a loan. High rates can be nothing more than a dealer's attempt to jack up the price you'll pay him, needlessly.

Moneysaver
Dealers may use proprietary matching programs to find the best finance rate, residual value, etc. Ask the dealer if he uses a program like this and have him find the best deal for you.

Bank alternatives

Credit Unions are tax-exempt competitors to traditional banks and are run by members. Historically, members needed to fit certain requirements to qualify to join, such as working in a certain industry, working for a certain company, or living in a specific area. The benefit is that their spartan way of doing business can lead to rates that are lower than you would pay at a traditional bank.

Even people who don't keep their savings in a credit union turn to one when seeking an auto loan. Nationwide, credit unions hold less than 10% of consumer savings, but account for almost a quarter of auto loans. You may be able to get a percentage point or two lower than with conventional bank financing.

Some of the pros and cons of Credit Unions are shown in Table 7.7.

TABLE 7.7 CREDIT UNIONS

Pros	Cons
May offer lower rates than banks	May require affiliation with a group or specific location of residency to join
Consumer-oriented philosophy and service	Minimum balances
	To save costs, some may offer fewer conveniences than banks (such as ATMs, where free withdrawals can be made)
	May require you to use your funds on deposit as security for loans over a few to several thousand dollars

Watch out for secured loans that use not only your car, but also perhaps your savings for collateral (and apply freezes on withdrawals below a certain level). Read the fine print.

Independent finance companies

Independent finance companies do billions of dollars in business every year. When you apply for financing with an Internet car buying service like Auto-By-Tel, you may be financed by one of them. Auto-By-Tel's acceptance company works with GE Capital, as well as Chase Manhattan Auto Finance and Triad Financial to finance cars.

Large independent financing firms may handle retail financing, leasing on new and used cars, and sub-prime financing (less-than-perfect credit customers) in their auto divisions, and large banks often have auto financing subsidiaries.

Unofficially...
Congressional action may mean that credit unions will become available to a wider slice of the population, rather than catering to niche interests as they do now. (Source: Credit Union Membership Acceptance Act, H.R. 1151, passed U.S. House of Representatives, April 1, 1998)

Timesaver
Check your yellow pages or your trade organization for credit unions you may be able to join. On the Web, look for a credit union in your area with the help of the National Credit Union Administration at www.ncua.gov.

Subsidiaries of subsidiaries abound in this business, and many smaller finance companies exist as well. Some deal only with dealers and others provide loans directly to the public. Although many strive to offer rates that are competitive with bank and other forms of financing, caution is advised. You should always compare the fine print of a conventional bank loan (as well as its rates) with what you're being offered by a finance company. Especially when dealing with a smaller firm, inquire about which dealers they do business with, and check out their reputation, just to be on the safe side.

You can find independent auto finance companies in the yellow pages, in newspaper ads, and increasingly on the Internet, as they have sought new venues in which to win over auto loan customers.

To apply for an auto loan over the Web, check links from major auto-shopping sites.

Unconventional financing sources

The reader is strongly advised to consider the ease with which conventional financing can be handled before resorting to anything more exotic. But unofficially, here are some other ways that people occasionally finance their cars, although the drawbacks may outweigh the benefits, and you should think it all through very carefully before deciding to proceed.

Friends and family. The benefit here is informality, potentially good lending terms, and a flexible payment schedule. The downside is that you may never hear the end of it from your gracious lender. Federal law allows a family member to lend as much as he wants, if you're paying an interest rate similar to what can be found in the marketplace, or up to ten grand annually without incurring gift taxes.

One little talked-about kind of bank loan that can be used to finance your car purchase is a home equity loan (or "home equity line of credit"). Borrowing against the value of your home can secure you a lower interest rate than a typical auto loan, and the interest is almost always tax-deductible. Because of that, a home equity loan is comparable to a conventional loan, but two to three percentage points lower. The savings can mean more than $1,000 on the cost of financing a typical new car. But be judicious, this is your home we're talking about here! (Among the drawbacks to using home equity, however, is the cost to establish a new line of credit—it may include having to pay for a title search or appraisal).

Then there's your life. That is, whole life insurance policies may permit borrowing at low rates. Check your policy for specifics, including a notice that the policy's death benefit drops with the balance!

Are you vested? Check your company's 401(k) plan or similar arrangement for details of borrowing against it. You may get a very low interest rate and have up to five years to pay the loan back. Similarly, margin loans are available from stockbrokers for up to a decent percentage of the worth of the securities held in your account.

The problem with all of these types of financing is that they use something other than the car as security, meaning that you're tying up other property (or, in the case of friends and family, guilt and favors) in the auto loan equation.

Moneysaver
Some people say cash is always best, others firmly believe that using your credit is the only way to go. Weigh both options because it always depends on the variables involved in your situation, and there are no short answers.

Bright Idea
Be very, very careful on this one, but consider it in special situations when you would pay cash... charge some car cost to a credit card that offers cash back or frequent flyer points. Then pay off the credit card immediately. Be aware, though, that dealers may be less willing to negotiate when you're paying by credit card.

Comparing cash, bank loans, and manufacturer financing

How do you weigh your financing options: how long a payment term to use and at what rate? There are many variables. It's probably best to consider your comfort and safety levels, and work from there.

1. Are you thinking of purchasing a car that, at an average interest rate (see earlier in this chapter) will take you no more than four years to pay off (five max for a new car, preferably three for a used one)? If not, find a cheaper car. Table 7.8 shows monthly payments at different interest rates.

2. Will the monthly payments be in a range you can comfortably afford? Many people seem to prefer spending no more than $300–$350 a month, although your comfort spot may be higher or much lower.

3. See who has the most competitive loan rates for the length and amount of the loan you want.

TABLE 7.8   MONTHLY PAYMENT (FOR EVERY $100 FINANCED)

Interest Rate	24 months	36 Months	48 Months	60 Months
4%	$4.34	$2.95	$2.26	$1.84
6%	$4.43	$3.04	$2.35	$1.93
8%	$4.52	$3.13	$2.44	$2.03
10%	$4.61	$3.23	$2.54	$2.12
12%	$4.71	$3.32	$2.63	$2.22
14%	$4.80	$3.42	$2.73	$2.33

Say you're considering a three-year loan, but you would rather have five years to pay off the car. You want to know what your extra costs will be. To compare two loan possibilities of varying lengths, use

Worksheet 7.1. Perhaps you've found a rate better than your bank's loan offer, and you're wondering whether it's worth your trouble to drive across town and fill out the paperwork. You can use Worksheet 7.1 for that as well.

WORKSHEET 7.1   COMPARING LOAN TERMS OR INTEREST RATES

1. Divide the amount to be financed by 100, and put the answer here: _____.

2. Multiply that figure by the dollar amount for your interest rate and selected term, shown in Table 7.8, and write the result here: _____. This is your monthly payment.

3. Multiply that figure by the number of months in the term, and write that result here: _____.

4. Subtract the amount to be financed (from Step 1) and put the result here: _____. This is your total financing cost over the term.

5. Repeat the steps for a loan term or rate you'd like to compare this one to, and see which has the lower total financing costs.

6. Subtract the lower figure from the higher one. The difference is the amount you'll save, and you can write that here: _____.

If you're caught in a quandary between getting a loan, paying cash, or leasing, you can get some idea about how those options compare by using Worksheet 7.2.

WORKSHEET 7.2   COMPARING CASH, LOANS, AND LEASING

Loan:

   $_____ Sales Tax & Down Payment

+ $_____ (Monthly Payment _____ × _____ Term (in months)

= $_____ Cost of Vehicle

− $_____ Estimated Resale Value (at end of term)

− $_____ Expected Earned Interest (on any amount of cash on hand as a result of not paying cash for the vehicle)

= $_____ Cost of this Option (at end of term)

Rough estimations are necessary when considering opportunity cost (and expected interest earned on any amount of cash on hand as a result of not paying cash for the vehicle).

Do your calculations with equivalent loan and lease terms.

Cash:

$\qquad$ Price of Car & Sales Tax

+ $\qquad$ Opportunity Cost (amount you would otherwise expect to earn on the money if invested or saved) Price of Car & Sales Tax $\qquad$ × expected interest rate to be earned $\qquad$% × (term of loan option in months) $\qquad$

= $\qquad$ Cost of Vehicle

– $\qquad$ Estimated Resale Value (at end of loan option term)

= $\qquad$ Cost of this Option (at same time as end of loan term)

Lease:

$\qquad$ Leasing Fees and Up-Front Payments

+ $\qquad$ Total of Monthly Payments (monthly payment $\qquad$ × lease term in months $\qquad$)

= $\qquad$ Cost of Vehicle

– $\qquad$ Expected Earned Interest (on any amount of cash on hand as a result of not paying cash for the vehicle)

= $\qquad$ Cost of this Option (at end of lease term)

Upcoming sections of this book, devoted to leasing, will tell you more about leasing terminology.

Typical financing for new, used, and leased cars

What's really out there in the marketplace? A sample scenario of the options available to a car shopper might go like this. Suppose that Mary, who's on a budget, can spend in the low teens on a car. She has her eye on a modest Asian import, and part of her is thinking that a domestic sedan a couple of years old might be a good choice, too.

Mary has decent credit, applies to her California bank, and checks out other financing sources. She can afford a car in the low teens, is thinking of a three-year loan, and can put 20% down on the car. She'll be borrowing an even $10,000. Her options could stack up this way (see Table 7.9).

TABLE 7.9   MARY'S (TYPICAL) FINANCING OPTIONS

	New Car	Two-Year-Old Car
Mary's Bank	9.25%	10.75%
Another Bank	10%	12%
Credit Union	8.5%	10%
Dealer Financing	3.9%*	9.9%
State Average	9.42%	11%

*promotional rate

By shopping around and, in this case, going with the promotional dealer offer to finance that import, Mary can save just over $1,000 versus the financing rate she can get from a bank down the street from her office, as shown in Table 7.10.

Coincidentally, her best deal on the used car is the same as that bank rate on the new car that is so much more expensive than the dealer's promoted rate. So if all other things are equal, including Mary's attraction to the cars, buying new with dealer financing will save her considerable money—more than $1,000.

If the dealership offers Mary a choice of that promotional rate or a $2,000 rebate, and Mary goes for the rebate (and decides to finance $8,000), buying the car will still cost her about $1,000 more in interest with a credit union loan, even considering the break she gets on taxes. The dealer's promotional financing is still a better idea.

TABLE 7.10   MARY'S FINANCING COSTS

	New Car	Two-Year-Old Car
Mary's Bank	$1,489.76	$1,743.20
Another Bank	$1,616.12	$1,957.04
Credit Union	$1,364.48	$1,616.12
Dealer Financing	$612.80	$1,599.20
State Average	$1,518.56	$1,786.04

Timesaver
Check your finan-
cial planning
software for a
"loan calculator"
that automatical-
ly determines
your monthly
payment for vari-
ous interest
rates. These can
also be found on
the Internet at
various sites.

Buying at the dealer promotional rate, Mary's monthly payments will be $295 for three years. She might consider one other choice: leasing the new car, which can perhaps cut her monthly payments in half if a competitive lease is offered. Mary knows that she will spend more on the car if she decides to buy it at the end of the lease instead of buying it out-right, but she's tempted by the idea of spending just $150 a month on a car payment. Part V, "The Lease Option," explains how she can factor those figures into her evaluation.

Loan types

Generally, the safest kinds of loans to stick with are those easiest to understand—simple, fixed interest loans, where what you see is what you get. Creative financing may benefit the lender more than the bor-rower. Some innovations can be helpful to the con-sumer, but the first rule is that you should be able to understand the type of financing you're getting—only then do you have a fighting chance of making a good deal.

Financing definitions

The lexicon of terms specific to financing is vast. Here are the primary ones you need to know as they pertain to your vehicle loan:

- **Principal:** The amount being financed (the cost of the car, for example) before fees and interest charges.

- **Rate (APR):** The percentage you'll pay in inter-est annually on the principal.

- **Term:** The length of the loan, usually described in months.

- **Fixed Rate:** A loan set at a certain annual interest rate that will not go up or down over the life of the loan.

- **Variable Rate (or Adjustable Rate):** A loan whose rate may change over its life, within the parameters of its "cap."

- **Cap:** The most that the rate can change on an adjustable rate loan. A cap may be specified as "1% annually" and "3% over the life of the loan," which means that a 10% loan can vary between 9% and 11% annually, but can't ever be less than 7% or more than 13%.

- **Balloon Contract:** A loan that is amortized just down to the expected end-term value, with a balance remaining that is to be paid at the end of the term in a lump sum.

- **Balloon Payment:** Not used with typical auto loans; a huge fixed dollar amount due at a certain time (beginning or end of the loan term), which allows other monthly installments to be kept low.

- **Simple Interest:** Interest calculated on principal; literally simple.

- **Rule of 78s:** A method of calculating loans that penalizes the borrower who wants to repay early. With this method, you pay more interest in the beginning months of a loan (compared to principal), so if you pay off early, you're not really saving interest expense.

Don't be afraid to talk to the loan officer thoroughly about terms of financing you're evaluating. Explain what you expect your financial situation to be like over the next few years—the plan the two of you come up with should be tailored to fit it.

Promotional financing

Car shoppers who are just starting out may get all excited at the prospect of "zero down and 1.9% financing!" Jaded consumers (who've been looking more than perhaps three days) barely raise an eyebrow.

Promotional financing can be legitimate, and you should check it out—particularly if it originates at the manufacturer. But often, what appear to be great deals in an ad aren't all they're described to be.

Individuals with poor credit might be lured by promises of easy credit, only to find that:

- the term of the loan offered is so short it's useless to them

- a prohibitively large down payment is required

- they may be charged a higher price for the car

- a loan might require a several-thousand-dollar "balloon payment" at the end of the term

- in order to qualify for the loan, they may be required to buy an extended warranty, insurance for their credit, or extras like rustproofing.

And no matter what your credit rating is, be skeptical of offers for 0% financing and things that sound too good to be true. There is some way that the lender will make money, such as by difficult requirements you aren't likely to meet (and resultant unexpected fees and penalties).

And after you have that loan...

Your attention to financing shouldn't end when you get your car and settle into forking over the monthly installments. If interest rates in the marketplace drop, contact your bank—it may make sense to refinance at a lower rate (but weigh the value of a lower rate against any prepayment penalties before you jump at refinancing).

And if your salary rises or expenses drop, perhaps paying off that loan more quickly than needed could be to your advantage. How do you tell if you should? Check the rates out there—if returns on what you consider to be safe investments are lower than the loan rate, it's in your favor to pay up now (provided there's not a prohibitive prepayment penalty).

The best way to ensure that everything will go fine with your financing is to handle it right at the outset—do your homework, check rates in your area, find preapproval on a bank or credit union loan, and then go see what the dealer has to offer.

Just the facts

- Average financing rates are about a percentage point higher for used cars than new (check your newspaper's business section for current averages).

- You should be able to get credit union or independent finance company financing that's a percentage point or two lower than comparable bank financing, but collateral requirements may be stricter.

- Simple interest, fixed-rate loans are the safest for the consumer.

- Cash sounds like a good idea, but it may not be the most practical way to pay for a car after opportunity cost and the high cost of other forms of consumer credit (as might be needed in an emergency) are considered.

Moneysaver
Make a note to yourself to check out savings and investment interest rates quarterly—it might make sense to refinance. And while you're doing that with your car, what about your home mortgage and your credit cards? Call lenders and ask for a better rate—shop around if they refuse.

The Basics of
Buying Used

GET THE SCOOP ON...
When buying used really is to your advantage
▪ Whether to go with a dealer or a private
party ▪ Avoiding (or at least winning) used car
lot games ▪ Getting a good deal via a dealer,
private party, or auction

Ups and Downs, Ins and Outs of Used Car Buying

Chapter 8

A used car can be a great way to save or get more car for your money. But surprisingly, selling used cars is more profitable for dealers than selling new ones, based on the purchase price. In fact on trade-ins, dealers gross almost $1,500 on average (source: National Automobile Dealers Association).

Dealerships can make money and you can save money buying used, and that can only mean one thing—there's a lot of breathing room between the initial price of a new car and the value of a used auto.

Some people are phobic about buying a set of wheels that another person has been driving, and for them the peace of mind of buying new or leasing may be worth the extra money. But for the rest of us willing to pinch pennies and hit the pavement, the trouble comes in sorting out when a used car is a

very good idea and when its benefits don't outweigh
the trouble.

Is buying used to your advantage?

At first glance, it seems certain that buying used can
give you an economic advantage. A new car's value
plummets as soon as it's driven off the lot. So why
not let someone else buy new and foot that hefty
chunk of depreciation? Then you can start ownership when the value's better.

Even cars that sport some of the best resale values around zip down that initial depreciation hill
quickly. Take, for instance, an import sedan with
estimated resale value (wholesale) two years down
the road at 63% of the original price—a very good
figure, but it still loses thousands to depreciation, as
Table 8.1 shows.

TABLE 8.1　THE DEPRECIATION MONSTER

1998 Sedan	Value	Resale Value Percentage	Depreciation Loss
MSRP new	$17,275		
2 years old	$10,825	63%	$6,450

If you think that's scary, sit down and think about
all the costs that those new car depreciation loss figures don't reflect—sales tax, for instance. Using the
current scenario, if your state sales tax is 8%, buying
the car new versus two years old costs you more than
$500 extra in sales tax alone.

Then think about the 8% or so interest you
might be paying—an extra few hundred dollars for
the first year's financing costs. Your insurance and
state personal property taxes can be higher, too, if
they're based on the value of the vehicle.

Taking all this a step further, let's see what happens to depreciation in the next four years of a car's
life span, shown in Table 8.2.

TABLE 8.2   TAMING THE DEPRECIATION MONSTER

1998 Sedan	Value	Approximate Resale Value Percentage	Depreciation Loss (since purchase)
MSRP new	$17,275		
2 years old	$10,825	63%	$6,450
3 years old	$9,625	56%	$7,650
4 years old	$8,650	50%	$8,625
5 years old	$7,750	45%	$9,525

Remember, a car goes from resale to wholesale as soon as it's driven off the lot, losing 10–14% of its value, depending on dealer margin.

In our example, the sedan is expected to lose $6,450 in value over the first two years of its life (a substantial portion of that as soon as it's driven off the lot), but it loses just $2,175 over the following two years, demonstrating that it stands to depreciate more than twice as much when new (when you consider the instant depreciation inherent immediately upon purchase).

Depreciation isn't the only issue, however. There are other things to consider—for example, new cars are covered by warranties. Years down the road, the driver must pay for repairs. And the need for those logically increases the older a vehicle gets. Which brings us to the topic of when a used car is a wise buy for you, and when it's not.

Moneysaver
Convertibles, cars with large engines, trucks, and vans tend to depreciate less than other vehicles. (Source: FinanCenter Inc./SmartCalc)

When a used car can be to your advantage

We talked in Chapter 3 about how to know if you're a good candidate for buying used, and that discussion dealt mainly with lifestyle and psychological factors—such as whether you tend to keep your cars a long time. Most people keep theirs four to six years, according to the National Automobile Dealers Association (NADA).

If you've never owned a used car before and aren't sure how you feel, look at other areas of your life. Are you a do-it-yourself kind of man or woman,

Timesaver
You can compare the specifications of any two cars at Microsoft CarPoint at www.carpoint. com.

Unofficially...
Some used car superstores now offer three- to five-day money-back guarantees, warranties, and flat pricing (employing non-commissioned salespeople). The trend is catching on among other dealers. (Source: Consumer Federation of America)

a bargain hunter, an antiques collector, perhaps? Those things indicate that you could do well with a used car, and may tolerate the need for a few repairs or imperfections in exchange for a find.

If, on the other hand, you're a meticulous modernist and avid style-watcher (who prefers brand new whenever possible), or if you're a bit too busy to devote time to finding the perfect used car or taking it in for occasional repairs, perhaps buying or leasing new is for you.

But let's "bottom line" it here—when is buying a used car really going to save you money? There are a few components that can make buying used advantageous:

1. Initial price savings over buying new (given the chunk of value that disappears as soon as a new car is driven off the lot and subsequent depreciation)

2. Cheaper insurance (sometimes)

3. Less to pay in sales tax

4. Less to pay financing charges on

You have to consider the total cost of ownership of the new car—a point we'll get to momentarily—compared to the used one (as well as psychological factors).

When a used car can be a disadvantage

A used car isn't necessarily the best deal on wheels when you don't really fit the criteria described in Chapter 3 (refer to Checklist 3.2) for used car ownership, or when the following are true:

Watch Out!
Financing rates on used cars are typically higher than on new vehicles, and the amount of time you can take to pay it off is usually shorter.

1. When very good incentives are underway for buying or leasing a new car you want

2. When you can get much better financing on a new car

3. When repair costs, gas charges, and hassles out-strip your monthly savings versus buying or leasing a new car (and remember that buyers of used cars have less lemon law protection than car buyers do)

4. When a used car would be difficult to resell—the more late model lease returns coming onto market, the less anybody wants older cars

Short of making a really bad decision, however, there are a few instances when buying used won't save you significant money over buying new.

One way to compare new vs. used
Just how much benefit will buying used offer over buying new? In terms of money, it's really the overall cost of car ownership that matters most.

You can estimate it yourself using Worksheet 8.1, although you'll have to hunt for some of the data you'll need and guess at some things as well. IntelliChoice, on the Internet at www.intellichoice. com, lists purchase prices along with expected five-year costs of ownership and operation.

WORKSHEET 8.1 ESTIMATING AND COMPARING TOTAL COST OF OWNERSHIP

New Car Make, Model, Year:	Used Car Make, Model, Year:
1. Add these items:	
$ _____ Expected Purchase Price	$ _____ Expected Purchase Price
+ _____ Sales Tax	+ _____ Sales Tax
+ _____ Total Financing Cost	+ _____ Total Financing Cost
= _____ "Buying Cost"	= _____ "Buying Cost"
2. Then add up these anticipated annual figures:	
$ _____ Insurance	$ _____ Insurance

Use Table 1.1. (in Chapter 1), if needed, to figure your approximate financing cost. Other data can be found using the sources mentioned in Chapter 4.

Check your favorite major car Internet site for resale values.

$ _____ State Property Tax	$ _____ State Property Tax
$ _____ Fuel Costs	$ _____ Fuel Costs
$ _____ Repairs	$ _____ Repairs
= _____ "Ownership Cost"	= _____ "Ownership Cost"

And multiply the Ownership Cost by 5:	And multiply the Ownership Cost by 5:
= _____ "5-Year Ownership Cost"	= _____ "5-Year Ownership Cost"

3. Add the final results of both:

$ _____ Buying Cost	$ _____ Buying Cost
+ _____ 5-Year Ownership Cost	+ _____ 5-Year Ownership Cost
= _____ "Buy & Own Subtotal"	= _____ "Buy & Own Subtotal"

4. Subtract the 5-year resale value (residual):

$ _____ Buy & Own Subtotal	$ _____ Buy & Own Subtotal
− _____ 5-Year Resale Value	− _____ 5-Year Resale Value
= _____ Total Cost of Ownership (5 Years)	= _____ Total Cost of Ownership (5 Years)

The worksheet lets you see, side-by-side, where a car's strong points are. New cars beat older ones hands down in the repair costs category because of warranties. Another thing to really consider is fuel efficiency.

If the used car you're thinking of stands to get few miles to the gallon and the newer one has great gas mileage, it adds up over the course of a year—and certainly over five. But it's very, very difficult for those potential new car pluses to balance out the high MSRP.

Where to buy used cars—more options than ever

One of the nice things about buying used is that you have a choice of where to get your car, depending on how you like to do business.

You can play it safe and buy from a reputable new car dealer who offers warranty coverage and a greater likelihood that your vehicle will be a lease return. But you'll pay for the privilege, literally full retail. Or you can buy from a used auto lot, or have you considered an ex-rental car?

You could seek to buy from a private party, get to meet that little old lady who only used the car to get to church on Sundays, and save some money over full retail, but you'll have to hunt for the right vehicle and take the burden of handling any repairs that may come up.

There's another option too...and only for the hardiest and most bargain-minded car shopper of all—to look for a car at auction. We don't recommend it, but if you're up for an adventure, it's sure to be one, and there's money if not time to be saved.

Only in the last case, would we recommend that you consider going with a buying service. That's because the intricacies and rules of used car auctions warrant it. The used car market otherwise, we think, is built for shoppers intent on saving by doing whatever footwork is necessary themselves.

Some things to consider when shopping each type of dealership, privately or at auction, are listed in Table 8.3.

> 66
>
> They consume more fuel than the average modern car. However, if kept in tune, their gas mileage is reasonable and probably better than most SUVs (sport utility vehicles). Some may lack shoulder harness seat belts. They need more maintenance as they get older, which can be a hassle. However, the repairs and parts are usually cheap.
>
> —Ken, owner of '67 Buick Skylark
>
> 99

TABLE 8.3   PROS & CONS OF USED CAR SOURCES

	Pros	Cons
New Car Dealer	good car condition	highest prices
	many lease returns	negotiation
	wide selection	
	financing available	
	warranties available	
Used Car Megastore	huge selection	retail prices
	good car condition	

Bright Idea
Every state has a new car lemon law, which requires manufacturers to repair, replace, or buy back chronically defective new cars. But only a handful of states have similar protection for those buying used cars. For which states have the best used car lemon law coverage, see Chapter 17.

	flat pricing (some)	
	mechanical check-over	
	warranties	
	financing (sometimes)	
Used Car Dealer	varied car condition	slightly lower prices
	some selection	negotiation
		no financing (often)
		no warranties (often)
Rental Car Dealer	wide selection (of certain models)	possible hard use
	warranties	limited car type
	mechanical check-over	
Private Party	low prices possible	footwork involved
	car history knowledge	repairs may be needed
	negotiation easier	no financing
	specific car search	no warranties
		do your own paperwork
Auction	low prices possible	footwork involved
		agent may be needed
		cash or credit
		limited pre-buy review

The way you shop for a used car depends on how much time you have available, as well as personal preference and the availability of things like used car megastores or auctions in your area.

Dealerships

Shopping for your used car at a new car dealer offers all the advantages of browsing at a nice store.

It's not a rummage sale, everything's usually in at least "good" condition, and there's a selection to choose from. If you are almost thinking of buying new or leasing, but want to save a little money on a recent model car, this may be your option. But, no, it's not cheap.

One recent addition to the used car selling circus is the vehicle certification program, in which manufacturers certify that a used car being sold gets a detailed checkout by a mechanic, and any necessary repairs are made—extended warranties are often part of the bargain. This type of certification is usually prominently displayed on the car, as it's a selling point to instill buyer confidence that a car is in great working shape. Though the posted price of a "certified used vehicle" may be higher, it's often worth considering.

Beyond the traditional dealership, there is the used car megastore, a recent and convenient trend. Expect acres of cars of all makes and models, often with fixed pricing and even warranties. The stores, usually chains like CarMax, AutoNation, and others, take in used cars from a variety of sources, check them out, sometimes spend hundreds refurbishing them, and put them all in one place for you to peruse.

Independent car dealers—used car lots, that is—buy cars at auction or from private parties. They're not typically known for having the highest quality standards across the board, but that's not to malign those reputable used car dealerships that choose good cars to begin with, abide by ethical practices (not turning the odometer back, etc.), and offer customers some good bargains with the help of low overhead and business savvy.

Moneysaver
Most consumers think that they have a "three day right to cancel" option when they buy a car, but there are no state laws granting that blanket privilege. However, used car superstores advertise their own voluntary cancellation plans.

Watch Out!
"As is" or "No warranty" used car sales are prohibited in 10 states (and the District of Columbia): Connecticut, Kansas, Maine, Maryland, Massachusetts, Minnesota, Mississippi, New York, Rhode Island, and West Virginia. (Source: Consumer Federation of America)

Moneysaver
Don't let a used car dealer sell you a warranty on a car that in actuality is still well covered by the factory warranty—check the owner's manual (call the carmaker, if necessary) to verify whether a warranty exists and whether it's transferable to you as a new owner.

Used car salesmen have their own bags of tricks, and used cars have more variable factors in terms of condition and real worth than new autos. Some factors that may affect how salesmen gear a sales pitch are:

1. Do you have a trade-in that he can consider?

2. Are you more interested in a low purchase price or low monthly payments?

3. Do you have figures in mind?

The object is to reveal as little as possible about your position (to reduce his ability to juggle figures to fit it) yet still give the salesman some idea of what you're looking for.

Assume that posted prices are of course higher than what the lot will sell cars for, and tell the salesman that you'd like to look around, you're not certain of price range, and you'd like to see sedans, for example—have him tell you about the cars before you discuss prices. And try to avoid discussing your trade-in at this point—it's best to negotiate the price of the car you want to buy separately. Later, you can decide whether you like his trade-in offer enough to accept it without having to renegotiate the entire car purchase.

A shopper is always at a disadvantage when mentioning monthly payments because the salesman can then dazzle with lowball rates, neglecting to mention the long-term or high interest rate of the loan he has in mind.

If you state a purchase price you're interested in, you run the risk of being shown a $13,000 car that he'll tell you is a $14,900 car because you said you wanted to spend "$15,000 or less." You're better off researching cars with acceptable prices, and then asking to see those models at the lot.

Because you'll likely be arranging your own financing, the used car dealer is at a disadvantage against the new car dealer—he can't make his profit there or, usually, aftersell you such things as undercoating. Used car warranties aren't a bad idea, but beware an attempt to be "aftersold" anything!

There's another option in used car shopping, and that's buying a rental car. "Wait," you say, "Why would I ever want to do that?!" Although they carry the drawback of having not one but perhaps hundreds of previous drivers, there are pluses:

- Rental cars may have had recommended maintenance performed more regularly than other preowned cars.

- Car rental agencies reselling their vehicles typically offer warranty coverage on them.

- These cars undergo a thorough inspection and, when needed, get repairs before being offered for sale.

- There's likely to be a decent selection of certain models—so if you've ever rented a car that you loved, this may be one place to look.

Check rental car 800 numbers for resale dealerships in your area, and see what they offer—perhaps no-haggle flat pricing, certified vehicles, acceptance of trade-ins, financing assistance, a return policy, and warranties. It's clear that both rental car companies and used car megastores are out to gain market share in the used car sales business, and they've been quite successful at it.

Some guidelines when dealer wheeler-dealing at any type of establishment include:

Watch Out!
Most used car dealers surveyed violate the Federal Trade Commission's Used Car Rule requiring dealers to post a Buyers Guide in each vehicle for sale. The Buyers Guide alerts shoppers to warranty coverages and becomes part of the sale contract. Small independent dealers were least likely to comply. If you don't see one, ask, and if the salesman won't get you one, consider doing business elsewhere. (Source: Consumer Federation of America)

1. Assume that there's at least $600 profit built into the price of any car for sale.

2. Don't expect to be offered what your trade-in is actually worth. Consider selling it yourself.

3. If you do decide to try to trade in your old car, insist on negotiating the cost of each car separately.

4. Know your numbers. Bring a used car price guide with you, and review the appropriate wholesale and retail figures privately before you decide to buy.

Private parties

This is undoubtedly the most time-consuming way to go about finding a used car, but with careful shopping, you can exchange that time for savings and the assurance that you'll know something of the vehicle's history. Some pros and cons of buying privately are shown in Table 8.4.

**TABLE 8.4   THE PROS AND CONS OF
BUYING PRIVATELY**

Pros	Cons
Firsthand knowledge of what the vehicle's been through, any quirks, etc. (though there's no guarantee the seller's going to be honest with you)	No warranties or guarantees (unless it's quite a late model—always ask the seller what warranty remains and check that it's transferable to you before you buy)
Sizable savings if you're a good shopper	Footwork, phone calls, tedium
Scan ads for perfect car for you—a certain color, year, and style	Less likely that the car has been through a mechanical check and that any needed repairs or maintenance have been taken care of—you'll have to deal with that too

> Paperwork involved is less
> standard, and although dealer
> paperwork may favor the dealer,
> there are also protections
> built in for you that you don't
> get with a private party sale

How do you brave the wilds of buying from an individual? The process can include:

- Shopping the classifieds (including online ads)

- Placing a "car wanted" ad yourself

- Buying from people you know who happen to be selling

- The drive-by

In most areas, a good newsstand or convenience store will carry specialty papers or guides full of nothing but used cars for sale, and some have pictures. The local Sunday paper, of course, is usually chock full of used cars ads.

No matter where you look, try to find ads that look legitimate—no "buy now" or phone numbers suspiciously repeated in six adjacent ads—that's a clear sign of a dealer trying to lure you to his lot.

Many local papers and some specialty guides have Web sites, and for the connected. This is a fast way to find what you're looking for—check online classifieds, especially *searchable* sections.

Tips for getting a good car through a private party:

1. **Find out why the car is being sold.** Good reasons include a new baby in the family, moving across the country, getting a company car, or anything that suggests a motive other than exasperation with constant repairs, or a huge looming and hidden mechanical problem.

Timesaver
An Internet search for used car ads can give you a good idea of low-to-high market prices, even if the ads aren't targeted toward your area. Bear in mind, however, that there is some price variation around the country.

Moneysaver
When you're seriously shopping for used cars from private individuals, try to block out some available time in your life—Sunday afternoons, perhaps, and an evening or two per week. The more quickly you're able to arrange a test-drive, the better your chances of buying a car at a great price.

2. **Favor one-owner cars** that are being sold by people who seem meticulous and responsible. A car being sold by the second owner isn't necessarily bad, but try to find out why the first owner sold it and anything else you can.

3. **Ask if the selling party has repair records** or an owner's log for the car, and review them in an informal way with the seller prior to purchase.

4. **Be thorough about inspecting the car** (that's what the next chapter is all about) and check the paperwork, which is much more informal than when buying from a dealer. (Chapter 15 goes over the papers you'll need to sign and walks you through the process.)

5. **Act quickly.** Good cars listed at great prices may sell fast. Call as soon as the ad appears in the paper, and if you aren't called back, keep trying.

6. **Prearrange financing.** Having a bank loan for a ballpark amount in the same month that you're seriously shopping will do two things: sway the buyer to sell to you (because you're prepared and the money's assured) and potentially let you handle all arrangements the same day that you decide to buy the car.

7. **Come prepared.** If you've seen the ad in a newspaper, get the wholesale value for that car and bring it with you. Or, if similar cars are being sold for less in another paper, bring those ads—showing the seller whatever's true may persuade him that your price range is reasonable.

If you're thinking about buying from a private party you know, make sure that you separate business and pleasure. While it's helpful to get candid information about a car's history, if it turns out to be a clunker, will you feel badly toward the person? Likewise, are you comfortable trying to drive a hard bargain with them? Don't immediately assume that buying from a friend or relative is the best idea for either of you.

Going once, going twice, going to an auction

Auto auctions are one place where dealers get the used cars they sell on their lots. Bank repossessions, unsold used cars, and other vehicles may wind up on the block. In fact, more than half of the used vehicles sold annually in this country pass through one of the more than 260 dealer-only auctions in operation. There are also U.S. Customs and other law enforcement agency auctions of stolen vehicles.

All kinds of vehicles wind up at auction, but don't expect the cream of the crop unless you really hunt—consider the sources. Can the individual consumer get in on these "wholesale" deals? Yes, but you will be working for the money you save. You may see ads for auto auctions tucked into the Sunday classifieds, on the Internet, and in the yellow pages.

Many are "dealer only" affairs featuring up to a few thousand cars at a time, geared toward the industry rather than the lonesome shopper. The way around that is to use an auction agent—someone who knows the ropes and will go to the auction for you (you're probably not allowed to go). He will receive a fee for the service (the goal is that the cost of the fee will be made up in the savings you get by buying an auction vehicle). Consider having an agent go with you to those auctions that you are allowed into, too. You'll find ads for them in similar spots, offering things like "10% over true wholesale," although agents may also work from a flat fee.

Bright Idea
Be polite—never more than with an individual seller are you relying on your own charm to clinch a sale at a good price.

Timesaver
Remember that auction bidding can go higher than pricing guides suggest, and you may be able to get as good a deal through a private party—without all the hassles and uncertainty.

Why auctions are enticing is illustrated in Table 8.5, which shows general estimates of prices that cars may be sold for, as compared to their approximate retail value (the price you might see at a dealer).

Remember that a retail price guide figure includes the costs of refurbishment on a used car and that you'll be responsible for any refurbishment needed when you buy at auction.

TABLE 8.5   SAMPLE AUCTION PRICES VS. APPROXIMATE RETAIL

Vehicle	Mileage	General Auction Price Approximation	Approximate Retail Value
Domestic sport utility vehicle '96	13,000	$18,000	$23,000
Japanese import sedan '96	26,000	$13,000	$16,500
Domestic economy car '97	10,000	$8,500	$11,000
Luxury European import '94	16,000	$16,500	$28,000

Among the things you need if you're really considering the auction option:

- Knowledge of what kind of car you want and how much you're willing to pay for it (auctions are for buyers, not shoppers)

- A very strong desire to save some money and willingness to put forward extra effort for it

- An agent whom you trust for the majority of auctions you're not allowed into

- If you're allowed on the lot, a flexible mechanic who can check out a car you're considering on short notice and possibly on a weekend (there's often a very limited window of time during which cars can be checked out on-site—half an hour, perhaps)

- Cash or prearranged financing

The difficulty of arranging bank financing on an as-yet-unseen auto means that cash or a credit card (with appropriate limit) are better options. But don't try to finance your auction car with credit card rates! Be prepared to pay the amount off immediately.

As you can see, the drawbacks of buying at auction are daunting. Table 8.6 lists some of the pros as well as the cons.

TABLE 8.6   SHOULD YOU BUY A CAR AT AUCTION?

Pros	Cons
Low wholesale pricing (thousands of dollars can be saved)	Footwork involved and unfamiliar procedures
Variety of vehicles to choose from	Auctions are usually open only to pros—you may have to have an agent do all auction work for you
You can impress your friends with the story if you do it successfully	Limited ability and time to inspect prior to purchase
	You won't have a choice of options on the car; you need to be flexible
	Financing is difficult if not impossible to arrange
	Vehicles of dubious origin—repos, salvaged from accidents, etc.—watch out for salvage titled cars, which may be available at auction (and should be clearly designated as such)—a salvage title can cause resale and insurability problems, and is sometimes why a car's available at what seems like a surprisingly low price
	Need to have vehicle and payable price in mind, then decide quickly
	You may be outbid
	Little recourse for any post-purchase problems

Cash-rich penny pinchers on the warpath for a bargain are the ideal auction buyers—even if you consider yourself one, strongly consider using an auction agent who knows the ropes!

The brave souls who still wish to try auction purchasing must consider another thing—the "clear title" problem. Cars that have problems in terms of knowing who the owners really are, or cars that have been in serious accidents or other cataclysms, hold what's called a "salvage title." Typically, if you try to resell a car with a salvage title:

1. No one will go near it (save mechanics who want to fix it up themselves and never sell it, or the entirely clueless).

2. You'll get, at best, 50% of the usual resale value for that car.

In other words, buyer beware! This is the chief problem with buying autos seized by law authorities and sold at their auctions.

So, how do you get a good deal at auction? Here are some ways:

1. One way to lower your risk of having to pay for potential problems is to buy a newer model car well within its manufacturer warranty period and mileage requirements.

2. Strongly consider using an auction agent who knows the ropes.

3. Set your acceptable mileage and cost slightly above round numbers. Many cars are sold at auction once they reach a round figure that reflects higher-than-average miles per year (about 15,000). Also, other bidders may have told their agents not to go above a certain rounded dollar amount or above a certain rounded mileage figure. Setting your stipulations slightly above those amounts puts you in a position to make a potentially successful bid.

4. Bring a used car price guide with you that shows wholesale and retail figures.

Bright Idea
The more popular the type of car you're looking for, the more likely you'll find it at auction.

5. Arrive early and inspect the cars outside—sometimes you can make a deal before a car goes up for bid.

The process of going to auction is shown in Table 8.7. It varies, depending on whether you're using an agent, and on how the agent and auction operate. Be prepared—an auction happens very fast, and some have as many as four lines of bidding going at once. It's no place for the faint-hearted.

TABLE 8.7 GOING TO AUCTION

Without an Agent	With an Agent
1. Locating and contacting an auction that allows individuals (newspaper ads for upcoming events, yellow pages, Internet searches).	1. Locating an agent (same places).
2. Being prepared to buy with cash (cashier's check) or credit.	2. Potentially depositing an escrow amount (to cover purchase cost) with the agent's account.
3. In some cases, checking lists of cars available for those you are interested in.	3. Filling out a bid sheet noting what models, years, mileage, and price ranges you'll consider, and with what options.
4. Preauction inspection opportunity (the day before or day of—bring price guides and a mechanic, if possible).	4. Agent notifies you of auctions with such vehicles available.
5. Bidding against competing buyers at the auction. If your bid is successful, pay on the spot and arrange post-purchase items like tag and insurance yourself.	5. On the day before or day of auction, he may do a preauction inspection of those cars.
	6. Dealer bids on cars of your choice with your given parameters at the actual auction.

Bidders typically get some indication about the condition of an automobile being sold at auction—a green light on the auction floor indicates good, yellow means some problems, and red means it's probably best to stay away.

> 7. Agent walks through purchase and post-purchase paperwork with you and refunds any excess in the escrow account (less his fee). You may come to the auction house to pick up the vehicle with a gate pass, or he may deliver it to you.

All in all, auto auctions tend to be chaotic places fit for only the staunchest of used car deal-hunters and professionals. If you do decide to try this option and find an auction you can attend yourself, make sure that you stick to your guns on price (and everything else) rather than getting caught up in the fever of runaway bidding.

No matter how you decide to buy your used car, research the pricing yourself, and give yourself time to find the vehicle you're really looking for. A little planning goes a long way toward saving you money.

Just the facts

- Expect to pay the most for a used car at a new car dealership, a bit less at an independent used car dealer, and less still either from a private owner or at auction.

- Look for a "certified used vehicle" indication for the best assurance that a car is in great shape.

- Shield yourself from repair costs by selecting a used vehicle still well within manufacturer warranty period and mileage restrictions.

- A used car is to your advantage only if it won't cost more in the long run than buying or leasing new—consider mileage efficiency, projected repair costs, and trade-in value first.

- If you decide to go the auction route, strongly consider using an auction agent.

GET THE SCOOP ON...
The right questions to ask sellers ▪ Doing your
own auto checkover ▪ What a mechanic's
prepurchase inspection should involve
▪ Telltale signs of car abuse

Before You Fall in Love—Inspect!

Chapter 9

It's easy to get giddy or just plain forgetful when what looks like the perfect used car is staring you in the face with its only-slightly-outdated headlamps gleaming in the sun. But take charge and be the steely one. Make sure that it passes your inspection before any money leaves your hands.

Getting information from the seller

You don't know where this car has been or what it has been through, so ask. Although it may take some prodding to get such prior-owner information from a dealer, you often can if you're serious about buying the car you're examining. With private parties, it's a different story, and you're more likely to hear the whole story of the vehicle with the gentlest of prodding, of course.

You can start "asking the right questions" even before you've seen the car for the first time—when you're speaking to a salesman or private seller on the phone. Touch on as many of the points in

Checklist 9.1 as is warranted, given your interest. It can save you time by screening vehicles in or out of the running.

Bright Idea
Try to keep your material questions about a car out of a "negotiating" mindset. You want honest answers, not for the salesman to simply tell you what he thinks you want to hear.

CHECKLIST 9.1　"HELLO, ABOUT THAT CAR FOR SALE..."

Questions for a Dealer	Questions for a Private Party
1. Verify year, make, model, price	1. Verify year, make, model, price
2. How negotiable is the price?	2. How negotiable is the price?
3. Mileage	3. Mileage
4. General condition	4. General condition
5. Major option packages and style (sedan, coupe, hatchback, convertible); engine size; manual or automatic	5. Major option packages and style (sedan, coupe, hatchback, convertible); engine size; manual or automatic
6. Color (exterior and interior)	6. Color (exterior and interior)
7. How long has the car been for sale?	7. How long has the car been for sale?
8. Where did the car come from? Trade-in? One owner? Auction? Lease return?	8. One owner? How long have they had the car?
9. What manufacturer warranty remains on the car; what warranty will be offered?	9. Why is the car for sale?
10. Name of the salesman, hours and location of the dealership	10. Does the car need any repairs?
	11. Is it still under warranty? For how long?
	12. Name and general location of seller; other phone numbers
	13. Convenient time for test-drive

Save any more Q & A for a site visit to see cars you're tempted to consider. Then what should you ask? Everything! And take notes.

Unanticipated questions to ask

The old saying "if a deal sounds too good to be true, it probably is" can be a cue for the car shopper. If anyone is selling a car at a lower price than the numbers indicate they should, be suspicious. And try to save some time by cutting to the chase with questions that should get to the bottom of it. (Try not to ask, "Why so cheap?" of course!)

A car below trade-in value may be a bona fide battered vehicle or at least a homeless one. Ask whether the title to the car is clear, ask again who owns it according to the title, and reiterate once more, "Does it have a salvage title?" A car with a salvage title, as we described in prior chapters, has usually been in an accident or a natural disaster. Such a car can be difficult or impossible to insure, and have a horrible resale value. Pass on these vehicles and head for the cream puffs.

Ask the seller for the VIN number of the car from the title and check it against the VIN on the driver's side dash, keeping a note of it. You can check with your state motor vehicle department to research a car's title history—to ensure that it isn't a salvaged car or "lemon buy-back."

Other questions you may want to ask a vehicle's seller include:

1. What was the car used for? Are those highway or city miles?

2. What quirks does the car have, if any? This may not change your mind about wanting the automobile, but it may help you be a tolerant owner.

3. Was scheduled maintenance performed?

4. Are there car care records that can be reviewed, or can you see a folder of maintenance- and repair-related bills?

5. How many miles does the car really get per gallon?

6. What grade of gasoline has been used in the car?

Unofficially...
Stewart sixty mile instrument. Lamps, five. Acetylene head lights, with generator, oil side and tail lamps. Horn, jack, tire kit, full set of tools. Accessories finished in black enamel and nickel.
—Grant Motor ad (1914)

7. Has the vehicle been kept in a garage, in a driveway, or streetside?

8. What regions of the country has the car spent its life in? (The drier, the better—less rust!)

9. What does the current owner love and hate about the car?

10. Has it ever been in an accident?

11. Has the car ever been recalled?

12. Any liens on the vehicle?

13. Has it been repainted?

Whatever questions you really want to ask, you may remember shortly after you've left the scene. Make sure that you've got adequate ways to contact the seller with any remaining questions—at work or via their pager, for instance. And, of course, a dealer is unlikely to know the answers to some of the more personal queries.

Interpreting the answers

What you want to hear from a car's seller is that there's an obvious reason why he's not keeping it, and that the reason has nothing to do with the car itself. Again, new babies in the family or a planned move to another state are both good signs—particularly if you hear an infant babbling in the background or see shipping boxes piled up in the living room window.

When talking with a dealer, accept answers with a grain of salt. But generally a car that's a lease return is a safe bet (if the mileage works out to 15,000 or fewer miles for each year of the car's age, it's a typical lease return). A trade-in is an acceptable idea as well. And if a car has been in stock for awhile without selling, wonder why.

Don't expect perfect answers to everything you ask. It's nice if a car has more highway miles than city, for instance, but city miles alone do not a clunker make. Ditto the gas grade used. What you should be trying to get is a general idea that the car was well cared for and a few tidbits to chew on.

A car with detailed maintenance records gets high marks, and the more expensive and exotic the car, the more important such records become. (If a butler is sent to retrieve the leather-bound versions, you're above your price range.)

Reviewing repair and maintenance expenses is an excellent idea, and, should you choose to buy the car, ask the current owner if you can make photocopies. That's foresight for a time in the future when your mechanic may ask, "Has this water pump ever been replaced?" Some repaired parts may be covered by warranty, but that won't do you any good unless you know and have proof.

Exterior inspection

It's amazing what a fresh coat of wax and some silicone can do for the average vehicle. No matter what car you're considering, look at it and then look at yours. There's likely to be a big shine difference. People who are selling cars (dealers included) dress them in their Sunday best by detailing them.

You should check all the details, so bring your glasses and go on the ding patrol during daylight hours.

What to look for

The outside appearance of a vehicle isn't just what you'll be presenting to your neighbors—it's also a clue to the way the car's been treated and any future problems that may crop up, such as rust.

Watch Out!
If you live in an area that's prone to snow and rain, or to very hot, bright days, the issue of whether a car has been garaged gets more serious. Paint and upholstery, not to mention the undercarriage and other parts prone to rust, fare better when protected. For extra assurance, ask the seller whether the car has ever been professionally rustproofed, although rustproofing is often routinely done before cars leave the factory.

Here's what to check for:

1. Is the entire painted body of the car smooth, shiny, and free of imperfections without signs of excessive abuse, or, particularly, rust?

2. Glance at the undercarriage; any rust? Everything look in order?

3. Is there plenty of tread on the tires in all positions, indicating even wear? Are the types of tires on the car all the same?

4. Make sure there are no wide gaps where the body of the car fits together.

5. Review for flaws everywhere.

6. How does the car look structurally? Any signs of past accidents?

7. Take a look under the hood. You want uncorroded battery cables, firmly positioned fan belts—and easy on the oil leaks. Check oil color and level.

8. Check the trunk, too. And make sure there's a spare tire.

9. Check for appropriate stickers, such as a state inspection decal.

If the outside inspection moves along fine, proceed to the next level and take the driver's seat, where there are even more things you should consider.

Interior inspection

Considering that this is where you will spend all of the time you have with your new toy, aside from occasionally washing it, be very sure that you're comfortable and not sitting in an inferior interior.

Your interior review is about more than comfort—check the car's instrumentation thoroughly.

What to look for

As you get into the vehicle, check the door sides for paint marks—a car that hasn't been repainted in a different shade is a better purchase. As you sit down, make sure that there's enough headroom, and that the steering wheel and seat position offer a good fit—not too snug or too loose. You can continue with Checklist 9.2. Have the keys with you, if possible, to try out items that need power.

CHECKLIST 9.2	INSIDE INSPECTION
General Appearance	Are the seats clean and free of cracks, cigarette burns, or stains?
	Are the carpets clean and not worn?
	Is the dashboard, headliner or visor faded or cracked?
	Is anything missing—like dash knobs?
Comfort	Are the seats comfortable and adjustable to a good driving position?
	How about the seatbelts?
	Is the vehicle too high or low to the ground for your taste? Can you get in and out comfortably?
	Are there accessories you'd like, such as decently-sized cup holders?
Safety	Can you see clearly over the dashboard and read the gauges?
	Are the lights, wipers, and other instruments comfortably reachable?
	How's visibility in all directions? Check windshield tint and what happens when you turn on the wipers; check the mirrors and their adjustments.

After all the other questions, sit back and ask, "Can I really see myself driving and owning this car?" Trust your instincts about interior creature comforts.

There are some things you should test in a car before you even leave the parking space on the lot. Turn the ignition on (not the engine, just the ignition) and check that all of the dash lights work properly. Also check power windows and locks, the radio (and cassette or CD player), the cigarette lighter, the wipers (and wiper fluid), the glove-box latch, and anything else the car has that matters to you.

How to spot car abuse

Cars that have had it hard tend to show it all over. A car with a pristine interior isn't as likely to have been manhandled on the road as one with obvious signs of interior wear.

Ditto broken things that either haven't been fixed or have been repaired only with stopgap solutions. Given broken dash knobs being held together with twist ties, who knows what's going on under the hood?

Regular wear is one thing. Floor mats get dirty and they are replaceable. But cigarette holes and their ilk show a disregard that should warn any potential buyer. Likewise, any serious exterior cosmetic defects.

Have someone else start the car and check the exhaust. Dark smoke can mean unburned fuel, and valve or carburetor problems, or that the car's burning oil. Better to consider cars that are nonsmokers!

Road testing

The goal of road testing is to cover a little bit of everything, if possible—hill and dale, a freeway, a couple of bumps, and a driveway or two. Rainy days and evenings are great, too—particularly for the second test-drive in a vehicle—as a challenge to see whether the car measures up to your exacting standards.

What to test

We suggest that you take an initial test-drive out of the gate to see how you like the car. Don't look for anything in particular. Just drive. Leisurely. Then briefly on a faster highway, and see what you think. Get used to the car.

If you're pleasantly impressed and it feels like this could already be your car, start putting it through its paces. At this point, we'll assume that you're in the car and ready to start making evaluations.

First, there are some general sensory items you should be aware of throughout the test: smoothness of ride, ease of handling and braking, engine power, and noise level. Then consider specifics (see Checklist 9.3).

Bright Idea
The procedures for setting up test-drives are described in Chapter 4, in case you want a quick review.

CHECKLIST 9.3	YOUR TEST-DRIVE
Power & Performance	Does the car respond well to your acceleration, without lagging, when shifting gears and otherwise?
	Is there enough oomph in the engine to get you safely onto a freeway from a stop or to pass a car, with the air on full?
	Try a steep hill with the air on full. Can the vehicle make it smoothly without shifting to a lower gear?
	If it's a four-wheel drive, try the same hill in a low gear with four-wheel drive engaged—it should feel smooth and full of torque power to climb nimbly.
Steering	Steering should be responsive and fluid, but not loose.
	Try a U-turn in an empty parking lot. The car should turn smoothly all the way through.

Be thoughtful in examining a car during a test-drive, but don't go overboard. You want a mechanic to look at it too, so take time to enjoy driving it rather than just stressing on every detail.

	When driving on a straight stretch, relax your hands slightly. The car should continue in a straight line, not pulling to either side.
Suspension	Is the ride what you want, on smooth surfaces and over bumps, at high speeds and low? Sports cars will have a firmer ride, luxury cars a more marshmallow-like ride, and there are all ranges in between... it's a matter of personal preference and tolerance.
	Does the car travel smoothly and hold together well on pronounced curves, or does it "skip" a bit?
Brakes	Find an empty area and push down firmly on the brake pedal. Automatic braking systems should bring the vehicle to a controlled stop without pulling right or left.
	Are you comfortable with the firmness or softness of the brakes, compared to what you're used to?
Parking	Try parallel parking the car. If you can't do it after a couple of tries, get something else.
	Can you comfortably park the car in a typical parking space?
	Are you comfortable gauging where the hood and trunk end? (Boxy cars equal defined lines. Melted-bar-of-soap shapes may be harder to estimate.)

Essentially, the more different driving conditions you can try out in the vehicle, the better. Braking in the rain is sure to be different than on dry streets. When driving at night, you need to be able to clearly see illuminated gauges, as well as be comfortable with the headlight pattern and brake light intensity.

What to listen for

The way a car sounds during a test-drive can give you as many clues about its health as your visual observations and sense of the ride. Listen for a smooth, clean startup and a relative absence of out-of-place noises. A healthy (but muted) acceleration growl sounds different from a straining transmission. Listen for engine pings as well, and notice how much the noise level increases as you accelerate from slower speeds to faster ones. There shouldn't be too distinct a difference.

Take part of your test-drive with the windows open and part with them closed. Listen to the air conditioner—is that a healthy fan motor? And try the stereo system, of course, at different levels of treble and bass, and in either position of the balance control (left to right). Check the front and rear speakers, to ensure that they're in good repair and not blown out, tinny, or with an otherwise distorted response.

After the test-drive

As soon as possible after you try out a car, make some notes on its performance, for comparisons to any other vehicles you'll drive and for future negotiations. Worksheet 9.1 can be used for once-over recollection.

WORKSHEET 9.1   TEST-DRIVE WORKSHEET

	Good	Okay	Poor	Observations
Exterior Appearance				
Interior Appearance				
Interior Comfort Level & Safety				

If you're displeased with a car's performance, try another engine size in the same model or ask about other options packages that may suit your preferences better.

	Good	Okay	Poor	Observations
Instrumentation & Accessories				
Ride				
Steering & Handling				
Braking				
Parking				
Acceleration & Shifting				
Noise Level				
Fit with Expectations				

The mechanic's inspection

It sounds incongruous that you're calling your mechanic now, in the interest of giving him less business later. But never consider buying a used car without having someone you trust—someone who knows cars—give it a mechanical review.

If the person trying to sell you a car won't consider letting you have your mechanic review it, look elsewhere. In a survey, salesmen were asked if their dealerships would allow a mechanic's review prior to purchase—either at the lot or mechanic's garage, and 92% said yes (source: Consumer Federation of America).

What is it?

The constituent components of a perfect prebuy review vary from mechanic to mechanic, as do the fees. You are essentially paying for a pair of expert eyes that look over the vehicle and perhaps catch signs of impending problems that you missed.

Of course, you probably don't have test equipment at home in your garage, but your mechanic has access to all sorts of interesting devices.

A typical mechanic's review may consist of checking the major operating systems of the auto, and it should, of course, include the mechanic's test-drive. This may cost you a little extra, it but can save much more in the end. You want him to check:

1. Brakes (pads and lines)

2. The frame and suspension (for rust and any signs of accident damage)

3. Cooling system

4. Wheel rims and alignment, bearings, tires

5. Battery and electrical system

6. Drive train

7. Exhaust system (particularly for state-required emissions-level inspections)

8. Transmission

9. Engine compression

Ask for your mechanic's informal comments, as well as his findings in writing. How much would he expect repairs to cost you over the next year? Does he consider the car to be in good shape, or does he suggest that you could do better? Your mechanic is your ally and a good sounding board for your auto buying thoughts.

Why it makes sense

You can't expect your mechanic to foresee your prospective car's entire future (or all currently clandestine problems). But a mechanical review should

Moneysaver
Every model line has its weak spots, and you can find out what they are with a Reliability Report available at Microsoft's CarPoint Web site (carpoint.com). Have your mechanic check anything that your desired model's prone to.

Bright Idea
Four-wheel-drive vehicles should have a front end, suspension, and transfer case check by a qualified mechanic—repairs can be expensive.

Timesaver
Try to prearrange a time during the week when you can shop and when your mechanic may be available to check over a car—rather than on the weekends, when many garages are closed and a mechanic may be reluctant to assist.

be able to alert you to major signs of impending doom that you could just as easily avoid by getting a different car. Metal filings in fluid indicate a part that's been getting serious wear, and the location of oil leaks can tell a mechanic whether you may be up for engine problems or just a couple of line seals.

Even if a review turns up nothing major, you can ask a seller to take responsibility for any minor repair needs that your mechanic has identified, or you can use it as a bargaining chip for a lower price. And used car shopping is stressful enough—this is one place where you can find some peace of mind.

Just the facts

- Road test a car under as many different driving conditions as possible—good and bad weather, day and night, freeways, hills, and at low speeds.

- Small bubbles in body paint can indicate a more serious problem underneath—rust.

- Most dealerships will allow your mechanic to review a vehicle you're considering, and you shouldn't consider buying without one.

The Lease Option

GET THE SCOOP ON...
The anatomy of a lease ▪ What leasing terms
mean in English ▪ When it makes the most
sense to lease ▪ Why lease prices that
look good may not be

Leaning Toward Leasing

Chapter 10

F ive hundred bucks, $639, topping $700?! Monthly installments on new vehicle purchases are looking more and more like apartment rent figures these days, and we mean apartments in nice neighborhoods. The rising cost of driving can intimidate anyone shopping for a new car—particularly if they have been out of the market for a few years.

So who wouldn't find the prospect of making two-thirds (or even less than half) the usual monthly new car payment alluring? That's the kind of benefit that leasing can offer, and it's a powerful persuader against cries of "But you'll never really own the car, it's a bad idea!"...

Hang on, dear reader, we'll sort this out in logical fashion and you can decide on which side of the fence your money is greener... the leasing side or the buying side.

The leasing trade-off

The arguments for and against leasing both sound convincing, and there's the leasing dilemma.

Assuming that the car is sold at the end of the purchase financing term or lease term, great deals can be comparable for some shoppers.

On the pro-leasing side of the coin, there's the old saying that one should only buy things that appreciate in value, but rent things that depreciate (or put as little money into them as possible). A car is a depreciating asset, as anyone who's ever bought or sold one knows well. When you invest in an appreciating asset (such as, one hopes, your home) your money grows in the form of equity. An extremely simplified example is shown in Table 10.1.

Say you're debating between buying a $28,000 new car that you will finance over four years or picking up a lease on the same vehicle. Let's further simplify the illustration by saying that you're considering a long lease—four years, equal to the amount of time it will take you to finance the car if you buy it.

TABLE 10.1   LEASE OR BUY A DEPRECIATING ASSET? (LIKE A CAR)

	Buying	Leasing
Purchase Price	$28,000	$28,000
10% Down Payment	$2,800	$2,800
Sales Tax	(6%)	(6%)
Amount to Be Financed	$26,712	$14,000 (based on 40% 48-month residual value)
Financing Rate	9%	9%
Total of Payments (48 months)	$31,907	$21,836
Difference		$10,071 less

(Taxes and other fees excluded for illustration purposes)

In our simple illustration, you might not have anything to drive at the end of that four-year lease (though a buyer gets equity), but you would have spent about ten grand less than if you bought the car, and had payments about $210 less.

Say you decide to lease and plow that extra $210 into your savings every time you mail off your installment, and you get a nice little rate of return of about 5%. Table 10.2 shows what would happen to your money.

TABLE 10.2   VALUE OF $210 SAVED MONTHLY AT 5% INTEREST OVER 48 MONTHS

At Start	$0
1 Year	$2,799
2 Years	$5,520
3 Years	$8,381
4 Years	$11,388

You come out more than $1,300 ahead from the savings alone (never mind that if you left it in a tax-deferred account for another 20 years at the same rate with no additional deposits it would grow to $30,215—not inflation-adjusted).

As you can see, restricting what you spend on a depreciating asset lets your money grow when put to work elsewhere, such as in a savings account generating decent interest. In this example, the $10,071 saved by leasing turns into $11,388 at the end of the lease term that way (through the compounding of interest—the idea that you'll be earning interest on not just the invested amount but also on the interest you've already earned on the invested amount).

So why isn't everyone leasing? Let's take the illustration a step further and see what happens at the end of the lease or financing term (see Table 10.3). Although the buyer will have a vehicle to drive free and clear at the end of his or her string of payments, the lessee must either find something

Unofficially...
Part of auto leasing's popularity has to do with changes in tax laws several years ago that impaired the deductibility of interest payments on car purchases.

else to drive or purchase the lease car, financing over more years.

TABLE 10.3   TAIL END OF THE TERM (LEASING OR FINANCING)

	Buying	Leasing
Residual Value of Car at End of Financing	$11,200	$11,200
Cost to Refinance and Purchase Car (assumes 10% down and 90% financing, at 10% for 48 months)	$0	$14,195

Given this scenario, a person who chooses to lease and then purchase at lease end will spend eight years paying off the car, at a cost of more than $4,000 above what he would have paid if he bought the car outright.

So who comes out ahead? It's hard to say. Remember that $11,388 that the leasing contract would save? If a lessee uses the saved money to buy this car outright, he or she will owe only a bit less than $500 in tax (assuming 6%) if using all of the saved money toward a cash purchase of the vehicle, making it close to even. Or he or she can assume a new lease and keep adding to savings.

Those who argue against buying a car emphasize that pouring more money than necessary into the purchase of a vehicle is not going to make any money for you, but just ties up cash you can be growing elsewhere.

Or even spending. There's the prospect of saving two or three hundred dollars a month on your payments. Three hundred extra bucks a month can roughly buy the following in the course of a year:

- a great television ($500)
- ten hours of massage therapy ($500)

- an updated wardrobe of clothes ($500)

- a respectable PC ($2,000) plus

- more than half-a-dozen of the hottest CDs to play ($100)

...and you would be driving the same new car.

On the flip side of the argument, leasing loses its luster for some when compared to used car purchases in particular. The first year of depreciation on a new car is a hard hit, but after that, the yearly losses slow. Someone who buys used, or even buys new and hangs onto that car quite awhile, builds equity and will in a few years have a drivable set of wheels and no payments at all to make.

The lessee ends up with less: nothing, to be exact, at the end of the lease term. If he or she wants to continue driving, he or she must continue forking over money for another new lease car (or buy the lease car at the end of the term and spend additional years making payments).

The beauty of leasing is that you're not paying for the car, you're paying for the depreciation over the time you use it. And conversely, the ugliness of leasing is that you're not paying for the car, you're paying for the depreciation over the time you use it! It's you who's getting that big first-year depreciation hit over and over, as you trade in your lease cars and get new ones.

So it's all in how you look at it. Let's take this further under the microscope and see if you can thrive as a future lessee.

Are you a candidate for leasing?

Some of us are better cut out to buy vehicles, others prefer to "rent" them long term, as you're really doing in a lease. The ideal lease candidate is a person who strongly prefers new cars over preowned vehicles, takes good care of his things, doesn't drive more than 15,000 miles per year, and expects to have a fairly predictable lifestyle and income for the next few years. He should be able to afford, or nearly afford, some kind of new car purchase. Do you have questions about whether you should really be considering a lease? Table 10.4 can help you answer some of them.

TABLE 10.4   ARE YOU AN IDEAL LESSEE OR BUYER?

Lessee	Buyer
Typically needs to drive no more than 15,000 miles annually	May drive more than 15,000 miles per year
Careful with car care (no dings)	Not necessarily as easy on cars
Can easily return car at end of lease term (won't move out of area, for example)	Prefers or needs flexibility in the amount of time car is kept
Prefers lower payments, but will be able to afford to release at end of lease term	Can handle higher payments (or plans to buy used)
Strong preference for a new car (acquires new cars every few years)	Keeps cars more than a few years
Doesn't mind the idea of being a "long-term renter"	Strong preference for ownership (even if the bank really owns the car during its payoff period)

What further distinguishes the difference between a lessee and a buyer? There are money and psychological factors to consider (refer to Chapter 3). And no one can afford to ignore either category.

Leasing and your head

No matter what else happens, you must be true to yourself. Start with your conscience and sensibilities. Try this quick test (Quiz 10.1) to double-check your disposition toward leasing.

QUIZ 10.1   ARE YOU PSYCHOLOGICALLY READY TO LEASE?

Answer the following questions true or false:

T or F	1. I'm nearly as happy renting a home as owning one.
T or F	2. I don't get attached to my possessions.
T or F	3. I have never given a pet name to a vehicle.
T or F	4. I'm usually on time for appointments and don't often stress about whether I'll be prompt.
T or F	5. Money and cars are means to an end.
T or F	6. I like following trends and fashion.
T or F	7. I can predict where I'll be and what I'll be doing in two years with some degree of certainty, and I'm comfortable with my plan.
T or F	8. Once I make a decision, I tend to stick with it rather than vacillate.
T or F	9. Antique hound? Collector? Not me! I like nice, new, clean things.
T or F	10. I agree with the statement, "It makes no sense to invest in something that depreciates."
T or F	11. Driving a new car makes me feel better than driving an older one.
T or F	12. My habits are fairly predictable.
T or F	13. I'm one of those people who says "today matters." I'll plan, but I live for the present.
T or F	14. I take good care of my things, but throw out or give away what's too worn or what I don't want anymore.
T or F	15. I feel relatively in control of my time and life.

If you answered "false" to three or more quiz questions, leasing may be against your grain—think it over very carefully before proceeding.

The psychology of leasing is a double-edged sword: you get the prestige and comfort of a new car with lower payments than buying; but it's not really your car, and at the end of the lease, you don't own anything. How you feel about those factors can affect the enjoyment of the car you'll be driving. Two or three years is a long time to cope with

Nothing is more fairly distributed than common sense: no one thinks he needs more of it than he already has.
—Descartes

Timesaver
Want a quick acid test of your leasing leanings? Think about the last time you rented a car. Did you make sure there was unlimited mileage or worry about going over the limit? Did you buy the daily collision damage waiver out of fear? If you had bad tinglings then, perhaps you're more of a buyer.

lessee's remorse, and you'll have little recourse if you really do change your mind.

Some of the personal issues you'll need to grapple with if you go for a lease include:

- Reconciling the concept that it's not really your car

- Coping with mileage limitations

- Factors that affect the return of your car, such as a move some distance away from the dealership where you leased the vehicle

By all outward appearances, your lease car is your car. Only you know the truth. There may be no difference at all between the way a perfectionist treats a lease car and how he treats a purchased one. But while the car is in your hands, you're responsible for its care. Normal wear and tear is allowed, but when possible, try to treat lease cars with some TLC.

Would you garage the car whenever possible, try to park it in spots where it's least likely to wind up with door dings, be gentle on the upholstery—generally, keep it as new-looking as possible? If not, maybe you're not the best person to be considering a lease. The difference is that an upholstery tear in an out-of-the-way spot might be annoying in a car you've purchased, but it can be costly in a car you've leased.

And while you're driving, at some point you are no doubt looking ahead to the end of the lease term, keeping your eye on other new cars that you may want to lease instead, or considering the benefits and drawbacks of purchasing your lease car at the end of the term. It's a different feeling from a car purchase, where your car is simply your car.

Watch Out!
According to your lease contract, you may need to bring the car in for scheduled maintenance or else risk potential complications involving "excessive wear and tear" charges. When purchasing, you would simply have the option to bring your car in for maintenance.

Which brings us to the topic of mileage. Take your current car into consideration. How long ago did you buy it? How many miles have you put on it since then? How many miles does that equal per year, and do you recall the annual mileage being roughly the same from year to year? We'll talk more in Chapter 11 about prepurchasing extra miles you may need, but bear in mind that it will increase your monthly payments.

Toward the end of your first year in a lease car (or perhaps quarterly, if you remember to), it's a good idea to take a look at how many miles you've driven. Will you be far off the mark at return time if you continue at the same rate? You may need to adjust your driving habits to accommodate the mileage requirements—that can mean changing plans for a long-distance vacation by auto or relying on another vehicle in the family for some regular transportation needs. The best policy is to prepurchase any extra mileage you think you'll need—so you don't have to worry or make alternate arrangements. Look at your past driving habits as a guideline (and factor in any recent changes in your commuting distance or other mileage).

Leasing and your wallet

The money aspect of leasing is of primary importance, of course. When you lease, you're in essence agreeing to say good-bye to a chunk of cash (hundreds to thousands of dollars) or to your trade-in at the onset of a lease, and every month to wave good-bye to more in the form of payments. The trade-off is that you get to drive that cool new car that no one else has driven, which shouldn't need repairs (at least during the period of the lease that the car's covered by a manufacturer warranty). But if you have a large down payment or a great trade-in, strongly consider buying instead of leasing—such up-front factors can bring an otherwise high month-ly purchase payment into line, and you'll be build-ing equity.

Another area to pause for reflection about is practicality. Are things so predictable in your life that you're comfortable estimating how many miles you'll drive in a year? And is there no reason you might need to change to a different type of vehicle in the next two to three years?

Leasing is an ideal way for some consumers to drive a new set of wheels and save some money on monthly payments. In that respect, the tight-budgeted may love leasing. But squeeze your eco-nomic situation a few more notches and leasing becomes more burden than benefit.

When leasing is a bad idea

Leasing doesn't make sense when you simply don't fit the profile of an ideal lessee and would be happi-er buying—whether new or used.

The short list of shoppers for whom leasing is not a practical option is shown in Table 10.5.

TABLE 10.5   LEASING IS IMPRACTICAL WHEN...

When	Why
Ability to make payments is in question	Those with any doubt about their ability to pay the set monthly installments for the lease term should consider buying used instead—you can resell in a pinch, but early lease return penalties are heavy.
Need for a car may change	Those whose need for a car may disappear during the next two or three years should con-sider the weight of lease return penalties too, such as

	anyone moving to a very urban setting with other transportation options.
Long-term budget is very tight	Those on the tightest budgets who need equity in a vehicle should consider buying used instead of leasing, particularly those whose financial burdens are expected to increase in two to three years.
Mileage is likely to be high	Those who expect to drive in excess of 12,000 (and definitely above 15,000) miles annually should consider purchasing instead, because of high excess mileage penalties at lease-end (although higher mileage leases are available).
Wear and tear on car is likely	Those who put vehicles to rough use (pickup trucks used in construction, etc.) probably fare better buying instead of worrying about excess wear and tear lease charges.
Vehicle must be modified	Those who need their business name painted on the side of a work vehicle should review terms carefully with the dealer before leasing—as should anyone else who may need to modify the vehicle. Leasing isn't built to fit this kind of consumer.

For the shopper looking at leasing as a way to save money on the cost of a new car, there are some additional points to consider before biting. Let the lessee beware—it is possible to pay more when leasing a car than when buying it. Common trip-ups include:

- Paying more than you should for a lease at the dealer (compare lease vs. purchase prices with Worksheet 11.1 in Chapter 11).

- Driving more than the allowed number of miles during the term of the lease (paying a dime to a quarter for each extra mile).

- Being liable for a large cash "early termination" penalty by defaulting on the lease or otherwise making an early return.

- Incurring a charge for excess wear and tear.

- Agreeing to a lease contract in which you are liable for the difference between the predicted residual value of the vehicle (determined at lease signing) and the car's actual fair market value at lease end.

Understanding leasing

Leasing bears more resemblance to renting than it does to buying. When you lease a car, the only thing you are "buying" is the right to drive the vehicle for a certain period of time. What you pay for is not the car itself, but the amount the car will depreciate over the time that you use it (plus some profit, taxes, and fees, of course).

When you decide to lease, a leasing finance company (or bank) actually buys the car, in effect, and then loans it to you. That part is analogous to what happens when you get a bank loan to finance a car you're buying.

Quick anatomy of a lease

There are three major players in a lease deal: you are the lessee, the dealer is the dealer, and the lease finance company or bank that's buying the vehicle is the lessor that holds title to the vehicle. Beyond that:

- Most leases are for 24, 36, or 48 months.
- Annual mileage allowance is typically no more than 15,000 (10,000–15,000).

Timesaver
Leasing isn't the simplest form of car acquisition. If you live for simplicity, it may not be your cup of tea. But if you tolerate complexity in your life well, you can be rewarded by having a new car to drive with relatively low payments to make on it.

- As with a car purchase, you usually make a sort of down payment on a lease at the beginning by laying out for some costs up-front, and then you make monthly payments throughout the term.

How much those monthly payments are depends largely on the four primary points of a lease:

1. How long the lease is for (the "Term").

2. What purchase price the lease is being based on ("Capitalized Cost"), and what the price is after figuring in any additions or subtractions, such as rebates, acquisition fees, taxes, etc. (to get the "Adjusted Capitalized Cost").

3. What "Interest Rate" you'll be paying on the financing ("Rent Charge," figured by using a number known as the "Money Factor").

4. The expected wholesale worth of the vehicle at the end of the lease term ("Residual Value").

(See the upcoming section on definitions in this chapter for detailed descriptions.)

There are two types of leases you should be familiar with:

- **Closed-end:** The common consumer lease, which presupposes the residual value of a vehicle at lease end, in which the lessor (finance company or bank) typically bears the risk of any difference between that and the actual value at lease end.

- **Open-end:** Beware of this type of lease, which may require you to pay the difference if the vehicle is worth less at the end of the lease than originally estimated. It is typically relegated to business leasing arrangements, not consumer auto leasing.

Unofficially...
As a rule of thumb, leasing and buying can be comparable, assuming that a buyer will sell his car once he finishes financing it, at the same time a lessee would make a lease car return.

The biggest chunk of money you will spend on your lease usually goes toward the car's depreciation. If it is expected to be worth 45% of its original MSRP at the end of the lease term, you pay for the other 55%.

The second biggest expense in a lease is the "lease charge" or "rent charge," which is similar to the interest that you might pay on a car loan when you're purchasing. You also pay tax on the cost of the lease (monthly payments and often a down payment as well, varying by state) and a variety of fees.

The major components of a lease, as you may encounter them, are shown in Table 10.6. They vary from lease to lease, and you should use this table only to familiarize yourself with the terms and procedures that can be used in a typical closed-end lease.

Some up-front items may be amortized over the life of the lease and included in monthly payments instead.

TABLE 10.6   WHAT'S IN A LEASE? YOUR UP-FRONT COSTS AND CREDITS ("TOTAL DUE AT LEASE SIGNING")

Cost	or Credit	About It	Example
acquisition fee		covers lessor's loan-processing costs; a similar charge may be called "assignment fee"	$475
destination charge			$420
security deposit		refunded at lease end	$400
tax		may be amortized over life of lease and included in monthly payments instead	$0 (see monthly payment)
title fees			varies by state
registration fees			varies by state
first monthly payment			$388

Cost	or Credit	About It	Example
any additional miles purchased			$0
required insurances			$0
advertising association fees		regional ad cost spread between area dealers (not all dealers participate)	$110
	rebate or other discount		$1,000
	value of trade-in		$2,200
	any additional down payment		$0

YOUR MONTHLY PAYMENT

Cost	About It	Example
monthly depreciation	total depreciation divided by term (in months)	$250
additional amortized amounts	anything you're financing beyond actual depreciation (such as dealer add-ons or charges not paid up front)	$0
rent charge	the "interest" you pay, also called "lease charge" or "monthly lease fee"	$116
tax	if not included in up-front payments	$22

Calculations of state and other applicable taxes are usually based on monthly payment amounts and often on down payments, but a number of states figure sales tax on the entire purchase price (and occasionally local authorities levy their own taxes).

YOUR LEASE-END COSTS AND CREDITS

Cost	or Credit	About It	Example
disposition fee		administrative fee if you decide not to buy the vehicle	
excess mileage charges			$0
excess wear and tear charges			$0

Cost	or Credit	About It	Example
	security deposit refund		$520

There are many opportunities within a lease for a dealer to make back money that you negotiate away. To bottom line what's happening and ensure that you get a fair deal, you need to know both the Net Capitalized Cost and the Net Interest Rate.

Learning the language of leasing

Leasing can seem like an entirely different world from buying, and it's important to have a good grasp of the terminology and workings of a lease contract.

Some primary concepts to get familiar with:

Watch Out!
Ask for an item-ization of what's included in your capital cost—make sure that the capital cost isn't overly inflated to negate the worth of your trade-in.

- **Acquisition Fee:** Also called "initiation fee," "assignment fee," or sometimes "loan fee," it's a sum due at the beginning of the lease to cover the lessor's costs of preparing it. (This is where they get you coming; the Disposition Fee is where they get you going.)

- **Advertising Association Fees:** A charge commonly added to the cost of your lease when the dealer participates in regional advertising for a certain make of car. The cost is divided between the dealers who participate.

- **APR (Annual Percentage Rate):** The interest rate used to figure lease payments; also called "base interest rate."

- **Capitalized Cost:** There are two costs: gross cap cost and adjusted cap cost. "Gross cap cost," what many lease numbers are be derived from, is the agreed price of the car plus any extras such as service plans, gap insurance, and other fees. "Adjusted (net) cap cost" is that less any reduction in the cost of the vehicle (a rebate, down payment, or the value of your trade-in). The way that this cost is computed may vary among leasing agents.

- **Capitalized Cost Reduction:** Your down payment on a lease (cash, the value of your trade-in, a rebate amount you choose to put toward up-front costs). The more you pay up front, the less your monthly payment will be. Consider minimizing your up-front payments to keep more cash at your disposal in your own bank account, but remember that monthly payments will be higher if you do, and there will also be an interest charge on that money.

- **Closed-End Lease:** A common type of consumer vehicle lease, in which the risk of a difference between residual and actual value at lease-end is borne by the lessor, not you.

- **Depreciation:** The reduction of a car's value. It's the largest single cost in a lease, and the difference between a car's original MSRP and its residual value at the end of the lease term.

- **Disposition Fee:** What you pay the lessor at lease end to cover his hassle of reselling the car.

- **Early Termination Charge:** A hefty penalty (can be thousands) that you pay for ending the lease before it's up—the earlier in the lease you do this, the bigger the charge. One reason for its high expense is that the initial depreciation a car experiences isn't paid for at the beginning of the lease, but is spread out over the entire lease. So bringing the car back early could leave a payment gap for the lessor. They'd prefer that you cover that cost.

Bright Idea
So what's the lowdown on depreciation? Refer to Chapter 6 for a discussion of it.

- **End-of-Lease Purchase Price:** Typically, leases offer lessees the option to buy the vehicle at the end of the lease term. The end-of-lease purchase price describes just that, how much you'll pay to actually buy the car at that point. It may be equal to the residual value of the car, but may also include extra fees.

- **Excess Mileage Charge:** What you pay at the end of the lease if you drove it more than the annual mileage allotment (usually 12,000–15,000 miles per year)—often 10–25 cents per mile.

- **Excess Wear-and-Tear Charge:** What you pay at the end of the lease if you treated the vehicle more roughly than normal.

- **Gap Insurance:** (Has nothing to do with where you shop for clothes.) Picks up where typical auto insurance leaves off: it covers the difference between what a car is worth and how much was paid on the lease (which may be less) in the event of the loss of the vehicle during the term. It covers your liability for expenses in such unavoidable circumstances and it is necessary when your lease contract doesn't include a Gap Waiver.

- **Gap Waiver:** Language included in some leases protecting you from gap charges (see Gap Insurance).

- **Lease Company:** The bank or other financial institution that is buying the vehicle from the dealer and leasing it to you. It may be a "captive finance company" affiliated with the manufacturer (such as Ford Motor Credit, Toyota Motor Credit, etc.), a bank, a bank-related institution, or an independent financing organization.

- **Lessee:** You, the person leasing.

- **Lessor:** Them, the people you're leasing from (the Lease Company). Not the dealer.

- **Money Factor:** The rate of the financing expense that is used to calculate your lease payment. It is equal to $\frac{1}{24}$ of the APR.

- **Net Interest Rate:** The total interest rate for the lease, deduced from the net capitalized cost.

- **Open-End Lease:** A lease in which the lessee is responsible for any difference between the pre-supposed residual value (on which your payments were based) and the actual residual value at the end of the lease term. Used in business arrangements; no longer part of the common lexicon of consumer leasing.

- **Option Discount Adjustment:** Manufacturer purchase discounts on certain option packages, which in leasing are described instead at full retail value for purposes of residual calculation. It's good because your residual is higher, meaning that you'll spend less on monthly payments. (However, bear in mind that some leasing companies limit values associated with overaccessorizing options that won't return value in the resale market, thus your "savings" may be limited).

- **Purchase Option:** Also called "lease-end purchase option." It means that you have the option to purchase the vehicle at the end of the lease, and it describes the terms.

- **Rent Charge:** Also known as a "lease charge," it describes what you're paying in financing expenses, as determined by the Money Factor.

Timesaver
Want to express an annual percentage rate as a money factor? Just express it as a decimal and divide it by 24. For example: 12% becomes (.12 ÷ 24) = .00500. To express a money factor as an APR, just multiply it by 24: (.00500 × 24) = .12 = 12%.

- **Residual Value:** What a leased car is expected to be worth, wholesale, at the end of the lease. It is expressed as both a percentage (always of MSRP) and as a dollar figure, and it may be called the "resale value."

- **Security Deposit:** A refundable amount that you pay at the outset of a lease, often close to a month's lease payment. You get it back at the end of the lease unless you're liable for other charges, which can be deducted from the security deposit amount.

- **Subsidized Lease:** Also called a "subvented" lease; a lease offer with a manufacturer's incentive attached—it can include a rebate, special interest rate, or special residual higher than guidebook numbers.

- **Term:** How long you are renting the car for (usually 24, 36, or 48 months).

- **Total Out-of-Pocket Cost:** Total of payments, fees, deposits, and cap cost reduction from the beginning to the end of the lease. Does not include tax, license, or registration.

- **Trade-in Allowance:** The worth you're being allowed for trading in your old vehicle.

- **Up-front costs:** Just that, what you pay up front (it often includes security deposit, down payment, advanced payment, and taxes).

End-of-lease payments

The pot of gold at the end of the lessor's rainbow may be you, driving back to turn in your leased car. How can you wind up owing money on a lease after you've made all those payments?

In an "open-ended" lease (now typically used just in business arrangements), you take the risk that the vehicle will be worth less than specified at the outset. With that kind of lease, you may get periodic payments that are lower than with the "closed-end" variety, in which the lessor, rather than yours truly, takes on the risk of a difference in residual price. With the closed-end lease, you won't owe.

You can also owe for running up too many miles on the odometer or for returning the vehicle in worse-than-acceptable shape.

You probably didn't take the time to try to talk the leasing agent out of or down from end-of-lease charges, such as the "disposition fee" for the cost of readying your car for resale.

Penalties apply

If you've ever listened to car lease commercials (and likely they've been catching your ear lately), the very fast, timid speech you hear at the very end—the audio version of fine print—is all about what's not included and penalties.

When you lease, you've got to toe the line and play by the rules. Three major kinds of penalties may apply:

1. Early Termination
2. Excess Mileage
3. Excess Wear and Tear

Let's take a look at them one by one.

Early termination penalties exist for a couple of reasons. The dealer dealt with you once, and his object was to get you to pay as much as possible and go away. He wants you to come back when you're ready to spend more money, and he doesn't want to give up any he's already gotten from you. If you could at any time return the car and get a prorated portion of your money back, think of the profit nightmare it would pose for him, not to mention the paperwork. It's just not practical to the current way of doing business.

But there's another reason behind the existence of early termination penalties. It's all because most leases have uniform payments over the lease term— you know how much you'll pay in each monthly installment.

When that lease car rolls off the lot for the first time with you behind the wheel, its value plummets (nothing personal). Instead of sticking you with that initial depreciation shock—"What?! My first monthly payment's $1,600?!"—the extreme price of newness is amortized, or spread out, over the life of the lease. In English, you're getting a phenomenal deal at the outset of your lease and paying way too much at the end. But it all evens out if you keep the car for the full term.

If you don't, your total lease payments may not equal the rapidly diminishing value of that car you're driving. Terminating the lease early in the term for whatever reason (your choice or your default) could theoretically leave the lessor in the lurch, not fully compensated for the value of the car by the time it's given back.

Mileage limitations are common with closed-end lease contracts. Any excess mileage will probably require an end-of-lease payment. You should negotiate mileage allowances with the leasing company before signing the contract (and always thoroughly read over your contract and absorb the information, including the fine print).

Unofficially...
Auto leases used to let the leasing company resell a car at auction in the event of early termination or default while charging the consumer for the difference. That method was too uncertain to result in "reasonable" charges in all cases. These days, leases contain complex calculations that measure the residual value of the car at return and the total of payments made.

The Consumer Leasing Act makes it all easier

We have the federal government to thank for a big, fat KISS. The Consumer Leasing Act is a law mandating "keep it simple, stupid!" by requiring certain information be given to consumers who lease, in a very understandable fashion.

Regulation M, issued by the Federal Reserve Board under the Consumer Leasing Act, details the precise language that must be used in consumer leases and their advertisements. Some states have enacted their own auto leasing laws requiring additional disclosures.

The Consumer Leasing Act applies to cars, trucks, and other forms of personal property (such as furniture, tools, etc.) leased by a consumer for personal, household, or family (but not business) use for more than four months. Businesses offering such leases have to give a written statement to the consumer before the lease is signed, containing the following information:

- The amount of security deposit or other advance payment required
- The number, frequency, and dollar amount of the regular payments
- Total dollar amount of the payments
- License, and registration fees and taxes
- A statement about who is responsible for maintenance and similar costs
- Insurance that is needed and must be paid for by the consumer, and insurance to be paid by the leasing company
- Express warranties on the item to be leased, if any
- Standards used to determine "wear and tear"

- Penalties for default and late payment

- Information on cancellation procedures and penalties

- Whether the lessee can buy the vehicle, and for how much

Consumer lease advertisements also have to disclose (conspicuously):

- Total security deposit or other initial payment required at lease outset

- Number, amount, schedule, and due dates of periodic payments in the lease

- Whether there's an option to purchase the vehicle at the lease end and, if there is, the price or method for determining the price

- If the lessee is responsible for the difference between the actual value of the car at the end of the lease and what it was estimated to be at the beginning of the lease (plus the method for figuring out that difference)

Lease price plumage (why it's deceptively attractive)

You're bound to come across some alluring ads in your lease-shopping exploits. Zero down? How can they do that?! Because almost every part of a lease is open to dollar manipulation, leases differ widely and can trumpet some amazing claims. But if the initial payment is low, you'll probably be asked to fork over more dough in payments or at lease end. Or if you see a low payment offer like $119 a month, does that mean you'll need to pay $4,000 up front? Probably something similar to that. It's like leaky plumbing...patch one hole and another one launches somewhere else.

Watch Out!
Although it's hard to imagine, some consumers have leased cars without realizing the contract was a lease. Partly because of that problem, the Federal Consumer Leasing Act requires that the financing structure be specifically described as a lease in lease ads.

If you're leasing for business, you may be offered, for instance, an open-ended lease with relatively low monthly payments compared with other lease offers. Not always a bad deal, but it can be uncertain and treacherous territory for the consumer who is used to the cut-and-dried, due to the amounts you may have to pay at the end of the lease term.

Just remember that there's no such thing as a free ride. Which is not to say you can't get a great lease deal—just that you have to be a smart consumer about it (ways to achieve that are the business of Chapter 11). Take a look at the Sample Lease Ad below for an example of lease offers and their bottom-of-the-page fine print disclosures.

Common misconceptions about leasing

So, Virginia, you say you were just leased a shiny, new car by a dealer? Not so, exactly. The dealer doesn't own your car while you drive it, typically the lease will belong to a bank that specializes in leases or a manufacturer leasing division such as Ford

Sample Lease Ad.

1998 Big M
BIGMOBILE

4 Dr. Sedan, Dual Airbags, AM/FM Audio System, Tilt, Tinted Glass & Much More!

$13,777 or $179 per mo.

+99 cents + tax 36 mos. Closed end lease. $869 cap reduction. Total to start $1662. Total payments $7348. 1 at these exact terms (123456)

Moneysaver
Different leasing companies offer better or worse lease packages, depending on a number of factors including their valuation of the car at lease end. The higher the residual value on file with a particular financial institution, the less expensive your lease is likely to be. Ask your dealer to see which lender offers the highest residual on the car you're interested in.

Motor Credit (if you're getting a Ford). The dealer is usually just the go-between, the middleman, your man in Havana. Or Poughkeepsie. What happens when you lease is that the financial institution purchases the vehicle from your dealer and leases it to you.

Just the facts

- You may be charged 10–25 cents for each mile driven over the allotment included in your lease (usually 10,000–15,000 per year).

- Beware of open-end leases (commonly relegated only to business leasing), where you bear the risk of a difference between presupposed and actual car value at the end of the term and can end up owing (look for typical consumer closed-end leases).

- The two biggest costs in a lease are typically depreciation and financing charges.

- Lease payments are determined largely by four factors: the term of the lease, the purchase price that the lease is based on, the rate you pay for financing the lease, and the expected residual value of the car at lease end.

GET THE SCOOP ON...
Running lease numbers ▪ Comparing a lease to
a purchase ▪ Similarities between car
purchase and car lease negotiations ▪
End-of-lease options

Shopping for a Great Lease

Chapter 11

About 3 out of every 10 gleaming new cars you see on the highway are driven by lessees. If you're interested in joining their ranks (after all, look at those proud faces), this chapter will tell you how to drive a great bargain.

Manufacturers and dealers have responded to America's enthusiasm for leasing by trying to make it more popular—leases now are often simpler than they used to be, and lessees have more help from the law, too.

In this chapter, we'll go over what to look for in a lease deal, explore your end-of-lease options (because they matter at the beginning), and warn you about some dangers to look out for.

What to look for in a lease deal

The good news about lease shopping is that you should approach it the same way that you approach a car purchase—negotiate the same points, and then add in a few extras.

Unofficially...
"Very few consumer transactions are as deceptively simple as entering into a new car lease, but this seemingly simple transaction is fraught with consumer risk..."
(Source: Center for the Study of Services/ LeaseWise)

Timesaver
Check the potential cost of the car you want with MicroSoft CarPoint at carpoint.com. An interactive sticker builder helps you sort out the maze of options and packages to build a detailed report with up-to-date MSRP and invoice pricing information.

The basics

Finding a cheap lease on a terrific set of wheels is a result of the hunt for these things:

- Car with a great resale value
- Low negotiated cash purchase price
- Modest rate of "interest"
- Absence of wacky dealer add-on fees

We might add one more item to the scavenger search: rebates, rebates, rebates.

You can find out which vehicles have the best resale values by checking your favorite automotive price annual or Internet site (and refer to Chapter 2 for more on that).

You'll probably have to haggle the low negotiated cash purchase price yourself—it's the first thing you should negotiate in a lease, and work your other numbers from there. Ask the dealer to see the interest rate on the lease he's offering, and negotiate that as low as possible, within a percentage point or less of what you would pay if you were buying. In other words, start the whole lease process as if you intend to purchase.

The area of your negotiations that is likely to require some consumer smarts and finesse is in the "wacky dealer add-ons" department. You want to try to pay as little as possible in the way of "acquisition fees" or other variable up-front charges. And, by the way, you want to ensure that just because the salesman agrees to trim some costs, they won't show up at the back end in the form of fees you'll have to pay when you return the car.

Some tips

One of the best ways to find a great lease is to look for those that are manufacturer-subsidized. A manufacturer that really wants to move those cars will offer rebates or generous lease terms. Sometimes they're called "subvented" leases (they often include high residual values) on cars expected to be easily resold after you turn them in at lease end. In recent years, some lease offers have been so generous with high residuals that lease financers are now suffering huge losses. The residuals that they guaranteed reflected higher expectations than what the resale market actually delivered. Lessees got a better deal than they would have if lessors had kept more conservative expectations.

Tucked away inside leasing practices is something that works like a rebate, but doesn't come out and call itself that. You know already that how much you pay for a lease is determined in part by the residual, or resale, value of the vehicle at the end of the lease term.

Market conditions vary, and cars can sell at prices healthily above their stated residuals (even considering markup on the residual). So, sometimes dealers are willing to fix a dollar figure higher than the stated residual for what they'll pay for the car at lease return time. The higher that number goes, the less you pay over the life of the lease. By offering this kind of hidden rebate, a dealer may be willing to forgo some of the future profit on the resale of the car in order to move it off his lot (sacrificing good numbers later for good numbers immediately).

Where you can find lease deals

Leases are all over. You see the ads; you know the dealers. You have some options for finding that car and the financing arrangement that accompanies it.

Moneysaver
CarDeals, a newsletter of national automotive rebates and incentives, is available for $7 from the Center for the Study of Services at (800) 475-7283. You can also order the newsletter and find out more information from their Web site at www.checkbook.org.

Traditional auto dealerships offer lease deals on the cars they sell, and they make money whether you buy or lease. So if a car is for sale, just ask about lease arrangements.

For convenience seekers and the car-shopping phobic

A number of "name brand" leases claim to have the competitive edge and dibs on simplicity. Check your favorite manufacturer for its touted lease package, which may include relatively low rates and terminology training wheels for the uninitiated. Look for brochures advertising similar well-packaged leases while you're at the dealership, or check your car manufacturer's Web site.

Turning to those who show the net interest rate for popular leases can be a useful plan. Intelli-Choice, on the Web at www.intellichoice.com, lists "Gold Star Leases" that represent evaluations of the lowest cost leases available.

If you really like the idea of a lease, hate the idea of negotiating one yourself, and have a little faith in your fellow man, there's another alternative you can try. The nonprofit Center for the Study of Services runs LeaseWise, (800) 475-7283, a service that can do the dirty work for you. It's not inexpensive—the charge is a whopping $290, but LeaseWise strives to get consumers better deals than they can on their own.

It works this way: Once you've decided on the make, model, style, lease term, and annual mileage of the vehicle you want to lease, you call the service, charge the fee to your credit card, and allow some time for LeaseWise's consumer savings elves to do their thing. The time needed varies. Currently it's about two weeks.

The elves look at a database of dozens of lease plans and figure out which will produce the lowest monthly payment for you. Then they solicit bids from dealers in your area (at least five), in essence asking the dealers to compete for your business. The dealers must commit to a markup or markdown from Factory Invoice Cost, and all additional fees and add-ons are itemized and fully disclosed.

The LeaseWise elves analyze the dealers' offers and send you a report, including detailed dealer quote sheets and the name of the manager responsible for the price commitment. You're also sent the factory invoice cost information for your type of vehicle (what the elves worked from) and detailed financial terms for each dealer's recommended lease plan (as well as details of their lowest cost lease plan, if the terms are different).

After you've plowed through that mass of paperwork, you call the bidding dealership of your choice, talk with the designated manager responsible for offering those presumably impeccable lease terms, and make arrangements on your own to execute your lease.

The benefits can be great over blindly accepting the first lease deal that might come your way without the service's help. Customer testimonials include the guy who says he saved over ten grand on a three-year Lexus lease versus quotes he found on his own, and folks who've saved a couple to a few thousand on less luxy vehicles versus the lease deals they were offered before trying the service.

We would like to think that a bit of shopping fortitude and some good statistical backup can let you find the same deals independently. But if you like the chutzpah of having a consumer advocacy group

Watch Out!
As a general rule, don't lease a car for longer than its manufacturer warranty to avoid being saddled with repair expenses (consider opting for an extended warranty that covers your lease term).

do your bidding (literally) and wish to spare the necessary money, it's an interesting option.

One thing that everyone can learn from this service is the value of serious shopping at multiple dealerships. LeaseWise notes that its own bidding process has led to offers with differences of more than $5,000 between low and high bids on a Lexus LS400 lease, more than $3,800 on a Ford Explorer, almost $3,000 on a Mercedes S420, and just over a grand on a Honda Accord (for three-year leases).

You may also see ads for independent lease agents listed in your phone directory, newspaper, or on the Internet.

Seeking out good promotional rates and avoiding bad ones

Despite warnings about misleading ones, lease advertisements are a good clue for you that a car is on sale. There's some reason that money is being spent to say "come get this car," and often it means that a manufacturer rebate is on. Read over the fine print in lease ads—if a lease seems too cheap to be for real, it probably is. Along with putting big-dollar disclosures at the bottom of the ad and things like "zero down" in bold print, dealerships may list in fine print "three at this price," which means there's an excellent chance you'll be lured to the dealership to be pitched a much higher-priced lease.

Strategies

Since lease and car negotiations involve so much of the same aspects, you should treat them as such. And remember these points:

- Negotiate the purchase price of the car first
- Don't be led into discussions of "How much do you want to pay per month?"

Watch Out!
A word about down payments in leasing. Keep them as low as possible if you live in a state where sales tax is computed not on the monthly payment but the entire lease amount. And otherwise keep them as low as possible if you can earn an interest rate better than your rate of state sales tax.

- Negotiate the rate you will pay for financing the lease
- Negotiate the residual value of the vehicle
- Negotiate the value of your trade-in
- Negotiate the fees tacked onto the lease arrangement

Running the numbers

Will a lease you're offered be advantageous to you over a purchase deal you're offered? Some of that depends on the personal factors we went over in the last chapter.

Deciding between lease and finance deals

Once you have a lease deal offer in hand, take a look at it versus deciding to purchase. What are the practical comparisons? Think carefully about the points in Table 11.1

TABLE 11.1   LEASING PROS AND CONS

Pros	Cons
Lower monthly payments than buying a new car.	Payments are not building equity.
You can get a nicer car for your money (versus buying new).	You won't have any car at the end of your lease term.
If you're comfortable with the idea of always making a monthly car payment, leasing lets you drive newer cars.	You'll always be making payments, and may have to come up with additional money down the next time you lease.
Perhaps never having to take your car in for repairs.	You may have to adhere to regularly scheduled maintenance requirements.
Tax benefits for business use.	Tax laws are not as liberal as they used to be with leasing (particularly more expensive leases).
No worries about how much your car might depreciate with closed-end leases (resale values locked in ahead-of-time).	Hefty charges for exceeding annual mileage limitations (usually about 15,000 miles per year): 10–25 cents per extra mile.

Pros	Cons
No deciding what to do with your trade-in vehicle when you get a new car.	Less-familiar terms and procedures to walk through at the dealership for first-time lessees.
"Trying out" a vehicle for a couple of years before you decide whether you want to buy it (though you'll pay for the privilege).	You may not be able to modify the vehicle (such as putting business signage on a van).
	Hefty charges for early lease return (for instance, if you decide you need a different type of vehicle).

Those on the tightest budgets should consider buying used over leasing, as should anyone whose expenses will rise or income will drop after the next two to three years. Who could be in that category? Those who are planning families or a return to school, getting ready to buy a home, or about to retire, to name a few.

Let's say Eric is going on to medical school after a few productive years in the work world. He's looking forward to a great salary, but that's several years down the road. For now, he's going to economize and decides that a domestic economy car is the thing. Should he lease a new one, buy a new one, or buy a used one?

Being the brilliant left-brained guy he is, Eric has run the numbers on a somewhat sporty 1998 economy model that has a nice little package of extras with an MSRP of $11,995. He may go for a long lease (four years) or consider buying used. Eric, of course, will be haggling, but worked out the initial numbers based on MSRP.

On the new economy model, Eric will get a promotional manufacturer rebate of $1,000 (for lease or purchase), and plans to put $1,500 down (either as a down payment on the purchase or a "cap cost reduction" on the lease). Assuming that he gets 7.5% financing, here's how Eric's choices work out (see Table 11.2). If Eric buys used, he's considering a two-year-old similar car that he can get for a mere $6,500.

Timesaver
Compare a lease to a loan using Worksheet 7.2 in Chapter 7.

TABLE 11.2   ERIC'S ESCORT—BUY NEW, USED, OR LEASE?*

	Buy New	Lease	Buy Used
Purchase Price	$11,995	$11,995	$6,500
– Rebate	–$1,000	–$1,000	
– Down Payment	–$1,500	–$1,500	–$1,500
– Four-Year Residual (for lease)		–$4,678 (39% of MSRP)	
+ Various Potential Leasing Fees		+$500	
= Amount to Be Financed	$9,495	$5,317	$5,000
Interest Rate	7.5%	.00313 (Market Money Factor)	10%
Sales Tax (6%)	$660	$372 (calculated on the monthly payment)	$390
Monthly Payments	$246 (48 months)	$138 (48 months)	$137 (48 months)
Anticipated Resale Value at End of Financing	$4,678 (39% of MSRP)	$4,678 (39% of MSRP)	$3,480
Eric's Equity at End (how much value he's left with)	$4,678	$0	$3,480

*Prices exclude title, taxes and license fee for simplicity of illustration

Eric would spend almost $5,200 more buying the new economy car versus the used one or the lease. Considering the value he's left with at the end of the purchase ($4,678), Eric in this case dismisses the idea of buying new and ponders between buying used and leasing. His monthly payments would be within a couple of dollars, but if he buys the used car, at the end of four years, he'll have a six-year-old vehicle worth $3,480 (although he'll probably have to shell out for some post-warranty repairs). Right now, Eric is thinking, "Say that $480 goes toward repairs, I'm left with $3,000," and dividing that up over four years to evaluate whether it's worth an extra $750 a year to him to drive a new car instead of one he buys when it's two years old.

Determining the real cost of your lease

What's the bare minimum you need to know to calculate a lease payment? Check the cost of traditional financing with the cost of the lease before making a decision. To estimate the total cost related to traditional financing, add the total of the down payment, amount financed, finance charges, cost of insurance, and estimated repairs and maintenance. For the total cost of the lease, include all lease charges plus any other required costs such as insurance, repairs, and maintenance.

Use Worksheet 11.1 to make your own calculations.

WORKSHEET 11.1   YOUR LEASE CALCULATOR

Fill in the appropriate information:

	Sample	Your Figures
Term	36 months	_____ months
MSRP	$20,000	$_____
Cap Cost (sell price)	$19,000	$_____
Residual	$10,000 (50%)	$_____ (_____%)
State Sales Tax Percentage	.06 (6%)	_____ (_____%)
Money Factor (from Table 11.3)	.00400	_____

Then figure your lease costs:

	Sample	Your Figures
Total Depreciation (cap cost – residual)	$9,000	$_____
Monthly Depreciation (total dep. ÷ term)	$250	$_____
Monthly Lease Fee [money factor × (cap cost + residual)]	$116	$_____
Monthly Rent (monthly depreciation + monthly lease fee)	$366	$_____

And arrive at a final figure:

	Sample	Your Figures
Total Monthly Payment (monthly rent × sales tax percentage)	$387.96	$_____

(Source: *Automotive Lease Guide*)

Find MSRPs and residuals in your favorite auto price magazine annual, on the Web with LeaseSource at www. leasesource.com, or at other major auto sites.

Use the information in Table 11.3 with Worksheet 11.1. It shows the monthly interest dollars needed to keep the yield indicated.

TABLE 11.3   MONEY, MONEY, MONEY FACTORS

	Money Factor	Yield*
(Cap Cost + Residual) ×	.00325	7.8%
(Cap Cost + Residual) ×	.00350	8.4%

(Cap Cost + Residual) ×	.00375	9.0%
(Cap Cost + Residual) ×	.00400	9.6%
(Cap Cost + Residual) ×	.00425	10.2%
(Cap Cost + Residual) ×	.00450	10.8%
(Cap Cost + Residual) ×	.00475	11.4%
(Cap Cost + Residual) ×	.00500	12.0%
(Cap Cost + Residual) ×	.00525	12.6%

(Source: Automotive Lease Guide)
*Yield will vary slightly with length of lease

Customizing your lease deal

What, Joe, you say you're all ready to lease, you're a perfect candidate, but you've just gotta drive more than a thousand miles a month? Don't put yourself in a position to pay up to 25 cents for every mile you're over the limit at lease end. Buy those extra miles, say 10,000 more, up front at a lower cost.

You may wince at what it does to your monthly payment, but in reality you could wind up spending just over half what you would otherwise—perhaps eight or nine cents per mile instead of 15 or 20. And if you don't use the extra miles, according to some lease contracts, you can be reimbursed. That's an important point to look for and discuss with the lessor if you expect to need extra miles.

Likewise, seek out leases that allow a generous mileage allotment up front (without resorting to extra coverages).

Used car leasing

If new cars depreciate more dramatically than used cars and leasing is basically paying for depreciation, then a really economical deal must be leasing a used car, right?

We wish it were that simple, but the auto industry isn't very accommodating on that point.

Surprisingly, you won't necessarily save money, and could even pay more. Because manufacturers are eager to move their new cars, rebates can be found on many new models, but not on used ones. What you can get by careful planning for a new car lease will probably beat out a used car lease.

You can check with a new car dealer about leasing a late model car that may have been a lease return itself. And some used car lots specializing in luxury vehicles may offer their own used-car lease programs.

So what about used vehicle leasing? If you're in the market for a used car, negotiate the buy price; after you've got a solid offer, you can always ask the dealer to run some lease numbers for you as well.

End-of-lease options

It seems like only yesterday that you picked up that gleaming new set of wheels, and already it's time to go back to the dealership. You've grown a little attached to the creature, and somewhere in the back of your mind you're wondering if you should buy it (although it's not common for lessees to buy their own lease vehicles). Probably more prominently in your mind is the question of whether you'll owe anything else or will be getting out of the lease free and clear.

Considering your options

First, let's limit your losses. If you have the typical sort of "closed end" lease, aside from its use in calculating your monthly payment, it shouldn't matter what the residual value of the car is if you're not interested in keeping it. You shouldn't owe the difference between what the expected residual value of the car was predicted to be and what it really turned out to be. You can be out "clean" there.

If, however, you're a businessperson who opted for an "open ended" lease, you're probably feeling vulnerable. As well you should. It's you who will owe money if the car has depreciated faster than originally expected. How to mitigate that little snafu? It's Regulation M to the rescue. When the value of the vehicle realized on sale is subtracted from that previously predicted residual value, it can't exceed the cost of three monthly payments without being presumed unreasonable (unless it's due to excessive use).

When you lease a motor vehicle, the lease documents state its residual value. When you return the vehicle, the dealer will either sell it or appraise it. Depending on the sale proceeds or the appraised value in comparison to the vehicle's residual value, you may or may not have to make an end-of-lease payment and, depending on whether a right to a refund was in your contract, you can be entitled to a refund. If the residual value is greater than the vehicle's sale proceeds or appraisal value, you have to make up the difference through an end-of-lease payment to the leasing company under an open-ended lease.

When buying your leased car makes sense

If, at the end of your lease, you decide that you love the car because it's a known commodity, buy it if the numbers work out. A purchase at term's end makes sense when what the car could actually sell for is above the residual stated in your closed-end contract. If it is worth much more than your purchase option indicates, you can technically buy it and resell it at a profit if you wish. If, on the other hand, your purchase option says that the car is worth $15,000 at lease end, and similar cars are selling for just $13,000, it doesn't make sense to purchase your lease—save money and get one of those $2,000 cheaper equivalent cars.

So what if you turn the car in early?

We talked in the previous chapter about the penalties that apply if, forbid, you decide to turn in your leased car before its term is up or if you otherwise default.

How reasonable is the early return penalty provision in a lease? A good reasonableness "rule" to use is to compare the used car value of the vehicle at the time you turn it in to the total of payments you've made until that time. A penalty that's significantly in excess of the difference could be a Consumer Leasing Act violation.

Just the facts

- Prepay additional mileage that you expect to need, and pay about half of what you would at lease end if you exceed allotments.

- Look for manufacturer-subsidized leases (rebates, etc.), a high resale value, a low negotiated cash purchase price, a low financing rate, and a relative absence of dealer add-on charges.

- Make sure you understand what the different aspects of your lease entail so that you won't face high costs when you return the car at the end of term.

- Begin your lease negotiations as if you were purchasing—negotiate a low cash purchase price and make sure the interest rate you're being charged on the lease is within about a point of the interest rate you'd get if you were buying.

Negotiating

GET THE SCOOP ON...
Where cash negotiating has power • Basic sales-
man tricks • Countermaneuvers you can make
• Talking the private seller down in price

PART VI

Negotiating with the Dealership or Private Seller

Chapter 12

G ood consumer that you are, you've deduced about how much you should spend for your target vehicle, and now it's time to go persuade a dealer that they really, really should sell or lease it to you for that amount. Or you're running through newspaper ads looking for the perfect cream puff used vehicle, and you need to persuade a private party to sell you the car at a good price—a much less intimidating prospect for most.

Dealer tools and tricks of the trade

The car salesman you're about to meet spends his days making as much money as possible for himself and the dealership. He's the definition of capitalism. Which is not to say that he won't also be helpful in honestly locating a car that fits you.

He has his repertoire of persuasive lines and concepts, and so should you. We'll begin with his arsenal.

Basic negotiating tactics

Before you arrive on the lot, the salesman's brain is already awash with numbers. He has a working idea of how many cars he needs to sell to meet his quota, and knows which models are slow movers and which the dealership can barely keep in stock.

He's been through motivational and sales training, been coached by his sales manager, and been polished by all the previous sales he's ever made. He's a selling machine, a pro—at least much of the time. What he typically does to make a sale:

1. Sizes up the customer visually

2. Warms up the customer with initial approach; makes her feel at ease

3. Directly qualifies the customer—what can she afford; what does she need or want?

4. Plays show-and-tell—presents and demonstrates the merchandise in all its glory, and takes a test-drive

5. Asks for the sale

6. Overcomes objections

7. Negotiates the price, if necessary

8. Closes the sale

9. Closes the aftersell (undercoating, extended warranties, etc.)

When you set foot on the premises, the salesman's first step is to visually "qualify" or size you up as a potential customer. Do you look like you have money to pay for a high-end car, are you lolling by the convertibles like a curious window-shopper rather than a serious buyer? Are you alone or with a spouse? Couple shopping is an indication of seriousness.

As the salesman approaches you, he may greet you warmly and ask, "What kind of car are you looking for today?" His objective is to get you to buy as soon as possible. He may tell you off the bat that a certain model is on special, if he thinks it will accelerate your interest. But during this initial phase, the salesman is largely waiting for you to tell him why it is you stopped at his dealership, and show some focus on a particular model or two, so he can launch into real selling. As you browse by a couple or a few cars on the lot, you'll probably find him briefly interjecting positive points about the vehicles like a talking price sticker.

The sooner he takes control of the situation, the better for him. When you finally pause by a certain sedan and show interest, you may find yourself as the audience for a rehearsed sales talk that the salesman has given over and over and over before, designed to draw you in.

The sales process can be controlled by questions, and a good salesman is a master of the art:

"How much do you want to spend per month?" lets the seller steer you toward a car with the correct payment range, but not mentioning actual price gives him tons of leeway in hiding profit. Salesmen often try to qualify what type of buyer a customer is, depending what they base their decision-making on:

- Specific car purchase price
- Monthly payments
- Value accepted for a trade-in
- Cost range
- Financing rates
- Pure emotion

> 66
> Keep the golden mean between saying too much and too little.
> —Publius Syrus, 42 B.C.
> 99

Of course, some combination of these is most likely. A shopper who negotiates the specific purchase price of a car is far ahead of other types of consumers, who are more likely to be led down that path lined with expensive primroses.

The monthly payment buyer can be shown an enticing range of cars he can drive for a certain dollar amount each month. The trumpeting of "affordability" is only a veneer here, though, because, in theory, monthly payments can go on forever.

Although it's important to get a good return on your trade-in (see the next chapter on factoring your old car into the deal), it's also important to remember that a great price here can mean that profits are hidden elsewhere in the sales package—you have to check every component.

The cost-range shopper is at a particular disadvantage because, for instance, his desire to spend $15,000 on a car may lead a salesman to show him a car worth $13,000, but marked up to $15,000. This kind of shopping ignores the real numbers relevant to specific cars.

Timesaver
Financing rates, while obviously quite important, are negotiation points best dealt with after the actual selling price of the car has been established.

The buyer who is shopping for a car without the benefit of having done preliminary research is in the worst position of all—impulse buying is best left to trinkets, not big-ticket items. If you want an emotional boost, buy a hot fudge sundae instead, and crunch those numbers when it comes to your new car.

Signs of a skilled salesman

A good salesman works with speed and clarity, deftly moving the customer along the sales pipeline from initial qualification toward final closing. He also has a vast working knowledge of the cars for sale on the lot, the financing arrangements available, and other tidbits of information that can be valuable to the consumer, as well as his own position.

As long as you can be sure that you're being offered a deal, this is the best kind of relationship possible between salesman and buyer—one where both parties seek to share some information to fill their needs at the least disadvantage to the other.

A skilled salesman, realizing that you're a cost-conscious consumer who is unlikely to buy without a very good deal, may even suggest waiting a day or two to buy because of a manufacturer rebate taking effect. The rationale is a good one—the more "off" you're allowed on the car by the manufacturer, the more profit he hopes you'll allow him. The name of the game is not only negotiation, but also communication.

At the outset, a skilled salesman will be catering toward your needs, helping you move things along in the decision department. So you're interested in a four-door only? And what color? We have these models... oh, you like this one... He will treat you with respect, but may assume whatever role you're likely to respond to best—paternal, affable, logical. And that sets the style and tone for the rest of the sell.

A disaffected salesman may appear apathetic to your needs by not being helpful and doing little to close the sale—making you do all the work. An unskilled salesman may:

- Be nervous
- Have little knowledge of the cars he's selling
- Launch into a sales speech that the customer realizes is canned

> **"**
> Let every eye negotiate for itself And trust no agent.
> —William Shakespeare, *Much Ado About Nothing*
> **"**

- Flit between sales points with no cohesive line, such as asking for the sale at an inappropriate juncture

- Quote numbers that are patently wrong

You may run into a "hard sell" sort of salesman—the kind who gives a customer little breathing room for making appropriate decisions and insists on having it his way (take the "or the highway" option here). Signs of the hard sell include:

- Time limitations—act now, this offer expires in five minutes

- Unwillingness to demonstrate a range of models or options, or respond appropriately to any request you have

- An "authority figure," or having a stern paternal approach to conversation points

- The "I'm doing you a favor" approach, replete with take-it-or-leave-its

- Constant reiteration about who you are and what you want ("You don't want that one, you want this one. You're a muscle car driver!")

Most customers can do without this sort of belligerence.

Your tools and tactics

You want to come across as a serious shopper who is buying soon, and you want the salesman to pay attention to you. Arriving at the dealership in a car likely to be your trade-in (rather than your spouse's one-year-old model) may help, and if you have the title to the vehicle visibly with you, that's a sure sign of seriousness. If the car's clean and not loaded with stuff, that's another indicator that you may want to

Bright Idea
Effective approaches on the car lot begin before you arrive. Dress neatly in clothes that don't belie your income level as very low or very high. Bring a small notebook and pen—you may use them either for making notes or as a sort of prop. Also bring your research materials (car price annual, price comparisons you've worked out, ads, etc.) but don't keep them in plain view of the sales staff, at least not initially (you want to get bottom dollar, but not necessarily advertise your penny-pinching so blatantly to a salesman).

leave it with the dealership and drive off in something new.

Do your own sizing-up of potential salesmen as you walk into the showroom or survey the lot. Who you make initial eye contact with may determine who sells you your car. Catching your eye makes you a certain salesman's property. Master the art of peripheral vision and use your gut instincts, then head for the salesman who you have the best hunch about if more than one looks approachable.

As the salesman greets you and asks what he can do, don't give yourself away as either a super-ready sale or a browser (unless you are ready to buy and simply want his bottom dollar on the model of your choice—see the section "The 'just sell me the car, I'm done browsing' approach" up ahead in this chapter for specific tactics you can use in that case). Tell him you're interested in seeing this model or that model, or models of a certain type. Be evasive about questions to which you're not ready to give an answer. Are you a cash buyer? To that question, hedge with, "Well, I'd be interested in seeing what financing plans you might have."

The salesman may engage you in what seems like casual conversation. When he asks "Are you married?" your answer is an indicator of seriousness. If you are, why are you alone on the lot if you're serious? Some indication that your spouse is unavailable for a good reason or easily available at buy time may help. "She works just around the corner at such-and-such," for instance.

Bringing a friend with you can be to your benefit as well, if he's willing to play with you in some negotiating roles—the good cop/bad cop routine, for instance, or as the doubting Thomas, skeptical of the worth of a car you'll be negotiating on the same day. In a world of mostly male car salesmen, does it help to have a male along if you're female? (What about a female if you're male?!) We'll leave to you the decisions about whether to play any gender cards—take along whoever you think will be of the most help.

General tactics to consider using during the early part of your visit with the salesman:

- Be evasive but reasonable when asked questions you feel it would be better not to answer yet.

- Do give the salesman some parameters for the vehicle you'd like—don't make him guess or play psychic hotline.

- Don't give away that you can or will pay cash.

- Discuss the cost of cars by total price, not monthly payments.

- Try to keep the initial parts of your conversation directed toward your choices in vehicles—discuss the cars generally in your range first, and specifics of prices only when you're more certain.

Whoa, Bessie! Getting off the one-way sales track

If you're stuck on a one-way sales track that's going somewhere expensive fast, you need to meet the salesman at his own game. Meet every close-'em question with an appropriate stalling response (see Table 12.1).

TABLE 12.1

Salesman's "close-'em" question	Your stalling response
So this is the vehicle you want. Can I write it up?	There are good points to this model, but I like that model, too. Let's go take a look.

So, if I can get you this model and package for $19,800, you'll buy it today?	There are a couple of options packages I like. How much under $19,800 can you go on this one?
I can only give you the $19,800 price if you buy today—our sale was only supposed to run through Thursday. Are you going to buy the car today?	If you can knock some additional money off of that price, I'll consider buying it.

Price haggling

When you know you want a specific car and the salesman suspects it too, you've reached the price-haggling portion of your visit. The smart consumer has been commitment-phobic to this point, and should continue to be so until very late in the game.

For every attempt the salesman makes to get you to agree, you have to restate his supposition as a counter question, which is better than restating it as a negative. This concept is at the heart of some world peacekeeping efforts—it's negotiation diplomacy that allows each side to save face.

"So you'll buy the car if I can get $500 off that price?" can be met with "How much lower than a $500 discount can you go?" Rather than be pinned down to buying a car at a stated price, you're implying (as diplomatically as possible) that the case is that you won't buy it otherwise. But you're not coming out and saying that, lest the salesman, heaven forbid, thinks you're rude and instinctively goes on the defensive.

A word on using leading questions yourself: Some customers are quick studies who model and reflect the tone and type of response that a salesman gives them. Those battered and exasperated by leading salesman questions pushing them toward a sale closing might consider using a bit of the salesman's

Watch Out!
Beware of the leading salesman question. "Do you want to buy the red one or the green one?" traps you conversationally into a buying position. Head these off at the pass—with a comment such as "Let's look at what options are available on each."
Remember, the salesman has a full quiver of overshooting arrows to work with.

own medicine. When the salesman suggests, "So you'll buy the car if I can get $500 off the price?", a customer is free to respond with "Are you going to do better than $500 off the price or are you going to include a better options package for that $500 off?"

This method can be a good negotiating tool with some salesmen and it can backfire with others, so use it judiciously. Use it with the wrong shrewd salesman and you may find that he pulls out his or her real negotiating tactics and stonewalls yours. If that happens, kick back to a less carnivorous course and become, once again, the contrite customer looking to work toward the best option for you both. You'll assuage the ego, and with any luck, the salesman will unconsciously start to adopt the same style and attitude.

Remember, there is more than one piece to the profit puzzle, and your dollar-figure negotiations are just the beginning of your task. The variables include:

- Purchase price of the car
- Value of your trade-in
- Options you get on the car and their prices
- Financing arrangements and rates
- Aftersell items (like rustproofing, extended warranties, etc.)

Never go into a salesman's cubicle to do serious price negotiating without knowing your spending limitations, including what you can reasonably afford for monthly payments, as well as how good a financing deal you can get elsewhere.

The power of your checkbook and cash negotiating

We've said that you may not want to reveal at the outset that you're a cash customer because then you're letting the salesman know he has to keep the purchase price of a car (or other variables) high due to his lack of financing profit potential with you.

If you are flexible on the percentage you can pay in cash, you can use that as a negotiating tactic too. If a salesman isn't coming down in price enough for you, before you've even discussed financing arrangements, now may be the time to bring it up. For instance, you can say, "If you can go lower on that figure, I can finance part of the car through you."

The "just sell me the car, I'm done browsing" approach

If you are thoroughly familiar with the model of the car you want to buy and its options, and you've calculated exactly how much you want to spend, you can try a shortcut approach that may save time for both you and the dealer.

Go into a dealer's showroom, say hello to the salesman who meets you there, and ask for the sale. You're turning his usual procedure on its head by doing so ("What, a customer is asking ME to sell her a car?!"). Briefly summarize your case—for instance, if you've decided you can pay $300 over dealer invoice, say something like, "Hello. I've been researching, I took some test-drives, I'm ready to make a deal on a Toyota Corolla and finance it through you, if you will take $300 above dealer cost on it." (Of course, you would still want to do a test-drive to check out that particular car before purchasing or leasing it.)

If the salesman hems and haws, politely but firmly indicate that you're not interested in any variations on the deal you suggested, and you're prepared to go elsewhere if necessary. Ask him to

Moneysaver
Your cash position is perhaps strongest when you're buying a used car from a private party—someone who does not want delays or snafus (see "Negotiating used cars with individuals," later in this chapter).

check with the sales manager on the low-profit deal and tell him that you'd like to buy today. Don't necessarily state it, but make it clear to him that you can just as easily try the dealership across town. He must be convinced that you know what you want, and have plenty of options as to where to get it.

If the salesman says yes to your purchase request off the bat, still ask him to verify that the sales manager will go for the deal, and clarify that you're not interested in any add-ons and at what percentage rate and terms you're talking about getting financing. You should be prequalified with your bank and have a very good idea about what another dealership would offer you in terms of interest rates. You should also factor any promotions and rebates into the price, of course. If the conversation is going well and this is a dealer you may well want to do business with, you can briefly discuss your trade-in, but do that only after you know the score on pricing for the car you want to get. (Bear in mind that the dealer will really need to take a look at your trade-in before pinning any serious numbers on it.)

When may this approach work?

- At a high-volume dealership particularly, where the sales staff is used to quick decision-makers and where profits rely on a huge number of cars with relatively low markup leaving the lot

- When dealerships or salesman need to reach their quotas (at month's end, for example)

- With a car that the dealership would like to get off the lot—a model soon to become last year's, a style or color that's not the hottest-seller, or something that has an options package no one else is going for, but you want

- With vehicles that the dealership doesn't typically get a very high markup on (for instance, luxury cars and sport utility vehicles)

- When extra profit is coming to the dealer because you're financing with him (and not necessarily an unreasonable amount—when you're asking a dealership for the "favor" of a cheap car price, letting them make the financing money that your bank might otherwise make is a legitimate negotiation plus)

- When you are dealing with an intelligent and sensible salesman who realizes you mean what you say

- When the offer you're making includes some fair amount of profit for the salesman and dealership (there's low, and there's just insulting)

- When you're leasing and thus stand the chance of becoming a repeat customer (after all, you have to come back to the dealership to turn the vehicle in at lease-end)

- When another dealership has already offered you a deal almost as good

- When you've got a trade-in in great shape that the dealership will have no problem reselling at a profit (but make sure you get a fair price for it)

- When you're a great credit risk

- When you're clearly a fast, simple sale—you have your trade-in title with you, are ready to make the down payment, and clearly have your papers in order

- When there's a new, hungry salesman (a beginner, for instance) on the lot, who's only happy to just sell a car, no matter how little profit he gets

- When you come across as a customer they want to please, rather than an annoying wheeler-dealer wannabe

- When you've misfigured and they're actually going to make a whole lot more on the deal than you've estimated (perhaps you missed a rebate that's in effect?)

You can just as easily see when your bottom-dollar offer isn't as likely to fly:

- At "boutique" dealerships, where the selling style is to get top dollar on a smaller number of vehicles leaving the lot instead of selling a huge number of cars

- On vehicles selling so well that they're hard to keep in stock (and may have to be ordered from the factory)

- When you are going with a bank loan, so the dealership and the salesman won't have the benefit of additional profit from financing

- When you're not sure and aren't ready to close the sale that day

- When there are problems with your trade-in, such as not having clear title, or it's a real clunker they couldn't possibly resell on their lot

- When salesmen are under comparatively little pressure to make deals at low profit margins, such as immediately after a big sale blitz where profits were made and quotas met

- When the dealership's busy and there are prospects likely to generate more profit who are browsing the lot

Bright Idea
If you find a great salesman willing to work with your bottom-dollar deal, consider relaxing the rules a little and ask him for a counteroffer—if you're flexible on the options your car will have, ask him if there's a version of your desired model that he'd particularly like to get off the lot and could offer an even further discount on.

- On high profit-margin vehicles, where there's a huge dollar difference between your lowball offer and the potential windfall generated by the average buyer of that vehicle

- When you run into an ill-informed or obstinate salesman, and there's no chance of an end run against his hyperbolic defense strategies (although you can look for the sales manager and try to speak directly, asking in private for another salesman to handle the deal—some may be amenable to save a potential sale)

- When the offer you're making is just too lowball and they sneer

- When they're the only dealership within a 300-mile radius

- When your credit situation is iffy at best, more likely a nightmare

- When you look and sound like a problem child who's going to ask for the moon, take all of their time and offer them very little in return, or if you annoy the salesman

Another option in the direct "I wanna buy" approach is to check whether a "one-price" dealer accommodates your desired price. Since these dealerships are geared toward consumers who don't want to haggle, the short and sweet approach won't likely elicit protests there.

A number of auto buying sites on the Internet feature direct links to local dealers, as well, and you may be able to e-mail them directly with your request (something to try perhaps, but not rely on—go for good old-fashioned in-person footwork).

Improving the deal you get

What can you do to improve the deal you get on a car? Consider these pointers, some of which work out to the advantage of you, the salesman, and the dealer (see Checklist 12.1).

CHECKLIST 12.1   BETTERING YOUR DEALERSHIP DEAL—WHAT WORKS?

_____ 1. Choose equivalent dealer financing over a loan from an outside bank.

_____ 2. Shop when rebates and other discounts are in effect.

_____ 3. Be flexible about options packages (and even models)—what cars does the dealership most need to move that you like?

_____ 4. Shop near the end of quota periods, such as the last part of the month.

When you're negotiating for a used car

Used cars aren't like new cars, with a very much fixed value versus the other options out there. Used cars vary in terms of their condition, availability, worth of the options they're equipped with, and amount the seller paid for them.

Negotiating used cars with dealers

When negotiating with a new car dealer on a used car, you don't know what he shelled out to acquire it. You can hope the car you want:

- Is a lease return on which the dealership has already made significant profit

- It's a trade-in attached to some other customer's sale, on which the dealer made a generous profit

- It was bought at auction (perhaps someone defaulted on payments and a bank repossessed it and then auctioned it off)

Moneysaver
Refer to Chapter 4 for the best times of year to shop for the lowest prices.

Many of the tactics you can use with new car negotiations still apply with used car negotiations, and there are other points you can use to your advantage.

If you happen to be looking for a domestic sport utility vehicle and see one while driving by your local import car dealer (which doesn't have its own line of four-wheel drives), you may be able to get a better deal on it because it's an atypical vehicle for the dealership. Think about it. People come to that dealership looking for cars—probably the same import brand. The dealer may hardly ever see a truck shopper, and he may be glad to move that domestic sport utility, making room for yet another import sedan he knows won't be sitting on his lot for weeks or months.

CHECKLIST 12.2   BETTERING YOUR USED CAR DEAL AT A DEALERSHIP—WHAT WORKS?

____ 1. Choosing equivalent dealer financing over a loan from an outside bank.

____ 2. Buying a vehicle atypical to the dealership.

____ 3. Being flexible on options packages, colors (and even models)—what cars does the dealership most need to move that you like?

The used car lot is a different creature altogether from the new car dealer. Bear in mind that some of the largest used car sellers with the best choices offer no-negotiation pricing. The haggle-phobic can always choose this option.

Like the new car salesman, the infamous used car salesman will try to qualify you, including what type of buyer you are—monthly payments, cost range, etc. As with new car negotiating, stick to figuring out the lowest possible purchase price of a car first, and save the monthly payment math for later.

What if you have an import sedan now and want that preowned domestic sport utility? If you can find one on the lot of a dealer with the same-brand vehicle as the one you own, consider trading in your good-condition used car there, and take that domestic sport utility off his hands. The bigger the dealer, the better your odds.

Of course, before going to any dealer, you should already have an idea of what your acceptable price range is for a car, and which models fall within its boundaries.

Negotiating used cars with individuals

Negotiating with a private seller for a used car can be a welcome relief from the world of professional closers. But it carries its own brand of frustrations.

Rather than having a choice of cars to peruse on a lot, you've searched in the newspaper (or wherever), found a car to your liking, taken the trouble to come see it, and now you're considering buying it.

Point one: the seller knows you're pretty interested to have gotten this far.

Point two: cars being sold by private parties may go quickly if the price is fair.

How do you get as good a deal as possible on the vehicle? It depends on what the seller's all about, and using some sales tactics yourself may help. Qualify the seller—what is it he wants out of the car? What's the car's story? The seller may or may not have an accurate idea of the car's worth.

Perhaps the seller bought a new car and was considering trading the old one in on the deal, only to find that the dealer offered him a lowball price that just didn't seem right. This seller may accept a relatively low price for the car, as long as it beats the dealer's trade-in offer. Ask questions.

The advertised price of a used car for sale by a private party is often quite negotiable. And depending on how long the car's been advertised, the seller may be willing to come down from the quoted price significantly—no one wants his money tied up in a car he's trying to unload, not to mention the inconvenience of showing it.

> 66
> I hate negotiating for a car. I test drove a Miata and liked it. It was a good price because they wanted to sell it quickly. She said the price, I said done, and that was it—I was very lucky!
> —Ben, an Englishman, on his American car-buying experience
> 99

In situations where the individual seller of a used car sounds like a reasonable person, we advise bringing lots of handy aids with you, which you can pull out when you need to convince the seller your price is fair, and close the sale. Remember, whoever's selling a used car is a consumer just like you.

When you go out for a serious look at a car (it could be your second visit to test-drive that particular one, for instance), bring along documentation showing the wholesale value of that vehicle with those options (a used car price guide or an Internet search can get these figures for you—see Chapter 6 for pricing details). Also bring along the publication in which you saw the car ad listed, and whatever local paper has the most similar cars listed.

Your aim with this is, where necessary, to educate the seller on the worth of their car, in a helpful, not know-it-all, way. How did he decide on the price that he listed the car for? There are many different answers to that question, and showing a seller what wholesale value actually is can be an eye-opener.

If possible, try to get the car for wholesale value, as a dealer would when accepting the vehicle as a trade-in. Or you can offer a couple hundred dollars above the wholesale trade-in figure, depending on how great the car looks and how much you'd really have to pay for it at retail, as well as the availability and desirability of that model and its options.

If cars like the one you want to buy are listed for sale at a variety of low prices in the paper, show the seller (on the other hand, if his price is lower, keep the paper under wraps). The best thing you can do to strengthen your position is to come up with a listing of many similar cars, all going for low amounts, and back that up with a pricing guide's wholesale price. Let the numbers themselves convince the seller.

Cash is the great persuader when it comes to buying used from an individual. If three potential buyers come to see the car in a given weekend, the one who can come up with a cashier's check (cash) beats the customer who says "I'll need to check with my bank."

Maximizing your dealership visit

Bright Idea
If you need to get a bank loan and are shopping seriously via private individuals, at least pre-arrange a bank loan for the approximate value of the car you want to get, as it will go some distance in convincing the seller that you can actually pull off the financing.

As you go head-to-head with a salesman, nothing will save you as much as knowing his bottom line. To get the most out of your trip to the dealer, make your preshopping research pay off for you:

1. Know how much a dealer is likely to accept for a car (see chapters 6 and 14).

2. Know what a reasonable financing rate is for your situation by getting preapproval for a bank loan before your dealer visit.

3. Negotiate your way up from dealer invoice, not down from sticker price.

4. Negotiate the price of the car, financing, and the value of your trade in separately.

5. Use effective strategies when dealing with the salesman—countering leading questions with questions, for instance.

What's your best option? Don't be pushed into a deal. Think on it. Once you think you've got a solid offer, demand time to evaluate it—come back later in the afternoon, take half an hour to yourself in private at the dealership… and compare what you're seeing against other options by using the methods already described earlier in this book. Don't make a deal until you're ready, and until you've thoroughly run the numbers.

Just the facts

- You can better your deal by agreeing to bank-equivalent (or lower) financing at the dealer in exchange for price concessions.

- Keep your cards a little hidden—it's better, for instance, to not reveal up front that you're a cash buyer.

- Derail leading sales questions ("So if I lower the price $500, you'll buy?") with counter-questioning ("How much lower than that can you go?")

- Cash on the spot can be a great negotiating tactic, particularly when you're buying used from a private party.

GET THE SCOOP ON...
How to unload your old car yourself ▪
Alternatives to trading your car in ▪ What
makes the most financial sense ▪ What to do if
you have a lease car now

Factoring Your Old Car into the Deal

You've been driving your present car how long now? Long enough! Or you wouldn't be shopping for a different set of wheels. Maybe you just want to get rid of the thing, and you're yearning for the pristine interior of a brand spanking new automobile (or at least, a brand spanking newer one).

Before you lose your head, remember that your feelings are typical of many car shoppers. And because it's easy to focus on your new vehicle, not your old one, there's a loophole there where money can fall out.

The difference between what you may get by trading your old car in or selling it yourself could be a thousand dollars, or more than $10,000 if yours is a luxury model, based on the difference between wholesale trade-in and retail values.

In this chapter, along with emphasizing that you should pay attention to your trade-in and get a good price for it, we'll show you how and give you some

Chapter 13

263

66

A pessimist sees
the difficulty in
every oppor-
tunity. An
optimist sees the
opportunity in
every difficulty.
—Winston
Churchill

99

special advice in the event you've got a lease car
now.

Options for your old car

Generally you're likely to fall into one of a few categories with respect to your present set of wheels, and
which one determines how you should approach the
trade-in question:

- Lease return

- Very recent model used car (1–3 years)

- Midrange used car (4–6 years)

- Older used car (7+ years)

Also affecting your choices are the condition the
car is in, the mileage, and of course market factors
related to the desirability of the brand and model.

No matter what your situation, chances are you
want to:

1. Get a fair price for your car

2. Dispose of it quickly with as little hassle as
   possible

You also of course have the option of keeping
your present car, an option families needing more
than one set of wheels might consider. In that case,
you should also consider carefully which of your present vehicles you want to keep most, and which
would be better to sell.

If you have a very new car now, still under manufacturer warranty, you're probably also still making
payments on it. We have to stop and ask you here,
why do you want to get rid of it? Getting rid of a new
used car poses a pair of problems:

1. If you're still financing, you may technically owe
   more on the car than what you can sell it for,
   because it has depreciated faster than you could

pay it off. Called being "upside-down" on payments, it means you could sell the car and still owe money on the loan.

2. If you're considering getting rid of your new car because the financing rate is too high, you should see what kind of financing you have before deciding it's a good idea to trade it in. If your loan is a simple interest one, that's good news (you might also consider simply refinancing the simple interest loan you've got, but at a lower rate if feasible). If your loan abides by the "Rule of 78" (look for check boxes and terms in your loan and car purchase paperwork), that's bad news. A "Rule of 78" loan is one in which the interest is paid off in much greater proportion before the principal. You could have been making payments for many months, and still owe the entire value of the car.

Watch Out!
Rule of 78 loans favor the lender, not the borrower. This is typically a dealer financing arrangement—and you should refuse it if possible—go for a simple interest loan instead, so you could save if you decide to pay it off early.

Beyond those potential, substantial difficulties, there are the positive points that new cars are easier to resell, and thus a dealer to whom you trade in the car may look favorably at having it in stock (though you might consider selling the vehicle yourself).

A midrange used car, one that's perhaps four to six years old, is also a viable, resellable vehicle. But the large number of lease returns populating dealer lots these days are likely to be one or more years newer—a midrange car is less desirable to many people and thus to dealers. Your circumstances are bettered when the car has been kept in good condition, without very high miles, and if the model's body style hasn't changed significantly.

Older used vehicles are not the easiest for new car dealers to resell, and when a dealer accepts a car like this as a trade-in, it may go straight to auction, where it's resold to a used car lot. Here the dealer accepts it as a trade simply because you're getting a new car from him—he doesn't want to look at his prospects for reselling the vehicle. He, like you, wants to get rid of the car, and offers you only as little as possible for it. Then he has to deal with the nuisance of disposing of it. Slightly newer autos that have been beaten up or have high mileage may be treated similarly.

If your car is a lease return, you still have options at trade-in time, largely depending on two things: whether you have a closed-end or open-ended lease, and consumer protections that help you get fair market value for your lease car. See the section "What to do if you have a lease car now" later in this chapter.

Moneysaver
There are exceptions to the off-to-the-glue-factory mentality regarding older cars. Certain models stay in demand for long periods of time in what is either a bona fide collector's market, or in something approaching it.

Trading it in

Perhaps the best reason for trading in your car rather than selling it is a little-thought-of point: in many states when you buy a car and trade one in on it, you pay sales tax only on the difference in price. At 6% state sales tax, even a $10,000 trade-in could absolve you of $600 in taxes.

If you decide to trade in your old car, the easiest way to get it out of your driveway, you obviously want a fair price for it. But "fair" is a relative term here. On a car that a dealer can resell for significantly more money, fair may be anything from the least you will accept to the highest a dealer can afford, while still ensuring he makes a little money at resale time.

That difference between "wholesale" and "retail" used car rates (see Chapter 6 on pricing for more detail) means you can use your trade-in as leverage when negotiating the price of your new vehicle.

Say your domestic sedan carries a wholesale trade-in value of $10,775 but a retail value of $13,305, a difference of $2,530. Provided it's in good shape with decent mileage, a dealer knows he can sell your car for close to its retail value. That means if he wanted to, he could offer you more than trade-in value. If the only cost to the dealer is an hour of detailing and the carrying expense of actually having it on the lot, and he gives you trade-in value, he stands to make $2,530 in profit.

Many customers who think they're negotiating a decent price on their new car, even those who go to the trouble of deducing real dealer cost, will lose money by accepting less than what they should for a trade-in.

A good policy is to, as we've said, negotiate the purchase price of the vehicle you're getting first, then negotiate the value of your trade in and the rate you'll get on financing separately, so there's less opportunity for a dealer to change variables and hide profits.

Selling it yourself

For those willing to forgo the convenience of trading their used car in to a dealer, the reward is a potentially much higher price for selling a vehicle on one's own.

Using again the example of a 1996 domestic sedan with a trade-in expectation of $10,775 but a retail value of $13,305, your potential "profit" above trade-in value is $2,530. Yes, you'll have to run an ad—some are free, some you pay for by the day or week and some go for a fixed price—but two-and-a-half grand may be worth your trouble to show the car to a few interested buyers. Bear in mind, however, when selling your car yourself you will be missing the potential sales tax break a trade-in could provide toward the car you get. See Chapter 16 for more on how a buyer should handle details of purchasing your vehicle, such as sales tax.

Keeping it

Keeping your used car is another option you can consider. Whether this works out for you depends on your budget and whether you have space to keep the vehicle. Extra expenses of hanging on to a used car include:

1. Extra insurance cost (though you may get a discount for covering two cars on the same policy)

2. Double registrations and tags

3. Parking expense (if, for instance, you live at an apartment complex where you've used your allotted spaces already)

4. If your old car isn't entirely paid for, the rest of its financing

5. Repairs and maintenance on that second vehicle

Reasons you might consider (or use to rationalize) keeping your present vehicle as well as the new one include:

▪ Having an extra vehicle on hand for use by other members of the family—your spouse or perhaps a teenager approaching driving age.

▪ Different uses from the new car you're considering. You can retire an older sport utility vehicle for use only on mountain trips or as a weekend vehicle. Also consider, if appropriate, relegating one of the vehicles entirely to business use. Consult your tax advisor and IRS publications for the benefits, which could be substantial.

Timesaver
If you really want to trade a vehicle in rather than selling it yourself, try to get at least the going trade-in rate (see Chapter 2 for pricing sources), and not less than $300 below that amount, when you're making mileage and options adjustments.

■ If you're deciding to lease a car for a relatively short term and want to keep your old car as an optionally drivable vehicle after the lease term ends.

Should you keep your old car? It's a personal decision, and the indecisive can rationalize, "I can always sell it later." But to calculate the financial benefits and detractors, try Worksheet 13.1.

WORKSHEET 13.1   SHOULD I KEEP MY PRESENT CAR TOO?

$ _____ Additional annual insurance (call your agent for a quote—remember to use the older "trade-in" vehicle as the "additional" car for quote purposes)

+ _____ Expected regular annual maintenance costs (oil changes, etc.)

+ _____ Reasonable annual allowance for repairs (if car isn't under warranty)

+ _____ Yearly allocation for personal property insurance on the vehicle (if applicable)

+ _____ Any remaining financing or loan amount on the older vehicle (monthly payments × 12)

+ _____ Cost of tags, registration annually

+ _____ Any additional parking costs (annual)

= _____ Total Cost of Keeping Second Car

Consider relegating your old car entirely to use by your business, if appropriate, for potential tax savings, but this may only make sense if you don't intend to switch it back to personal use at a later date. Check with your tax advisor for specifics.

Weigh your worksheet answers, which gave you annual costs, against factors such as how much the car's worth, whether you can really afford the monthly budget implications, especially in light of the new car loan you're likely going to be paying, and the "opportunity cost" of the money you'll be spending keeping the car.

If the additional approximate amount works out to $4,000, for instance, even if that can be covered in your budget, what could that $4,000 invested or used elsewhere bring you? And what about the value of the car? If the car itself is worth $12,000, over the four-year-life of your new auto loan, keeping it would cost $28,000! And the $12,000 value could have been going toward a huge reduction in the amount of interest expense you would otherwise have to pay on your new car.

Keep your present car only if you really need it, and where possible, relegate it to business use for tax savings.

Other options for your old car

Huh? Besides trading it in, selling it yourself, or keeping it, what could you possibly do with your old car? Give it away. That's right. If you have an old vehicle you don't think is worth your time and effort to sell, consider donating it to one of a number of non-profit organizations, and reaping the tax benefits.

Alternately, if you're trying to save money here, but you're just a bit lazy, consider finding a used car dealer who will take your vehicle on consignment, minus a percentage for selling the car for you. Check your yellow pages.

Deciding what to do

Given your options for your old car, you need to make a decision which you'll choose. First, you can ensure you have a firm grip on the possibilities with a quick test (Quiz 13.1).

QUIZ 13.1   TEST YOUR TRADE-IN KNOWLEDGE

1. You're not finished financing a car and are thinking about trading it in. But refinancing it at a lower rate might be a good idea if:

   a)   You have just a fraction of the financing left to pay

   b)   You have a simple interest loan

   c)   You have a Rule of 78 loan

2. Keeping your old car after you buy another is:

   a) A federal income tax benefit whether you have a business or not

   b) Always cheaper in the long run

   c) An expensive proposition given what its value could reduce your new car financing by.

3. If the other parts of your new car purchase have already been negotiated to bottom dollar, a dealer will typically offer you what for your trade in:

   a) 92% of full retail value if you'll let him go that low

   b) Wholesale trade-in value (or lower, perhaps)

   c) A similar car

4. Trading in a lease car is:

   a) Easy because you never actually have any choice as to what a fair price is—it's always mandated at the outset of a lease

   b) Safest because you're always assured of having a big amount of money to put toward your next lease

   c) About as variable as trading in a purchased car, with a closed end lease where you have the option to buy

How did you do? Taking a look at the questions one by one:

1. The best answer is (b). If you have a simple interest loan, refinancing may make sense, if the fees involved in refinancing don't outweigh your savings over the remaining life of the loan.

Bright Idea
Those wishing to cut costs on the upkeep of a second vehicle might consider reducing or eliminating collision coverage costs on the older vehicle—but only after carefully weighing the drawbacks against benefits. Eliminating collision coverage altogether works best only with vehicles of lesser worth and in situations where they are either not driven at all or very little.

(a) is not the best answer because refinancing fees may altogether negate the value of refinancing at a lower rate if there's little left to refinance, and (c) is not the best answer, because a Rule of 78 loan means you're stuck paying off largely the interest first, and principal last.

2. The correct answer is (c). Keeping your old car as a second vehicle involves substantial costs, such as insurance coverage and, where applicable, personal property taxes. The biggest expense could be the opportunity cost wrapped up in its value—you could be substantially reducing the cost of financing your new car by using the proceeds from your old car as a down payment.

3. In our earlier domestic sedan example, trade-in value was about 81% of retail value, and a "fair" dealer trade-in price is considered to be just that, the wholesale "trade in" price, so (b) is the correct answer. (If, however, your trade-in car is a hot seller worth a nice price in the current local market, a dealer could offer you more to seal the deal—you should search for one willing to go with slimmer margins, more of a likelihood if you're buying your new car from a dealer representing the same manufacturer.)

4. Trading in your lease car only looks like a set proposition. Consumer protection laws allow you to get an outside estimate of a car's worth, and market conditions could make it favorable to buy the car, so (c) makes the most sense. See the upcoming section "What to do if you have a lease car now," dealing specifically with lease returns.

The benefits and drawbacks of trading your vehicle in, selling it yourself, keeping it, and giving it away are summarized in Table 13.1.

TABLE 13.1   PROS AND CONS OF YOUR OLD CAR OPTIONS

Trading In	Selling Yourself	Keeping the Car	Selling on Consignment	Donating It
Easy	Involves work	Easy	Easy, if you find a consignment lot	Easy
Low to middling $ benefit	Most $ benefit	Most additional cost involved	Middling to high $ benefit, less sale commission	$ benefit depends on tax situation
New cars with low mileage favored	Low mileage, late model cars may be easiest to sell	Older cars with low estimated $ value less costly to keep in terms of taxes and insurance, but repairs can add up	Different lots handle different types of cars	An option for hard-to-sell vehicles
Good, it's gone! Simple car transition	Penny-pinching satisfaction	Sentimental value and convenience	Compromise between selling it yourself and trading it in	Good Samaritan factor

So you've decided to trade it in

Perhaps you've decided your time and trouble in selling a vehicle just doesn't match up to the ease with which you can trade in your present car to a dealer. And perhaps that dealer is willing, all other things being equal, to give you a pretty good rate on your old car—at least one you won't feel "taken for a ride" by.

Watch Out!
Never let the keys to your trade-in out of sight at a dealership, or give them to a salesman so he can take a look at the car. Go use the keys yourself. An old trick of the trade is to "accidentally" misplace a car shopper's keys, trapping them at the dealership until they can be sold a car. Yes, really.

As you go through negotiations about your old car, here are some things to keep in mind.

Your perspective vs. the dealer's

You and the dealer are approaching your trade-in from opposite sides of the table. To you, your car may be something you saved for and worked hard to buy, an automobile you've been proud to drive for years and which you've treated carefully. In your mind it's a cream puff.

In the salesman's mind, it's baggage. Used cars may be sold by different salesmen in a different lot (or at least a different section). New cars with their shine appeal and high sticker prices offer more opportunity for profit. Taking in your old car is something the dealer does "as a favor" (or so it seems) to seal a deal with a new car buyer.

To the dealer, the vehicle in effect is worth wholesale—for he can get other similar cars at wholesale via an auction, or some other bloke or lady deciding to trade in their vehicle.

How your used car factors into price negotiation on your new car

If you fail to attempt to negotiate the allowance a dealer will give you for your trade-in, you will almost certainly be setting him up to make a large profit on you in that department, which doesn't mean he won't seek to profit from you in other areas of the sale.

As we've said before, when you're buying a vehicle, first negotiate the purchase price of the car separately—don't allow the salesman to consider your trade-in in an initial offer spiel—there are too many variables, too many fudge factors.

If you've reached what you believe is a reasonable price for the car you intend to purchase, move on to the down payment, which may include cash, but should first include your trade-in. Before you've told the salesman exactly how much other cash you can afford to pay up front on the car, figure out how much he'll let you have for your old one.

When you get an offer, if it's below Blue Book wholesale, tell the salesman and ask why he's offering you that low a price—you need to put him on alert gently that you have no intention of being bamboozled at this juncture.

Once you've gotten at least a wholesale trade-in offer, we suggest moving on to discuss financing without alerting the dealer you may want more money from that trade. What financing rate can you get? Iron out the rest of the specifics of the deal— you know you can buy the car you want for $20,200 at a promotional financing rate of 6.9% over 48 months, for instance, assuming you'll put the $7,450 wholesale trade-in value of your car toward it. Clarify any fees. . . and then move back to negotiating your trade-in. If there are similar vehicles on the lot going for $10,000, you know the dealer is making at least $2,550 on the markup (less some minor fixing up and carrying costs).

Now, if you're considering paying cash for that down payment, mention it. "You know, I think I'd like to keep my trade-in car. . . it's worth more to me than $7,450," you can say, "Let's go ahead with the sale, but I'll put that $7,450 down in cash and my (wife, husband, other relative) can drive my old car."

The dealer doesn't want you to do that, and will probably put up all manner of protest—you've just chopped a big chunk of profit out of what he thought was a sweet deal. Now, as he fiddles around

> 66
> They asked me really basic stuff about the trade-in, major mechanical problems, things like that. They started the car, didn't even look under the hood, and gave me $500 more than I thought I deserved for it.
> —Barney, traded in his car
> 99

Moneysaver
Demand for used cars tends to be higher during spring and early summer, when you should consider selling the car yourself. But dealers don't usually account for the seasonal difference between whole-sale trade-in and real market retail values, so a dealer won't necessarily offer you less in winter than he would in spring.

for a way to jack up the total cost of your new car again, don't let him. Stick to discussing the value of your old car and get the best deal you can out of him. Mention (if it's true) you've heard your particular model, year, and mileage level vehicle is a pretty hot seller, and that other similar cars on the lot are going for substantially more than he's offered.

Generally, you should avoid putting much money into repairs for a car you're trading in, by the way. Small repairs that seem to make a big difference, yes—because it takes away the salesman's "how can we sell that thing, we're going to have to pour money in to fix it" argument. But big dollars? No. You'll be paying retail for the repairs, and getting close to wholesale for your car. It's cheaper for the dealer to make the repairs.

So you've decided to sell your old car yourself

Maybe you're willing to spend a little time and effort for potentially a decent cash windfall over and above what a dealer will offer you.

At least you're going to give it a try. What next? The steps include:

1. **Estimate the value of your old car.** Check for resale values with *Kelley Blue Book* or another used car pricing guide or Internet site—start with retail, rather than wholesale or trade-in, figures, and compare them to classified ad prices for similar cars to determine your initial selling price. You may get closer to trade-in value, but you can start out asking near retail if the car's in great shape.

2. **Gather relevant papers.** Make sure you have title and registration for the vehicle, check with your

bank regarding procedures if you still have an auto loan out.

3. **Run an ad** in your daily local paper's classifieds, or consider a photo-and-ad in a local monthly publication—other possibilities include Internet classifieds sites (often free), weekly papers, etc. Post a sign with the make, year, selling price, and your phone number in the car window if you like (but don't obstruct your view!).

4. **Show the car** to potential buyers.

5. **Negotiate price** if necessary.

6. **Seal the deal** and make sure all sales paperwork is filled out correctly. It may require bank visits.

7. **Make appropriate changes** to your insurance, handle return of tags to your state (unless they're going on your new car), etc.

Deciding on a price

At what rate should you price the car for sale? If you're not in a hurry and the car is truly in fine shape with no need for repairs, try full retail. Many used car buyers have no idea what wholesale and retail rates are, and would just as happily buy from you at retail as they might from a dealer at retail. In effect, what you're giving them is the convenience of knowing where that used car they want actually is. Rather than cruise dealers looking for one that happens to carry the '96 or '97 sedan they've been hankering for, your ad shows there's a nice one available in the color they like, nearby, and for how much.

You, of course, when shopping for a used car to buy from a private party, would not think of paying retail since you don't have to—other used cars are

Bright Idea
Baffled by classified ad terminology? *A/C* means "air conditioning," *dr* is "door," *hb* is "hatchback," *hp* is "horsepower," *obo* is "or best offer," *pb* is "power brakes," *pd* "power doors," *pl* "power locks," *pw* "power windows." Check current classified ads for other abbreviations you can use to save space (and thus perhaps cost) in an ad you run.

available for purchase from private parties for barely above wholesale. The seller may himself be someone who was going to trade in the car, but didn't like
the dealer trade-in offer and simply wanted to see if
a private buyer might offer him a little bit more.

With a classified ad running for full retail (and
maybe a window sign for passersby) or what rate
other similar cars are listed for in the classifieds, you
have room to negotiate downward a bit with a buyer
and still make a "profit" over trade-in. If the ad runs
a couple of weeks and the car doesn't sell, you can
adjust your price accordingly.

When should you sell it?

Ideally, sell your used car before you actually buy
your new one, if and only if you're buying a new car.
You've checked with a couple of dealers and discov-
ered what they would offer you as a trade-in rate—
or you've decided to dispense with the idea of trading it in, altogether, knowing you can make more
money with a private buyer. You should also know
what new car you want to buy, perhaps you're waiting a couple of weeks for a rebate offer to kick in—
whatever, you're ready to pounce.

Getting rid of your old car before you get your
new one, when you can arrange it, will save you the
expense of insuring two cars and the potential trouble of dealing with two sets of tags. You can check
with your insurer about the cost of covering two cars
at once, but there will be an expense there (see
Chapter 18 for more on insurance).

If timing the perfect segue sounds too tricky, buy
your new car first but make arrangements with the
dealer to actually take delivery and possession of it
in two weeks to a month—giving you time to sell
your old car—if you can stand not having your new

car immediately and the dealer will agree. This may work particularly well when you're getting a car so in demand it has to be factory-ordered anyway.

Sealing the deal

Before showing your old car, make sure it's clean and invest a little elbow grease in detailing with shine products for both interior and exterior, not to mention under the hood, where you can consider using a spray-on degreaser, but don't get any on your outside paint, and make sure to cover the distributor cap first, so it will start after you hose off the degreaser.

What, you don't know what a distributor cap is? You might have your under-the-hood region cleaned (steam cleaned perhaps) and get a detailing job from a full-service car wash, if you think the change in appearance will help convince a car buyer. It's also a good idea to use the best grade of gasoline for the smoothest running while your car's being test-driven. Of course, after all this, you run the risk of now wanting to keep your shiny, seemingly newer, old set of wheels.

Still selling? When you do find the perfect buyer, make sure you're protected as you make the transaction.

If selling a car to a cash buyer, insist on a certified check or cashier's check, available for a few dollars from banks, guaranteed by the bank. If your buyer is getting bank financing, speak with the loan officer in person if possible to make sure the bank's procedures are followed to a "T." If you still have a loan with the bank for the car you're selling, check with their loan department about specific procedures.

Watch Out!
Keep your bill of sale and related papers at least a year—you could need it to prove, for instance, that you're no longer the owner and thus don't owe personal property taxes on it anymore.

The bill of sale for your used vehicle can protect you as well. Particularly if you've modified the car at all, you need to make sure you're selling it "as is" and that you bear no responsibilities for any malfunctions, and that you're not implying any warranties.

A sample bill of sale is shown below. Yours should include at minimum:

- Year, make, and model of your car
- Vehicle Identification Number (check the driver's side dash area for this)
- Mileage
- Your name
- Buying party's name
- Price
- Date
- Statement whom the vehicle is being sold by, to and for how much
- Disclaimer that vehicle is being sold "as is"
- Signatures of both parties, with date (and notarization if possible, for extra safety)

Check the front and back of the title you'll be transferring for places to sign, and photocopy all sale documents, including checks. Check with your bank loan officer and state Department of Motor Vehicles about any other specifics you may need to address, before you sell the car!

Bill of Sale

I, _____ (seller's full name), hereby sell one _____ (year, make and model), VIN # _____ (Vehicle Information Number), with mileage of _____ (odometer mileage) to _____ (buyer's full name) for the sale price of $_____ (sale price), on this date, _____ (mm/dd/yy).

This vehicle is sold "as is", with no representation made as to fitness or mechanical condition.

Signed:

_____ (seller signs)   _____ (buyer signs)

_____ (seller name)   _____ (buyer name)
_____ (seller address)   _____ (buyer address)
_____   _____
_____   _____

Date: _____   Date: _____

You should also inquire at your state DMV of any special procedures. In California, for instance, the following is required:

Release of Liability: When the owner of a California registered vehicle sells or transfers title of interest in the vehicle, the seller must complete a Notice of Release of Liability (REG 138) and submit it to the department within 05 calendar days. This releases the owner from civil or criminal liability for any parking, abandonment, or operation of the vehicle occurring after the transfer date. The vehicle record is not permanently changed, however, until the department receives a completed application for transfer of title with appropriate fees from the new owner.

When selling your old car, you need not only the bill of sale, but also the title to hand over to the new owner. Don't forget to remove your license plates, either. Your sale could require trips to two banks. . . the buyer must go get a certified check or cashier's check made out to you for the full price of the car, and if you still have a loan at your bank, the buyer should then go with you to settle up the paperwork for transferring title and handing over the check. Remember to cancel your insurance coverage for the car being sold as well, and check Chapter 16 for a word about registration.

What to do if you have a lease car now

If this is your first lease, and you're about to turn that baby in for a totally new set of wheels, there are some things you should know.

In a typical closed-end lease, the best kind for most consumers, you're often given the option to purchase the car for a certain amount, generally the

Timesaver
Check your state Department of Motor Vehicles Web site for details on what's necessary when you sell your car—some even have blank forms you can print out, and it's a lot faster than waiting in line at a DMV site.

anticipated residual value of the vehicle at the end of the lease, as determined at the beginning of the lease. If you've had the vehicle for three years, a lot may have happened to market factors. The car may be more or less in demand than what was thought so many months ago.

If your "option to buy" figure is less than the profit you could make if selling the car on the market privately, consider buying the vehicle for that prestated amount. Remember to factor in the sales tax you would owe to purchase it outright (or initiate purchase financing), and some temporary insurance costs to cover it. If you're in this situation and not sure you want to get another lease car, consider buying the car and delaying your decision—you stand to make money on that lease car when you do sell it.

The disposition fee due at the end of your lease to cover the expenses of selling the car is something you should try to negotiate your way out of, by the way, if you're buying the car and reselling it yourself. If you're buying it and keeping it, the resale obviously isn't taking much effort from the dealer! And use common sense regarding any other charges you're asked to pay—excess mileage or even wear charges don't make sense if the dealer isn't getting the car back. Make a strong case for dismissal of those charges, and don't forget your security deposit.

Just the facts

- Trading in your vehicle can sometimes reduce how much sales tax you'll owe on your new car—many states base it only on the difference between the trade-in's value and the new car's price.

■ Selling a car yourself will probably bring you the best price, though other options include trading it in, putting it on consignment with a dealer, keeping the car, or even donating it to charity.

■ The gap between wholesale trade-in (that a dealer might offer you) and retail (that he might get for reselling the car) can be over $10,000 on luxury models, and upwards of $1,000 even on less pricey vehicles.

■ If selling your car yourself, be certain to draw up a bill of sale that includes appropriate information and a disclaimer that the vehicle's being sold "as is."

■ If you're returning a lease car at the end of its term, consumer protection laws allow you the right to an independent appraisal of its value.

Making the Deal

PART VII

Deciding How Much to Pay

Chapter 14

You're done shopping and you're ready to get hold of that new set of wheels, or newer set of wheels as the case may be. After your preliminary negotiating you think you've found a dealer who you can agree with, and you're proceeding toward that narrow light at the end of the tunnel, which you hope is the sun reflecting off the hood of your new car on its first Sunday afternoon drive.

In this chapter, we'll help you make that crucial decision of how much to pay and give you some strategies to nail down a final number to your liking. You should also beware that while the first part of your car-buying experience is finishing, the back end holds perils all its own.

How much profit should the dealer make?

What a fair price is varies, not only by market conditions and dealers, but also by what the consumer considers "fair" to be. For some tightwads, it's absolute bottom dollar. For others, it's simply not getting gouged—the value of saving a bit more money is outweighed at some point by the stress of having to negotiate for it.

Previous chapters of this book have gone into more detail about how you can calculate prices, but you can consider these rules of thumb. For cars not more than a few thousand dollars above the average new car cost, say up to the high twenties, paying just a few hundred dollars atop dealer cost makes sense.

Auto pricing experts suggest offering more than that as the vehicle price approaches $40,000—perhaps $500 to $1,000 over invoice. And as the price of a new car heads even further into luxury land, so does the cut that the middleman gets. If you're spending more than $40,000 on a new car, it's figured you can part with perhaps $2,000–$3,000 atop dealer cost.

By careful shopping, you can, of course, find situations where dealers will take less—even less than invoice, due to rebates and other incentives. When in doubt, start low—negotiating your way back down is much harder than starting low and working upward.

As assurance that you'll get the best price, don't forget the points in Checklist 14.1.

CHECKLIST 14.1 IMPROVE YOUR NEW CAR PRICE

_____ 1. Always research dealer cost on your new car and keep research materials with you that have all the relevant figures.

_____ 2. Check for rebates and other incentives that may be in effect on your vehicle, but which the dealer won't necessarily reveal.

_____ 3. When possible, shop when your vehicle's most likely to be on sale or when the dealer is most likely to want to move it (Chapter 4 has more on that).

_____ 4. At the dealership, negotiate from the dealer cost up, not sticker price down; and avoid being drawn into sales pitches concentrating on "what monthly payment you can afford."

The bottom line—whether buying or leasing

Two factors should determine how much you decide to spend on a vehicle: what your own budget limitations are, and how low an overall price the dealer is willing to offer you in relation to the worth of the car to your needs.

How to decide on your spending limits

In Chapter 3, we went over what a successful car budget entails—and that means making allowances for costs such as the of insurance, taxes, maintenance, fuel, and repairs; as well as the financing costs and the price of the vehicle itself.

Review major spending limit concepts in Table 14.1.

Bright Idea
Check newspaper ads, even if you think you've found your dealer. They can alert you to incentives you haven't heard of yet.

TABLE 14.1 SPENDING LIMIT POINTERS

What percentage of my income?	Some may spend 7% of their income or less on total transportation-related expenses. Some consumer counselors advise not to exceed about 15%.
How much per month?	Many people are comfortable not exceeding about $350 per month in payments. Figure your threshold based on income percentage—and a hard look at your budget.
Should I consider leasing, buying new, or buying used?	When you have a comparable purchase and lease deal, the costs may work out very similarly for those who keep their cars only a few years. The longer you typically keep a car, the worse a leasing deal will look. And buying used may give you the longest-term

PART VII ■ MAKING THE DEAL

Don't forget to factor in all of your auto-related expenses when deciding how much to spend per month— insurance and taxes may add up...but, on the plus side, you can get a car with a better mileage rating and much-reduced repair expenses.

	value, but it depends on your specific situation and car-keeping habits.
What happens to my payments if I lease rather than buy new?	When leasing, monthly payments may be $2/3$ of new car purchase payments, and some dip to under half the amount.
Any hidden things that can affect my spending limits?	Absolutely. Among them, potentially much higher insurance costs on a new car that's worth more than your present vehicle, personal property taxes based on the value of your vehicle, the financing rate you can secure, and the list goes on.

Determining what the dealer will accept before you bargain

If you go into your final negotiation round armed with inside information the dealer doesn't think you know, you're much better off than the average car buyer. Getting down to that soft spot of a fair price may still take some doing, but having your numbers in order should make the task easier.

How much the dealer will accept depends on factors including:

1. How much money a dealership needs to make on each car to turn a decent profit (is it a high volume dealer or one that sells fewer cars, but typically at a premium?)

2. The status of any rebates or other incentives

3. The market demand for the car you're getting (can the dealers barely keep it in stock, or can they not get the thing off the lot?)

4. Whether the dealer will make any money on you via financing, and whether he expects you'll go for back-end goodies like rustproofing

5. How much dealer holdback is already included in the dealer invoice price figure (refer to Chapter 6 for that analysis), and bear in mind that dealers don't typically consider this part of their profit bag—its relevance may arise only in the most competitive dealmaking

6. What competing dealers in the area are offering

Make sure that you've reviewed the appropriate numbers via Chapter 6's pricing advice, and that you've drawn your conclusions and are literally keeping them on a pad tucked in your pocket or purse.

Final price negotiation strategies

The psychology of closing a car deal isn't most people's favorite topic. Until now, you and the salesman have probably had a pretty reasonable time of it, with no real antagonism between the two of you.

As you get into the final stretch, however, you may need to pull out the big consumer guns to seal the deal the way you want it.

Consider the strategies in Table 14.2.

TABLE 14.2   FINAL PRICE NEGOTIATIONS

Salesman's Pitch	Your Strategy
"How much do you want to spend per month—we can get your payments lower with leasing."	"I'm not negotiating based on the monthly payment. Let's keep to the purchase price."
"If I come down $500, will you buy the car?"	"How much lower can you go?"
	"If you're only coming down $500, I'll need the same options package, but with the larger engine."
"We're already giving you an unbeatable deal with that rebate."	"But that's a manufacturer's rebate; what's to keep me from going to [name their competitor]?"

Bright Idea
Remember, it may be advisable not to mention until very late in the game that you plan to pay for a substantial portion of your new car in cash. It tells the dealer that he won't be making much if any money by financing you and that you've got enough big bucks to be shown the really pricey models.

Never be afraid to walk away from a deal if the salesman really isn't meeting your terms.

"This is the lowest I can go. If you'll take this offer, I can have you driving that car in half an hour."	"I need more time, and I'm tired. I'll think about coming back another time."
"This is a very hot model; it's not going to stay on the lot through the weekend. You should buy it now."	"I'm not sure this model is worth that much to me. How much lower can you go on the price?"
"That's the absolute bottom dollar I can get. My sales manager won't let me go any lower."	"If you can get $300 lower on that, I'll consider financing with you."

Remember that countering a leading question with a question prevents you from being drawn further into a deal you're not ready to make. If you seem to back away in terms of interest in the car, you may short-circuit a salesman's canned routine. If he's trying to squeeze dollars out of you on that glossy new coupe, get a glazed look and mumble something like, "You know, I'm almost wishing I was getting that sedan now (name a cheaper car on their lot)." Or pipe up with, "I wonder how much one of those a couple of years old would cost instead?" Going from a done deal to no deal tops the list of salesman nightmares. He may wake up and give you what you want.

End-game car-buying pointers:

1. Be sure to first negotiate a solid purchase price.

2. Then, separately negotiate the value of your trade-in.

3. Separately negotiate your financing rate, type, and terms.

Final lease negotiation strategies

You should be taking essentially the same steps in final lease negotiations as with buying—you're working first for the lowest purchase price, then the value of your trade, and then the best possible lease rate instead of interest rate and loan terms.

As you go into the homestretch, here's how to tweak the price of that lease:

1. Make the salesman check with more than one financing entity to find the one that lists the best residual value for the vehicle—the higher that residual, the lower the monthly payments you should make. If you're a brave soul and know that the market value for your particular model of car is running high, ask the dealer to list an even higher guaranteed residual (if you're not planning to buy at lease end).

2. Be sure to carefully review leasing disclosures and check the math for any "hidden" profit that the dealership may try to make.

3. Are you planning to drive the car lightly? Ask about discounts for using fewer than the specified number of miles—but only if you are sure you won't use them.

4. Take time now to persuade the dealership out of lease return, resale, or any other charges associated with your purchase option.

Moneysaver
When you discuss a lease, make sure that you clarify what they're pitching you—it should be a closed-end lease in which your costs at return time are known.

Last-ditch efforts, fortitude, and phobia

You're at the point now where the sales manager either accepts or rejects your offer. There's a wonderful moment that comes when you realize that he knows he's given it his best shot, and that you're not about to budge. Things start happening quickly, and the objective turns to speeding along the sale before you change your mind. Oh, until you walk out the door, you're in danger of being sold something else, but if you handled things this well so far, you should do fine with the rest.

As a customer, you need to remember that the people you're negotiating with at the dealership are human, too—and some of them may have huge egos. Whether you want to run the risk of truly offending them is up to you—we advise against it as a matter of personal policy. Coming up with a brash last-ditch negotiation tactic is less advisable when you deal with a truly customer-focused dealership, but perhaps less offensive when the dealership seems populated with difficult personalities. But if that's the case, why are you buying a car there? Given the odds that you may need to return for maintenance or have to deal with these people otherwise, we advise that you instead find a dealer you can work with.

How good dealerships handle this stuff—and their evil twins

At the kind of dealership you want to be giving your business to, negotiations are designed to be in the best interest of the dealer, but not in an out-of-line way. If the salesman doesn't tell you patent untruths, that's good. If dealings are in the gentlemanly (or gentlewomanly, as the case may be) sport of negotiation, without true intimidation or emotional games, that's very good. An ideal salesman at a fair dealership will—at least somewhat—lay it on the line with you—how can you both walk away with the best deal? Working a little bit together on the matter can have some rewards. For instance, a salesman who clues you in to a rebate a few days down the road might win your favor enough to have the privilege of writing up your deal.

But some dealerships fall far short of the golden standard. As a consumer, if you've done your homework, you'll be able to spot lies that fly by other

Unofficially... Car sales isn't known as the industry with the least turnover. There's a high burnout rate (it's not an easy job!). Quotas can eliminate under-performers from the profession. But a good car salesman can top professionals in some respected fields with annual wage rates. The best performers are rewarded with fully-paid exotic vacations—on which, of course, they're exposed to more motivational training.

shoppers. A single lie should make you question whether you're doing business with the right people. If you decide to proceed, make explicitly sure that you double-check every single written point and item of math before you sign. When a sales manager or salesman resorts to intimidation ("Why are you wasting my time?!") or emotional role-playing (good cop/bad cop between the sales manager and salesman), a potentially harrowing experience is in the making. Keep your keys on your person and get them to the ignition of your intended trade-in as quickly as possible. Find someone else to work with—a good dealer can give you just as good a deal (and possibly better) than one where rotten attitudes prevail.

Cover your rear—avoiding being back-ended in the deal

Once you handle the basics of buying or leasing a car and set up the financing, you're verbally faced with decisions about extras. Our best advice is to avoid them all and save yourself some money.

You approach the "back end" of the sale. The good news is that you're almost finished. The bad news is that there are still plenty of places to be tripped up.

Once again, what's the back end?

The back end is, simply put, the rear part of the sale that includes all the little extras you didn't see before. After you thoroughly review and sign the paperwork to buy the car, if you're presented with costs and fees that were not previously discussed, say no. The time to negotiate back-end (aftersell) fees is when they appear—don't forewarn the salesman that he won't make those extra profit dollars.

66

Undercoating is a slam dunk. It's a last ditch effort to get profits they can charge you $600 for. I never sold a car that wasn't undercoated at the factory, anyway.
—Alan, former new car salesman

99

Exploits of the F&I man

If you buy at a dealership, you still have a battle ahead of you—getting past the F&I manager (remember, that's Financing & Insurance), the sales manager, and out that door with your new car with as little monetary leakage as possible.

Before you and the salesman part ways and you face his comrades in capitalism, ask him to write down the figures you've agreed to. It's something you can at least wave in front of the sales or F&I manager if they try to convince you that you really agreed to something else.

When the salesman leaves to retrieve or check with the sales manager on this final deal, a number of things can happen —your best bet is to stay vigilantly on guard and stick to your guns.

If the salesman returns and says he made a mistake and gave you an offer too low, tell him you're not interested in going any higher than what you've already agreed to, and be ready to walk. Keep an eye on your personal belongings, by the way, and keep your old car keys with you at all times, as we urged you before.

Much back-and-forth restating of the final amounts may legitimately lead you to ask to speak to the sales manager. This is the "cut to the chase" option because the sales manager is the one with authority to okay the deal. Problem is, he may be a lot better at the salesman's own game. If he offers you any deal that's not as good as the best one you discussed with the salesman, make moves to leave, and do.

When you're at the "paperwork about to be drawn up" stage, ask again for the salesman's (preferably the sales manager's) total list of costs of the deal. You're likely to be presented either with a short list that includes the purchase price, financing terms and rate, and trade-in allowance (which means they ignored your real question); or you'll get a full list of previously unheard-of items, ranging from "dealer preparation" fees to "document preparation" fees, etc. It may be helpful now to reiterate to the sales manager or salesman that you intend to pay none of them. How much you snip off their cost depends largely on how strong your stomach for stonewall negotiating is.

Your advantage at this stage lies in three areas: one, the sales manager knows he can sell you a car. Two, he knows he's making some profit, and exactly how much. At this stage, his negotiation goals are to tweak profits. The third advantage is that of time—the sales manager and salesman have invested theirs in you, as you have in them, and they would be foolish to let you walk away now.

The next stop is the desk of the F&I man, whose job is to arrange financing and insurance for you, and profit for the dealership. Insurance? Yes, they'll sell it to you. And we advise you in most cases go to your insurance agent instead.

The first type of insurance to avoid is credit life insurance, in which your survivors gain benefits toward paying off the vehicle should something happen to you. If you already have life insurance, rely on that and don't duplicate. Even if you don't carry life insurance, isn't it unlikely that you'd need this policy?

Another kind of insurance you may be offered is disability insurance, wherein your payments may be covered should something horrible, short of death, happen to you. Even health insurance is sometimes

Watch Out!
Be wary of leaving the dealership in your new car without enough insurance on your old car to cover it. Chapter 18 tells you how typical insurance procedures work.

298   PART VII ▪ MAKING THE DEAL

offered at dealerships. If you feel you need anything that's offered, check other insurance sources at a less pressing time before you decide to go with a dealership's offer.

Along with the "insurances" part comes the "financing" part, where the terms of your loan (or lease) are detailed, and you'll also be offered extended warranty coverage on your vehicle. If you lease, you probably won't have the vehicle long enough to warrant this excess coverage; if you buy but plan to keep the car only a few years, it may be extraneous, too.

For longer-term owners, extended warranty protection may not be the worst bet, however, as long as it is truly manufacturer-backed. Ask whether the warranty coverage is transferable to another owner in the event of a sale—an extended warranty can easily make your car more appealing to a potential buyer when the time comes to sell.

Extended warranty protection makes the most sense when you buy a car that either has notoriously expensive repair needs (such as some fancier imports) or has not-so-hot reliability ratings. Should you bite? Read up on warranties in Chapter 17.

Realities of those add-ons and options

You may very well be charged a "Dealer Prep" fee, for which you might pay $100 or $200. This charge covers the supposed cost of getting the car ready for you. Can you negotiate it? You can try. If a dealer fears that he'll lose the sale when you question the validity of a dealer prep fee, he may dispose of it or at least come down in price. If he won't negotiate it, consider it the most expensive car wash you'll ever have.

Dealer prep fees can include anything from your first oil change to a state inspection check to a loaner car for warranty service work. When possible and when in doubt, write it out. Your object at the back end is to back out of everything you can, except getting that car.

Before you choose the optional rustproofing protection that you're pushed to get, consider where you live. If it's a dry place with little rust potential, consider saying no. If you'll keep the car only a few years, consider saying no. If you're a long-term buyer, consider rustproofing only if you really can afford it (and remember that the need for rustproofing at a dealer has been a subject of debate). Sometimes rustproofing is already included in the price of the car—it's performed before the car makes an appearance on the dealer's lot. Often, some rustproofing has already been done at the factory (as one car pundit puts it, "Cars just don't rust like they used to"). If you're just not sure whether you should fork over more cash, you can always have rustproofing applied later at an independent shop.

You can probably apply auto-store versions of protective sprays a dealer promises he has or can put on the interior of your car. Avoid paying for this item. Get a can of fabric or leather protectant yourself.

If you're being sold a vehicle that lacks something you really want—say air conditioning—and the dealer says he can install it for you, think twice, and then think a third time. You may be better off continuing your search for a new vehicle that already has factory-installed air. And if you have to have air installed, check your aftermarket options before deciding to let the dealer do it. Bear in mind

Watch Out!
Check the corrosion section of your new car warranty to discern what's really allowed in aftermarket rustproofing without impairing warranty coverages.

Bright Idea
If you want a car with a feature that's not found in the dealer's inventory (he's out of A/C?), see if you can arrange factory ordering for a car with your desired accouterments rather than agree to an aftermarket installation.

that appearances and function may be best when a part is installed at the factory—try to get the car you want, preoutfitted.

Avoid being blindsided after the sale

After you sign your paperwork, don't, for heaven's sake, agree to any other charges (as you'll read about in the next chapter). Once you've signed, you've signed, and you should stop very short of letting any additions be tacked on.

It's also important to do a full inspection when you take final delivery of the car. As we'll remind you again, don't sign those final delivery acceptance papers if a single thing isn't as you agreed or is sporting a problem.

Before you move on...

Take a final look at your situation—are you really ready to sign this deal? Checklist 14.1 can help.

Remember, a lease isn't necessarily a cheaper option—monthly payments will be lower, but over the longest haul, buying may work out more economically. But if you don't want to ante up for high new car purchase payments, leasing is one option you should consider.

CHECKLIST 14.1   READY TO DEAL?

_____ 1. Are you certain that the car you're negotiating is really the vehicle you want and need?

_____ 2. Can you comfortably afford to purchase (or lease) this vehicle; and handle insurance, taxes, and other costs without seriously impairing your financial life?

_____ 3. Is the price you're offered the best you think you can get?

_____ 4. Are you sure about what you want to do with your old vehicle? If you're trading it in, is the price you're being offered fair?

_____ 5. Have you already made inquiries to your insurer?

_____ 6. Have you already gotten preapproval and a rate quote for a bank loan (or other financing)? Which is your best financing option?

_____ 7. Are you certain that you want to buy this car instead of lease it?

_____ 8. Have you factored any current loan on your trade-in into the deal? Is the title clear on your trade-in?

_____ 9. Do you have the necessary down payment?

_____ 10. If you're a minor, are your parents signing off on your choices? And no matter what your age, is your vehicle choice and expense acceptable to your family (especially if the finances are joint)?

Just the facts

- Rules of thumb about how much to pay over dealer cost go up with the price of the car—from adding up to a few hundred dollars (for cars up to the high $20,000s) to as much as $2,000–$3,000 on expensive luxury models.

- Consider negotiating your way out of add-ons like rustproofing, extra insurance, and other fees.

- Counter a salesman's leading questions by phrasing your answers as questions—or at least by not giving concrete answers.

- Your position is strongest the closer you are to a sale—although that's when the salespeople pull out their best tricks. But they know you're serious and they don't want to lose a deal.

GET THE SCOOP ON...
Documents involved in a car purchase or lease ▪
What to make sure you have with you at deal
time ▪ A final predeal checklist ▪ Important
questions to ask at deal time

Anatomy of a Deal

Chapter 15

You may be biting your nails, but you're not
sure whether it's with anticipation or ner-
vousness. You're making a deal on a car—
that's a big change in your life—and it involves a
hefty wallet full of change too.

So many papers to sign! (So many places you
could be duped if you're not careful.) How to wade
through it? Bring your boots... in this chapter, we'll
explain the documents you're likely to encounter,
and give you some pointers.

What to expect at signing time

You've agreed verbally with a salesman about the
terms of a deal—essentially the purchase price, your
financing term and interest rate, and the value for
your trade-in.

If you're buying used, you've covered the ground
described in Part IV of this book, and if you're buying used from a private seller, lucky you—you have
some less intimidating ground to cover (but more
footwork!).

Presumably, you survived your first encounter with the sales manager and even the F&I man. You sit there, while somewhere in the inside offices of the dealership documents are being prepared that will probably chain you to a payment for what appears to be the foreseeable future. You breathe a sigh of relief that you've gotten this far, but keep your senses tuned because you're really approaching the most important point of the entire affair.

Did you bring with you the items in Checklist 15.1?

CHECKLIST 15.1   DEALMAKER'S SURVIVAL KIT

____ 1. Notepad and pen

____ 2. Calculator

____ 3. Reading glasses if you need them

____ 4. An astute companion

____ 5. Trade-in

____ 6. Title and registration for your trade-in, as well as any loan or lease papers that apply to it; insurance papers, too

____ 7. Checkbooks (and even a credit card for any incidentals you wish to pay for that way)

____ 8. I.D. (your driver's license and other forms of I.D.)

____ 9. Phone book

____ 10. This book (a copy of the checklists, at least!)

____ 11. Other research materials you used to determine which car to get and for how much

____ 12. A ride home (in case you don't take delivery today)

Plowing through the necessary paperwork

What will you be asked to sign? There are some documents common to all types of car deals, whether a new car purchase, a new car lease, or a used car purchase. Because the main document, the sale or lease agreement, depends on the particular deal you

---

If it's possible to have a trustworthy, intelligent companion with you at signing time, do it. Not only is it invaluable to have someone on your side with whom to discuss aspects of the deal (or to bring up points you may have missed), a second set of ears gives you a witness should anything run amiss.

Moneysaver
Why bring your trade-in to the dealership with a full tank of gas? And try to time your car deal-making close to your registration expiration date. You won't pay for a new year.

make, we'll cover those major items first, and then move on to the more common ground.

Purchase papers

The bill of sale is the official document that says who's buying what, and for how much. You saw a version used for the private sale of a used car in Chapter 13 (see the Bill of Sale figure on page 280), when we discussed selling your old vehicle on your own. If you're buying a used car from an individual, you'll probably be asked to sign a similar document.

Buying a new or used car from a dealer involves a more elaborate version of a bill of sale, which may resemble the one on the following three pages. It may also be called a purchase order, sales agreement, sales contract, retail buyers order, or invoice.

The major items you're likely to see on this document include:

- Basics, such as the name of the seller, buyer, addresses, and date, as well as the delivery date of the vehicle

- Details about the vehicle being purchased and the trade-in (VIN number, odometer reading, year/make/model, new or used, color, body style, options package, etc.)

- Pricing information, including the purchase price of the vehicle, any charges for dealer handling and delivery, cost of license and title, trade-in allowance, cash or credit card down payment, taxes, and any miscellaneous fees

- Basic warranty disclaimers, implying that the dealer itself may offer no warranty (it's up to the manufacturer)

- Details of optional insurances and indications, if any, that you authorize

Timesaver
Buying from a private party? Your best option is to bring your own blank form, in case you'll be dealing with a consumer who is not quite as savvy as you.

Watch Out!
Got any ideas about buying your car in a state where there's no sales tax? Watch out for the use tax monster. When you take your new baby home and register it, the state tax authorities will bill you for the sales tax it would have gotten if you'd shopped closer to home, in your own state.

Sample Dealer
Bill of Sale
(page 1).

PRE-COMPUTED INTEREST
MOTOR VEHICLE CONTRACT AND SECURITY AGREEMENT

Buyer's Name Joe Carbuyer	Agreement No. 12345678
Buyer's Residence or Business Address	Stock No. 12345
1234 Shady Lane Carcity, CA 12345	Sales Agent John Q. Salesman
	Date 7/2/98
Co-Buyer's Name and Address	Source LOCAL
	Home Phone (123) 456-7890
Date of Contract July 2, 1998	Business Phone

Contract language: The words 'we', 'us' and 'our' refer to the creditor (seller) named below or, upon assignment, its assignee. The words "you" and "your" refer to the buyer and co-buyer if any named herein. We sell you the vehicle described below on credit. The credit price is listed as the "Total Sale Price", The "Cash Price" is also listed. By signing this contract you choose to buy the "vehicle" on credit and agree to pay Total Sale Price, according to schedules, terms and agreements on the front and back of this contract. If this contract is signed by a buyer and co-buyer, each person is individually and jointly responsible for all contract agreements.

SEE OTHER SIDE OF THIS CONTRACT FOR ADDITIONAL TERMS AND AGREEMENTS:

NEW/USED	YEAR	MAKE	CYL	DIESEL/ GAS/OTHER	BODY STYLE	MODEL	ODOMETER READING
new	1998	BigM	6	gas	coupe	BigM Mobile	25
VIN	COLOR	TRIM	TIRES	TRANS	KEY	LIC NO	ROS NO.
0BMBM01A2BC012345	russet red	beige cloth			no	new	1234567

APR (Credit Cost as Annual Rate)	Finance Charge (Amount credit will cost)	Amount Financed (Amount of credit provided to you)	Total of Payments (Amount you will have paid after completing all scheduled payments)	Total Sale Price (Total cost of purchase on credit, including down payment of $3,371.08)
9.50%	$4,902.29	$18,847.51	$23,719.80	$27,120.88

Payment Schedule

Number of Payments	Amount of Payments	When Payments Are Due
One Payment of	None	
One Payment of	None	
59 Payments	395.83	Monthly, beginning July 2, 1998
One Final Payment	395.83	June 2, 2003

Security: You are giving a security interest in goods purchased.
Late Charges: For payments more than 10 days late you may be charged 5% of the late amount.
Prepayment: If you pay early, you may be entitled to a refund of a portion of the finance charge.
See contract documents for additional information regarding nonpayment, default, any required prepayment in full before the scheduled date and prepayment refunds.

Notices: Names and addresses of all persons to whom notices required or permitted by law to be sent are at top of this form. If you are buying a used vehicle with this contract, as indicated in the description of the vehicle above, federal regulation may require a special buyers guide to be displayed on the window.
(THE INFORMATION ON THE WINDOW FORM FOR THIS VEHICLE IS PART OF THIS CONTRACT. INFORMATION ON THE WINDOW FORM OVERIDES ANY CONTRARY PROVISIONS IN THE CONTRACT.)

- Details about dealer financing if you get it
- Places for both you and the dealer representative to sign and date the agreement
- Fine print, possibly on the back of the invoice, detailing restrictions and specifics related to the points on the front

Make sure that all options you're getting with a vehicle are itemized on the purchase order—if they are not represented clearly in the paperwork, an unscrupulous dealer could switch cars on you.

Sample Dealer Bill of Sale (page 2).

STATEMENT OF INSURANCE
NOTICE: No person is required as a condition of financing the purchase of a motor vehicle to purchase, or negotiate, any insurance through a particular insurance company, agent or broker.
You have requested Seller to include in the balance due under this agreement the following insurance. Insurance is to expire: WITH__ BEFORE__ AFTER__ the due date of the final installment. Buyer requests seller to procure insurance upon the described property against fire, theft, and collision for the term of this agreement. Any insurance will not be in force until accepted by the insurance carrier.
$ none ded. comp., fire & theft ____ mos. $ none
$ none deductible collision ____mos. $ none
Bodily injury $_____ limits ____mos. $ none
Property damage $_____ limits ____mos. $ none
Medical_____ mos. $ none
_____ mos. $ none
TOTAL VEHICLE INSURANCE PREMIUMS $ none

The foregoing declarations are hereby acknowledged.
Date 7/2/98 Seller
Buyer

Broker Fee Disclosure
If this Contract reflects the retail sale of a new motor vehicle the sale is not subject to a fee received by an autobroker unless the following is checked:
____ Name of Autobroker receiving fee, if applicable:
_____
_____

NOTICE OF RESCISSION RIGHTS
If buyer signs here, the provisions of paragraph "K" on the reverse side shall be applicable to this contract.
Buyer's Signature
Co-Buyer's Signature

CREDIT INSURANCE
AUTHORIZATION AND APPLICATION
You voluntarily request the credit insurance checked below, if any, and understand that such insurance is not required. You acknowledge disclosure of the cost of such insurance and authorize it to be included in the balance payable under the security agreement. Any returned or refunded credit insurance premiums shall be applied to sums due under this contract. Only the persons whose names are signed below are insured.

Credit Life_____ Mos. Premium $ none
Joint Life_____Mos Premium $ none
Credit Disability_____Mos. Premium $ none
Total Credit Insurance Premiums $ none (b)

____ You want Credit Life Insurance
X You do not want Credit Life Insurance
____ You want Credit Disability Insurance (Primary Buyer Only)
X You do not want Credit Disability Insurance
____ You want Joint Credit Life Insurance

You are applying for the credit insurance noted above. Your signature means you agree that: (1) You are not eligible for insurance if you have reached your 65th birthday. (2) You are eligible for disability insurance only if working for wages or profit 30 hours a week or more on the Effective Date. (3) Only Primary Buyer is eligible for disability insurance.

DISABILITY INSURANCE MAY NOT COVER CONDITIONS FOR WHICH YOU HAVE SEEN A PHYSICIAN IN THE LAST 6 MONTHS (see "Total Disabilities Not Covered" in your policy or certificate).

Date 7/2/98 Primary Buyer
Age 24
Date_____ Co-Buyer
Age_____

Itemization of Amount Financed		
1 A. Cash Price Motor Vehicle and Accessories (A)		$19,160.00
1. Cash Price Vehicle	$16,680.00	
2. Cash Price Accessories	$2,480.00	
B. Document Preparation Charge (B) (not a governmental fee)		$35.00
C. Smog Fee Paid to Seller (c)		none
D. Sales Tax (on A+B+C)		$1,538.59
E. Luxury Tax		none
F. Service Contract (optional)*		$1,020
G. Other		none
To whom paid_____		
TOTAL CASH PRICE (A to G) (1)		$21,798.59
*We may retain, or receive, a portion of amount.		
2 PUBLIC FEE AMOUNTS		
A. License (A)		$420.00
B. Registration (B)		Incl
C. Smog Impact Fee (C)		none
TOTAL OFFICIAL FEES (A+B+C)(2)		$420.00

3 INSURANCE AMOUNTS		
Total premiums per Statement of Insurance (a + b)* (3)		none
4 STATE SMOG CERT. FEE (4)		none
5 TOTAL (1 to 4) (5)		$22,218.59
6 A. Trade-In		
Yr: 91 Make: Jeep		
Model: Wrangler (A)		$3,000.00
VIN: 0BMBM01A2BC012345		
Odometer: 83,853		
B. Less Pay Off (B)		$4,628.92
C. TRADE-IN (A less B) (C)		-$1,628.92
D. Deferred downpayment due before 2nd installment (D)		none
E. Manufacturer's Rebate (E)		none
F. Remaining cash downpmt. (F)		$5,000
TOTAL DOWNPAYMENT (6C+D+E+F) (6)		$3,371.08
7 AMOUNT FINANCED (5 less 6) (7)		$18,847.51

Leasing papers

There is no such thing as a "standard" leasing contract, but the basic elements are identifiable. Your lease contract might resemble the example on page 309.

Starting from the top, a typical leasing contract will include: your name as lessee; the lessor's name, which may be simply stated as the dealer, although he is the middleman in the deal; and addresses and phone numbers for both of you.

At some point, you'll see language that gets to the heart of the matter, along the lines of:

Bright Idea
Find the sales papers relating to previous car purchases or leases in your family, and spend half an hour reviewing them over coffee before you go to the dealership. Remember how it went—you may decide how to do things differently this time.

PREPAYMENT REFUND: Any refund for prepayment in full will be calculated as follows:
__ according to the Actuarial Method __ according to the Sum of the Periodic Time Balances X according to the Rule of 78s
(If no selection is checked calculation method for prepayment refund will be the Sum of the Periodic Time Balances)

VEHICLE USE: X Personal, Family or Household __ Commercial or Agricultural

OFFICIAL FEES (Not Financed): The Buyer will pay estimated fee(s) of $10.00 to appropriate public authority to transfer registration after full payment.

OPTION: __ You pay no finance charge if the amount financed, item 7, is paid in full on or before _____,
19_____. SELLER'S INITIALS: _____

SELLER ASSISTED LOAN: FOR THIS LOAN, BUYER MAY BE REQUIRED TO PLEDGE SECURITY AND WILL BE OBLIGATED FOR THE INSTALLMENT PAYMENTS ON SECURITY AGREEMENT AND LOAN.
Proceeds of Loan - From N/A   Amount $ none Finance Charge $ none Total $ none
Payable none installments of $ none $ none from this loan is described in (6D) above.

SERVICE CONTRACT (Optional) You request a service contract with the following company for the term indicated. Cost is shown in item (1F) above.
Company BigManufacturer AllProtect Term 100,000 miles or 84 Months
Buyer Joe Carbuyer (X) Joe Carbuyer

If you have a complaint regarding this sale, try to resolve it with the seller. Complaints regarding unfair or deceptive practices or methods by the seller may be referred to the city attorney, the district attorney, or the Department of Motor Vehicles, Division of Investigations and Occupational Licensing for your state. After this contract is signed, seller may not alter financing or payment terms unless you agree in writing to the change. You do not have to agree to any change, and it is an unfair or deceptive practice for the seller to make unilateral changes.

Buyer's Signature X Joe Carbuyer   X_____

The minimum public liability insurance limits provided in law must be met by everyone purchasing a vehicle. If you are uncertain whether your insurance policy will cover your newly bought vehicle in an accident, contact your insurance agent.

Warning: Your present policy may not cover collision damage or may not provide for full replacement costs for the vehicle being bought. If you do not have full insurance coverage, supplemental coverage for collision damage may be available through your insurer or through selling dealer. Unless otherwise noted, coverage you obtain through dealer protects only the dealer, usually up to amount of unpaid balance after vehicle repossession and resale. For advice on full coverage to protect you in event of loss or damage to vehicle, contact your insurer or its agent. The buyer shall sign to acknowledge that buyer understanding these public liability terms and conditions.

s/s   (X) Joe Carbuyer   X_____

NO COOL-OFF PERIOD
This state's law does not provide for a cancellation period for vehicle sales. You cannot later cancel this contract simply for change of mind, belief the vehicle costs too much, or desire to acquire a different vehicle. After you sign below, you may only cancel this contract with the seller's agreement or for a legal cause, such as fraud or misrepresentation.

Buyer acknowledges (1) before signing agreement buyer read both sides of contract and received a legible copy, completely filled-in, and that (2) buyer received a copy of all other documents buyer signed during negotiations pertaining to contract.
Buyer's Signature (X) Joe Carbuyer   **Co-Buyer's Signature** X_____
Seller BigManufacturer   Address 123 Automall Way
                              By Jan Salesmanager (Jan Salesmanager) Title Mgr.

Truth in Lending Copy
1. This document is to be provided to BUYER prior to signing 2. Both buyer and seller sign this copy after contract is signed.

"You," (the "Lessee" and "Co-Lessee," if applicable) agree to lease from Lessor the following Vehicle. If more than one Lessee executes this Lease, each Lessee will be individually liable for the entire amount owing under this Lease...

You'll see a description of the vehicle you're leasing—the year, make, model, body style, odometer reading, Vehicle Identification Number, and probably a check box noting that it's new, used, or a demo.

You'll also see a description of your trade-in vehicle, if you have one, which may include the year, make, and model; as well as a dollar-figure

Watch Out!
Those consumer protective lease disclosure laws only apply to lease deals under $25,000 (and that last longer than four months).

Sample Lease Contract.

BigMCredit

Vehicle Lease Agreement   Approval #1234567
Lease Date: 7/1/98

Lessor Name & Address	Lessee Name & Address
BigDeal BigM Motors 1234 AutoMall Way Cartown, CA 12345	Owen Forlong 123 Payment Street Cartown, CA 12345
Dealer Number: (123) 456-7890	County: Car County

Garaging Address, if different: _____

"You", (the "Lessee" and "Co-Lessee", if applicable) agree to lease from Lessor the following Vehicle. If more than one Lessee executes this Lease, each Lessee will be individually liable for the entire amount owing under this Lease. Lessor will assign this Lease and leased Vehicle to BigManufacturer Credit, a division of MegaManufacturer Credit, Inc., or its assignee (the "Holder").

Lease Vehicle Description

Year: 1998
Make: BigM
Model: BigMMobile

Gross Trade-in Allowance: $2,471.02
Amount Owed on Trade-in: $_____
Net Trade-in Allowance: $2,471.02

Payment Calculations

1. **Amount Due at Lease Signing or Delivery:**
$2,471.02

3. Other Charges (not part of monthly payment)

A. Turn-in Fee $250.00
B. _____ $_____
C. TOTAL $250.00

2. **Monthly Payments**

A. Your first monthly payment in the amount of $326.77 is due July 1, 1998,
followed by monthly payments in the amount of $326.77 due on the 1st of
every month, beginning August 1, 1998.
B. The total of your monthly payments: $11,763.72

4. **Total of Payments** (amount paid by lease end):

$14,157.97

(Section 1 plus Section 2(B) plus Section 3(C) less Section 5(A)(3) less Section 5(A)(4)

5. _____ **Amount Due at Lease Signing or Delivery Itemization**
A. Amount Due at Lease Signing or Delivery:

		B. How the Amount Due at Lease Signing or Delivery is Paid:	
1. Capitalized Cost Reduction:	$1,578.98	1. Net Trade-in Allowance:	$2,471.02
2. Taxes on Cap Cost Reduction:	$130.27	2. Rebates, Non-Cash Credits:	$none
3. First monthly payment:	$326.77	3. Cash Amount:	$none
4. Refundable Security Deposit:	$none	4. Credit Card Amount:	$none
5. Title Fees:	$none	5. TOTAL :	$2,471.02
6. Registration Fees:	$435.00		
7. License Fees:	$none		
8. Sales Tax:	$none		
9. _____: $_____			
10. _____: $_____			
11. TOTAL:	$2,471.02		

6.   **How Your Monthly Payment is Determined:**

A. Gross Capitalized Cost. Agreed Vehicle value $19,800 and any other items you pay for over the term of the lease (including fees, taxes, insurance, outstanding prior balance, service agreements etc.) $20,250

B. Capitalized Cost Reduction. The total of any cash, noncredit, rebate or net trade allowance you pay in order to reduce Gross Capitalized Cost $1,578.98

C. Adjusted Capitalized Cost. Used to calculate your Base Monthly Payment $18,671.02

D. Residual Value. Vehicle value at lease end $11,871.90

E. Depreciation and Amortized Amounts. Amount charged for value decline in vehicle during normal usage, and other items paid over term of lease $6,799.12

F. Rent Charge. Amount charged beyond amortized amounts and depreciation $4,068.20

G. Base Monthly Payment Total. Depreciation + Amortized Amounts + Rent Charge $10,867.32

H. Lease Term. Number of months of your lease   36

I. Base Monthly Payment $301.87

J. Sales Tax $24.90

K. Total Monthly Payment $326.77

Early Termination: You may face a sizable charge for ending this lease before the expiration of its term, up to several thousand dollars, depending on when the lease is terminated. The earlier the lease is ended, the greater this charge will probably be.

7. **Excessive wear** charges may apply based on standards of normal use and excess miles beyond 45,000 allowed lease term miles with maximum odometer reading of 45,002 at a charged rate of $0.12 per mile.
YES____ NO _ X ____ Mileage allowed includes 0 over the lease term purchased at $0.12 per mile, included in your payment.

8. **Lease-End Purchase Option**. You have the option to purchase this vehicle at the end of the lease term for the purchase price of $11,871.90 and a fee of none and all amounts owed under this lease, plus any official fees and taxes due in connection with purchasing the vehicle.

9. **Other Important Terms**. See the front and back of this lease for additional information on early termination, your options in purchasing the vehicle, maintenance responsibilities, warranties, insurance, security interests if applicable, and late and default charges.

Lease contracts are often particularly complex, and every one is unique.

calculation of your net trade-in allowance (the gross trade-in allowance—how much they offer for your used car—less any amount you owe on the trade-in).

The calculations section can tell you some hard numbers you need to know. These may include the following, as shown in the figure on the next page.

1. The amount due at lease signing or delivery

2. Monthly payment details, including the amount of each, due dates, and the total of your monthly

payments (the date and amount of your first
payment due may also be noted here)

3. Other charges that can apply, such as a disposi-
    tion fee (here described as a "turn-in fee"), if
    you don't opt to buy the car at the end of the
    lease

4. Total payments—the amount you will pay by the
    end of the lease)

Basic Lease
Calculations
Section (Sample
Lease Document).

Payment Calculations	
1. **Amount Due** at Lease Signing or Delivery: $2,471.02	3. **Other Charges** (not part of monthly payment) A. Turn-in Fee $250.00 B. _____ $_____ C. TOTAL $250.00
2. **Monthly Payments** A. Your first monthly payment in the amount of $326.77 is due July 1, 1998, followed by monthly payments in the amount of $326.77 due on the 1st of every month, beginning August 1, 1998. B. The total of your monthly payments: $11,763.72	4. **Total of Payments** (amount paid by lease end): $14,157.97 (Section 1 plus Section 2(B) plus Section 3(C) less Section 5(A)(3) less Section 5(A)(4)

What does that initial "amount due at lease signing or delivery" entail? Yours may include items like
those shown in the figure on the next page.

Here, the capitalized cost reduction is listed,
along with any taxes that may be due on it (many
states make you pay tax on the "down payment" portion of a lease, remember, as well as the monthly payments—and some states tax the entire price of the
vehicle as if it were being sold, not just the depreciation aspect). Your first monthly payment is usually
due now, along with any security deposit, title fees,
registration fees, and license fees.

The second portion of the itemization you may
see shows how the amount that's due now is going to
be paid—that's where any rebates may appear, along
with the amount of any cash down payment you

Bright Idea
Consider making
your cash down
payment with a
credit card for
which you earn
frequent flyer
miles, cash back,
or other bene-
fits—just remem-
ber to make sure
that your limit's
high enough and
that you pay it
off by the next
due date!

2.	Amount Due at Lease Signing or Delivery Itemization	
A. Amount Due at Lease Signing or Delivery:		**B. How the Amount Due at Lease Signing or Delivery is Paid:**
1. Capitalized Cost Reduction:	$1,578.98	
2. Taxes on Cap Cost Reduction:	$130.27	1. Net Trade-in Allowance: $2,471.02
3. First monthly payment:	$326.77	2. Rebates, Non-Cash Credits: $none
4. Refundable Security Deposit::	$none	3. Cash Amount: $none
5. Title Fees:	$none	4. Credit Card Amount: $none
6. Registration Fees:	$435.00	5. TOTAL : $2,471.02
7. License Fees:	$none	
8. Sales Tax:	$none	
9. _____ :	$_____	
10. _____ :	$_____	
11. **TOTAL:**	$2,471.02	

Itemization of Amount Due at Lease Signing or Delivery (Sample Lease Document).

make (even by credit card!), and your net trade-in allowance.

How is your monthly payment determined? A sample lease section devoted to that topic is shown in the figure on the following page.

In this example, the capital cost reduction (your up-front payment), is subtracted from the gross capitalized cost to arrive at the adjusted (or "net") capitalized cost. It is from this figure that your monthly payment cost is derived.

The expected residual value of the vehicle at the time you'll be returning it appears next, and is subtracted from the adjusted capitalized cost to arrive at a figure representing the car's depreciation and "amortized amounts," which are those things other than the car itself that you've chosen to pay for over the long haul rather than at the initiation of the lease.

From there, we go to your rent charge, the monthly financing expense you have for the privilege of driving the vehicle. It is added to the "depreciation and any amortized amounts" section to arrive at your total base monthly payments. Divide that by the number of months in your lease and voilà! You've got your base monthly payment. With us so far?

Timesaver
Refer to Part V of this book for details of leasing terms such as "rent charge" and "capital cost reduction."

How Your
Monthly Payment
is Determined
(Sample Lease
Document).

6.	*How Your Monthly Payment is Determined:*	
A. Gross Capitalized Cost. Agreed Vehicle value $19,800 and any other items you pay for over the term of the lease (including fees, taxes, insurance, outstanding prior balance, service agreements etc.)		$20,250
B. Capitalized Cost Reduction. The total of any cash, noncash credit, rebate or net trade allowance you pay in order to reduce Gross Capitalized Cost		$1,578.98
C. Adjusted Capitalized Cost. Used to calculate your Base Monthly Payment		$18,671.02
D. Residual Value. Vehicle value at lease end		$11,871.90
E. Depreciation and Amortized Amounts. Amount charged for value decline in vehicle during normal usage, and other items paid over term of lease		$6,799.12
F. Rent Charge. Amount charged beyond amortized amounts and depreciation		$4,068.20
G. Base Monthly Payment Total. Depreciation + Amortized Amounts + Rent Charge		$10,867.32
H. Lease Term. Number of months of your lease		36
I. Base Monthly Payment		$301.87
J. Sales Tax		$24.90
K. **Total Monthly Payment**		$326.77

Now that a base monthly payment has finally been deduced, it gets slapped on your state sales tax percentage to come out as the "total monthly payment."

Following all this in our example are some "bad news" specifics—what happens if you don't toe the line. You may see a warning about early termination penalties that could cost you thousands. The excessive wear and use clause says that you could be charged for returning the car in iffy shape. It's packaged with the excessive mileage clause, which notes the charge for extra miles that you drive over [whatever the entire term of the lease allows] at a rate of [whatever number of cents] per mile. If you've opted for extra miles at a lower additional cost, that may appear here.

If you have the option to purchase the vehicle at the end of the lease, that will be stated, along with the price and any likely purchase option fees (these are negotiable, of course).

Your lease may also contain an itemization of gross capitalized cost and details of service contract arrangements. Expect plenty of fine print on the back of your lease, in less friendly, simple language.

Contract concepts that you need to become familiar with when leasing your vehicle include:

Unofficially...
A consumer organization surveyed member agencies on the single most needed important new consumer protection. Among the suggestions was to allow early termination of auto leases for members of the military who are relocated or civilians going out of state for employment reasons.

- **Required insurance coverages,** which mandate that you have full coverage and a reasonable deductible. You might not need this much insurance when buying rather than leasing (but it may not be a bad idea anyway). Gap insurance will likely also either be mandated by the lease or included within it (without you having to pay an outside insurer). This covers the difference between what you've paid on the lease and what the car's worth (after your insurance company makes its payment) if the car is totaled or stolen.

- **Excessive wear and tear clauses,** saying essentially that you have to be kind to the car and keep it well-maintained so that someone else will want to buy it when you return it at lease end. Or you'll owe a big penalty.

- **Excessive mileage.** You're given an allotted number of miles that you can drive during the term of your lease, usually 10,000–15,000 annually. Extra miles will cost you, and the excessive mileage language spells out how much.

- **Early-termination penalties,** which make it extremely prohibitive to do anything but turn in your car when you agree to, and not before. In Chapter 10, we discussed why this penalty exists (primarily because of the huge initial drop in the value of a car during the first year of its life). You're paying equal installments, remember, so that initial cost is spread out over the life of the lease. Early-termination penalties usually require you to pay not only the penalty fee, but also any remaining depreciation on the car and a disposition fee of a few hundred dollars (to cover the cost of reselling the car). The

Moneysaver
You can often prepay for mileage you expect to use at a much lower per-mile rate, perhaps 8 cents per mile instead of 15, for instance.

wholesale value of the car at the time you make early termination is factored in; it's called the car's "realized value."

■ **Option to buy:** This part of a lease states how much you can expect to pay for a vehicle at the end of your lease if you're given the option to buy it. If the vehicle is really resellable for more than the residual listed in your lease, you should consider buying and reselling it for a profit.

Even with the new lease disclosure laws, there's a lot about a lease you won't necessarily find printed on it— sometimes including the rebates you got, the money factor used, or even capital cost.

Your "first payment" on a lease car is typically due when you sign the lease, and successive payments are due on the first of the month thereafter. You'll also probably be asked to pay a security deposit of about the same amount as a monthly payment; your lease paperwork should say that you'll get the money back at the end of the lease term, unless fees (such as excessive wear fees) are charged against it.

Similar to getting a mortgage on your home, you'll be asked to pay "points" on an auto lease, except that they're called "acquisition fees." That's the charge the leasing company applies to cover its costs of starting up the lease.

Your car title

The title is the state document of legal vehicle ownership. When you pay cash for a car, the title of the vehicle should be transferred to you—and procedures for doing so are usually listed on the title itself. A title will typically contain the kind of information shown in the figure on the following page.

STATE NAME
CERTIFICATE OF TITLE
(MOCKUP ONLY - NOT A REAL TITLE)

12345678901

AUTOMOBILE
VEHICLE ID NUMBER   YR / MODEL / MAKE   PLATE NUMBER
1ABCD23E4CT567890   93 BIGM   123456
BODY TYPE MODEL   AX   UNLADEN WEIGHT   FUEL
UT   G
TRANSFER DATE   FEES PAID   REGISTRATION EXP.   ISSUE DATE
                   $371   10/8/98   11/3/97
YR FIRST SOLD / CLASS / YR   MO   EQUIPMT/TRUST NO.
                          BK 93   BY
MOTORCYCLE ENGINE NO.   ODOMETER DATE   ODOMETER READING
                                  10/07/1997   51324 MI
                                  ACTUAL MILEAGE

REGISTERED OWNER(S)
TOM CAROWNER
1234 TOM'S DRIVE
CARCITY, STATE 12345

I certify under penalty of perjury under the laws of This State, that the signature(s) below releases interest in the vehicle.

1a._____   X_____
      DATE   SIGNATURE OF REGISTERED OWNER
1a._____   X_____
      DATE   SIGNATURE OF REGISTERED OWNER

Federal and State law requires you state mileage upon transfer of ownership. Failure to complete or providing a false statement may result in fines and/or imprisonment.
Odeometer now reads _____ miles and to the best of my knowledge reflects the actual mileage unless one of the following statements is checked.
WARNING: ___ Odometer reading not actual mileage
                ___ Mileage exceeds odometer's mechanical limits
I certify under penalty of perjury under the laws of This State the foregoing is true and correct.

DATE	TRANSFEROR/SELLER SIGNATURE(S)	DATE	TRANSFEREE/BUYER SIGNATURE(S)
	X		**X**
PRINTED NAME OF AGENT SIGNING FOR A COMPANY		PRINTED NAME OF AGENT SIGNING FOR A COMPANY	

IMPORTANT
READ CAREFULLY
Any change of Lienholder (security interest holder) must be reported to the Department of Motor Vehicles within 10 days.
LIENHOLDER(S)

                                        2. X_____
                                        Signature releases interest in vehicle.
                                        Date of release_____

                                                          TS 12345678

                     123456

Typical Title Information.

In simple person-to-person vehicle sales, a car's title may contain the basics of the transaction, as if it were an invoice. Protect yourself by insisting that a formal bill of sale be written up. (An example is shown in Chapter 13.)

When you trade in your old car, you transfer title to the dealership by signing the title over. Always check your title and related state papers for specific procedures your state may require that you follow, whether buying, selling, or leasing.

When you finance a vehicle and thus don't own it yet (or won't own it—as in leasing), the bank or entity that really bought the vehicle (who you are paying off) holds the title. After your last payment is made, the title can be yours.

Among the items that a title will list are:

- Vehicle indentification number (VIN)
- Name and address of the registered owner
- Odometer reading and date
- Statement of the amount of fees paid
- Plate number
- Expiration date of registration
- Year and make of vehicle
- Date of registration issue
- Number identifying the title document
- Procedures for transfer of title

Insurance

During the few days prior to your purchase, when you're narrowing in on the vehicle you want, you should call your insurance company as well as others to shop for quotes on the type of vehicle you want. Ask them about specific procedures for getting insurance on your new car and removing insurance from your trade-in. You need to have the appropriate insurance in order before you drive your new car, but your full coverage policy may give you some time to put in the paperwork on the switch.

If you intend to take care of insurance matters during the same day you purchase your car, make your dealership visit during the morning on a day when your insurance agent is open and can handle the matter, or at least take last-minute phone calls. (See Chapter 18 for more about insurance coverages.)

Warranty

If you buy a new car, look for papers detailing what's covered under the manufacturer's warranty and

Watch Out!
Insurance on a new vehicle that's worth more money can be substantially higher than on your old car. Make sure you've checked insurance quotes and factored that in to your budget before you make a deal.

how long the warranty will be in effect. Some manufacturers offer extended warranties for an additional price.

The length of a new car warranty varies. Some manufacturers provide coverage for four years/ 50,000 miles (or even longer, particularly in the luxury car sector); others may offer a warranty of only two years/24,000 miles.

If you're buying used, you may also be able to get a manufacturer's warranty if going through a dealer, or a third-party warranty if going through a used car lot or even a private party. (Check Chapter 17 for details of which "extra" warranties you should consider, and when.)

Financing

Although your vehicle purchase order will typically contain some financing details, expect a large sheet or even a packet of paperwork pertaining just to your financing.

If you're going through a dealer for financing, everything can probably be handled there, on the spot. If you're getting outside financing, through your bank, for example, you may need a post-dealership visit trip to sign the appropriate paperwork. The figure on the following page is a sample car loan form a bank might give you—but each financing entity has its own procedures and blanks to fill in—observe yours closely.

Along with appropriate names, addresses, and the date, details may include:

- The annual percentage rate you will pay
- The total sum of the loan
- The amount of each payment
- When payments, including the first one, are due

Sample Bank Loan Agreement.

The Bank

Name and Address of Borrower(s)	Officer Initials	Loan No.	Date
John Carshopper 123 ABC St. Carcity STATE 12345			7/1/98

PROMISSORY NOTE, DISCLOSURE STATEMENT AND SECURITY AGREEMENT

In this Promissory Note, Disclosure Statement and Security Agreement the words Borrower, you, your and yours mean each and every person signing this document. The words Bank, We, Us, Our and Ours refer to The Bank.
(Office)___Carcity___.
For value received, the undersigned Borrower, if more than one jointly and severally promise to pay to the order of The Bank at its office at ___Carcity_____ the sum of _Five Thousand Eight Hundred Thirty Three and 80/100_____ Dollars ($ _5,833.80_____) payable according to the payment schedule and subject to terms and conditions set forth in this document.

ANNUAL PERCENTAGE RATE	FINANCE CHARGE	FINANCED AMOUNT	PAYMENTS TOTAL
13.085%	$1,049.31	$4,784.49	$5,833.80

Your payment schedule:

Number of Payments	Amount of Payments	Due Dates
36	$162.05	monthly beginning 7/1/98

INSURANCE: Credit life insurance and credit disability insurance is not required to obtain credit and won't be provided unless you sign and agree to the terms. By signing this document you acknowledge you have the option of assigning any other policies you own or may procure for the purpose of covering this loan.

Type	Premium	Signature
Credit / Single / Life / Joint	N/A	I want credit life insurance_____
Credit Life & Disability Insurance	N/A	I want credit life and disability insurance_____

Security: You're giving a security interest in:
_x_ Goods purchased
___ Funds on deposit with us
___ Your principal place of residence
_x_ Other _1993 Ford Escort_____
___ This is an unsecured loan
Filing Fee $ _____
Late Charge: If required payment is not made within 10 days of the due date, the charge will be 5% of the late payment.
Prepayment: If you pay off your loan before it is due you may receive a refund of part of the finance charge.
SECURITY: Borrower grants The Bank a security interest in the property described below, and any proceeds coming into your possession by virtue of insurance. Such property is subject to all terms, provisions and conditions set forth on the reverse side. Borrower warrants that the property is owned by them and is free of all other liens and security interests except_____
Property (collateral): _____ 1993 Ford Escort #1ABCD23D4ST567890

Itemization of amount financed (TOTAL FINANCED$ 4,784.49)

$ 4,777.29	Amount given to borrower directly	$	Amount paid on your account
Amounts paid on your behalf:			
$ 7.20	State documentary stamps	$	State Intangible Tax	$	Filing and recording fees
$	Insurers	$	Credit Bureaus	$	Prepaid Finance Charge

The finance charge is interest calculated over the term of the loan at the rate of _12.5%_ per annum plus a fee of _$50.00_ as reimbursement for costs of loan origination.

Borrowers make the agreements set forth in all sections of this document and acknowledge they received a fully completed copy prior to signing.

EXECUTED under seal on the date first written above

_____ Witness   _____Borrower's Signature (SEAL)
_____ Witness   _____Borrower's Signature (SEAL)

- The number of payments you'll make
- Optional insurance you can buy or decline
- The security being used to back up the loan—a typical loan uses your vehicle as collateral
- Whether funds on deposit with the institution may also be used to back up the loan
- Filing and other loan-origination fees
- State documentary stamp charges and any taxes
- The amount of any charges for late payments, and when they become effective
- Details about your prepayment options

- The way your interest is calculated—a simple interest loan, for instance, or a Rule of 78 loan

- A basic description of the vehicle being financed and the VIN number

- A place for signatures and notarization

- The specific terms of the loan (check for fine print on the back)

Walking through terminology and fine print

It's important that you spend time reading everything in your packet of deal papers, as laborious as that can be. What is stated on the front may look simple (or not!), but important terms relating to those calculations and statements are often on the flip side—a huge list of "what ifs" and "what you must dos."

You can ask the sales manager for interpretations of specific clauses you aren't sure about, but don't rely on his verbal answers as the ultimate truth. They may be correct, but it's an unknown whether the sales manager himself is thoroughly familiar with every nook and cranny of legal matters pertaining to the deal. Take some time to reason the fine print out yourself. If you feel you must rely on an interpretation by the sales manager, ask him to write up and sign a statement describing the interpretation as an addendum to the deal agreement.

Important points to clarify and questions to ask before you sign the papers vary, according to the situation. Make your own list and don't forget to include:

1. Are the prices exactly what you agreed to— including the value allowed for your trade-in?

Moneysaver
Be particularly careful of the way your interest is computed... with a Rule of 78 financing arrangement, you wind up paying off more of the interest before you get to paying off the bulk of the principal. (Review Chapter 7 for more details on financing).

Are the numbers "solid," with no language indicating that they could vary once you've signed the papers?

2. Is the vehicle you want the same vehicle you're signing a bill of sale for? Very carefully, go over everything: the engine size, body style, color, and options included. Again, make sure that all options and specifics of the vehicle are listed within signed paperwork—right on the purchase order. Check the VIN number of the actual car against the VIN number listed on your paperwork, and do a visual inspection to make sure that vehicle really is equipped with everything the seller says it has.

3. Make sure that any rebates or discounts appear on the paperwork, and that there's no misleading figuring, indicating that you may owe more than already discussed as a cash down payment.

4. Ensure that anything the salesman or sales manager promised appears clearly within any paperwork that must be signed by a dealership representative.

5. Check for double-charging, particularly when you're leasing. Is the cost of a warranty really figured into the capitalized cost, and then tacked on at the end as well? Use that calculator.

6. When will the vehicle be delivered? Make sure the date is spelled out in your contract as well.

Before closing the deal

By now, you've gone over every document, preferably in private with an astute companion, and you're getting ready to sign on the dotted line. You jotted down any questions you have and kept your calculator handy for sorting out some points. What to do?

66
With every one of my friends, I have to go to the dealership with them—everyone's scared!
—Jonathan, who works in the auto leasing industry
99

Recheck everything! This transaction is a landmark one in your financial life.

Recheck the checklist

Use Checklist 15.2 to remind you of some of the territory you need to cover. Every deal is different—it's up to you to cover everything—and, by the way, it involves a walk back out to your new vehicle too.

CHECKLIST 15.2   BEFORE YOU SIGN...

Checking the Car

_____ 1. Does the VIN number listed match the VIN number on the actual car?

_____ 2. Do you see verification in the VIN or elsewhere on the vehicle (check the driver's side door) that the car is the same year stated on your contract papers?

_____ 3. What does the odometer read? Is it the same mileage as that listed in your contract?

_____ 4. If you're leasing, does the contract description of the miles allowed take into account the actual odometer reading?

_____ 5. Does the car have all the options listed? What about floor mats? Check the owner's manual, dealer brochures for new cars, and your options itemization to ensure that you have everything!

_____ 6. Are you being given all keys to the vehicle (two sets if it's a new one)?

_____ 7. Is there an owner's manual and are there maintenance records?

_____ 8. Does the amount of gasoline in the tank compare to what's listed on the sales invoice?

Checking Your Trade-In

_____ 9. What about the odometer reading on your trade-in—has it been correctly entered in the paperwork?

_____ 10. Has the VIN number of your trade-in been correctly entered on paperwork?

_____ 11. Did you get all of your possessions out of your trade-in?! What about the license tags?

Checking the Paperwork

_____ 12. Is every blank accounted for and filled in?

_____ 13. Are numbers identical on all pieces of paperwork (VIN numbers on finance contracts and purchase agreements, mileage, pricing, etc.)

_____ 14. Are the finance charges and other charges exactly what you agreed to? Does the language indicate that you have qualified for those rates (it doesn't say "pending qualification" or something similar)?

_____ 15. Is the type of financing what you agreed to (simple interest, Rule of 78 interest, etc.)? Is the rate what you agreed to?

_____ 16. Are there fees that you didn't agree to included in the documents?

_____ 17. Check the math. Is it correct? Is any undisclosed amount "hidden" in the numbers?

_____ 18. When leasing, are Consumer Leasing Act disclosures made?

_____ 19. Review any warranty agreements. Are they signed by a representative of the dealership?

_____ 20. Are any exceptions or modifications that you or anyone at the dealership verbally agreed to spelled out thoroughly on paper, and signed?

_____ 21. What about insurance? Make arrangements for it before taking delivery of the car.

_____ 22. Has a dealership representative arranged for registration and license tags? Do you see the documents—what about a temporary tag in the window?

_____ 23. What about any state-required safety or smog inspections, and their certification papers?

_____ 24. Before you sign, have you read all the fine print on the back of every form?

_____ 25. Is there clear agreement about when you will take delivery of the car?

_____ 26. Has the dealership representative signed wherever appropriate on all papers?

_____ 27. Do you have copies of all the paperwork?

When to proceed with caution (or walk away)

Our checklist assumes that you're proceeding with the deal right through leaving your John Hancock on the dealer documents, handing over (probably) a check, and turning in your old car.

But, if at the signing stage of the game something seems the slightest bit fishy, stop. No matter how many annoyed looks you get from the salesman, if something isn't exactly as you discussed or if there's something you don't fully understand, refuse to go further with the paperwork until you get a chance privately to sort it out.

And then go home, in your trade-in. Fifteen minutes of being made to feel like the most unreasonable consumer on the planet beats the socks off of a misstep involving half your annual salary and a multi-year payment commitment with a piece of machinery that you'll be getting very intimate with.

Common pitfalls at the end-stage of the car-deal process usually result from overlooking something you should be paying attention to. Run through the math. Don't give up trying to negotiate the cost of extras that may be slapped on at the last moment. Make sure that the vehicle you're getting has everything that you were told it would have.

Your rights under the law

What if you're afraid that you've just scorched your savings? Isn't there some sort of cooling-off period? What if your lips curl with that puckering feeling and you start to smell citrus? You do have post-purchase rights. (Chapter 17 outlines lemon laws.)

But if something is amiss immediately after the sale, don't waste any time sorting it out—seconds can matter. (Read over the procedures outlined in Chapter 16 about taking delivery.)

Moneysaver
When leasing, don't forget to negotiate the end-of-lease aspects (better now than later!), such as insisting on a higher stated residual value, if appropriate, which can lower your monthly payments. Check your research materials for what your options might be.

Examine the car thoroughly, bit by bit, and insist on a final test-drive. If anything at all is amiss, don't accept delivery—tell the dealer representative that the problems must be remedied before you'll sign for delivery of the vehicle. Don't rely on a dealer's word that the problem can and will be fixed after you've taken delivery. He might back up his word, but why take chances?

What happens next?

Once you sign, they sign, and you slump back in the sales manager's customer chair, he or the salesman should advise you about procedures for taking the car home. This can be an occasion for a little proud grandstanding on their part because they want you to leave as a happy customer (and not come back with chagrin or problems later).

Delivery may be that day or the next day. If you've factory ordered the car, its delivery date should be clearly stated in your paperwork, although we advise only putting a refundable deposit down; don't finish the full sale process until you see the car in the "flesh." If you need to leave a refundable deposit for a vehicle, by the way, make sure "refundable" is clearly noted on the check. Never make a deposit for a substantial amount—just a bit to show good faith, and get a clearly written (and signed) note from the dealer stating what the deposit is for and that it's fully refundable, immediately upon your demand, prior to the signing of all sale documents. (The next chapter discusses taking delivery of your new car.)

You will leave the dealership with a package of papers that can include those in Checklist 15.3.

CHECKLIST 15.3   DO YOU HAVE ALL OF THE NECESSARY COPIES?

____ 1. Bill of sale or lease agreement

____ 2. Financing Agreement

____ 3. Temporary tags (or your own from the trade-in) and registration

____ 4. Warranty

____ 5. Receipts for money exchanged

____ 6. Photocopies of your checks (that you've requested)

____ 7. Any other documents you signed or supporting paperwork

Although a car deal can often be handled quickly, plan to do it early in the day when possible, and when you won't be rushed to be somewhere else at a given time.

Just the facts

■ Run through all the math yourself before you sign any papers, and make sure that the figures are exactly what you previously agreed upon.

■ Some charges may mysteriously appear for the first time in the final papers you're signing. Don't be afraid to argue a dealer out of incidentals that are designed to jack up the cost of your car; ask him to retype the agreement, if necessary.

■ Visually check the car's VIN number and stated options, etc., against the paperwork prior to signing.

■ Bring a calculator, a notepad, and an astute companion (among other things) with you at deal time.

GET THE SCOOP ON...
Why your car purchase or lease isn't done yet •
What to do before you sign for vehicle delivery
• Handling taxes, tags, and registration • What
to expect from here with a good dealership

Taking Delivery and Beyond

This chapter opens with a worrisome warning. Some in-the-know car industry veterans recommend not taking delivery of your new car until at least a day—or longer—after you've signed the paperwork. Sure, it's helpful to take a reflective look at the documents in private, before you've put mile one on that car. But what could happen?

If the rate of credit you were quoted wasn't stated as a rate you "qualified for," a loophole may exist that can set your loan or lease at a much higher figure and dramatically complicate your situation once you've already taken the car home, and perhaps left your trade-in at the dealer.

Do not take a car away from a dealership (or anywhere else) with anything on your paperwork that contains the phrase "subject to loan approval." That means the deal isn't done, and you could be entangled in unfortunate results. Make sure that you actually have the appropriate financing approval, and that you've checked over your paperwork thoroughly, word by word, before you drive off in that car. Don't feel silly about being meticulous.

Now, on with things. In this chapter, we'll of course talk about how and when you will be taking delivery of your new set of wheels (or that used set of wheels that's about to become your pride and joy), and what you should expect. And we'll also deal a bit with what to do if it wasn't what you expected...as well as how manufacturers keep tabs on dealers.

Following up: Getting tags, registration, insurance

When you're buying or leasing a car from a dealership, all that effort you spent negotiating should pay off a bit in the ease with which tags and other post-sale matters are handled.

Tags and registration

Moneysaver
You may be able
to use your cur-
rent vehicle's
tags on your new
car—check with
the dealer or
your state.

Although procedures vary by state (check your DMV for specifics), often at sale time you will pay the nominal tag fee and be given a temporary tag on the spot. The dealer may have the responsibility of sending in the appropriate paperwork; within a few weeks, the state DMV sends you permanent plates.

When you're not going through a dealer that is set up to thoroughly handle post-sale matters, we can't emphasize enough the need to check your state's requirements. In California, for instance, a section of the law states that you must notify the DMV (within five calendar days) when you sell or transfer your vehicle. A form called the Notice of Release of Liability is used to notify the DMV that the vehicle has been sold or transferred. Without it, you're not adequately protected from civil or criminal actions involving the vehicle after the sale date.

You may need the following to register a used vehicle with your state:

1. Surrender of the old title, which shows the assignment to you as the purchaser and the release of all liens (if applicable)

2. Bill of sale

3. Current insurance card

4. Safety or smog certification (varies by state)

5. Odometer statement (may be noted on title or bill of sale)

6. Sales tax information

7. Money for sales tax and registration fees

As noted, along with getting tags and registration sorted out for your vehicle, you may be required to have certification showing that the vehicle has passed state safety or smog inspection. With a new car, this may be handled by the dealer. On a used car, check for stickers indicating when the vehicle last went through inspection and when the next one is due. Also ask the seller for back-up paperwork relating to the inspection.

Taxes

You may already have paid state sales tax on your vehicle purchase if buying through a dealer (check your paperwork). If you bought a used car from a private party, sales tax on your purchase of a used vehicle might be payable at the time you get your registration for the vehicle, so be prepared—and check with the state to make sure of procedures.

Watch Out!
Some states have impact fees running in the hundreds of dollars for cars that are bought out-of-state. Think twice and double-check before buying outside state borders.

Timesaver
If you're phone-phobic because of hold times at the DMV, check your state's Web site for information instead—you may even be able to download forms or complete them online. Use the format of www. YOURSTATE ABBREVIATION.gov (for instance, Connecticut is www.ct.gov). Then access the state's motor vehicle department from there.

You also may have state personal property taxes to consider—check your previous vehicle's property tax notices to ensure that you're current on those taxes before you try to get registration for your new set of wheels.

Ensuring happy delivery... it's a car!

All of your hard work and careful consumerism leads to one thing... getting into the driver's seat of your new set of wheels, knowing it's finally yours.

Technically, it's probably still the bank's, or the lease company's, but, resume the music—we won't let that bother us now. It may seem that your whole life is taking on a new, clean-lined, shiny gloss.

But before you let your head rise too far into the clouds, put your feet on the ground and make sure that this moment goes right, too.

A customer-focused dealership does everything by the book to welcome you as a customer. Haggling is over, and they want a continued relationship with you on good terms. They'd like to see you again sometime down the road. You bought (or leased) once, so maybe they can retain your business.

In many cases, delivery of your vehicle can be arranged for the same afternoon you finalize the paperwork. You may drive the vehicle home yourself (do so only if the deal paperwork is clearly wrapped up, and you are in the clear regarding insurance and other matters). Otherwise, arrangements may be made for a dealer representative to deliver the car to you the same or the next day. If you've factory ordered, the dealership has already advised you how long it will be until your car arrives, and how it's going to be delivered. Try to avoid charges for this service—and definitely don't accept any after the deal paperwork has gone through.

What are trouble signs? An unscrupulous dealer can deliver a car to you that's not what you agreed to buy—the same in every way, perhaps, but without the options you understood you would get. That's why it's important to make sure that every option is clearly itemized on the purchase order itself. Otherwise, you run the risk of being told a price you paid (not full sticker, likely) didn't include those options. It's rotten, but it happens.

When you do take delivery of the car, wherever that may be, you are asked to sign a document "accepting delivery." This is a key final paper in the sales process, and you shouldn't proceed unless you're sure that everything's in order—you don't have to. If the car doesn't have something it's supposed to or isn't running properly, don't sign—call the dealer and demand to have the situation remedied. If he won't, tell him you want to cancel the deal for nonperformance.

Some of the things you should review before accepting delivery of your vehicle include those in Checklist 16.1.

CHECKLIST 16.1 BEFORE YOU ACCEPT DELIVERY...

____ 1. Is the VIN and all other information on the delivery paperwork identical to what's on the car and on your deal papers?

____ 2. Is the mileage consistent with your paperwork?

____ 3. Is the car clean and with all necessary accessories assembled and installed? Is there a spare tire, jack, etc.?

____ 4. Does the car have all the options and the correct size engine you made the deal for?

____ 5. Check the delivery papers for any agreement to charges—don't go for anything except "I accept delivery of this vehicle."

Watch Out!
Don't forget about your old tags or toss them—contact your state Department of Motor Vehicles about proper procedures for returning the license plates to them.

You can use test-drive checklists, found earlier in this book, for the most thorough delivery review.

____ 6. Sit in the driver's seat. Does everything work (switches, knobs, headlamps, radio, etc.)?

____ 7. Is the owner's manual in the glove box?

____ 8. Are you being supplied with two sets of keys (and all the keys the car needs—doors, ignition, gas cap, trunk, any security devices)?

____ 9. Insist on a short test-drive before signing. Does the car run well?

____ 10. Are temporary tags and registration with the vehicle? How about paper for state inspections, as needed?

Dealing with buyer's remorse

About a month into your new wheels, the time comes for your next payment and you begin to realize the depth of your financing commitment for the privilege of having that automobile in your driveway. Your insurance bill might arrive around the same time, with a substantially larger payment due than was on your old car.

Now, if everything's wonderful with your new car, the pride of ownership may help allay the write-a-big-check discomfort. But what can you do about serious buyer's remorse? There's probably not much, unfortunately, outside of the options outlined in the next chapter's section on legal issues.

Selling a new car soon after you've bought or leased it will set you back, with huge amounts of depreciation and other charges to cover. Contact the dealer if you seriously want out. Hope for a customer-focused creative solution, but don't expect one. If you bought a used car, selling isn't such a horrible proposition. If you paid retail for the vehicle, you may lose some of the premium above wholesale when selling it yourself, but perhaps not. Whatever your state sales tax percentage is can be a guide to your expense in getting rid of the vehicle—if it's 6% and you bought a $20,000 car, that's $1,200.

Be advised, too, that if you got a Rule of 78 loan, most commonly a dealer entity, paying off the loan early won't necessarily save you much because of the way interest is computed. Weigh all the factors before you act—including the plus side of selling… if you have a simple interest loan, selling your used vehicle might be "worth" the sales tax hit to you, given what you might save in financing costs or insurance premiums.

Customer satisfaction

How happy were you with the way the dealer treated you? Did you get a follow-up phone call from the salesman after delivery, just to make sure that everything was in order?

Manufacturers have an obvious interest in knowing how their affiliated dealerships treat customers, and how they are evaluated with followup questionnaires. Why are we telling you about this now? Because if you bought a new car from a dealership, you may get evaluation forms from the manufacturer in the mail periodically during your first two years of ownership.

The questionnaires rank things like how well the sales and managerial staff treated you, how much they knew about the product line, and how well the staff answered your vehicle questions. You'll be asked for general comments about service, the dealership's appearance, and the condition of the vehicle when you got it.

If you got great service, say so. If you got rotten service, say so. And while you're at it, for particularly stunning examples in either category, a letter to

> **66**
> Honest disagreement is often a good sign of progress.
> —Mahatma Gandhi
> **99**

the dealership and your local Better Business
Bureau might be a nice idea.

Just the facts

- Ensure that everything about your new car is
  exactly as your deal described it before signing
  to accept delivery.

- Check with your state's motor vehicle department about tag and registration procedures,
  taxes, and returning your old tags.

- Take time to respond to a manufacturer's survey
  about a dealership; if the service was wonderful
  or terrible, send a note to your local Better
  Business Bureau.

After the Sale

GET THE SCOOP ON...
What warranties cover and how long they last ▪
What used car warranties are all about ▪ How to
handle scheduled maintenance—and when
you have to ▪ How to know if you're driving an
official lemon, and what to do

PART VIII

Warranties, Repairs, and Lemon Laws

Chapter 17

Congratulations! You've survived your car deal. Now it's just you, that shiny hood, cozy seat, lots of horses, and the open road. Well, that and a lot of papers stuffed in your glove box or in your file box at home, one of which may be a warranty.

If you bought a new or late model used car, in the coming months and years you'll be checking all that paperwork for information on what scheduled maintenance is covered by your agreement—when is that thing supposed to get its first tune-up? What about an oil change? And should anything go wrong, it's back to the warranty papers to discern what's covered.

If this happens a lot, you may start to worry that not only did you get a bad deal, you got a lemon. So what do you do in that case, besides hang your head and cry? In this chapter, we'll tell you what lemon laws are all about, describe some of your other car-related rights, and of course we'll get into that warranty/maintenance/repair arena so you'll know where you stand. Hopefully though, everything will go just fine with your new purchase (or lease), and your car will get no closer to lemonhood than via the air-freshener scent at the car wash.

Warranties

Although you pay a premium for buying a car new, it's probably a welcome relief to think that you may be freed from most major repair responsibilities for a couple or even a few years. Not only do new car parts have less wear, they're usually warranty-protected.

What's in a warranty?

Some may be called "bumper to bumper" warranties when they include a number of major systems—but they still may be "limited" warranties in effect—you won't know for certain until you've examined the entire warranty agreement. General provisions you may find in your warranty include those in Table 17.1.

TABLE 17.1   WARRANTY CATEGORIES

Basic Coverage	Other than normal wear and maintenance items, basic coverage can include all major systems and some extras.
Power train	Your car's engine, transmission, and drive axle are major parts of the power train, although not all components attached to the power train may be covered. Aspects of front- and rear-wheel drive may be included; even seat belts and airbags may appear in this category.
Corrosion protection	Warranty for rust-through of sheet metal
Accessory warranty extras	May apply to manufacturer-approved
Federal emission coverage	Protects from costs related to meeting emissions requirements

State inspection	Often a guarantee by the dealer that your car will pass its first state motor vehicle inspection.

Manufacturer warranties differ from those backed entirely by the dealer, in which you may have only one choice for where to obtain service. Yet another category of warranty is the independent coverage type, sponsored by an outside firm. A dealer may try to sell you this type of warranty, too.

Warranties aren't typically 12 months/12,000 miles (whichever comes first) any more. Warranties that are double and quadruple that length are easily found among major manufacturers.

Aside from extended warranty options backed by carmakers, manufacturer warranties typically do not cost the consumer extra. They may be transferable from one owner to another during the warranty period, and you should check your paperwork regarding these provisions when buying a new car. An extended warranty may even be available from the manufacturer on a used car—in particular, so-called "certified" used cars that are typically lease returns (ask your dealer). Some mega-used car lots and rental car agencies that resell their cars offer reasonably warranties as well.

Should you buy an independent or dealer warranty? A warranty from a reputable service-oriented dealer may be helpful, but make sure that you don't duplicate the coverages contained in a manufacturer warranty, and that there's no extended manufacturer warranty available, which may be preferable. Independent warranty companies aren't necessarily unscrupulous by nature, but be careful—make sure that procedures for warranty repairs are reasonable, the company's solvent, and the systems you want

Moneysaver
Problem with a new car passing state inspection? Your dealership may be required by state law to cover all repairs necessary for it to pass.

Watch Out!
Don't assume
that a car has a
full warranty just
because of a
notation or win-
dow sticker...
ask to see the
warranty papers,
make sure they're
signed by an
appropriate rep-
resentative, and
read the fine
print about what
they actually
cover to avoid
being duped.

covered are covered before you bite. The dealer selling you a used car may have information about available warranty plans; your mechanic may know, too.
Also check the Internet for listings.

Secret warranties

A "secret warranty program" may exist, in which a
manufacturer routinely performs free repairs on
cars with persistent problems even after the official
warranty has expired, in order to avoid bad publici-
ty and a potential recall. But the consumer will have
to pursue this kind of free repair on his own. (Only
a few states make manufacturers notify car buyers
about secret warranties.)

You can spot the opportunity for repair under a
secret warranty by finding the related Technical
Service Bulletin, or "TSB." When a problem
becomes common for a certain make or model vehicle, a Technical Service Bulletin is developed by the
manufacturer. It details appropriate repair procedures.

Maintenance and repair

Taking care of your vehicle is the best way to ensure
its long life and as-low-as-feasible repair bills for you.
Your owner's manual should state recommended
maintenance intervals—and the good news is:
newer cars are being manufactured that require less
frequent maintenance.

Scheduled maintenance

When you buy a new car, certain maintenance may
be included free under your warranty at a certain
mileage or length of ownership; and when you lease,
you may be required to meet these deadlines—the
dealer wants to make sure when you return that
lease car that it's in resellable shape.

Although many new cars are designed to need little upkeep during their first years of life, scheduled maintenance—whether included free or not—can help your vehicle stay in its best shape over the long haul. Keep a car record book, and when you do have scheduled maintenance performed, save the receipts and log what the service was. At resale time, a car with complete records can sometimes command a higher price or sell more quickly than similar, less-well-documented ones.

When having maintenance tasks performed at the dealer, call a few days in advance to make an appointment, ask about loaner cars available while your car's in service, if necessary, and clarify the price or absence of price involved in the maintenance you're scheduling.

Although necessary maintenance varies by car model and manufacturer recommendation, oil changes may be recommended at least every 5,000–10,000 miles (some experts suggest every 3,000 miles) and tune-ups every 30,000 miles, although some new vehicles may go even 100,000 miles without one. It's a good idea to check your fluid levels frequently. Some auto care experts say to flush your radiator annually, and check your belts and hoses every couple of months. As for tire maintenance—a visual tread check (by you or a full-service gasoline attendant) is a good idea periodically. Windshield wipers may work best if replaced every six months. Use your judgment and follow your mechanic's advice on many of these suggestions, but don't skimp on the oil changes—follow your car manual's service recommendations, and keep a diary of when service is performed for easy reference.

Moneysaver
Ask your mechanic to check for TSBs (Technical Service Bulletins), or do so yourself at the National Highway Traffic Safety Administration's Web site at www.nhtsa.dot.gov, as well as other places on the Web.

Bright Idea
There are plenty of Web sites designed to help the consumer figure out auto repairs—have a look via your favorite search engine.

Warranty repairs

If there's something amiss with your vehicle, it may take a visit to your dealership's service department before you can determine whether the repair is actually covered under your warranty. Make sure that you don't authorize non-warranty repairs before finding out what's wrong, how much it costs, and why it's not covered under warranty.

Try these initial procedures for handling warranty repair problems:

1. First, consult your warranty booklet or owner's manual to read up on covered repairs.

2. Next, attempt to resolve the problem with the dealer from whom you got the vehicle.

If you still can't resolve the problem, you may be able to request arbitration from the manufacturer or pursue other legal avenues.

Excessive or unfixed car problems: Did you just buy a lemon?

It's a nightmare for the car buyer and even for lessees—nothing seems to work right and repair after repair is necessary, whether covered by warranty or not. How do you know if your new car is a lemon?

Although lemon laws are different from state to state, they cover cars that cannot be repaired, despite multiple attempts. A manufacturer is generally given a "reasonable" allowance of repair attempts during the warranty period, and if the vehicle still isn't fixable, the manufacturer may be required to replace it or reimburse the buyer or lessee for the purchase price, whichever the consumer prefers.

If you wonder whether you bought a lemon, read through the following section on lemon laws, and check with your state government for details of the lemon law that covers you.

Legal issues

No one wants to think of the possibility of a serious problem with a brand new vehicle or a new used one. But forewarned is forearmed, and you do have some consumer protections. That doesn't mean that something's going to happen automatically. You don't have to just stand up for your rights—often, you have to put up a fight for them.

Risks and rights

What can happen to sour a car purchase or lease? A lot. Typical complaints that may be under the jurisdiction of your state motor vehicle department include:

- Odometer fraud
- Dealer didn't transfer registration to buyer within specified time period (60 days in California, for instance)
- Dealer overcharged for DMV fees
- Counterfeit, fraudulent, or forged DMV documents
- Other fraudulent misrepresentations
- Violations of sales financing regulations
- Violations of leasing regulations

Just because you may not be happy with your new car or the terms of its purchase, doesn't mean you necessarily have recourse, as described in Table 17.2.

TABLE 17.2　REALITY CHECK

Cooling Off Periods	You don't necessarily have any mandated 72-hour cooling off period that allows you to return the car for a refund. Cooling-off periods are most often seen with other types of purchases and in special situations.
"As-Is"	It means "as is," and it's your responsibility to have a trusted mechanic go over the car so you're certain you're willing to accept it without warranty, "as is."
Canceling Sales Contracts	You may still have to make payments, as required by a contract, after you decide that you don't want the vehicle (even if you insist on returning it). Contact an attorney.
Lemon Laws	May require much more repair effort than you think before they kick in.
Warranties	They don't cover everything; you may be responsible for some repair costs.

Situations involving monetary amounts up to a few thousand dollars may be handled in small claims court (check your government pages in the phone book and call about procedures) for a nominal fee. An astute consumer may be able to handle this himself, but always consider the value of having an attorney represent you.

Many manufacturers offer buyers and lessees the chance to arbitrate disputes over new vehicle warranties, an option that can be less expensive and more informal than traditional courts. Call your state government's attorney general division for referrals to state arbitration programs or check your state's Web site.

Recalls

You may periodically see in a newspaper or magazine that a certain manufacturer is recalling one of its models for a certain year because of an unreliable part or some other problem. What exactly is a recall? How do you know if your car's being recalled?

The National Highway Transportation Safety Administration is responsible for investigating potential vehicle design and manufacturing defects. A recall occurs once a manufacturer is held responsible for making repairs that are necessary to restore vehicles to a safe working condition. Notices are sent out, but not all owners may hear about the recall or bring their vehicle in for free repair. The U.S. Department of Transportation reported that the response during a recent recall campaign only accounted for 68–72% of the vehicles affected.

Recalls may be related to the safety of the vehicle, and may be minor or major. Out of oodles of vehicle recalls, for instance, a recent one affected almost 1.75 million cars and trucks for a variety of problems, including airbag deployment irregularities and potential fire hazards.

Lemon laws and lemon aid

Lemon laws may help out the truly exasperated. They are in force in every state, but they may differ so you should research those applicable to where you live before proceeding. Table 17.3 outlines some lemon law basics.

Timesaver
Check for recall information at the National Highway Transportation Safety Administration's Web site (www.nhtsa.dot. gov). Some commercial car sites also list recall information. Or call your manufacturer.

TABLE 17.3   LEMON LAWS

Who do lemon laws apply to?	Generally speaking, those whose (typically new) cars have repeatedly been in for service, yet remain essentially unfixable or have numerous needed repairs off the bat.
What if I have a used car or I'm leasing?	Some states have lemon laws that pertain to lessees and used car buyers.
When do lemon laws kick in?	This varies state by state. In California, for example, lemon law presumption requires:
	1. The manufacturer or its agents to have made four or more attempts to repair the

Your state's lemon law is part of its civil code, by the way, in case you ever want to go look up the exact text. Reference departments of larger libraries are good places to find the code, and you may find excerpts of it at your state's Web site.

same problem (or the vehicle's been out of service more than 30 days, all totaled, while being repaired for any number of problems).

2. The four repair attempts or 30 days out of service have occurred within 12 months of the vehicle's delivery to the consumer or 12,000 miles on the odometer, whichever occurs first.

3. The problems are covered by the warranty; substantially reduce the vehicle's use, value, or safety to the consumer; and are not caused by abuse of the vehicle.

4. If required by the warranty materials or by the owner's manual, the consumer has directly notified the manufacturer about the problem(s).

What might be my next step, after efforts with the manufacturer?	An arbitration board can force the manufacturer into action—but look for a state-sponsored arbitration board over an industry-sponsored one.
Where can I find out more information?	Try your state attorney general's office or consumer affairs division.

How to proceed, and deciding whether you should

When you're evaluating whether to try to enforce your legal rights regarding a vehicle deal, consider carefully whether it's worth your time and effort (it could take a lot of both). There's also the prospect of attorney fees.

However, it's in the best interest of all consumers if consumer protection laws are supported by individuals who use them when appropriate, and wherever a large amount of money is involved. When you have so much wrapped up in a new car purchase, not doing whatever you can is ludicrous.

Your first course of action should be to fully understand what you're dealing with. Is it a lemon law situation, a simple breach of contract, a scam? Do some research—check with your local Better

Business Bureau, your state Department of Motor Vehicles, and whatever other agencies are necessary. Do a little Internet research—find out what the law really says. And where time limits (such as statutes of limitations) apply to your case, make certain that you act well within the time frame, or all could be for naught.

Often, a consumer armed with the right information and a serious but not vindictive attitude may be able to persuade a dealer (or other entity tied up in the problem) to iron things out rather than risk court. When in doubt, find a high-level manager (perhaps the dealership general manager, for instance) and seek mutual resolution.

Whenever possible, have an additional party with you as a witness to conversations. Send letters by certified mail and keep copies. Eliminate hearsay.

Your problem may require legal assistance to work out; if it does, solicit an attorney recommendation from someone you know and trust. Check your government pages in the phone book for an official legal aid society if you can't afford an attorney, and consider arbitration as one way to cut legal fees. Remember, no matter what you decide, you should stay abreast of every legal move made on your behalf, get to know your case and the law inside and out, and work closely with your representative. Just as with making a car deal, being an educated consumer in the legal realm greatly increases your chances of successful resolution.

Just the facts

- Lemon laws exist in all states, mainly cover new cars, and generally apply when a car requires a number of repairs for the same problem or a

Bright Idea
If your warranty is about to expire, consider taking your car to a good mechanic for a final check of covered systems. If a problem is beginning in one of the systems, having it fixed while still under warranty can save you big bucks.

Unofficially...
If you want something done right, do it yourself!
—age-old maxim

variety of repairs that tie it up in the shop for an extended period.

- You may be required to have scheduled maintenance performed when leasing a car.

- Recalls may happen more commonly than you think—check with your automobile's manufacturer or The National Highway Transportation Safety Administration Web site at www.nhtsa. dot.gov.

- An implied warranty may exist for a common and persistent problem, so don't be afraid to press a dealership's service department to make repairs for something that's technically not covered in your warranty.

GET THE SCOOP ON...
What insurance you have to have ▪
How much you should consider ▪ What really
affects your rates ▪ How to arrange insurance
for your new car

Auto Insurance

Now that you're getting a new set of wheels to drive, you need to make sure that you protect its value, as well as do what you can to ensure your own economic safety and that of your passengers, other drivers, and the owners of property that could be damaged if something unforeseen happens.

This chapter will brief you on basic auto insurance coverages, give you some tips to save money on your policy, and help you figure out exactly how much insurance coverage you actually need.

Procedures for getting insurance on your new car

The prudent shopper will have already called her insurance company and shopped around at others for new vehicle rates before she actually makes a deal. It also pays to ask your insurer (and check your own policy) about the recommended procedures for actually switching insurance from your old car to your new car.

If you're getting a vehicle you plan to take home the same day, don't even think of doing so without getting the okay from your insurer first. Your full-coverage policy may protect your new vehicle as you drive it off the lot and you may have a month to actually arrange coverage on the new car, but first verify the extent of your coverage and your responsibilities in switching the policy over with an insurer's representative. Some bare-bones policies won't protect your new car, and you should allow at least a day or two between sealing the deal and taking delivery to get full insurance coverage set up with an agent.

Typical insurances and costs

The cost to insure a vehicle has traditionally differed by hundreds of dollars depending on location—from just a few hundred dollars on average in some parts to close to a thousand in others—and many people pay much higher-than-average rates. How much you spend is determined by factors such as:

- The coverages you get
- Your driving record
- How many miles you drive
- How long you've been licensed
- Your age
- What kind of car you have
- Where you live

And we'll get to other things that affect your insurance rates shortly. What does a rate quote look like? A sample is shown on the next page but remember, rates will vary greatly from person to person!

AutoCity Consumer Insurance
1234 Consumer Pkwy.
Auto City, CA 12345
(123) 456-7890

Sample Insurance
Rate Quote.

```
          AUTOMOBILE INSURANCE RATE QUOTATION

                                    Page 1 of 1
                                    July 1, 1998

JOE CARBUYER

The following annual premiums are subject to any changes
that might arise from a revision of rate schedule.

AUTO                     USE                 MILEAGE
1 1993 BigM Bigmobile    Pleasure            7,000

COVERAGES                LIMIT OF LIABILITY   PREMIUMS
-----------------------------------------------AUTO 1--
LIABILITY                $300,000 each accident  $692.80
MEDICAL PAYMENTS         $5,000                  $ 58.40
UNINSURED MOTORISTS      $300,000 each accident  $238.40
DAMAGE TO YOUR AUTO      Actual Cash Value less
                           a deductible of:
                         AUTO 1
1. Collision                $500               *$387.40
2. Other than
   Collision Loss           $500                $215.20
TOWING AND LABOR         $   75 each disablement $  6.40
---------------------------------------------------------
*WAIVER OF COLLISION DEDUCTIBLE             INCLUDED
INCREASED TRANS EXPENSES $30 DAY/$900 MAXIMUM  $ 20.00
---------------------------------------------------------
              TOTAL PREMIUM THIS AUTO      $1,618.40

TOTAL ANNUAL PREMIUM       $1618.40

Up to ten installments are permitted under the installment
plan. Details will be included with your policy.
```

Unofficially...
How big is the problem of uninsured motorists? The state of California estimated during a recent year that insured motorists paid a billion dollars—10% of their premiums—to cover the cost of accidents involving uninsured motorists. (Source: California Department of Insurance, 1995)

What different coverages mean

Six typical risks that may be covered in an auto insurance policy are listed in Table 18.1.

TABLE 18.1   TYPICAL COVERAGE CATEGORIES

1. Bodily injury liability	For injuries that you might cause to another person
2. Medical or PIP (Personal Injury Protection)	For injuries that can occur to occupants of the policyholder's vehicle (PIP can sometimes cover medical payments, loss of wages, and the expense of replacing services usually performed by a person who can't perform them due to an accident.)

3. Property damage liability	For damage you do to another person's property
4. Collision	For damage that happens to the car of the policyholder from a collision
5. Comprehensive	For damage to the car of the policyholder when a collision with another car isn't involved (may cover fire, theft, earthquake, floods, falling objects, etc.)
6. Uninsured motorist coverage	For treatment of policyholder injuries after a collision with a driver who doesn't have insurance

Additional types of insurance are also available within the scope of your policy, such as reimbursement for a rental vehicle during the time you're having repairs done due to an insurance loss. Likewise, towing charges, emergency road service, gap coverage (more on that momentarily), and special coverages for your electronic equipment (even your cassettes or CDs).

How much do you need?

Deciding how much coverage to allow yourself is a very individual process. When you're uncertain, opt for safety.

New vs. older cars and collision coverage

You should ensure that you have appropriate collision and comprehensive coverages any time you're making payments on a vehicle, to protect yourself. And strongly consider this type of coverage on all but the oldest vehicles of least worth. Even if the insurance value of your vehicle isn't a lot, consider the difficulty that losing use of it would pose to your financial situation.

Ask yourself if the cost of the deductible and the annual payment you'll need to make toward this part of your insurance warrants coverage, or

Moneysaver
Want to save on your car insurance? Fight that ticket...your costs in doing so can be far less than the additional premium required with a mark against you.

whether it would be about the same as simply paying for repairs yourself. But don't leave yourself in a situation where your transportation abilities would truly be impaired in the event of an accident without appropriate coverage.

Although Collision and comprehensive coverage aren't the cheapest parts of an insurance policy, you can try to economize by opting for a higher deductible.

Medical payments coverage, for those injured in your vehicle, may or may not be a great idea. Before you opt for automobile medical payments coverage, check your regular health insurance policy to make sure you're not duplicating coverages.

Uninsured and underinsured motorist coverage should strongly be considered; it can protect you and your passengers when another party with no insurance or extremely limited coverage is at fault in the accident.

Required coverages

Many states require drivers to carry at least a certain minimum amount of liability insurance: for bodily injury, property damage, and personal injury protection coverage. Your state Department of Motor Vehicles can advise you about what's required where you live, or check with your prospective insurer or the state's insurance department.

State minimum requirements for liability coverage are generally just part of what industry experts may recommend. For most people, bodily injury liability coverage of $100,000 per person, $300,000 per accident, and $50,000 property damage liability coverage should be considered. No fault and PIP (personal injury protection) insurance requirements vary by state as well.

Timesaver
What's required in the way of auto insurance? Check your state's Web site for links to its insurance department. You'll also find insurance information at Insurance News Network at www.insure.com.

Gap coverage may be required in certain types of car financing arrangements, such as leases. Again, this coverage typically protects the financing company for the difference between what you've paid on the car and what it's worth if it's stolen or totaled. Your financing agreement spells out how much coverage you must have, and who's responsible for paying for it (sometimes gap insurance is built into the lease itself).

Cover your assets

It's an unpleasant topic to think about, but if you have significant assets—a home, some types of businesses, investments, etc.—consider carrying more than the typical liability insurance coverage. This helps to protect you if someone tries to sue, knowing that you have a lot they could try to obtain.

A combination of decent assets and low insurance coverage could even set you up for bankruptcy if you're liable in an accident. The greater your assets, the more tempted another party may be to sue. You may want to get an insurance policy allowing more than $100,000 per person, $300,000 per accident, and $50,000 property damage liability coverage.

If you have very little in the way of assets, should you have as little liability coverage as possible? No. You could still face bankruptcy if a judgment was great enough, and even that might not protect you from claims.

Look out for lapses

Letting your insurance expire can set you up for a nightmare of legal trouble and monetary expense. Keep current! You may have a month's grace period for making payments, but check with your

Bright Idea
Do you have adequate insurance? Consider how you would feel in the injured party's position. Don't skimp on the opportunity to protect your fellow man, and while you're at it, be a careful driver.

individual insurer before assuming anything. If you're moving, make sure that the insurer has your new address promptly. Not having state-mandated insurance can result in suspension of your license, and once you've let your insurance lapse, it can be much harder and more expensive to re-up.

Shopping for auto insurance

Auto insurance rates can vary significantly, depending on where you live. Often, insurance is handled by agents representing one or more different insurance groups, and those agents (check your yellow pages) can assist you in selecting a company (depending on which will accept you—some have stringent "good driver" requirements).

What determines your rates

Auto insurers determine basic rates for private passenger auto insurance from the cost of settling claims resulting from past auto accidents and losses. In other words, they take the historical perspective.

Your driving record is a major factor in the rates you get. If you've had previous accidents or other strikes against your driving record, you can be kicked up to a higher payment category. Even a single accident or "motor vehicle conviction" can jack up the expense, so toe the line.

Insurers also use the number of miles you drive annually as an indication of your likelihood of being involved in a claim. Short-distance commutes and vehicles used solely for leisure are a plus.

One big frustration a driver can't do much about is the age problem—younger drivers pay substantially more than older drivers, based on the number of years they've been licensed drivers. And

Unofficially...
Typically, drivers pay $5,800 or more for auto insurance during the time they own their vehicles.
(Source: *Consumer Reports*)

males pay higher rates than females if they've been driving less than several years.

Also consider the location in which you live. Insurers do. If there's a high statistical occurrence of accidents or other claim events, expect to pay more (cities tend to be highest, low-crime and rural locales lowest).

Two or more autos insured with the same company can bring discounts, as can being married! This latter point applies mainly to drivers who've had their license less than several years.

When one driver in a family is the principal driver and another family member only an occasional driver (such as a teenager using their parents' car), lower rates can apply for occasional operators.

And although younger people stand to spend more for auto insurance than their seniors, those who've been driving less than several years can sometimes get a break if they're "good students." To qualify, a driver generally must be at least 16 and a full-time high school or college student. Evidence may be asked for to prove that the student has met one or more of these requirements:

1. Ranks in top 20% of the class
2. Has a "B" grade average
3. Has at least a three-point average on a four-point grading scale
4. Made the "Dean's List" or "Honor Roll"

Taking a qualified driver training course can make a difference as well, for those new to the art.

How to find good, cheap auto insurance companies
Making the effort to comparison shop usually yields a surprising variation in rates There can be hundreds of dollars of difference between companies for the same coverage.

Watch Out!
Audio or phone equipment that you use in your vehicle may not be covered under your auto insurance policy. Check yours to see if the equipment must be "permanently installed" to qualify.

Start with word of mouth. Do you know anyone who is both satisfied with their insurer and pays low rates? Check magazine articles, consumer publications (and Internet sites) for rankings of who's best and who's cheapest. And use your local phone directory. If you're a member of an auto club, check with them as well.

How can you save money, no matter what company you insure with? The following points may help you trim your insurance bill, although all are not without their tradeoffs.

1. Ask for higher deductibles on collision and comprehensive insurance. You may save 15–30% by upping your deductible from $200 to $500 (source: Insurance Information Institute).

2. Make sure you ask about discounts that you may be eligible for because you have a good driving record, have state-of-the-art safety equipment on your car (automatic seat belts, air bags, ABS brakes…), always garage your vehicle, are over 50, have taken a driver-training course, have an anti-theft device on your car, etc. If you're a student, study! Some insurers even offer discounts for those with good grades.

3. Drive a car that doesn't jack up your insurance rates. Those that are frequently involved in accidents, are expensive to repair, or are often stolen may require higher insurance premiums due to increased risk. You may also find that a more powerful engine leads to increased rates, so check before you buy and ask your prospective insurer to check for variations on the car you're considering. You could save.

Moneysaver
Want to cut your car insurance rates? Age quickly. Discounts are often available for seniors.

Watch Out!
If you have questions about the company you're considering as an insurer, check with your local Better Business Bureau and also check their financial rating with a service that ranks insurers (call your library's reference section).

Moneysaver
Want to get a car
that won't cost a
lot to insure?
Check with the
Insurance
Institute for
Highway Safety,
1005 North Glebe
Road, Arlington,
VA 22201, and
ask for the
Highway Loss
Data Chart. You'll
find some eye-
opening informa-
tion about which
cars are most
frequently
stolen, and other
rate-affecting
statistics.

4. Consider dropping collision and comprehensive coverage if you have an old, low-worth car. A general rule of thumb is that if the car's worth less than $1,000, collision and comprehensive coverage don't make sense in light of your deductibles and annual insurance costs.

5. Don't drive much. Yes, that's right—some insurers offer a discount if you clock only a tiny number of annual miles.

6. Insure all cars in the family with the same insurer. Discounts may apply, but also inquire of your agent what can happen to your insurance rates if another driver, under the same policy, incurs insurance claims or even gets tickets.

7. Move on up to a better part of town or get that place in the country. Urbanity usually spells much higher insurance premium costs. Moving even a few miles to an area with a lower level of auto thefts and other losses can save you hundreds.

8. Consider bundling your insurance—having homeowner and auto insurance with the same company can provide discounts.

9. Periodically check to see if you could be getting a lower rate with another good insurer—and switch if the savings are great.

Avoiding insurance repair hassles

Should you actually have to use your insurance coverage—if you're involved in an accident or your vehicle is vandalized, for instance—use these tips to ensure that you avoid repair or other insurance-related hassles:

- Always keep your insurance card with you, and put another in the glove box.

- Call your insurance company as soon as a possibly covered event happens—clarify with them the exact procedures you should follow (do you have to file a police report, for instance), and get the name and direct phone number of the representative you speak with.

- Get estimates before filing a claim. If your deductible is $500 and the work will certainly cost no more than $600, consider the advisability of not filing an insurance claim (to protect your rates).

- Check with your insurer about whether you're required to have your vehicle repaired with an insurer-approved facility.

Bright Idea
The industry-sponsored Insurance Information Institute's Web site at www.iii.org can lead you to a number of helpful auto insurance links.

Just the facts

- Those with high asset levels should consider additional liability protection against lawsuits.

- Check immediately with your insurer whenever a potential claim situation arises, to make sure that you follow proper procedures that can ensure coverage.

- Some insurances are required by state law, and when leasing (or using other forms of financing), you may be required to have full coverage, including gap insurance.

- To lower your insurance cost, consider higher deductibles, and, by the way, what kind of car you decide to get can have a big effect on your rates!

Car Pricing Guide

The following listing of invoice and retail prices appears courtesy of Chek-Chart's *New Car Cost Guide.*

Year	Mfr.	Make	Code	Model	Invoice Price	Retail Price
1998	Acura	CL	YA314WJW	2.3 CL Coupe 2-Door (5-speed Manual)	$20,159	$22,310
1998	Acura	CL	YA324WJW	2.3 CL Coupe 2-Door (4-speed ECT Automatic)	$20,882	$23,110
1998	Acura	CL	YA315WJW	2.3 CL Coupe 2-Door w/Premium Package (5-speed Manual)	$21,108	$23,360
1998	Acura	CL	YA325WJW	2.3 CL Coupe 2-Door w/Premium Package (4-speed ECT Automatic)	$21,831	$24,160
1998	Acura	CL	YA224WJW	3.0 CL Coupe 2-Door (4-speed ECT Automatic)	$22,870	$25,310
1998	Acura	CL	YA225WJW	3.0 CL Coupe 2-Door w/Premium Package (4-speed ECT Automatic)	$24,090	$26,660
1998	Acura	Integra	DC434WPBW	RS Sport Coupe 3-Door (5-Speed Manual)	$14,475	$16,200
1998	Acura	Integra	DC444WPBW	RS Sport Coupe 3-Door (4-Speed Automatic)	$15,190	$17,000
1998	Acura	Integra	DC435WMBW	LS Sport Coupe 3-Door (5-Speed Manual)	$17,155	$19,200
1998	Acura	Integra	DC445WMBW	LS Sport Coupe 3-Door (4-Speed Automatic)	$17,870	$20,000
1998	Acura	Integra	DC436WMBW	GS Sport Coupe 3-Door (5-Speed Manual)	$18,630	$20,850
1998	Acura	Integra	DC446WMBW	GS Sport Coupe 3-Door (4-Speed Automatic)	$19,345	$21,650
1998	Acura	Integra	DC238WMBW	GS-R Sport Coupe 3-Door (5-Speed Automatic)	$19,032	$21,300
1998	Acura	Integra	DC239WMBW	GS-R Sport Coupe 3-Door w/Leather Seating Surfaces (5-Speed Manual)	$19,747	$22,100
1998	Acura	Integra	DB755WMBW	LS Sedan 4-Door (5-Speed Manual)	$17,870	$20,000
1998	Acura	Integra	DB765WMBW	LS Sedan 4-Door (4-Speed Automatic)	$18,585	$20,800
1998	Acura	Integra	DB756WMBW	GS Sedan 4-Door (5-Speed Manual)	$19,121	$21,400

1998	Acura	Integra	DB766WMBW	GS Sedan 4-Door (4-Speed Automatic)	$19,836	$22,200
1998	Acura	Integra	DB858WMBW	GS-R Sedan 4-Door (5-Speed Manual)	$19,300	$21,600
1998	Acura	Integra	DB859WMBW	GS-R Sedan 4-Door w/Leather Seating Surfaces (5-Speed Manual)	$20,014	$22,400
1998	Acura	NSX	NA213WPKW	NSX Hard Top 2-Door (6-Speed Manual)	$73,357	$84,000
1998	Acura	NSX	NA123WPKW	NSX Hard Top 2-Door (4-Speed ECT Automatic)	$73,357	$84,000
1998	Acura	NSX-T	NA216WPKW	NSX-T Open Top 2-Door (6-Speed Manual)	$76,850	$88,000
1998	Acura	NSX-T	NA126WPKW	NSX-T Open 2-Door (4-Speed ECT Automatic)	$75,850	$88,000
1998	Acura	RL	KA967WJW	Sedan 4-Door w/Navigation System	$37,727	$43,200
1998	Acura	RL	KA966WJTW	Sedan 4-Door w/Premium Package & Navigation System	$40,172	$46,000
1998	Acura	RL	KA965WJTW	Sedan 4-Door w/Premium Package	$38,425	$44,000
1998	Acura	RL	KA964WJW	Sedan 4-Door	$35,980	$41,200
1998	Acura	SLX	9C427WF34	Sport Utility 4-Door 4WD	$32,250	$36,300
1998	Acura	TL Sedan	UA265WJW	2.5 Base Sedan 4-Door	$27,431	$30,700
1998	Acura	TL Sedan	UA364WJW	3.2 Base Sedan 4-Door	$29,619	$33,150
1998	Audi	A4	8D25I4	1.8T Sedan 4-Door FWD	$20,942	$23,790
1998	Audi	A4	8D25V4	2.8 Sedan 4-Door FWD	$24,944	$28,390
1998	Audi	A4	8D55VK	Avant Wagon 4-Door FWD	$26,839	$30,465
1998	Audi	A4	8D55V5	Avant Quattro Wagon 4-Door AWD	$27,646	$31,040
1998	Audi	A6	4B24VA	Sedan 4-Door	$29,697	$33,750
1998	Audi	A6	4A53U8	Wagon 4-Door	$30,250	$34,400

Year	Mfr.	Make	Code	Model	Invoice Price	Retail Price
1998	Audi	A8	4D22UA	3.7 Sedan 4-Door FWD	$50,183	$57,400
1998	Audi	A8	4D228B	4.2 Quattro Sedan 4-Door 4WD	$56,795	$65,000
1998	Audi	Cabriolet	8G74U8	Convertible 2-Door (ex. CA, MA, & NY)	$30,424	$34,600
1998	BMW	3-Series		318ti Coupe 3-Door	$19,225	$21,390
1998	BMW	3-Series		318i Sedan 4-Door	$22,930	$26,150
1998	BMW	3-Series		323is Coupe 2-Door	$25,160	$28,700
1998	BMW	3-Series		323iC Convertible 2-Door	$30,410	$34,700
1998	BMW	3-Series		328i Sedan 4-Door	$29,010	$33,100
1998	BMW	3-Series		328is Coupe 2-Door	$29,095	$33,200
1998	BMW	3-Series		328ic Convertible 2-Door	$36,355	$41,500
1998	BMW	3-Series		M3 Coupe 2-Door	$34,780	$39,700
1998	BMW	3-Series		M3 Sedan 4-Door	$34,780	$39,700
1998	BMW	5-Series		528i Sedan 4-Door	$34,490	$38,900
1998	BMW	5-Series		540iA Sedan 4-Door	$44,225	$50,500
1998	BMW	5-Series		540i Sedan 4-Door	$46,675	$53,300
1998	BMW	7-Series		740i Sedan 4-Door	$54,495	$61,500
1998	BMW	7-Series		740iL Sedan 4-Door	$57,345	$65,500
1998	BMW	7-Series		750iL Sedan 4-Door	$80,610	$92,100
1998	BMW	Z3		1.9 Roadster 2-Seater 2-Door	$25,915	$29,425
1998	BMW	Z3		2.8 Roadster 2-Seater 2-Door	$31,455	$35,900

1998	Buick	Century	S69/1SA	Custom Sedan 4-Door	$17,013	$18,215
1998	Buick	Century	Y69/1SD	Limited Sedan 4-Door	$18,303	$19,575
1998	Buick	Le Sabre	P69/1SA	Custom Sedan 4-Door	$20,555	$22,465
1998	Buick	Le Sabre	R69/1SD	Limited Sedan 4-Door	$23,598	$25,790
1998	Buick	Park Avenue	W69/1SA	Base Sedan 4-Door	$27,761	$30,675
1998	Buick	Park Avenue	U69/1SE	Ultra Sedan 4-Door	$32,173	$35,550
1998	Buick	Regal	B69/1SA	LS Sedan 4-Door	$19,165	$20,945
1998	Buick	Regal	F69/1SD	GS Sedan 4-Door	$21,676	$23,690
1998	Buick	Riviera	D07/1SA	Coupe 2-Door	$29,413	$32,500
1998	Buick	Skylark	J69/R9C	Custom Sedan 4-Door (Fleet Only)	$15,337	$16,230
1998	Cadillac	Catera	6VR69	Sedan 4-Door w/Cloth Trim	$28,800	$29,995
1998	Cadillac	Catera	6VR69	Sedan 4-Door w/Leather Trim	$31,244	$33,610
1998	Cadillac	Deville	6KD69	Base Sedan 4-Door	$34,646	$37,695
1998	Cadillac	Deville	6KE69	d'Elegance Sedan 4-Door	$37,940	$41,295
1998	Cadillac	Deville	6KF69	Concours Sedan 4-Door	$38,855	$42,295
1998	Cadillac	Eldorado	6EL57	Base Coupe 2-Door	$35,378	$38,495
1998	Cadillac	Eldorado	6ET57	Touring Coupe 2-Door	$39,221	$42,695
1998	Cadillac	Seville	6KS69	SLS Sedan 4-Door	$39,038	$42,495
1998	Cadillac	Seville	6KY69	STS Sedan 4-Door	$43,155	$48,995
1998	Chevrolet	Astro Passanger Van	CM11006/1SA	Passanger Van 2WD, 111\WB	$18,167	$20,074
1998	Chevrolet	Astro Passanger Van	CL11006/1SA	Passanger Van 4WD, 111\WB	$20,248	$22,374

Year	Mfr.	Make	Code	Model	Invoice Price	Retail Price
1998	Chevrolet	Astro Van	CM11005/1SE	Van 111\W B, Rear-Wheel Drive	$17,503	$19,340
1998	Chevrolet	Blazer	CS10516/1SA	2 WD 2-Door Tailgate, 100.5\ WB	$19,605	$21,663
1998	Chevrolet	Blazer	CS10506/1SA	2 WD 4-Door Tailgate, 107\ WB	$20,985	$23,188
1998	Chevrolet	Blazer	CT10516/1SA	4 WD 2-Door Tailgate, 100.5\ WB	$21,404	$23,651
1998	Chevrolet	Blazer	CT105606/1SA	4 WD 4-Door Tailgate, 107\ WB	$22,784	$25,176
1998	Chevrolet	C1500 Pickup Extended Cab 2WD	CC10753/E63/1SA	Fleetside Cheyenne Décor (6.5-ft Box) 141.5\ WB	$16,061	$18,355
1998	Chevrolet	C1500 Pickup Extended Cab 2WD	CC10953/E63/1SA	Fleetside Cheyenne Décor (8-ft Box) 155.5\ WB	$16,756	$19,150
1998	Chevrolet	C1500 Pickup Extended Cab 2WD	CC10753/E62/1SB	Sportside Silverado Décor (6.5-ft Box) 141.5\ WB	$20,212	$23,099
1998	Chevrolet	C1500 Pickup Regular Cab 2WD	CC10703/E63/1SW	Fleetside Work Truck (6.5-ft Box) 117.5\ WB	$13,512	$14,390
1998	Chevrolet	C1500 Pickup Regular Cab 2WD	CC10903/E63/1SW	Fleetside Work Truck (8-ft Box) 131.5\ WB	$13,801	$15,250
1998	Chevrolet	C1500 Pickup Regular Cab 2WD	CC10703/E63/1SA	Fleetside Cheyenne Décor (6.5-ft Box) 117.5\ WB	$14,311	$16,355
1998	Chevrolet	C1500 Pickup Regular Cab 2WD	CC10903/E63/1SA	Fleetside Cheyenne Décor (8-ft Box) 131.5\ WB	$14,573	$16,655
1998	Chevrolet	C1500 Pickup Regular Cab 2WD	CC10703/E62/1SA	Sportside Cheyenne Décor (6.5-ft Box) 117.5\ WB	$14,814	$16,930
1998	Chevrolet	C2500 Pickup Extended Cab 2WD	CC20753/C5Z	Fleetside (6.5-ft Box), 141.5\ WB	$17,892	$20,448

Year	Make	Model	Code	Description		
1998	Chevrolet	C2500 Pickup Extended Cab 2WD	CC20953/C6P	Heavy-Duty Fleetside (8-ft Box), 155.5\ WB	$17,920	$20,484
1998	Chevrolet	C2500 Pickup Regular Cab 2WD	CC20903/C5Z	Fleetside (8-ft Box), 131.5\ WB	$15,603	$17,832
1998	Chevrolet	C2500 Pickup Regular Cab 2WD	CC20903/C6P	Heavy-Duty Fleetside (8-ft Box), 131.5\ WB	$16,517	$18,880
1998	Chevrolet	C3500 Pickup 2WD	CC30903/1SA	Regular Cab Fleetside (8-ft Box), Single Rear Wheels, 131.5\ WB	$16,638	$19,019
1998	Chevrolet	C3500 Pickup 2WD	CC30953/1SA	Extended Cab Fleetside (8-ft Box), Dual Rear Wheels, 155.5\ WB	$19,637	$22,442
1998	Chevrolet	Camaro	1FP87/1SA	Coupe Base	$15,222	$16,625
1998	Chevrolet	Camaro	1FP87/1SF	Coupe Z28	$18,730	$20,470
1998	Chevrolet	Camaro	1FP67/1SD	Convertible Base	$20,244	$22,125
1998	Chevrolet	Camaro	1FP67/1SH	Convertible Z28	$25,117	$27,450
1998	Chevrolet	Cavalier	1JC37/1SA	Coupe 2-Door Base	$10,855	$11,610
1998	Chevrolet	Cavalier	1JC37/1SD	Coupe 2-Door RS	$12,033	$12,870
1998	Chevrolet	Cavalier	1JC37/1SK	Coupe 2-Door Z24	$14,689	$15,710
1998	Chevrolet	Cavalier	1JC69/1SF	Sedan 4-Door Base	$11,042	$11,810
1998	Chevrolet	Cavalier	1JF69/1SH	Sedan 4-Door LS	$13,324	$14,250
1998	Chevrolet	Cavalier	1JF67/1SL	Convertible 2-Door Z24	$18,148	$19,410
1998	Chevrolet	Corvette	1YY07/1SA	Coupe 2-Door	$32,808	$37,495
1998	Chevrolet	Corvette	1YY67/1SB	Convertible 2-Door	$38,872	$44,425
1998	Chevrolet	Crew Cab	CC30943/1SA	Crew Cab 4-Door 2WD (8-ft Box), 168.5\WB	$19,377	$22,149

Year	Mfr.	Make	Code	Model	Invoice Price	Retail Price
1998	Chevrolet	Crew Cab	CK30943/1SA	Crew Cab 4-Door 4WD (8-ft Box), 168.5\WB	$22,154	$25,323
1998	Chevrolet	Express Van	CG11406/1SA	1500 135\WB	$19,916	$22,761
1998	Chevrolet	Express Van	CG21406/1SA	2500 135\WB	$21,103	$25,261
1998	Chevrolet	Express Van	CG21706/1SA	2500 155\WB	$22,891	$26,161
1998	Chevrolet	Express Van	CG31406/1SA	3500 135\WB	$22,353	$25,550
1998	Chevrolet	Express Van	CG31706/1SA	3500 155\WB	$23,140	$26,450
1998	Chevrolet	K1500 Pickup Extended Cab 4WD	CK10753/E63/1SA	Fleetside Cheyenne Décor (6.5-ft Box) 141.5\WB	$18,686	$21,355
1998	Chevrolet	K1500 Pickup Extended Cab 4WD	CK10953/E63/1SA	Fleetside Cheyenne Décor (8-ft Box) 155.5\WB	$19,381	$22,150
1998	Chevrolet	K1500 Pickup Extended Cab 4WD	CK10753/E62/1SB	Sportside Silverado Décor (6.5-ft Box) 141.5\WB	$22,837	$26,099
1998	Chevrolet	K1500 Pickup Regular Cab 4WD	CK10703/E63/1SW	Fleetside Work Truck (6.5-ft Box) 117.5\WB	$16,860	$18,630
1998	Chevrolet	K1500 Pickup Regular Cab 4WD	CK10903/E63/1SW	Fleetside Work Truck (8-ft Box) 131.5\WB	$17,150	$18,950
1998	Chevrolet	K1500 Pickup Regular Cab 4WD	CK10703/E63/1SA	Fleetside Cheyenne Décor (6.5-ft Box) 117.5\WB	$16,936	$19,355
1998	Chevrolet	K1500 Pickup Regular Cab 4WD	CK10903/E63/1SA	Fleetside Cheyenne Décor (8-ft Box) 131.5\WB	$17,198	$19,655
1998	Chevrolet	K1500 Pickup Regular Cab 4WD	CK10703/E62/1SA	Sportside Cheyenne Décor (6.5-ft Box) 117.5\WB	$17,439	$19,930

Year	Make	Model	Code	Description		
1998	Chevrolet	K2500 Pickup Extended Cab 4WD	CK20753/C6P	Heavy-Duty Fleetside (6.5-ft Box), 141.5\ WB	$20,638	$23,590
1998	Chevrolet	K2500 Pickup Extended Cab 4WD	CK20953/C6P	Heavy-Duty Fleetside (8-ft Box), 155.5\ WB	$20,749	$23,717
1998	Chevrolet	K2500 Pickup Regular Cab 4WD	CK20903/C6P	Heavy-Duty Fleetside (8-ft Box), 131.5\ WB	$18,927	$21,635
1998	Chevrolet	K3500 Pickup 4 WD	CK30903/1SA	Regular Cab Fleetside (8-ft Box), Single Rear Wheels, 131.5\ WB	$19,263	$22,019
1998	Chevrolet	K3500 Pickup 4 WD	CK30953/1SA	Extended Cab Fleetside (8-ft Box), Dual Rear Wheels, 155.5\ WB	$22,096	$25,253
1998	Chevrolet	Lumina	1WL69/1SA	Base Sedan 4-Door	$15,779	$17,245
1998	Chevrolet	Lumina	1WL69/1SC	LS Sedan 4-Door	$17,609	$19,245
1998	Chevrolet	Lumina	1WN69/1SE	LTZ Sedan 4-Door	$18,067	$19,745
1998	Chevrolet	Malibu	1ND69/1SA	Base Sedan 4-Door	$14,338	$15,670
1998	Chevrolet	Malibu	1NE69/1SD	LS Sedan 4-Door	$16,900	$18,470
1998	Chevrolet	Metro	1MR08/1SA	Base Hatchback Coupe 3-Door	$8,153	$8,655
1998	Chevrolet	Metro	1MR08/1SD	Lsi Hatchback Coupe 3-Door	$8,812	$9,455
1998	Chevrolet	Metro	1MR69/1SA	Lsi Sedan 4-Door	$9,371	$10,055
1998	Chevrolet	Monte Carlo	1WW27/1SG	LS Coupe 2-Door	$16,282	$17,795
1998	Chevrolet	Monte Carlo	1WX27/1SJ	Z34 Coupe 2-Door	$18,570	$20,295
1998	Chevrolet	Prizm	1SK19/1SA	Base Sedan 4-Door	$11,465	$12,043
1998	Chevrolet	Prizm	1SK19/1SB	Comsumer Marketing Sedan 4-Door (CA, ID, OR & WA Only)	$14,394	$15,120
1998	Chevrolet	Prizm	1SK19/1SE	Lsi Sedan 4-Door	$13,474	$14,614

Year	Mfr.	Make	Code	Model	Invoice Price	Retail Price
1998	Chevrolet	S10 2WD Fleetside Models	CS10603/E63	Base Regular Cab (6-ft), 108.3\WB	$11,338	$11,998
1998	Chevrolet	S10 2WD Fleetside Models	CS10803/E63	Base Regular Cab (71/3-ft), 117.9\WB	$11,966	$12,662
1998	Chevrolet	S10 2WD Fleetside Models	CS10603/E63	LS Regular Cab (6-ft), 108.3\WB	$11,927	$13,179
1998	Chevrolet	S10 2WD Fleetside Models	CS10803/E63	LS Regular Cab (71/3-ft), 117.9\WB	$12,245	$13,530
1998	Chevrolet	S10 2WD Fleetside Models	CS10653/E63	LS Extended Cab (6-ft), 122.9\WB	$13,783	$15,230
1998	Chevrolet	S10 2WD Sportside Models	CS10603/E62	LS Regular Cab (6-ft), 108.3\WB	$12,358	$13,655
1998	Chevrolet	S10 2WD Sportside Models	CS10653/E62	LS Extended Cab (6-ft), 122.9\WB	$14,213	$15,705
1998	Chevrolet	S10 4WD Fleetside Models	CT10603/E63	Base Regular Cab (6-ft), 108.3\WB	$15,631	$16,541
1998	Chevrolet	S10 4WD Fleetside Models	CT10803/E63	Base Regular Cab (71/3-ft), 117.9\WB	$15,945	$16,873
1998	Chevrolet	S10 4WD Fleetside Models	CT10603/E63	LS Regular Cab (6-ft), 108.3\WB	$16,002	$17,682
1998	Chevrolet	S10 4WD Fleetside Models	CT10803/E63	LS Regular Cab (71/3-ft), 117.9\WB	$16,389	$18,109
1998	Chevrolet	S10 4WD Fleetside Models	CT10653/E63	LS Extended Cab (6-ft), 122.9\WB	$17,722	$19,582

Year	Make	Model	Code	Description		
1998	Chevrolet	S10 4WD Sportside Models	CT10603/E62	LS Regular Cab (6-ft), 108.3\WB	$16,409	$18,132
1998	Chevrolet	S10 4WD Sportside Models	CT10653/E62	LS Extended Cab (6-ft), 122.9\WB	$18,129	$20,032
1998	Chevrolet	Suburban	CC10906/1SA	C1500 2WD, 131.5\WB, Tailgate Body	$22,361	$25,065
1998	Chevrolet	Suburban	CK10906/1SA	K1500 4WD, 131.5\WB, Tailgate Body	$24,363	$28,155
1998	Chevrolet	Suburban	CC20906/1SA	C2500 2WD, 131.5\WB, Tailgate Body	$23,743	$27,139
1998	Chevrolet	Suburban	CK20906/1SA	K2500 4WD, 131.5\WB, Tailgate Body	$26,018	$29,739
1998	Chevrolet	Tahoe 2WD Models	CC10516/1SA	Base 2-Door, 111.5\WB	$20,913	$23,900
1998	Chevrolet	Tahoe 2WD Models	CC10706/1SB	LS 4-Door, 117.5\WB	$22,988	$29,700
1998	Chevrolet	Tahoe 4WD Models	CK10516/1SA	Base 2-Door, 115.5\WB	$23,188	$26,500
1998	Chevrolet	Tahoe 4WD Models	CK10706/1SB	LS 4-Door 4WD, 117.5\WB	$28,263	$32,300
1998	Chevrolet	Tracker	CE10367/1SA	Convertible 2-Door 2WD	$13,000	$13,655
1998	Chevrolet	Tracker	CJ10367/1SA	Convertible 2-Door 4WD	$13,952	$14,655
1998	Chevrolet	Tracker	CE10305/1SA	Hardtop 4-Door 2WD	$14,147	$14,860
1998	Chevrolet	Tracker	CJ10305/1SA	Hardtop 4-Door 4WD	$143,856	$15,605
1998	Chevrolet	Venture Cargo Van	1UM06/1SJ	Extended Wheelbase 3-Door	$18,253	$20,169
1998	Chevrolet	Venture Cargo Van	1UM16/1SJ	Extended Wheelbase 4-Door	$18,787	$20,759
1998	Chevrolet	Venture Passenger Van	1UN06/1SA	Regular Wheelbase Minivan 3-Door	$18,325	$20,249
1998	Chevrolet	Venture Passenger Van	1UN16/1SA	Regular Wheelbase Minivan 4-Door	$19,393	$21,429
1998	Chevrolet	Venture Passenger Van	1UM06/1SE	Extended Wheelbase Minivan 3-Door	$19,610	$21,669

Year	Mfr.	Make	Code	Model	Invoice Price	Retail Price
1998	Chevrolet	Venture Passenger Van	1UM16/1SE	Extended Wheelbase Minivan 4-Door	$20,144	$22,259
1998	Chrysler	Cirrus	JACP41/26K	Lxi Sedan 4-Door	$17,794	$19,460
1998	Chrysler	Concorde	LHCH41/22C	LX Sedan 4-Door	$19,511	$21,305
1997	Chrysler	LHS	LHCP41/26J	Sedan 4-Door	$27,702	$30,225
1998	Chrysler	Sebring	FJCS22/21G	Coupe 2-Door LX	$15,498	$16,840
1998	Chrysler	Sebring	FJCP22/24J	Coupe 2-Door Lxi	$19,133	$20,925
1998	Chrysler	Sebring	JXCH27/24A	Convertible 2-Door JX	$18,892	$20,575
1998	Chrysler	Sebring	JXCP27/26D	Convertible 2-Door Jxi	$23,578	$25,840
1998	Chrysler	Town & Country	NSYP52/25F	Front Wheel Drive (FWD)4-Door SX Mid-Size Wagon (ex. CA/CT/MA/NY)	$24,218	$26,680
1998	Chrysler	Town & Country	NSYP52/28F	Front Wheel Drive (FWD)4-Door SX Mid-Size Wagon (CA/CT/MA/NY Only)	$24,218	$26,680
1998	Chrysler	Town & Country	NSYP53/28P	Front Wheel Drive (FWD)4-Door LX Maxiwagon (CA/CT/MA/NY Only)	$24,619	$26,135
1998	Chrysler	Town & Country	NSYS53/29Y	Front Wheel Drive (FWD)4-Door LXi Maxiwagon	$28,799	$31,885
1998	Chrysler	Town & Country	NSCP53	All Wheel Drive (AWD)4-Door LX Maxiwagon	$27,259	$30,135
1998	Chrysler	Town & Country	NSCS53/29Y	All Wheel Drive (AWD)4-Door Lxi Maxiwagon	$30,889	$34,260
1998	Chyrsler	Town & Country	NSYP53/25P	Front Wheel Drive (FWD)4-Door LX Maxiwagon (ex. CA/CT/MA/NY)	$24,619	$27,135
1998	Dodge	Avenger	FJDH22/21A	Base Coupe 2-Door	$13,965	$15,185
1998	Dodge	Avenger	FJDS22/21D	ES Coupe 2-Door	$15,989	$17,460

Year	Make	Model	Code	Description		
1998	Dodge	Caravan	5NSKL52/22S	50 States Base, 112\WB	$15,845	$17,412
1998	Dodge	Caravan	NSKH52/26A	ex. CA/CT/MA/NY SE, 112\WB	$19,255	$21,290
1998	Dodge	Caravan	NSKP52/25J	ex. CA/CT/MA/NY LE, 112\WB	$22,546	$25,030
1998	Dodge	Caravan	NSKH52/28A	CA/CT/NY Only SE, 112\WB	$19,425	$21,490
1998	Dodge	Caravan	NSKP52/28J	CA/CT/NY Only LE, 112\WB	$22,546	$22,546
1998	Dodge	Dakota Club Cab	AN1L31/21W	2WD Club Cab (6.5-ft Box), 131\WB	$14,665	$16,170
1998	Dodge	Dakota Club Cab	AN5L31/23W	4WD Club Cab (6.5-ft Box), 131\WB	$17,854	$19,755
1998	Dodge	Dakota Regular Cab	AN1L61/21W	2WD Regular Cab (6.5-ft Box), 112\WB	$11,818	$12,975
1998	Dodge	Dakota Regular Cab	AN1L62/21W	2WD Regular Cab (8-ft Box), 124\WB	$12,223	$13,435
1998	Dodge	Dakota Regular Cab	AN5L61/23W	4WD Regular Cab (6.5-ft Box), 112\WB	$15,355	$16,955
1998	Dodge	Durango	DN5L74	Sport Utility 4WD 4-Door	$23,316	$25,610
1998	Dodge	Grand Caravan 2WD	NSKL53/24S	(ex. CA/CT/MA/NY) Base, 119\WB	$18,270	$20,125
1998	Dodge	Grand Caravan 2WD	NSKH53/26A	(ex. CA/CT/MA/NY) SE, 119\WB	$20,171	$22,285
1998	Dodge	Grand Caravan 2WD	NSKP53/25J	(ex. CA/CT/MA/NY) LE, 119\WB	$23,462	$26,025
1998	Dodge	Grand Caravan 2WD	NSKP53/25M	(ex. CA/CT/MA/NY) ES, 119\WB	$24,460	$27,180
1998	Dodge	Grand Caravan 2WD	NSKL53/28S	(CA/CT/MA/NY Only) Base, 119\WB	$18,653	$20,575
1998	Dodge	Grand Caravan 2WD	NSKH53/28A	(CA/CT/MA/NY Only) SE, 119\WB	$20,341	$22,485
1998	Dodge	Grand Caravan 2WD	NSKP53/28J	(CA/CT/MA/NY Only) LE, 119\WB	$23,462	$26,025
1998	Dodge	Grand Caravan 2WD	NSKP53/28M	(CA/CT/MA/NY Only) ES, 119\WB	$24,460	$27,180
1998	Dodge	Grand Caravan AWD	NSDH53/29D	SE, 119\WB	$23,922	$26,580
1998	Dodge	Grand Caravan AWD	NSDP53/29K	LE, 119\WB	$26,328	$29,285
1998	Dodge	Grand Caravan AWD	NSDP53/29M	ES, 119\WB	$27,131	$30,210

Year	Mfr.	Make	Code	Model	Invoice Price	Retail Price
1998	Dodge	Intrepid	LHDH41/22C	Base Sedan 4-Door	$18,050	$19,685
1998	Dodge	Intrepid	LHDP41/24L	ES Sedan 4-Door	$20,524	$22,465
1998	Dodge	Neon	PLDL22/23A	Coupe 2-Door Competition	$10,405	$11,000
1998	Dodge	Neon	PLDH22/21D	Coupe 2-Door Highline	$10,415	$11,255
1998	Dodge	Neon	PLDL42/25A	Sedan 4-Door Competition	$10,589	$11,200
1998	Dodge	Neon	PLDH42/21D	Sedan 4-Door Highline	$10,595	$11,455
1998	Dodge	Pickup Ram 1500 Club Cab	BE1L31/23A	2WD Club cab 2-Door ST (6.5-ft Box), 139\WB	$16,649	$18,975
1998	Dodge	Pickup Ram 1500 Club Cab	BE1L32/23A	2WD Club cab 2-Door ST(8-ft Box), 155\WB	$16,887	$19,255
1998	Dodge	Pickup Ram 1500 Club Cab	BE6L31/23A	4WD Club cab 2-Door ST (6.5-ft Box), 139\WB	$19,434	$22,205
1998	Dodge	Pickup Ram 1500 Club Cab	BE6L32/23A	4WD Club cab 2-Door ST(8-ft Box), 155\WB	$19,715	$22,535
1998	Dodge	Pickup Ram 1500 Quad Cab	BE1l33/23A	2WD Quad cab 4-Door ST (6.5-ft Box), 139\WB	$17,296	$19,725
1998	Dodge	Pickup Ram 1500 Quad Cab	BE1L34/23A	2WD Quad cab 4-Door ST(8-ft Box), 155\WB	$17,534	$20,005
1998	Dodge	Pickup Ram 1500 Quad Cab	BE6L33/23A	4WD Quad cab 4-Door ST (6.5-ft Box), 139\WB	$20,072	$22,955
1998	Dodge	Pickup Ram 1500 Quad Cab	BE6L34/23A	4WD Quad cab 4-Door ST(8-ft Box), 155\WB	$20,352	$23,285

Year	Make	Model	Code	Description		
1998	Dodge	Pickup Ram 1500 Regular Cab	BR1L61/21W	2WD Ram Regular Cab WS (6.5-ft Box), 119\WB	$13,232	$14,485
1998	Dodge	Pickup Ram 1500 Regular Cab	BR1L61/21A	2WD Ram Regular Cab ST (6.5-ft Box), 119\WB	$14,306	$16,260
1998	Dodge	Pickup Ram 1500 Regular Cab	BR1L62/21W	2WD Ram Regular Cab WS (8-ft Box), 135\WB	$13,469	$14,755
1998	Dodge	Pickup Ram 1500 Regular Cab	BR1L62/21A	2WD Ram Regular Cab ST (8-ft Box), 135\WB	$14,548	$16,545
1998	Dodge	Pickup Ram 1500 Regular Cab	BR6L61/23A	4WD Ram Regular Cab ST (6.5-ft Box), 119\WB	$17,373	$19,815
1998	Dodge	Pickup Ram 1500 Regular Cab	BR6L62/23A	4WD Ram Regular Cab ST (8-ft Box), 135\WB	$17,662	$20,155
1998	Dodge	Pickup Ram 2500 Club Cab	BE2L31/25A	2WD Club cab 2-Door ST (6.5-ft Box), 139\WB	$18,617	$21,290
1998	Dodge	Pickup Ram 2500 Club Cab	BE2L32/25A	2WD Club cab 2-Door ST(8-ft Box), 155\WB	$18,778	$21,480
1998	Dodge	Pickup Ram 2500 Club Cab	BE7L31/25A	4WD Club cab 2-Door ST (6.5-ft Box), 139\WB	$21,415	$24,535
1998	Dodge	Pickup Ram 2500 Club Cab	BE7L32/25A	4WD Club cab 2-Door ST(8-ft Box), 155\WB	$21,576	$24,725
1998	Dodge	Pickup Ram 2500 Quad Cab	BE2L33/25A	2WD Quad cab 4-Door ST (6.5-ft Box), 139\WB	$19,264	$22,040
1998	Dodge	Pickup Ram 2500 Quad Cab	BE2L34/25A	2WD Quad cab 4-Door ST(8-ft Box), 155\WB	$19,426	$22,230
1998	Dodge	Pickup Ram 2500 Quad Cab	BE7L33/25A	4WD Quad cab 4-Door ST (6.5-ft Box), 139\WB	$22,052	$25,285

Year	Mfr.	Make	Code	Model	Invoice Price	Retail Price
1998	Dodge	Pickup Ram 2500 Quad Cab	BE7L34/25A	4WD Quad cab 4-Door ST(8-ft Box), 155\WB	$22,214	$25,475
1998	Dodge	Pickup Ram 2500 Regular Cab	BR2L62/25A	ST Regular Cab 2WD (8-ft Box), 135\WB, 8800# GVWR	$17,069	$19,510
1998	Dodge	Pickup Ram 2500 Regular Cab	BR7L62/25A	ST Regular Cab 4WD (8-ft Box), 135\WB, 8800# GVWR	$20,016	$22,925
1998	Dodge	Pickup Ram 3500 Quad Cab	BE3L34/25A	ST 2WD 4-Door (8-ft Box), 155\WB, Dual Rear Wheels	$20,875	$23,395
1998	Dodge	Pickup Ram 3500 Quad Cab	BE8L34/25A	ST 4WD 4-Door (8-ft Box), 155\WB, Dual Rear Wheels	$23,009	$26,410
1998	Dodge	Pickup Ram 3500 Regular Cab	3500BR3L62/25A	ST 2WD (8-ft Box), 135\WB, Dual Rear Wheels	$18,165	$20,800
1998	Dodge	Pickup Ram 3500 Regular Cab	BR8L62/25A	ST 4WD (8-ft Box), 135\WB, Dual Rear Wheels	$20,769	$23,810
1998	Dodge	Ram Van	AB1l11/22C	1500 Models Van, 109\WB	$15,677	$17,855
1998	Dodge	Ram Van	AB1l12/22C	1500 Models Non-Maxi Van, 127\WB	$15,715	$17,900
1998	Dodge	Ram Van	AB1l13/22C	1500 Models Maxivan, 127\WB	$17,577	$20,090
1998	Dodge	Ram Van	AB2L12/26C	2500 Models Non-Maxi Van, 127\WB	$17,322	$19,790
1998	Dodge	Ram Van	AB2L13/26C	2500 Models Maxivan, 127\WB	$18,686	$21,395
1998	Dodge	Ram Van	AB3L12/26C	3500 Models Non-Maxi Van, 127\WB	$18,316	$20,960
1998	Dodge	Ram Van	AB3L13/26C	3500 Models Maxivan, 127\WB	$19,081	$21,860
1998	Dodge	Stratus	JADH41/21A	Base Sedan 4-Door	$13,638	$14,840

1998	Dodge	Stratus	JADP41/21J	ES Sedan 4-Door	$16,512	$17,665
1998	Dodge	Viper	SRDS27/21A	R/T Convertible 2-Door 2-Seat	$57,520	$64,000
1998	Dodge	Viper	SRDS29/21A	GTS Coupe 2-Door 2-Seat	$59,720	$66,500
1998	Dodge	Wagon	AB1L51/22C	1500 Wagon, 109\WB	$18,546	$20,450
1998	Dodge	Wagon	AB2L52/26C	2500 Wagon, 127\WB	$19,985	$22,865
1998	Dodge	Wagon	AB3L53/26B	3500 Maxi-Wagon, 127\WB	$22,285	$22,570
1998	Eagle	Talon	FJXL24/21X	Base Hatchback 2-Door	$13,435	$14,505
1998	Eagle	Talon	FJXH24/21A	ESi Hatchback 2-Door	$14,173	$15,275
1998	Eagle	Talon	FJXP24/23D	TSi Turbo Hatchback 2-Door FWD	$17,069	$18,460
1998	Eagle	Talon	FJFS24/25F	TSi Turbo Hatchback 2-Door AWD	$19,119	$20,715
1998	Ford	Contour	P65	LX Sedan 4-Door	$13,544	$14,460
1998	Ford	Contour	P66	SE Sedan 4-Door	$14,501	$15,860
1998	Ford	Contour	P68	SVT Sedan 4-Door	$20,325	$22,405
1998	Ford	Crown Victoria	P72	Commercial Fleet Sedan 4-Door (Fleet Only)	$20,448	$21,905
1998	Ford	Crown Victoria	P73	Base Sedan 4-Door	$19,566	$20,935
1998	Ford	Crown Victoria	P74	LX Sedan 4-Door	$21,568	$23,135
1998	Ford	Econoline Cargo Van	E14	E-150 Van Regular Cargo Van	$16,847	$19,220
1998	Ford	Econoline Cargo Van	E24	E-250 Van Regular Cargo Van	$17,123	$19,545
1998	Ford	Econoline Cargo Van	S24	E-250 Van Super Cargo Van	$17,718	$20,245
1998	Ford	Econoline Cargo Van	E34	E-350 Van Regular Cargo Van	$19,342	$22,155
1998	Ford	Econoline Cargo Van	S34	E-350 Van Super Cargo Van	$20,174	$23,135
1998	Ford	Econoline Club Wagon	E11	Regular Club Wagon XL Base (8 Passenger)	$19,002	$21,755

Year	Mfr.	Make	Code	Model	Invoice Price	Retail Price
1998	Ford	Econoline Club Wagon	E31	Regular Club Wagon XL Heavy-Duty (12 Passenger)	$21,454	$24,640
1998	Ford	Econoline Club Wagon	E11	Regular Club Wagon XLT Base (8 Passenger)	$20,655	$23,700
1998	Ford	Econoline Club Wagon	E31	Regular Club Wagon XLT Heavy-Duty (12 Passenger)	$23,043	$26,510
1998	Ford	Econoline Club Wagon	S31	Super Club Wagon XL (15 Passenger)	$22,912	$26,355
1998	Ford	Econoline Club Wagon	S31	Super Club Wagon XLT (15 Passenger)	$23,737	$27,325
1998	Ford	Escort	P11	ZX2 Coupe 2-Door Cool	$10,857	$11,580
1998	Ford	Escort	P11	ZX2 Coupe 2-Door Hot	$12,222	$13,080
1998	Ford	Escort	P10	Sedan 4-Door LX	$10,630	$11,330
1998	Ford	Escort	P13	Sedan 4-Door SE	$11,813	$12,630
1998	Ford	Escort	P15	Wagon 4-Door SE	$12,905	$13,830
1998	Ford	Expedition	U17	2WD Sport Utility 4-Door XLT	$24,737	$28,225
1998	Ford	Expedition	U17	2WD Sport Utility 4-Door Eddie Bauer	$27,939	$32,055
1998	Ford	Expedition	U18	4WD Sport Utility 4-Door XLT	$26,947	$28,225
1998	Ford	Expedition	U18	4WD Sport Utility 4-Door Eddie Bauer	$30,233	$34,690
1998	Ford	Explorer	U22	2WD 2-Door Models Sport, 102\WB	$18,119	$19,880
1998	Ford	Explorer	U32	2WD 4-Door Models XL, 112\WB	$19,598	$21,560
1998	Ford	Explorer	U32	2WD 4-Door Models XLT, 112\WB	$22,353	$24,690
1998	Ford	Explorer	U32	2WD 4-Door Models Eddie Bauer, 112\WB	$26,022	$28,860
1998	Ford	Explorer	U32	2WD 4-Door Models Limited, 112\WB	$28,490	$31,665
1998	Ford	Explorer	U24	4WD 2-Door Models Sport, 102\WB	$20,623	$22,725

1998	Ford	Explorer	U34	4WD 4-Door Models XL, 112\WB	$21,287	$23,480
1998	Ford	Explorer	U34	4WD 4-Door Models XLT, 112\WB	$24,117	$26,695
1998	Ford	Explorer	U34	4WD 4-Door Models Eddie Bauer, 112\WB	$27,786	$30,865
1998	Ford	Explorer	U34	4WD 4-Door Models Limited, 112\WB	$30,255	$33,670
1998	Ford	Explorer	U35	AWD 4-Door Models XLT, 112\WB	$24,117	$26,695
1998	Ford	Explorer	U35	AWD 4-Door Models Eddie Bauer, 112\WB	$27,390	$30,415
1998	Ford	Explorer	U35	AWD 4-Door Models Limited, 112\WB	$29,859	$33,220
1998	Ford	Mustang	P40	Coupe 2-Door Base	$14,747	$16,070
1998	Ford	Mustang	P42	Coupe 2-Door GT	$18,307	$20,070
1998	Ford	Mustang	P47	Coupe 2-Door Cobra	$23,256	$25,630
1998	Ford	Mustang	P44	Convertible 2-Door Base	$18,752	$20,570
1998	Ford	Mustang	P45	Convertible 2-Door GT	$21,867	$24,070
1998	Ford	Mustang	P46	Convertible 2-Door Cobra	$25,748	$28,430
1998	Ford	Pickup F-150	F17-120	F-150 Pickup Regular Cab Styleside 2WD Standard (6.5-ft Box), 120\WB	$13,521	$14,785
1998	Ford	Pickup F-150	F17-139	F-150 Pickup Regular Cab Styleside 2WD Standard (8-ft Box), 139\WB	$13,776	$15,075
1998	Ford	Pickup F-150	F17-120	F-150 Pickup Regular Cab Styleside 2WD XL (6.5-ft Box), 120\WB	$13,952	$15,815
1998	Ford	Pickup F-150	F17-139	F-150 Pickup Regular Cab Styleside 2WD XL (8-ft Box), 139\WB	$14,207	$16,115
1998	Ford	Pickup F-150	F17-F120	F-150 Pickup Regular Cab Styleside 2WD XLT (6.5-ft Box), 120\WB	$16,205	$18,465

Year	Mfr.	Make	Code	Model	Invoice Price	Retail Price
1998	Ford	Pickup F-150	F17-139	F-150 Pickup Regular Cab Styleside 2WD XLT (8-ft Box), 139\WB	$16,460	$18,765
1998	Ford	Pickup F-150	F17-120	F-150 Pickup Regular Cab Styleside 2WD Lariat (6.5-ft Box), 120\WB	$18,275	$20,900
1998	Ford	Pickup F-150	F17-139	F-150 Pickup Regular Cab Styleside 2WD Lariat (8-ft Box), 139\WB	$18,530	$21,200
1998	Ford	Pickup F-150	F07-120	F-150 Regular Cab Flareside 2WD XL (6.5-ft Box), 120\WB	$14,812	$16,825
1998	Ford	Pickup F-150	F07-120	F-150 Regular Cab Flareside 2WD XLT (6.5-ft Box), 120\WB	$17,064	$19,475
1998	Ford	Pickup F-150	F07-120	F-150 Regular Cab Flareside 2WD Lariat (6.5-ft Box), 120\WB	$19,133	$21,910
1998	Ford	Pickup F-150	F18-120	F-150 Regular Cab Styleside 4WD Standard (6.5-ft Box), 120\WB	$16,399	$18,055
1998	Ford	Pickup F-150	F18-139	F-150 Regular Cab Styleside 4W Standard (8-ft Box), 139\WB	$16,653	$18,345
1998	Ford	Pickup F-150	F18-120	F-150 Regular Cab Styleside 4WD XL (6.5-ft Box), 120\WB	$16,834	$19,205
1998	Ford	Pickup F-150	F18-139	F-150 Regular Cab Styleside 4WD XL (8-ft Box), 139\WB	$17,089	$19,505
1998	Ford	Pickup F-150	F18-120	F-150 Regular Cab Styleside 4WD XLT (6.5-ft Box), 120\WB	$18,797	$21,515
1998	Ford	Pickup F-150	F18-139	F-150 Regular Cab Styleside 4WD XLT (8-ft Box), 139\WB	$19,052	$21,815

Year	Make	Model	Code	Description		
1998	Ford	Pickup F-150	F18-120	F-150 Regular Cab Styleside 4WD Lariat (6.5-ft Box), 120\WB	$20,868	$23,950
1998	Ford	Pickup F-150	F18-139	F-150 Regular Cab Styleside 4WD Lariat (8-ft Box), 139\WB	$21,123	$24,250
1998	Ford	Pickup F-150	F08-120	F-150 Regular Cab Flareside 4WD XL (6.5-ft Box), 120\WB	$17,484	$19,970
1998	Ford	Pickup F-150	F08-120	F-150 Regular Cab Flareside 4WD XLT (6.5-ft Box), 120\WB	$19,448	$22,280
1998	Ford	Pickup F-150	F08-120	F-150 Regular Cab Flareside 4WD Lariat (6.5-ft Box), 120\WB	$21,517	$24,715
1998	Ford	Pickup F-150	X17-139	F-150 Supercab Styleside 2WD Standard (6.5-ft Box), 139\WB	$21,517	$24,715
1998	Ford	Pickup F-150	X17-157	F-150 Supercab Styleside 2WD Standard (8-ft Box), 157\WB	$15,849	$17,430
1998	Ford	Pickup F-150	X17-139	F-150 Supercab Styleside 2WD XL (6.5-ft Box), 139\WB	$16,027	$18,255
1998	Ford	Pickup F-150	X17-157	F-150 Supercab Styleside 2WD XL (8-ft Box), 157\WB	$16,282	$18,555
1998	Ford	Pickup F-150	X17-139	F-150 Supercab Styleside 2WD XLT (6.5-ft Box), 139\WB	$18,483	$21,145
1998	Ford	Pickup F-150	X17-157	F-150 Supercab Styleside 2WD XLT (8-ft Box), 157\WB5	$18,738	$21,445
1998	Ford	Pickup F-150	X17-139	F-150 Supercab Styleside 2WD Lariat (6.5-ft Box), 139\WB	$20,553	$23,580
1998	Ford	Pickup F-150	X17-157	F-150 Supercab Styleside 2WD Lariat (8-ft Box), 157\WB	$20,808	$23,880

Year	Mfr.	Make	Code	Model	Invoice Price	Retail Price
1998	Ford	Pickup F-150	X03-139	F-150 Supercab Flareside 2WD XL (6.5-ft Box), 139\WB	$16,779	$19,140
1998	Ford	Pickup F-150	X03-139	F-150 Supercab Flareside 2WD XLT (6.5-ft Box), 139\WB	$19,133	$21,910
1998	Ford	Pickup F-150	X03-139	F-150 Supercab Flareside 2WD Lariat (6.5-ft Box), 139\WB	$21,203	$24,435
1998	Ford	Pickup F-150	X18-139	F-150 Supercab Styleside 4WD Standard (6.5-ft Box), 139\WB	$18,779	$20,760
1998	Ford	Pickup F-150	X18-157	F-150 Supercab Styleside 4WD Standard (8-ft Box), 157\WB	$19,035	$21,050
1998	Ford	Pickup F-150	X18-139	F-150 Supercab Styleside 4WD XL (6.5-ft Box), 139\WB	$19,214	$22,005
1998	Ford	Pickup F-150	X18-157	F-150 Supercab Styleside 4WD XL (8-ft Box), 157\WB	$19,469	$22,305
1998	Ford	Pickup F-150	X18-139	F-150 Supercab Styleside 4WD XLT (6.5-ft Box), 139\WB	$21,573	$24,780
1998	Ford	Pickup F-150	X18-157	F-150 Supercab Styleside 4WD XLT (8-ft Box), 157\WB	$21,828	$25,080
1998	Ford	Pickup F-150	X18-139	F-150 Supercab Styleside 4WD Lariat (6.5-ft Box), 139\WB	$23,103	$26,580
1998	Ford	Pickup F-150	X18-157	F-150 Supercab Styleside 4WD Lariat (8-ft Box), 157\WB	$23,358	$26,880
1998	Ford	Pickup F-150	X08-139	F-150 Supercab Flareside 4WD XL (6.5-ft Box), 139\WB	$19,864	$22,770

Year	Make	Model	Code	Description		
1998	Ford	Pickup F-150	X08-139	F-150 Supercab Flareside 4WD XLT (6.5-ft Box) 139\WB	$22,223	$25,545
1998	Ford	Pickup F-150	X08-139	F-150 Supercab Flareside 4WD Lariat (6.5-ft Box), 139\WB	$23,753	$27,345
1998	Ford	Pickup F-250 (Under 8500# GVWR)	F27	2WD Regular Cab Styleside Models Standard (8-ft Box), 139\WB	$15,259	$16,760
1998	Ford	Pickup F-250 (Under 8500# GVWR)	F27	2WD Regular Cab Styleside Models XL (8-ft Box), 139\WB	$15,691	$17,860
1998	Ford	Pickup F-250 (Under 8500# GVWR)	F27	2WD Regular Cab Styleside Models XLT (8-ft Box), 139\WB	$17,872	$20,425
1998	Ford	Pickup F-250 (Under 8500# GVWR)	F27	2WD Regular Cab Styleside Models Lariat (8-ft Box), 139\WB	$19,402	$22,225
1998	Ford	Pickup F-250 (Under 8500# GVWR)	X27	2WD Supercab Styleside Models Standard (6.5-ft Box), 139\WB	$17,019	$18,760
1998	Ford	Pickup F-250 (Under 8500# GVWR)	X27	2WD Supercab Styleside Models XL (6.5-ft Box), 139\WB	$17,455	$19,935
1998	Ford	Pickup F-250 (Under 8500# GVWR)	X27	2WD Supercab Styleside Models XLT (6.5-ft Box), 139\WB	$19,945	$22,865
1998	Ford	Pickup F-250 (Under 8500# GVWR)	X27	2WD Supercab Styleside Models Lariat (6.5-ft Box), 139\WB	$21,475	$24,665
1998	Ford	Pickup F-250 (Under 8500# GVWR)	F28	4WD Regular Cab Styleside Models Standard (8-ft Box), 139\WB	$17,947	$19,815
1998	Ford	Pickup F-250 (Under 8500# GVWR)	F28	4WD Regular Cab Styleside Models XL (8-ft Box), 139\WB	$18,382	$21,025
1998	Ford	Pickup F-250 (Under 8500# GVWR)	F28	4WD Regular Cab Styleside Models XLT (8-ft Box), 139\WB	$20,464	$23,475

Year	Mfr.	Make	Code	Model	Invoice Price	Retail Price
1998	Ford	Pickup F-250 (Under 8500# GVWR)	F28	4WD Regular Cab Styleside Models Lariat (8-ft Box), 139\WB	$21,994	$25,275
1998	Ford	Pickup F-250 (Under 8500# GVWR)	X28	4WD Supercab Styleside Models Standard (6.5-ft Box), 139\WB	$19,707	$21,815
1998	Ford	Pickup F-250 (Under 8500# GVWR)	X28	4WD Supercab Styleside Models XL (6.5-ft Box), 139\WB	$20,145	$23,100
1998	Ford	Pickup F-250 (Under 8500# GVWR)	X28	4WD Supercab Styleside Models XLT (6.5-ft Box), 139\WB	$22,537	$25,915
1998	Ford	Pickup F-250 (Under 8500# GVWR)	X28	4WD Supercab Styleside Models Lariat (6.5-ft Box), 139\WB	$24,067	$27,715
1999	Ford	Pickup F-250 Super Duty	F20-137	2WD Regular Cab XL (8-ft Box), 137\WB	$16,362	$18,520
1999	Ford	Pickup F-250 Super Duty	F20-137	2WD Regular Cab XLT (8-ft Box), 137\WB	$17,535	$19,900
1999	Ford	Pickup F-250 Super Duty	F20-137	2WD Regular Cab Lariat (8-ft Box), 137\WB	$18,938	$21,550
1999	Ford	Pickup F-250 Super Duty	F21-137	4WD Regular Cab XL (8-ft Box), 137\WB	$18,997	$21,620
1999	Ford	Pickup F-250 Super Duty	F21-137	4WD Regular Cab XLT (8-ft Box), 137\WB	$20,170	$23,000
1999	Ford	Pickup F-250 Super Duty	F21-137	4WD Regular Cab Lariat (8-ft Box), 137\WB	$21,573	$24,650
1999	Ford	Pickup F-250 Super Duty	X20-142	2WD Super Cab XL (6 3/4-ft Box), 142\WB	$17,854	$20,275

Year	Make	Model	Code	Description		
1999	Ford	Pickup F-250 Super Duty	X20-158	2WD Super Cab XL (8-ft Box), 158\WB	$18,024	$20,475
1999	Ford	Pickup F-250 Super Duty	X20-142	2WD Super Cab XLT (6 3/4-ft Box), 142\WB	$19,027	$21,655
1999	Ford	Pickup F-250 Super Duty	X20-158	2WD Super Cab XLT (8-ft Box), 158\WB	$19,197	$21,855
1999	Ford	Pickup F-250 Super Duty	X20-142	2WD Super Cab Lariat (6 3/4-ft Box), 142\WB	$20,429	$23,305
1999	Ford	Pickup F-250 Super Duty	X20-158	2WD Super Cab Lariat (8-ft Box), 158\WB	$20,599	$23,505
1999	Ford	Pickup F-250 Super Duty	X21-142	4WD Super Cab XL (6 3/4-ft Box), 142\WB	$20,489	$23,375
1999	Ford	Pickup F-250 Super Duty	X21-158	4WD Super Cab XL (8-ft Box), 158\WB	$20,659	$23,575
1999	Ford	Pickup F-250 Super Duty	X21-142	4WD Super Cab XLT (6 3/4-ft Box), 142\WB	$21,662	$24,755
1999	Ford	Pickup F-250 Super Duty	X21-158	4WD Super Cab XLT (8-ft Box), 158\WB	$21,832	$24,955
1999	Ford	Pickup F-250 Super Duty	X21-142	4WD Super Cab Lariat (6 3/4-ft Box), 142\WB	$23,064	$26,405
1999	Ford	Pickup F-250 Super Duty	X21-158	4WD Super Cab Lariat (8-ft Box), 158\WB	$23,234	$26,605
1999	Ford	Pickup F-250 Super Duty	W20-156	2WD Crew Cab XL (6 3/4-ft Box), 156\WB	$19,320	$22,000
1999	Ford	Pickup F-250 Super Duty	W20-172	2WD Crew Cab XL (8-ft Box), 172\WB	$19,490	$22,200

Year	Mfr.	Make	Code	Model	Invoice Price	Retail Price
1999	Ford	Pickup F-250 Super Duty	W20-156	2WD Crew Cab XLT (6 3/4-ft Box), 156\WB	$20,493	$23,380
1999	Ford	Pickup F-250 Super Duty	W20-172	2WD Crew Cab XLT (8-ft Box), 172\WB	$20,663	$23,580
1999	Ford	Pickup F-250 Super Duty	W20-156	2WD Crew Cab Lariat (6 3/4-ft Box), 156\WB	$21,896	$25,030
1999	Ford	Pickup F-250 Super Duty	W20-172	2WD Crew Cab Lariat (8-ft Box), 172\WB	$22,066	$25,230
1999	Ford	Pickup F-250 Super Duty	W21-156	4WD Crew Cab XL (6 3/4-ft Box), 156\WB	$21,955	$25,100
1999	Ford	Pickup F-250 Super Duty	W21-172	4WD Crew Cab XL (8-ft Box), 172\WB	$22,125	$25,300
1999	Ford	Pickup F-250 Super Duty	W21-156	4WD Crew Cab XLT (6 3/4-ft Box), 156\WB	$23,128	$26,480
1999	Ford	Pickup F-250 Super Duty	W21-172	4WD Crew Cab XLT (8-ft Box), 172\WB	$23,298	$26,680
1999	Ford	Pickup F-250 Super Duty	W21-156	4WD Crew Cab Lariat (6 3/4-ft Box), 156\WB	$24,531	$28,130
1999	Ford	Pickup F-250 Super Duty	W21-172	4WD Crew Cab Lariat (8-ft Box), 172\WB	$24,701	$28,330
1999	Ford	Pickup F-350 Super Duty	F30-137	2WD Regular Cab, Single Rear Wheels (SRW) XL (8-ft Box), 137\WB	$16,991	$19,260
1999	Ford	Pickup F-350 Super Duty	F30-137	2WD Regular Cab, Single Rear Wheels (SRW) XLT (8-ft Box), 137\WB	$18,492	$21,025

Year	Make	Model	Code	Description		
1999	Ford	Pickup F-350 Super Duty	F30-137	2WD Regular Cab, Single Rear Wheels (SRW) Lariat (8-ft Box), 137\WB	$19,767	$22,525
1999	Ford	Pickup F-350 Super Duty	F31-137	4WD Regular Cab, Single Rear Wheels (SRW) XL (8-ft Box), 137\WB	$19,626	$22,360
1999	Ford	Pickup F-350 Super Duty	F31-137	4WD Regular Cab, Single Rear Wheels (SRW) XLT (8-ft Box), 137\WB	$20,918	$23,880
1999	Ford	Pickup F-350 Super Duty	X30-142	2WD Super Cab, Single Rear Wheels (SRW) XL (6 3/4-ft Box), 142\WB	$18,772	$21,355
1999	Ford	Pickup F-350 Super Duty	X30-158	2WD Super Cab, Single Rear Wheels (SRW) XL (8-ft Box), 158\WB	$18,942	$21,555
1999	Ford	Pickup F-350 Super Duty	X30-142	2WD Super Cab, Single Rear Wheels (SRW) XLT (6 3/4-ft Box), 142\WB	$20,272	$23,120
1999	Ford	Pickup F-350 Super Duty	X30-158	2WD Super Cab, Single Rear Wheels (SRW) XLT (8-ft Box), 158\WB	$20,442	$23,320
1999	Ford	Pickup F-350 Super Duty	X30-142	2WD Super Cab, Single Rear Wheels (SRW) Lariat (6 3/4-ft Box), 142\WB	$21,547	$24,620
1999	Ford	Pickup F-350 Super Duty	X30-158	2WD Super Cab, Single Rear Wheels (SRW) Lariat (8-ft Box), 158\WB	$21,717	$24,820
1999	Ford	Pickup F-350 Super Duty	X31-142	4WD Super Cab, Single Rear Wheels (SRW) XL B (6 3/4-ft Box), 142\W	$21,407	$24,455
1999	Ford	Pickup F-350 Super Duty	X31-158	4WD Super Cab, Single Rear Wheels (SRW) XL (8-ft Box), 158\WB	$21,577	$24,655
1999	Ford	Pickup F-350 Super Duty	X31-142	4WD Super Cab, Single Rear Wheels (SRW) XLT (6 3/4-ft Box), 142\WB	$22,699	$25,975
1999	Ford	Pickup F-350 Super Duty	X31-158	4WD Super Cab, Single Rear Wheels (SRW) XLT (8-ft Box), 158\WB	$22,869	$26,175

Year	Mfr.	Make	Code	Model	Invoice Price	Retail Price
1999	Ford	Pickup F-350 Super Duty	X31-142	4WD Super Cab, Single Rear Wheels (SRW) Lariat (6 3/4-ft Box), 142\WB	$23,974	$27,475
1999	Ford	Pickup F-350 Super Duty	X31-158	4WD Super Cab, Single Rear Wheels (SRW) Lariat (8-ft Box), 158\WB	$24,144	$27,675
1999	Ford	Pickup F-350 Super Duty	W30-156	2WD Crew Cab, Single Rear Wheels (SRW) XL (6 3/4-ft Box), 156\WB	$20,123	$22,945
1999	Ford	Pickup F-350 Super Duty	W30-172	2WD Crew Cab, Single Rear Wheels (SRW) XL (8-ft Box), 172\WB	$20,293	$23,145
1999	Ford	Pickup F-350 Super Duty	W30-156	2WD Crew Cab, Single Rear Wheels (SRW) XLT (6 3/4-ft Box), 156\WB	$21,623	$24,710
1999	Ford	Pickup F-350 Super Duty	W30-172	2WD Crew Cab, Single Rear Wheels (SRW) XLT (8-ft Box), 172\WB	$21,793	$24,910
1999	Ford	Pickup F-350 Super Duty	W30-156	2WD Crew Cab, Single Rear Wheels (SRW) Lariat (6 3/4-ft Box), 156\WB	$22,898	$26,210
1999	Ford	Pickup F-350 Super Duty	W30-172	2WD Crew Cab, Single Rear Wheels (SRW) Lariat (8-ft Box), 172\WB	$23,068	$26,410
1999	Ford	Pickup F-350 Super Duty	W31-156	4WD Crew Cab, Single Rear Wheels (SRW) XL (6 3/4-ft Box), 156\WB	$22,546	$25,795
1999	Ford	Pickup F-350 Super Duty	W31-172	4WD Crew Cab, Single Rear Wheels (SRW) XL (8-ft Box), 172\WB	$22,716	$25,995
1999	Ford	Pickup F-350 Super Duty	W31-156	4WD Crew Cab, Single Rear Wheels (SRW) XLT (6 3/4-ft Box), 156\WB	$23,837	$27,315
1999	Ford	Pickup F-350 Super Duty	W31-172	4WD Crew Cab, Single Rear Wheels (SRW) XLT (8-ft Box), 172\WB	$24,007	$27,515

Year	Make	Model	Code	Description		
1999	Ford	Pickup F-350 Super Duty	W31-156	4WD Crew Cab, Single Rear Wheels (SRW) Lariat (6 3/4-ft Box), 156\WB	$25,112	$28,815
1999	Ford	Pickup F-350 Super Duty	W31-172	4WD Crew Cab, Single Rear Wheels (SRW) Lariat (8-ft Box), 172\WB	$25,282	$29,015
1999	Ford	Pickup F-350 Super Duty	F32-137	2WD Regular Cab, Dual Rear Wheels (DRW) XL (8-ft Box), 137\WB	$17,812	$20,225
1999	Ford	Pickup F-350 Super Duty	F32-137	2WD Regular Cab, Dual Rear Wheels (DRW) XLT (8-ft Box), 137\WB	$19,312	$21,990
1999	Ford	Pickup F-350 Super Duty	F32-137	2WD Regular Cab, Dual Rear Wheels (DRW) Lariat (8-ft Box), 137\WB	$20,587	$23,490
1999	Ford	Pickup F-350 Super Duty	F33-137	4WD Regular Cab, Dual Rear Wheels (DRW) XL (8-ft Box), 137\WB	$20,540	$23,435
1999	Ford	Pickup F-350 Super Duty	F33-137	4WD Regular Cab, Dual Rear Wheels (DRW) XLT (8-ft Box), 137\WB	$21,832	$24,955
1999	Ford	Pickup F-350 Super Duty	F33-137	4WD Regular Cab, Dual Rear Wheels (DRW) Lariat (8-ft Box), 137\WB	$23,107	$26,455
1999	Ford	Pickup F-350 Super Duty	X32-158	2WD Super Cab, Dual Rear Wheels (DRW) XL (8-ft Box), 158\WB	$19,757	$22,515
1999	Ford	Pickup F-350 Super Duty	X32-158	2WD Super Cab, Dual Rear Wheels (DRW) XLT (8-ft Box), 158\WB	$21,258	$24,280
1999	Ford	Pickup F-350 Super Duty	X32-158	2WD Super Cab, Dual Rear Wheels (DRW) Lariat (8-ft Box), 158\WB	$22,533	$25,780
1999	Ford	Pickup F-350 Super Duty	X33-158	4WD Super Cab, Dual Rear Wheels (DRW) XL (8-ft Box), 158\WB	$22,487	$25,725
1999	Ford	Pickup F-350 Super Duty	X33-158	4WD Super Cab, Dual Rear Wheels (DRW) XLT (8-ft Box), 158\WB	$23,778	$27,245

Year	Mfr.	Make	Code	Model	Invoice Price	Retail Price
1999	Ford	Pickup F-350 Super Duty	X33-158	4WD Super Cab, Dual Rear Wheels (DRW) Lariat (8-ft Box), 158\WB	$25,053	$28,745
1999	Ford	Pickup F-350 Super Duty	W32-156	2WD Crew Cab, Dual Rear Wheels (DRW) XL (6 3/4-ft Box), 156\WB	$21,156	$24,160
1999	Ford	Pickup F-350 Super Duty	W32-172	2WD Crew Cab, Dual Rear Wheels (DRW) XL (8-ft Box), 172\WB	$21,326	$24,360
1999	Ford	Pickup F-350 Super Duty	W32-156	2WD Crew Cab, Dual Rear Wheels (DRW) XLT (6 3/4-ft Box), 156\WB	$22,657	$25,925
1999	Ford	Pickup F-350 Super Duty	W32-172	2WD Crew Cab, Dual Rear Wheels (DRW) XLT (8-ft Box), 172\WB	$22,827	$26,125
1999	Ford	Pickup F-350 Super Duty	W32-156	2WD Crew Cab, Dual Rear Wheels (DRW) Lariat (6 3/4-ft Box), 156\WB	$23,932	$27,425
1999	Ford	Pickup F-350 Super Duty	W32-172	2WD Crew Cab, Dual Rear Wheels (DRW) Lariat (8-ft Box), 172\WB	$24,102	$27,625
1999	Ford	Pickup F-350 Super Duty	W33-156	4WD Crew Cab, Dual Rear Wheels (DRW) XL (6 3/4-ft Box), 156\WB	$23,672	$27,120
1999	Ford	Pickup F-350 Super Duty	W33-172	4WD Crew Cab, Dual Rear Wheels (DRW) XL (8-ft Box), 172\WB	$23,842	$27,320
1999	Ford	Pickup F-350 Super Duty	W33-156	4WD Crew Cab, Dual Rear Wheels (DRW) XLT (6 3/4-ft Box), 156\WB	$24,964	$28,640
1999	Ford	Pickup F-350 Super Duty	W33-172	4WD Crew Cab, Dual Rear Wheels (DRW) XLT (8-ft Box), 172\WB	$25,134	$28,840
1999	Ford	Pickup F-350 Super Duty	W33-156	4WD Crew Cab, Dual Rear Wheels (DRW) Lariat (6 3/4-ft Box), 156\WB	$26,239	$30,140

Year	Make	Model	Code	Description		
1999	Ford	Pickup F-350 Super Duty	W33-172	4WD Crew Cab, Dual Rear Wheels (DRW) Lariat (8-ft Box), 172\WB	$26,409	$30,340
1999	Ford	Pickup F-350 Super DutyPickup	F31-137	4WD Regular Cab, Single Rear Wheels (SRW) Lariat (8-ft Box), 137\WB	$22,193	$25,380
1998	Ford	Ranger	R10-112	2WD Regular Cab Models XL (6-ft Box), 112\WB	$10,880	$11,435
1998	Ford	Ranger	R10-118	2WD Regular Cab Models XL (7-ft Box), 118\WB	$11,312	$11,905
1998	Ford	Ranger	R10-112	2WD Regular Cab Models XLT (6-ft Box), 112\WB	$12,025	$13,255
1998	Ford	Ranger	R10-118	2WD Regular Cab Models XLT (7-ft Box), 118\WB	$12,508	$13,805
1998	Ford	Ranger	R10-112	2WD Regular Cab Models Splash (6-ft Box), 112\WB	$13,556	$14,995
1998	Ford	Ranger	R14-126	2WD Supercab Models XL (6-ft Box), 126\WB	$13,464	$14,890
1998	Ford	Ranger	R14-126	2WD Supercab Models XLT (6-ft Box), 126\WB	$13,908	$15,395
1998	Ford	Ranger	R14-126	2WD Supercab Models Splash (6-ft Box), 126\WB	$14,990	$16,625
1998	Ford	Ranger	R11-112	4WD Regular Cab Models XL (6-ft Box), 112\WB	$14,864	$15,765
1998	Ford	Ranger	R11-118	4WD Regular Cab Models XL (7-ft Box), 118\WB	$15,296	$16,235
1998	Ford	Ranger	R11-112	4WD Regular Cab Models XLT (6-ft Box), 112\WB	$15,580	$17,295
1998	Ford	Ranger	R11-118	4WD Regular Cab Models XLT (7-ft Box), 118\WB	$16,099	$17,885
1998	Ford	Ranger	R11-112	4WD Regular Cab Models Splash (6-ft Box), 112\WB	$16,873	$18,765
1998	Ford	Ranger	R15-126	4WD Supercab Model Splash (6-ft Box), 126\WB	$17,604	$19,595
1998	Ford	Ranger	R15-126	4WD Supercab Model XL (6-ft Box), 126\WB	$15,646	$17,370
1998	Ford	Ranger	R15-126	4WD Supercab Model XLT (6-ft Box), 126\WB	$16,886	$18,780
1998	Ford	Taurus	P52	Sedan 4-Door LX	$16,965	$18,345
1998	Ford	Taurus	P52/60E	Sedan 4-Door SE	$17,761	$19,455
1998	Ford	Taurus	P54	Sedan 4-Door SHO	$26,194	$28,920

Year	Mfr.	Make	Code	Model	Invoice Price	Retail Price
1998	Ford	Taurus	P57	Wagon 4-Door SE	$19,328	$21,205
1998	Ford	Windstar	BAE	Van 3-Door	$16,472	$18,110
1998	Ford	Windstar	A51	3.0L Wagon 3-Door	$17,977	$19,380
1998	Ford	Windstar	A51	GL Wagon 3-Door	$19,068	$21,060
1998	Ford	Windstar	A51	LX Wagon 3-Door	$23,683	$26,305
1998	Ford	Windstar	A51	Limited Wagon 3-Door	$26,587	$29,605
1998	GMC	Jimmy	TS10516	2WD Model 2-Door Tailgate, 100.5\WB	$19,716	$21,786
1998	GMC	Jimmy	TS10506	2WD Model 4-Door Tailgate, 107\WB	$21,600	$23,867
1998	GMC	Jimmy	TT10516	4WD Model 2-Door Tailgate,100.5\WB	$21,515	$23,774
1998	GMC	Jimmy	TT10506	4WD Model 4-Door Tailgate, 107\WB	$23,399	$25,855
1998	GMC	Pickup Sierra C-K 1500	TC10703/E63/1SL	C1500 Pickup Regular Cab 2WD Wideside Special (6.5-ft Box), 117.5\WB	$13,575	$15,000
1998	GMC	Pickup Sierra C-K 1500	TC10903/E63/1SL	C1500 Pickup Regular Cab 2WD Wideside Special (8-ft Box), 131.5\WB	$13,865	$15,320
1998	GMC	Pickup Sierra C-K 1500	TC10703/E63/1SA	C1500 Pickup Regular Cab 2WD Wideside SL Décor (6.5-ft Box), 117.5\WB	$14,372	$16,425
1998	GMC	Pickup Sierra C-K 1500	TC10903/E63/1SA	C1500 Pickup Regular Cab 2WD Wideside SL Décor (8-ft Box), 131.5\WB	$14,634	$16,725
1998	GMC	Pickup Sierra C-K 1500	TC10703/E62/1SA	C1500 Pickup Regular Cab 2WD Sportside SL Décor (6.5-ft Box), 117.5\WB	$14,875	$17,000
1998	GMC	Pickup Sierra C-K 1500	TC10753/E63/1SA	C1500 Pickup Extended Cab 2WD Wideside SL Décor (6.5-ft Box), 141.5\WB	$16,122	$18,425

Year	Make	Model	Code	Description		
1998	GMC	Pickup Sierra C-K 1500	TC10953/E63/1SA	C1500 Pickup Extended Cab 2WD Wideside SL Décor (8-ft Box), 155.5\WB	$16,818	$19,220
1998	GMC	Pickup Sierra C-K 1500	TC10753/E62/1SC	C1500 Pickup Extended Cab 2WD Sportside SLE Décor (6.5-ft Box), 141.5\WB	$20,273	$23,169
1998	GMC	Pickup Sierra C-K 1500	TK10703/E63/1SL	K1500 Pickup Regular Cab 4WD Wideside Special (6.5-ft Box), 117.5\WB	$16,924	$18,700
1998	GMC	Pickup Sierra C-K 1500	TK10903/E63/1SL	K1500 Pickup Regular Cab 4WD Wideside Special (8-ft Box), 131.5\WB	$17,213	$19,020
1998	GMC	Pickup Sierra C-K 1500	TK10703/E63/1SA	K1500 Pickup Regular Cab 4WD Wideside SL Décor (6.5-ft Box), 117.5\WB	$16,997	$19,425
1998	GMC	Pickup Sierra C-K 1500	TK10903/E63/1SA	K1500 Pickup Regular Cab 4WD Wideside SL Décor (8-ft Box), 131.5\WB	$17,259	$19,725
1998	GMC	Pickup Sierra C-K 1500	TK10703/E62/1SA	K1500 Pickup Regular Cab 4WD Sportside SL Décor (6.5-ft Box), 117.5\WB	$17,500	$20,000
1998	GMC	Pickup Sierra C-K 1500	TK10753/E63/1SA	K1500 Pickup Extended Cab 4WD Wideside SL Décor (6.5-ft Box), 141.5\WB	$18,747	$21,425
1998	GMC	Pickup Sierra C-K 1500	TK10953/E63/1SA	K1500 Pickup Extended Cab 4WD Wideside SL Décor (8-ft Box), 155.5\WB	$19,443	$22,220
1998	GMC	Pickup Sierra C-K 1500	TK10753/E62/1SC	K1500 Pickup Extended Cab 4WD Sportside SLE Décor (6.5-ft Box), 141.5\WB	$22,898	$26,169
1998	GMC	Pickup Sierra C-K 2500	TC20903/C5Z	C2500 Regular Cab 2WD Wideside (8-ft Box), 131.5\WB	$15,664	$17,902
1998	GMC	Pickup Sierra C-K 2500	TC20903/C6P	C2500 Regular Cab 2WD Heavy-Duty Wideside (8-ft Box), 131.5\WB	$16,578	$18,950
1998	GMC	Pickup Sierra C-K 2500	TC20753/C5Z	C2500 Extended Cab 2WD Wideside (6.5-ft Box), 141.5\WB	$17,953	$20,518

Year	Mfr.	Make	Code	Model	Invoice Price	Retail Price
1998	GMC	Pickup Sierra C-K 2500	TC20953/C6P	C2500 Extended Cab 2WD Heavy-Duty Wideside (8-ft Box), 155.5\WB	$17,981	$20,554
1998	GMC	Pickup Sierra C-K 2500	TK20903/C 6P	K2500 Regular Cab 4WD Heavy-Duty Wideside (8-ft Box), 131.5\WB	$18,988	$21,705
1998	GMC	Pickup Sierra C-K 2500	TK20753/C6P	K2500 Extended Cab 4WD Heavy-Duty Wideside (6.5-ft Box), 141.5\WB	$20,699	$23,660
1998	GMC	Pickup Sierra C-K 2500	TK20953/C6P	K2500 Extended Cab 4WD Heavy-Duty Wideside (8-ft Box), 155.5\WB	$20,810	$23,787
1998	GMC	Pickup Sierra C-K 3500	TC30903	C3500 2WD Regular Cab Wideside (8-ft Box), 131.5\WB	$16,699	$19,089
1998	GMC	Pickup Sierra C-K 3500	TC30953	C3500 2WD Extended Cab Wideside (8-ft Box), 155.5\WB, Dual Rear Wheels	$19,698	$22,512
1998	GMC	Pickup Sierra C-K 3500	TK30903	K3500 4WD Regular Cab Wideside (8-ft Box), 131.5\WB	$19,324	$22,089
1998	GMC	Pickup Sierra C-K 3500	TK30953	K3500 4WD Extended Cab Wideside (8-ft Box), 155.5\WB, Dual Rear Wheels	$22,158	$25,323
1998	GMC	Pickup Sierra Crew Cab	TC30943	Crew Cab 4-Door 2WD (8-ft), 168.5\WB	$19,438	$22,219
1998	GMC	Pickup Sierra Crew Cab	TK30943	Crew Cab 4-Door 4WD (8ft), 168.5\WB	$2,215	$25,393
1998	GMC	Pickup Sonoma	TS10603/R9S	2WD Regular Cab Models SL Wideside (6.1-ft) Box, 108.3\WB	$11,351	$12,012
1998	GMC	Pickup Sonoma	TS10603/YC3	2WD Regular Cab Models SLS Sport Wideside (6.1-ft) Box, 108.3\WB	$12,100	$13,370
1998	GMC	Pickup Sonoma	TS10603/YC3	2WD Regular Cab Models SLS Sport Sportside (6.1-ft) Box, 108.3\WB	$12,530	$13,845

Year	Make	Model	Code	Description		
1998	GMC	Pickup Sonoma	TS10803/R9S	2WD Regular Cab Models SL Wideside (7.4-ft) Box, 117.9\WB	$11,979	$12,676
1998	GMC	Pickup Sonoma	TS10803/YC3	2WD Regular Cab Models SLS Sport Wideside (7.4-ft) Box, 117.9\WB	$12,418	$13,721
1998	GMC	Pickup Sonoma	TS10653/YC3	2WD Extended Cab Models SLS Sport Wideside (6.1-ft) Box, 122.9\WB	$13,956	$15,421
1998	GMC	Pickup Sonoma	TS10653/YC3	2WD Extended Cab Models SLS Sport Sportside (6.1-ft) Box, 122.9\WB	$14,386	$15,896
1998	GMC	Pickup Sonoma	TT10603/R9S	4WD Regular Cab Models SL Wideside (6.1-ft) Box, 108.3\WB	$15,644	$16,555
1998	GMC	Pickup Sonoma	TT10603/YC3	4WD Regular Cab Models SLS Sport Wideside (6.1-ft) Box, 108.3\WB	$16,175	$17,873
1998	GMC	Pickup Sonoma	TT10603/YC3	4WD Regular Cab Models SLS Sport Sportside (6.1-ft) Box, 108.3\WB	$16,582	$18,323
1998	GMC	Pickup Sonoma	TT10803/R9S	4WD Regular Cab Models SL Wideside (7.4-ft) Box, 117.9\WB	$15,958	$16,887
1998	GMC	Pickup Sonoma	TT10803/YC3	4WD Regular Cab Models SLS Sport Wideside (7.4-ft) Box, 117.9\WB	$16,562	$18,300
1998	GMC	Pickup Sonoma	TT10653/YC3	4WD Extended Cab Models SLS Sport Wideside (6.1-ft) Box, 122.9\WB	$17,895	$19,773
1998	GMC	Pickup Sonoma	TT10653/YC3	4WD Extended Cab Models SLS Sport Wideside (6.1-ft) Box, 122.9\WB	$18,302	$20,223
1998	GMC	Safari Cargo Van	TM11005/R9S	SL 2WD, 111\WB	$17,561	$19,404
1998	GMC	Safari Cargo Van	TL11005/R9S	SL AWD, 111\WB	$19,733	$21,804
1998	GMC	Safari Passenger Van	TM11006	SL 2WD, 111\WB	$18,225	$20,183

Year	Mfr.	Make	Code	Model	Invoice Price	Retail Price
1998	GMC	Safari Passenger Van	TL11006	SL AWD, 111\WB	$20,306	$22,438
1998	GMC	Savana Cargo Van	TG11405/R9S	1500 STD, 135\WB	$17,129	$19,576
1998	GMC	Savana Cargo Van	TG21405/R9S	2500 STD, 135\WB	$17,501	$20,001
1998	GMC	Savana Cargo Van	TG21705/R9S	2500 STD, 155\WB	$18,288	$20,901
1998	GMC	Savana Cargo Van	TG31405/R9S	3500 STD, 135\WB	$18,840	$21,535
1998	GMC	Savana Cargo Van	TG31705/R9S	3500 STD, 155\WB	$19,627	$22,435
1998	GMC	Savana Passenger Van	TG11406/R9S	1500 STD, 135\WB	$19,972	$22,825
1998	GMC	Savana Passenger Van	TG21406/R9S	2500 STD, 135\WB	$22,159	$25,325
1998	GMC	Savana Passenger Van	TG21706/R9S	2500 STD, 155\WB	$22,947	$26,225
1998	GMC	Savana Passenger Van	TG31406/R9S	3500 STD, 135\WB	$22,409	$25,614
1998	GMC	Savana Passenger Van	TG31706/R9S	3500 STD, 155\WB	$23,196	$26,514
1998	GMC	Suburban	TC10906	C1500 2WD, 131.5\WB	$21,988	$25,129
1998	GMC	Suburban	TK10906	K1500 4WD, 131.5\WB	$24,613	$28,129
1998	GMC	Suburban	TC20906	C2500 2WD, 131.5\WB	$23,370	$26,713
1998	GMC	Suburban	TK20906	K2500 4WD, 131.5\WB	$25,995	$29,713
1998	GMC	Yukon	TC10706/YE9	SLE 4-Door 2WD, 117.5\WB	$25,904	$29,604
1998	GMC	Yukon	TK10706/YE9	SLE 4-Door 4WD, 117.5\WB	$28,529	$32,604
1998	Honda	Accord	CG314WPBW	Coupe 2-Door w/4-CYL. Engine LX (5-speed Manual)	$16,162	$18,290
1998	Honda	Accord	CG324WPBW	Coupe 2-Door w/4-CYL. Engine LX (4-speed ECT Automatic)	$16,869	$19,090

Year	Make	Model	Code	Description		
1998	Honda	Accord	CG315WJW	Coupe 2-Door w/4-CYL. Engine EX w/Cloth Trim (5-speed Manual)	$18,380	$20,800
1998	Honda	Accord	CG325WJW	Coupe 2-Door w/4-CYL. Engine EX w/Cloth Trim (4-speed ECT Automatic)	$19,086	$21,600
1998	Honda	Accord	CG327WJW	Coupe 2-Door w/4-CYL. Engine EX ULEV w/Cloth Trim (4-speed ECT Automatic)	$19,086	$21,600
1998	Honda	Accord	CG315WJNW	Coupe 2-Door w/4-CYL. Engine EX w/Leather Trim (5-speed Manual)	$19,396	$21,950
1998	Honda	Accord	CG325WJNW	Coupe 2-Door w/4-CYL. Engine EX w/Leather Trim (4-speed ECT Automatic)	$20,103	$22,750
1998	Honda	Accord	CG327WJNW	Coupe 2-Door w/4-CYL. Engine EX ULEV w/Leather Trim (4-speed ECT Automatic)	$20,103	$22,750
1998	Honda	Accord	CG224WPBW	Coupe 2-Door w/V6 Engine LX (4-speed ECT Automatic)	$19,042	$21,550
1998	Honda	Accord	CG225WJNW	Coupe 2-Door w/V6 Engine EX (4-speed ECT Automatic)	$21,340	$24,150
1998	Honda	Accord	CF854WPBW	Sedan 4-Door w/4-CYL. Engine DX (5-speed Manual)	$13,343	$15,100
1998	Honda	Accord	CF864WPBW	Sedan 4-Door w/4-CYL. Engine DX (4-speed ECT Automatic)	$14,050	$15,900
1998	Honda	Accord	CG554WPBW	Sedan 4-Door w/4-CYL. Engine LX w/o Anti-Lock Brakes (5-speed Manual)	$16,162	$18,290
1998	Honda	Accord	CG564WPBW	Sedan 4-Door w/4-CYL. Engine LX w/o Anti-Lock Brakes (4-speed ECT Automatic)	$16,869	$19,090
1998	Honda	Accord	CG564WEW	Sedan 4-Door w/4-CYL. Engine LX w/ Anti-Lock Brakes (4-speed ECT Automatic)	$17,399	$19,690

Year	Mfr.	Make	Code	Model	Invoice Price	Retail Price
1998	Honda	Accord	CG555WJW	Sedan 4-Door w/4-CYL. Engine EX w/Cloth Trim (5-speed Manual)	$18,380	$20,800
1998	Honda	Accord	CG565WJW	Sedan 4-Door w/4-CYL. Engine EX w/Cloth Trim (4-speed ECT Automatic)	$19,086	$21,600
1998	Honda	Accord	CG667WJW	Sedan 4-Door w/4-CYL. Engine EX ULEV w/Cloth Trim (4-speed ECT Automatic)	$19,086	$21,600
1998	Honda	Accord	CG555WJNW	Sedan 4-Door w/4-CYL. Engine EX w/Leather Trim (5-speed Manual)	$19,396	$21,950
1998	Honda	Accord	CG565WJNW	Sedan 4-Door w/4-CYL. Engine EX w/Leather Trim (4-speed ECT Automatic)	$20,103	$22,750
1998	Honda	Accord	CG667WJNW	Sedan 4-Door w/4-CYL. Engine EX ULEV w/Leather Trim (4-speed ECT Automatic)	$20,103	$22,750
1998	Honda	Accord	CG164WPBW	Sedan 4-Door w/V6 Engine LX (4-speed ECT Automatic)	$19,042	$21,550
1998	Honda	Accord	CG165WJNW	Sedan 4-Door w/V6 Engine EX w/Leather Trim (4-speed ECT Automatic)	$21,340	$24,150
1998	Honda	Civic	EJ632WBW	Hatchback 3-Door CX (5-speed Manual)	$9,990	$10,650
1998	Honda	Civic	EJ642WPBW	Hatchback 3-Door CX (4-speed ECT Automatic)	$10,928	$11,650
1998	Honda	Civic	EJ634WPBW	Hatchback 3-Door DX (5-speed Manual)	$10,856	$12,100
1998	Honda	Civic	EJ644WPBW	Hatchback 3-Door DX (4-speed ECT Automatic)	$11,574	$12,900
1998	Honda	Civic	EJ612WPBW	Coupe 2-Door DX (5-speed Manual)	$11,287	$12,580
1998	Honda	Civic	EJ622WPBW	Coupe 2-Door DX (4-speed ECT Automatic)	$12,005	$13,380
1998	Honda	Civic	EJ712WPBW	Coupe 2-Door HX (5-speed Manual)	$12,022	$13,400

Year	Make	Model	Code	Description		
1998	Honda	Civic	EJ722WPBW	Coupe 2-Door HX (CVT Continuously Variable Transmission)	$12,920	$14,400
1998	Honda	Civic	EJ814WFW	Coupe 2-Door EX (5-speed Manual)	$13,682	$15,250
1998	Honda	Civic	EJ824WFW	Coupe 2-Door EX (4-speed ECT Automatic)	$14,400	$16,050
1998	Honda	Civic	EJ825WFW	Coupe 2-Door EX \A\ w/Anti Lock Brakes (4-speed ECT Automatic)	$14,938	$16,650
1998	Honda	Civic	EJ652WPBW	Sedan 4-Door DX (5-speed Manual)	$11,426	$12,735
1998	Honda	Civic	EJ662WPBW	Sedan 4-Door DX (4-speed ECT Automatic)	$12,144	$13,535
1998	Honda	Civic	EJ657WPBW	Sedan 4-Door LX (5-speed Manual)	$12,988	$14,750
1998	Honda	Civic	EJ667WPBW	Sedan 4-Door LX (4-speed ECT Automatic)	$13,706	$15,550
1998	Honda	Civic	EJ854WJW	Sedan 4-Door EX (5-speed Manual)	$14,786	$16,480
1998	Honda	Civic	EJ864WJW	Sedan 4-Door EX (4-speed ECT Automatic)	$15,504	$17,280
1998	Honda	CR-V	RD284WPBW	2WD Sport Utility 5-Door LX (4-speed Automatic)	$16,651	$18,350
1998	Honda	CR-V	RD174WPBW	4WD Sport Utility 5-Door LX (5-speed Manual)	$17,014	$18,750
1998	Honda	CR-V	RD184WPBW	4WD Sport Utility 5-Door LX (4-speed Automatic)	$17,740	$19,550
1998	Honda	CR-V	RD176WEW	4WD Sport Utility 5-Door EX (5-speed Manual)	$18,375	$20,250
1998	Honda	CR-V	RD186WEW	4WD Sport Utility 5-Door EX (4-speed Automatic)	$19,101	$21,050
1998	Honda	Odyssey	RA384WEW	LX Minivan 7-Passenger 5-Door	$21,039	$23,810
1998	Honda	Odyssey	RA386WEW	LX Minivan 6-Passenger 5-Door	$21,401	$24,220
1998	Honda	Odyssey	RA387WJW	EX Minivan 6-Passenger 5-Door	$22,798	$25,800
1998	Honda	Passport	9B214W2B1	2WD Models LX (5-speed Manual)	$20,135	$22,700
1998	Honda	Passport	9B224W2BA	2WD Models LX (4-speed Automatic)	$21,155	$23,850
1998	Honda	Passport	9B226W2EA	2WD Models EX w/Cloth Trim (4-speed Automatic)	$23,506	$26,500

Year	Mfr.	Make	Code	Model	Invoice Price	Retail Price
1998	Honda	Passport	9B227W2LA	2WD Models EX w/Leather Trim (4-speed Automatic)	$24,393	$27,500
1998	Honda	Passport	9B314W4B1	4WD Models LX (5-speed Manual)	$22,574	$25,450
1998	Honda	Passport	9B324W4BA	4WD Models LX (4-speed Automatic)	$23,594	$26,600
1998	Honda	Passport	9B315W4B1	4WD Models LX (5-speed Manual) w/Wheel Package	$22,929	$25,850
1998	Honda	Passport	9B325W4BA	4WD Models LX (4-speed Automatic) w/Wheel Package	$23,949	$27,000
1998	Honda	Passport	9B326W4EA	4WD Models EX w/Cloth Trim (4-speed Automatic)	$25,679	$28,950
1998	Honda	Passport	9B327W4LA	4WD Models EX w/Leather Trim (4-speed Automatic)	$26,566	$29,950
1998	Honda	Prelude	BB614WJW	Base Coupe 2-Door (5-speed Manual)	$20,667	$23,300
1998	Honda	Prelude	BB624WJW	Base Coupe 2-Door (4-speed Automatic Sequential Sport Shift)	$21,554	$24,300
1998	Honda	Prelude	BB615WJW	Type SH Coupe 2-Door (5-speed Manual)	$22,885	$25,800
1998	Hyundai	Accent	12393	Hatchback L 3-Door (5-speed Manual)	$8,622	$9,099
1998	Hyundai	Accent	12333	Hatchback GS 3-Door (5-speed Manual)	$9,175	$9,899
1998	Hyundai	Accent	12332	Hatchback GS 3-Door (4-speed Automatic)	$9,860	$10,654
1998	Hyundai	Accent	12343	Hatchback GSi 3-Door (5-speed Manual)	$9,918	$10,699
1998	Hyundai	Accent	12342	Hatchback GSi 3-Door (4-speed Automatic)	$10,602	$11,454
1998	Hyundai	Accent	12423	Sedan GL 4-Door (5-speed Manual)	$9,547	$10,299
1998	Hyundai	Accent	12422	Sedan GL 4-Door (4-speed Automatic)	$10,231	$11,054

Year	Make	Model	Code	Description		
1998	Hyundai	Elantra	41423	Sedan 4-Door Base (5-speed Manual)	$10,541	$11,499
1998	Hyundai	Elantra	41422	Sedan 4-Door Base (4-speed ECT Automatic)	$11,266	$12,299
1998	Hyundai	Elantra	41443	Sedan 4-Door GLS (5-speed Manual)	$11,245	$12,549
1998	Hyundai	Elantra	41442	Sedan 4-Door GLS (4-speed ECT Automatic)	$11,970	$13,349
1998	Hyundai	Elantra	41523	Wagon 4-Door Base (5-speed Manual)	$11,366	$12,399
1998	Hyundai	Elantra	41522	Wagon 4-Door Base (4-speed ECT Automatic)	$12,091	$13,199
1998	Hyundai	Elantra	41542	Wagon 4-Door GLS (4-speed ECT Automatic)	$12,545	$13,999
1998	Hyundai	Sonata	22403	Base Sedan 4-Door (5-speed Manual)	$13,444	$14,749
1998	Hyundai	Sonata	22402	Base Sedan 4-Door (4-speed ECT Automatic)	$14,235	$15,549
1998	Hyundai	Sonata	22422	GL Sedan 4-Door (4-speed ECT Automatic)	$14,735	$16,349
1998	Hyundai	Sonata	22432	GL V6 Sedan 4-Door (4-speed ECT Automatic w/Adaptive Control)	$15,636	$17,349
1998	Hyundai	Sonata	22452	GLS V6 Sedan 4-Door (4-speed ECT Automatic w/Adaptive Control)	$16,355	$18,549
1998	Hyundai	Tiburon	51323	Base Hatchback Coupe 2-Door (5-speed Manual)	$12,326	$13,599
1998	Hyundai	Tiburon	51322	Base Hatchback Coupe 2-Door (4-speed Automatic)	$13,051	$14,399
1998	Hyundai	Tiburon	51343	FX Hatchback Coupe 2-Door (5-speed Manual)	$13,198	$14,899
1998	Hyundai	Tiburon	51342	FX Hatchback Coupe 2-Door (4-speed Automatic)	$13,923	$15,699
1998	Infiniti	I30	95018	Standard Sedan (4-speed Automatic)	$25,683	$28,900
1998	Infiniti	I30	95758	Touring Sedan (5-speed Manual)	$27,676	$31,500
1998	Infiniti	I30	95718	Touring Sedan (4-speed Automatic)	$28,555	$32,500
1998	Infiniti	Q45	94318	Base Luxury Performance Sedan 4-Door	$42,569	$47,900
1998	Infiniti	Q45	94818	Q45t Luxury Performance Sedan 4-Door	$44,346	$49,900

Year	Mfr.	Make	Code	Model	Invoice Price	Retail Price
1998	Infiniti	QX4	71018	Luxury Sport Utility 4-Door 4WD	$31,666	$35,550
1998	Isuzu	Hombre	P14	2WD Pickup Regular Cab S (4-speed Automatic)	$11,517	$12,519
1998	Isuzu	Hombre	P15	2WD Pickup Regular Cab S (5-speed Manual)	$10,533	$11,449
1998	Isuzu	Hombre	P24	2WD Pickup Regular Cab XS (4-speed Automatic)	$11,749	$13,054
1998	Isuzu	Hombre	P25	2WD Pickup Regular Cab XS (5-speed Manual)	$10,786	$11,984
1998	Isuzu	Hombre	P54	2WD Pickup Spacecab XS w/2.2L 4-Cyl. Engine (4-speed Automatic)	$13,962	$16,235
1998	Isuzu	Hombre	P55	2WD Pickup Spacecab XS (5-speed Manual)	$13,042	$15,165
1998	Isuzu	Hombre	P64	2WD Pickup Spacecab XS w/4.3L V6 Engine (4-speed Automatic)	$14,955	$17,390
1998	Isuzu	Hombre	T35	4WD Pickup S Regular Cab (5-speed Manual)	$15,396	$17,107
1998	Isuzu	Hombre	T65	4WD Pickup XS Spacecab (5-speed Manual)	$17,353	$20,178
1998	Isuzu	Hombre	T64	4WD Pickup XS Spacecab (4-speed Automatic)	$18,066	$21,007
1998	Isuzu	Oasis	J54	S Minivan 5-Door	$20,708	$23,532
1998	Isuzu	Oasis	J64	LS Minivan 5-Door	$22,706	$25,802
1998	Isuzu	Rodeo	P45	2WD Models S 4-Cyl. (5-speed Manual)	$18,196	$17,995
1998	Isuzu	Rodeo	R44	2WD Models S V6 (4-speed Automatic)	$18,767	$21,950
1998	Isuzu	Rodeo	R45	2WD Models S V6 (5-speed Manual)	$17,912	$20,950
1998	Isuzu	Rodeo	R64	2WD Models LS V6 (4-speed Automatic)	$22,432	$26,390
1998	Isuzu	Rodeo	V44	4WD Models S V6 (4-speed Automatic)	$20,604	$24,240
1998	Isuzu	Rodeo	V45	4WD Models S V6 (5-speed Manual)	$19,754	$23,240

Year	Make	Model	Code	Description		
1998	Isuzu	Rodeo	V64	4WD Models LS V6 (4-speed Automatic)	$24,429	$28,910
1998	Isuzu	Rodeo	V65	4WD Models LS V6 (5-speed Manual)	$23,584	$27,910
1998	Isuzu	Trooper	L44	S 4-Door (4-speed Automatic)	$23,630	$27,800
1998	Isuzu	Trooper	L45	S 4-Door (5-speed Manual)	$22,568	$26,550
1998	Jaguar	XJ Series Sedans	2811	XJ8 Sedan 4-Door	$47,830	$54,750
1998	Jaguar	XJ Series Sedans	2851	XJ8 L Sedan 4-Door, Long Wheelbase	$52,198	$59,750
1998	Jaguar	XJ Series Sedans	2853	Vanden Plas Sedan 4-Door, Long Wheelbase	$55,736	$63,800
1998	Jaguar	XJ Series Sedans	2914	XRJ Supercharged Sedan 4-Door	$58,881	$67,400
1998	Jaguar	XK8	2840	Coupe 2-Door	$57,104	$64,900
1998	Jaguar	XK8	2830	Convertible 2-Door	$61,472	$69,900
1998	Jeep	Cherokee	XJTL72/23A	2WD 2-Door Sport Utility SE	$14,601	$15,540
1998	Jeep	Cherokee	XJTL72/25D	2WD 2-Door Sport Utility Sport	$16,454	$18,175
1998	Jeep	Cherokee	XJTL74/23A	2WD 4-Door Sport Utility SE	$15,568	$16,580
1998	Jeep	Cherokee	XJTL74/25D	2WD 4-Door Sport Utility Sport	$17,385	$19,210
1998	Jeep	Cherokee	XJTL74/26X	2WD 4-Door Sport Utility Classic	$18,608	$20,600
1998	Jeep	Cherokee	XJTL74/26H	2WD 4-Door Sport Utility Limited	$20,283	$22,570
1998	Jeep	Cherokee	XJJL72/23A	4WD 2-Door Sport Utility SE	$16,000	$17,055
1998	Jeep	Cherokee	XJJL72/25D	4WD 2-Door Sport Utility Sport	$17,803	$19,685
1998	Jeep	Cherokee	XJJL74/23A	4WD 4-Door Sport Utility SE	$16,962	$18,090
1998	Jeep	Cherokee	XJJL74/25D	4WD 4-Door Sport Utility Sport	$18,734	$20,720
1998	Jeep	Cherokee	XJJL74/26X	4WD 4-Door Sport Utility Classic	$19,961	$22,115
1998	Jeep	Cherokee	XJJL74/26H	4WD 4-Door Sport Utility Limited	$21,971	$24,480

Year	Mfr.	Make	Code	Model	Invoice Price	Retail Price
1998	Jeep	Grand Cherokee	ZJTL74/26E	2WD 4-Door Sport Utility Laredo	$23,507	$23,945
1998	Jeep	Grand Cherokee	ZJTL74/26G	2WD 4-Door Sport Utility Limited	$28,360	$31,460
1998	Jeep	Grand Cherokee	ZJJL74/26E	4WD 4-Door Sport Utility Laredo	$25,275	$27,915
1998	Jeep	Grand Cherokee	ZJJL74/26G	4WD 4-Door Sport Utility Limited	$30,533	$33,890
1998	Jeep	Grand Cherokee	ZJJL74/29U	4WD 4-Door Sport Utility Limited 5.9	$34,392	$38,275
1998	Jeep	Wrangler	TJJL77/23A	SE Soft Top 4WD	$13,504	$14,090
1998	Jeep	Wrangler	TJJL77/25C	Sport Soft Top 4WD	$15,804	$17,505
1998	Jeep	Wrangler	TJJL77/25G	Sahara Soft Top 4WD	$17,661	$19,615
1998	Kia	Sephia	14201	Base Sedan 4-Door (5-speed Manual)	$8,996	$9,995
1998	Kia	Sephia	14202	Base Sedan 4-Door (4-speed ECT Automatic)	$9,856	$10,970
1998	Kia	Sephia	14221	LS w/o Power Package 4-Door (5-speed Manual)	$9,791	$10,995
1998	Kia	Sephia	14222	LS w/o Power Package 4-Door (4-speed ECT Automatic)	$10,651	$11,970
1998	Kia	Sephia	14241	LS w/Power Package 4-Door (5-speed Manual)	$11,741	$13,325
1998	Kia	Sephia	14242	LS w/Power Package 4-Door (4-speed ECT Automatic)	$12,601	$14,300
1998	Kia	Sportage	42221	2WD Sport Utility 4-Door Base (5-speed Manual)	$13,541	$14,895
1998	Kia	Sportage	42222	2WD Sport Utility 4-Door (4-speed ECT Automatic)	$14,451	$15,895
1998	Kia	Sportage	42241	2WD Sport Utility 4-Door EX (5-speed Manual)	$15,580	$17,295
1998	Kia	Sportage	42242	2WD Sport Utility 4-Door EX (4-speed ECT Automatic)	$16,490	$18,295

Year	Make	Model	Code	Description		
1998	Kia	Sportage	42421	4WD Sport Utility 4-Door Base (5-speed Manual)	$14,770	$16,395
1998	Kia	Sportage	42422	4WD Sport Utility 4-Door (4-speed ECT Automatic)	$15,680	$17,395
1998	Kia	Sportage	42441	4WD Sport Utility 4-Door EX (5-speed Manual)	$16,500	$18,495
1998	Kia	Sportage	42442	4WD Sport Utility 4-Door EX (4-speed ECT Automatic)	$17,410	$19,495
1998	Land Rover	Discovery		LE Sport Utility 4WD	$30,705	$34,500
1998	Land Rover	Discovery		LSE Sport Utility 4WD	$33,820	$38,000
1998	Land Rover	Range Rover		4.0 SE 4-Door 4WD	$49,550	$56,000
1998	Land Rover	Range Rover		4.6 HSE 4-Door 4WD	$56,201	$63,500
1998	Lexus	ES 300	9000	Luxury Sport Sedan 4-Door	$26,745	$30,790
1998	Lexus	GS	9300	GS 300 Luxury Performance Sedan 4-Door	$31,964	$36,800
1998	Lexus	GS	9320	GS 400 Luxury Performance Sedan 4-Door	$38,461	$44,800
1998	Lexus	LS 400	9100	Luxury Sedan 4-Door	$44,800	$52,900
1998	Lexus	LX 450	9600	Sport Utility 5-Door 4WD	$41,809	$48,700
1998	Lexus	SC	9200	SC 300 Luxury Sport Coupe 2-Door (4-speed ECT-i Automatic)	$35,526	$40,900
1998	Lexus	SC	9220	SC 400 Luxury Sport Coupe 2-Door (5-speed ECT-i Automatic)	$42,243	$52,700
1998	Lincoln	Continental	M97	Sedan 4-Door	$35,524	$37,830
1998	Lincoln	Mark VII	M91	Base Coupe 2-Door (ex. California)	$34,524	$37,830
1998	Lincoln	Mark VII	M92	LSC Coupe 2-Door (ex. California)	$35,850	$39,320
1998	Lincoln	Mark VII	M91	Base Coupe 2-Door (California Only)	$33,634	$36,830
1998	Lincoln	Mark VII	M92	LSC Coupe 2-Door (California Only)	$34,960	$38,320

Year	Mfr.	Make	Code	Model	Invoice Price	Retail Price
1998	Lincoln	Navigator	U27/620A	Sport Utility 4-Door 2WD	$34,333	$39,310
1998	Lincoln	Navigator	U28/625A	Sport Utility 4-Door 4WD	$37,351	$42,860
1998	Lincoln	Town Car	M81	Executive Sedan 4-Door (CA/CT/MA/NY)	$34,373	$34,660
1998	Lincoln	Town Car	M82	Signature Sedan 4-Door	$35,992	$39,480
1998	Lincoln	Town Car	M82	Cartier Sedan 4-Door	$38,796	$42,630
1998	Mazda	626		DX Sedan 4-Door	$14,201	$15,550
1998	Mazda	626		LX Sedan 4-Door	$15,909	$17,650
1998	Mazda	626		LX-V6 Sedan 4-Door	$18,619	$20,665
1998	Mazda	626		ES-V6 Sedan 4-Door	$20,933	$23,240
1998	Mazda	Millenia		Cloth Sedan 4-Door	$25,581	$2,895
1998	Mazda	Millenia		S Sedan 4-Door	$31,533	$36,595
1998	Mazda	MPV		2WD Wagon 4-Door LX	$20,835	$23,095
1998	Mazda	MPV		2WD Wagon 4-Door ES	$23,827	$26,395
1998	Mazda	MPV		4WD Wagon 4-Door LX	$24,278	$26,895
1998	Mazda	MPV		4WD Wagon 4-Door ES	$26,080	$28,895
1998	Mazda	MX-5 Miata		Base Convertible 2-Door	$17,248	$19,125
1998	Mazda	MX-5 Miata		STO-Edition Convertible 2-Door (1997 .5 Model)	$20,306	$22,520
1998	Mazda	MX-5 Miata		M-Edition Convertible 2-Door	$22,077	$24,485
1998	Mazda	Pickup B Series		B2500 2WD Pickup SX Regular Cab, 112\WB	$10,122	$10,885
1998	Mazda	Pickup B Series		B2500 2WD Pickup SE Regular Cab, 112\WB	$11,395	$12,705

Year	Make	Model	Description		
1998	Mazda	Pickup B Series	B2500 2WD Pickup SE Cab Plus, 125\WB	$13,305	$14,845
1998	Mazda	Pickup B Series	B3000 2WD Pickup SE Cab Plus, 125\WB	$14,117	$15,795
1998	Mazda	Pickup B Series	B4000 2WD Pickup SE Cab Plus, 125\WB	$14,517	$16,245
1998	Mazda	Pickup B Series	B3000 4WD Pickup SX Regular Cab, 112\WB	$14,397	$15,415
1998	Mazda	Pickup B Series	B3000 4WD Pickup SE Regular Cab, 112\WB	$15,136	$16,945
1998	Mazda	Pickup B Series	B3000 4WD Pickup SE Cab Plus, 125\WB	$16,464	$18,430
1998	Mazda	Pickup B Series	B4000 4WD Pickup SE Cab Plus, 125\WB	$16,865	$18,880
1998	Mazda	Protégé	DX Sedan 4-Door	$11,473	$12,145
1998	Mazda	Protégé	LX Sedan 4-Door	$12,516	$13,545
1998	Mazda	Protégé	ES Sedan 4-Door	$13,974	$15,295
1998	Mercedes-Benz	C-Class	C230 Sedan 4-Door	$26,490	$30,450
1998	Mercedes-Benz	C-Class	C280 Sedan 4-Door	$30,800	$35,400
1998	Mercedes-Benz	CL-Class	CL500 Coupe 2-Door	$79,950	$91,900
1998	Mercedes-Benz	CL-Class	CL600 Coupe 2-Door	$117,710	$135,300
1998	Mercedes-Benz	CLK	CLK320 Coupe 2-Door	$34,670	$39,850
1998	Mercedes-Benz	E-Class	Sedan 4-Door E300 D Diesel	$36,370	$41,800
1998	Mercedes-Benz	E-Class	Sedan 4-Door E320 2WD	$39,580	$45,500

Year	Mfr.	Make	Code	Model	Invoice Price	Retail Price
1998	Mercedes-Benz	E-Class		Sedan 4-Door E320 AWD	$41,980	$48,250
1998	Mercedes-Benz	E-Class		Sedan 4-Door E430	$44,020	$50,600
1998	Mercedes-Benz	E-Class		Wagon 4-Door E320 2WD	$40,450	$46,500
1998	Mercedes-Benz	E-Class		Wagon 4-Door E320 AWD	$42,850	$49,250
1998	Mercedes-Benz	M-Class		ML320 Sport Utility 4-Door 4WD	$29,540	$33,950
1998	Mercedes-Benz	S-Class		S320 Sedan 4-Door Short Wheelbase (SWB)	$55,680	$64,000
1998	Mercedes-Benz	S-Class		S320 Sedan 4-Door Long Wheelbase (LWB)	$58,550	$67,300
1998	Mercedes-Benz	S-Class		S420 Sedan 4-Door Long Wheelbase (LWB)	$64,290	$73,900
1998	Mercedes-Benz	S-Class		S500 Sedan 4-Door Long Wheelbase (LWB)	$76,120	$87,500
1998	Mercedes-Benz	S-Class		S600 Sedan 4-Door Long Wheelbase (LWB)	$115,060	$132,250
1998	Mercedes-Benz	SL-Class		SL500 Coupe/Roadster 2-Door	$69,510	$79,900
1998	Mercedes-Benz	SL-Class		SL600 Coupe/Roadster 2-Door	$108,750	$125,000

Year	Make	Model	Code	Description		
1998	Mercedes-Benz	SLK		SLK230 Coupe/Roadster 2-Door 2-Seater	$34,540	$39,700
1997	Mercury	Cougar XR7	M62	Coupe 2-Door	$16,279	$17,830
1998	Mercury	Grand Marquis	M74	GS Sedan 4-Door (ex. CA & HI)	$20,455	$21,890
1998	Mercury	Grand Marquis	M75	LS Sedan 4-Door (ex. CA & HI)	$22,184	$23,790
1998	Mercury	Grand Marquis	M74/60C	GS Sedan 4-Door (CA & HI Only)	$20,892	$22,370
1998	Mercury	Grand Marquis	M75/60L	LS Sedan 4-Door (CA & HI Only)	$22,934	$24,615
1998	Mercury	Mountaineer	U52	Sport Utility 2WD 4-Door, 112\WB	$24,118	$26,680
1998	Mercury	Mountaineer	U54	Sport Utility 4WD 4-Door, 112\WB	$25,878	$28,680
1998	Mercury	Mountaineer	U55	Sport Utility AWD 4-Door, 112\WB	$25,878	$28,680
1998	Mercury	Mystique	M65	GS Sedan 4-Door	$14,911	$16,310
1998	Mercury	Mystique	M66	LS Sedan 4-Door	$16,099	$17,645
1998	Mercury	Sable	M50	GS Sedan 4-Door	$17,781	$19,445
1998	Mercury	Sable	M50/60L	LS Sedan 4-Door	$18,716	$20,495
1998	Mercury	Sable	M55	LS Wagon 5-Door	$20,399	$22,385
1998	Mercury	Tracer	M10	GS Sedan 4-Door	$10,698	$11,405
1998	Mercury	Tracer	M13	LS Sedan 4-Door	$11,932	$12,760
1998	Mercury	Tracer	M15	LS Wagon 4-Door	$13,292	$14,255
1998	Mercury	Villager	V14	GS Van 3-Door	$18,532	$20,450
1998	Mercury	Villager	V11	GS Wagon 3-Door	$18,843	$20,805
1998	Mercury	Villager	V11	LS Wagon 3-Door	$22,601	$25,075
1998	Mercury	Villager	V11	Nautica Wagon 3-Door	$24,211	$26,905

Year	Mfr.	Make	Code	Model	Invoice Price	Retail Price
1998	Mitsubishi	3000GT	GT24-B	Base Hatchback FWD (5-speed Manual)	$23,597	$27,770
1998	Mitsubishi	3000GT	GT24-B	Base Hatchback FWD (4-speed Automatic)	$24,353	$28,660
1998	Mitsubishi	3000GT	GT24-G	SL Hatchback FWD (5-speed Manual)	$28,848	$35,190
1998	Mitsubishi	3000GT	GT24-G	SL Hatchback FWD (4-speed Automatic)	$29,603	$36,110
1998	Mitsubishi	3000GT	GT24-K	VR-4 Twin Turbo Hatchback AWD (6 Speed Manual)	$37,905	$46,230
1998	Mitsubishi	Diamante	DM42-B	ES Sedan 4-Door	$23,776	$27,650
1998	Mitsubishi	Diamante	DM42-G	LS Sedan 4-Door	$28,087	$33,050
1998	Mitsubishi	Eclipse	EC24-G	Coupe 3-Door RS (5-speed Manual)	$13,761	$15,740
1998	Mitsubishi	Eclipse	EC24-G	Coupe 3-Door RS (4-speed Automatic)	$14,289	$16,430
1998	Mitsubishi	Eclipse	EC24-K	Coupe 3-Door GS (5-speed Manual)	$15,541	$17,880
1998	Mitsubishi	Eclipse	EC24-K	Coupe 3-Door GS (4-speed Automatic)	$16,158	$18,580
1998	Mitsubishi	Eclipse	EC24-P	Coupe 3-Door GS-T Turbo (5-speed Manual)	$19,093	$21,960
1998	Mitsubishi	Eclipse	EC24-P	Coupe 3-Door GS-T Turbo (4-speed Automatic)	$19,830	$22,800
1998	Mitsubishi	Eclipse	EC24-X	Coupe 3-Door GSX Turbo 4WD (5-speed Manual)	$21,767	$25,320
1998	Mitsubishi	Eclipse	EC24-X	Coupe 3-Door GSX Turbo 4WD (4-speed Automatic)	$22,498	$26,170
1998	Mitsubishi	Eclipse	EC28-K	Spyder Convertible 2+2 2-Door GS (5-speed Manual)	$17,340	$19,940
1998	Mitsubishi	Eclipse	EC28-K	Spyder Convertible 2+2 2-Door GS (4-speed Automatic)	$17,957	$20,650
1998	Mitsubishi	Eclipse	EC28-P	Spyder Convertible 2+2 2-Door GS-T Turbo (5-speed Manual)	$22,422	$25,780

Year	Make	Model	Code	Description		
1998	Mitsubishi	Eclipse	EC28-P	Spyder Convertible 2+2 2-Door GS-T Turbo (4-speed Automatic)	$23,160	$26,630
1998	Mitsubishi	Galant	GA41-B	DE Sedan 4-Door (5-speed Manual)	$13,952	$15,680
1998	Mitsubishi	Galant	GA41-B	DE Sedan 4-Door (4-speed ECT Automatic)	$14,728	$16,550
1998	Mitsubishi	Galant	GA41-G	ES Sedan 4-Door (5-speed Manual)	$15,565	$17,670
1998	Mitsubishi	Galant	GA41-G	ES Sedan 4-Door (4-speed ECT Automatic)	$16,248	$18,450
1998	Mitsubishi	Galant	GA41-K	LS Sedan 4-Door (4-speed ECT Automatic)	$21,509	$23,310
1998	Mitsubishi	Mirage	MG21-B	DE Coupe 2-Door (5-speed Manual)	$9,842	$10,830
1998	Mitsubishi	Mirage	MG21-B	DE Coupe 2-Door (4-speed Automatic)	$10,460	$11,550
1998	Mitsubishi	Mirage	MG21-G	LS Coupe 2-Door (5-speed Manual)	$12,725	$14,330
1998	Mitsubishi	Mirage	MG21-G	LS Coupe 2-Door (4-speed Automatic)	$13,343	$15,010
1998	Mitsubishi	Mirage	MG41-B	DE Sedan 4-Door (5-speed Manual)	$10,998	$12,360
1998	Mitsubishi	Mirage	MG41-B	DE Sedan 4-Door (4-speed Automatic)	$11,617	$13,070
1998	Mitsubishi	Mirage	MG41-G	LS Sedan 4-Door (5-speed Manual)	$11,836	$13,300
1998	Mitsubishi	Mirage	MG41-G	LS Sedan 4-Door (4-speed Automatic)	$12,454	$13,880
1998	Mitsubishi	Montero	MP45-B	Sport Utility 4-Door 4WD	$28,663	$33,530
1998	Mitsubishi	Montero Sport	MT45-B	2WD 4-Door ES (5-speed Manual)	$16,219	$18,030
1998	Mitsubishi	Montero Sport	MT45-G	2WD 4-Door LS (4-speed Automatic)	$19,361	$22,260
1998	Mitsubishi	Montero Sport	MT45-P	2WD 4-Door XLS (4-speed Automatic)	$24,670	$28,360
1998	Mitsubishi	Montero Sport	MT45-K	4WD 4-Door LS (4-speed Automatic)	$21,552	$24,780
1998	Mitsubishi	Montero Sport	MT45-X	4WD 4-Door XLS (4-speed Automatic)	$28,050	$32,250
1998	Mitsubishi	Montero Sport	MT45-K	4WD 4-Door ES (5-speed Manual)	$20,810	$23,920

Year	Mfr.	Make	Code	Model	Invoice Price	Retail Price
1998	Nissan	200SX	1158	Base Coupe (5-speed Manual)	$12,520	$13,149
1998	Nissan	200SX	1118	Base Coupe (4-speed ECT Automatic)	$13,282	$13,949
1998	Nissan	200SX	1258	SE Coupe (5-speed Manual)	$14,025	$15,399
1998	Nissan	200SX	1218	SE Coupe (4-speed ECT Automatic)	$14,754	$16,199
1998	Nissan	200SX	1458	SE-R Coupe (5-speed Manual)	$15,255	$16,749
1998	Nissan	200SX	1418	SE-R Coupe (4-speed ECT Automatic)	$15,984	$17,549
1998	Nissan	240SX	26158	Base Coupe (5-speed Manual)	$16,437	$18,359
1998	Nissan	240SX	26118	Base Coupe (4-speed ECT Automatic)	$17,153	$19,159
1998	Nissan	240SX	26258	SE Coupe (5-speed Manual)	$19,695	$21,999
1998	Nissan	240SX	26218	SE Coupe (4-speed ECT Automatic)	$20,411	$22,799
1998	Nissan	240SX	26358	LE Coupe (5-speed Manual)	$21,888	$24,449
1998	Nissan	240SX	26318	LE Coupe (4-speed ECT Automatic)	$22,605	$25,249
1998	Nissan	Altima	5658	XE Sedan 4-Door (5-speed Manual)	$14,265	$14,990
1998	Nissan	Altima	5618	XE Sedan 4-Door (4-speed Automatic)	$15,025	$15,790
1998	Nissan	Altima	5758	GXE Sedan 4-Door (5-speed Manual)	$15,646	$17,190
1998	Nissan	Altima	5718	GXE Sedan 4-Door (4-speed Automatic)	$16,373	$17,990
1998	Nissan	Altima	5958	SE Sedan 4-Door (5-speed Manual)	$16,638	$18,490
1998	Nissan	Altima	5918	SE Sedan 4-Door (4-speed Automatic)	$17,358	$19,290
1998	Nissan	Altima	5818	GLE Sedan 4-Door (4-speed Automatic)	$17,897	$19,890
1998	Nissan	Frontier	33058	2WD Pickup Regular Cab Standard (5-speed Manual)	$11,541	$11,990

Year	Make	Model	Code	Description		
1998	Nissan	Frontier	33558	2WD Pickup Regular Cab XE (5-speed Manual)	$12,560	$13,190
1998	Nissan	Frontier	33518	2WD Pickup Regular Cab XE (4-speed Automatic)	$13,560	$14,240
1998	Nissan	Frontier	53558	2WD Pickup Regular Cab XE (5-speed Manual)	$13,486	$14,640
1998	Nissan	Frontier	53518	2WD Pickup King Cab XE (4-speed Automatic)	$14,452	$15,690
1998	Nissan	Frontier	53258	2WD Pickup King Cab SE (5-speed Manual)	$16,385	$17,990
1998	Nissan	Frontier	53218	2WD Pickup King Cab SE (4-speed Automatic)	$17,341	$19,040
1998	Nissan	Frontier	33758	4WD Pickup Regular Cab XE (5-speed Manual)	$15,650	$19,990
1998	Nissan	Frontier	53758	4WD Pickup King Cab XE (5-speed Manual)	$16,567	$18,190
1998	Nissan	Frontier	53358	4WD Pickup King Cab SE (5-speed Manual)	$18,900	$20,990
1998	Nissan	Maxima	8458	GXE Sedan 4-Door (5-speed Manual)	$19,470	$21,499
1998	Nissan	Maxima	8418	GXE Sedan 4-Door (4-speed ECT Automatic)	$20,814	$23,249
1998	Nissan	Maxima	8258	SE Sedan 4-Door (5-speed Manual)	$20,916	$23,499
1998	Nissan	Maxima	8218	SE Sedan 4-Door (4-speed ECT Automatic)	$21,806	$24,499
1998	Nissan	Maxima	8618	GLE Sedan 4-Door (4-speed ECT Automatic)	$23,943	$26,899
1998	Nissan	Pathfinder	9258	2WD/Sport Utility 4-Door Models XE (5-speed Manual)	$21,610	$23,999
1998	Nissan	Pathfinder	9218	2WD/Sport Utility 4-Door Models XE (4-speed Automatic)	$22,510	$24,999
1998	Nissan	Pathfinder	9318	2WD/Sport Utility 4-Door Models LE (4-speed Automatic)	$27,418	$30,449
1998	Nissan	Pathfinder	9658	4WD/Sport Utility 4-Door Models XE (5-speed Manual)	$23,410	$25,999
1998	Nissan	Pathfinder	9618	4WD/Sport Utility 4-Door Models XE (4-speed Automatic)	$24,311	$26,999

Year	Mfr.	Make	Code	Model	Invoice Price	Retail Price
1998	Nissan	Pathfinder	9758	4WD/Sport Utility 4-Door Models SE (5-speed Manual)	$26,202	$29,099
1998	Nissan	Pathfinder	9718	4WD/Sport Utility 4-Door Models SE (4-speed Automatic)	$27,103	$30,099
1998	Nissan	Pathfinder	9818	4WD/Sport Utility 4-Door Models LE (4-speed Automatic)	$29,580	$32,849
1998	Nissan	Quest	10318	XE 7-Passenger	$20,560	$23,099
1998	Nissan	Quest	10418	GXE 7-Passenger	$23,186	$26,049
1998	Nissan	Sentra	42058	Sedan 4-Door Base (5-speed Manual)	$10,950	$11,499
1998	Nissan	Sentra	42158	Sedan 4-Door XE (5-speed Manual)	$12,761	$13,699
1998	Nissan	Sentra	42118	Sedan 4-Door XE (4-speed Automatic)	$13,506	$14,499
1998	Nissan	Sentra	42258	Sedan 4-Door GXE (5-speed Manual)	$13,494	$14,899
1998	Nissan	Sentra	42218	Sedan 4-Door GXE (4-speed Automatic)	$14,218	$15,699
1998	Nissan	Sentra	42458	Sedan 4-Door SE (5-speed Manual)	$15,168	$16,749
1998	Nissan	Sentra	42418	Sedan 4-Door SE (4-speed Automatic)	$15,892	$17,549
1998	Nissan	Sentra	42558	Sedan 4-Door GLE (5-speed Manual)	$14,263	$15,749
1998	Nissan	Sentra	42518	Sedan 4-Door GLE (4-speed Automatic)	$14,987	$16,549
1998	Oldsmobile	Achieva	3NL69/1SA	SL Sedan 4-Door	$16,835	$17,815
1998	Oldsmobile	Aurora	3GR29/1SA	Sedan 4-Door	$32,544	$35,960
1998	Oldsmobile	Bravada	3TV06/1SA	Sport Utility 4WD 4-Door	$27,734	$30,645
1998	Oldsmobile	Cutlass	3NB69/1SA	GL Sedan 4-Door	$16,287	$17,800

1998	Oldsmobile	Cutlass	3NG69/1SA	Gls Sedan 4-Door	$17,774	$19,425
1998	Oldsmobile	Eighty-Eight	3HN69/1SA	Base Sedan 4-Door	$20,857	$22,795
1998	Oldsmobile	Eighty-Eight	3HN69/1SB	LS Sedan 4-Door	$22,138	$24,195
1998	Oldsmobile	Intrigue	3WH69/1SA	Base Sedan 4-Door	$18,941	$20,700
1998	Oldsmobile	Intrigue	3WS69/1SB	GL Sedan 4-Door	$20,222	$22,100
1998	Oldsmobile	LSS Sedan	3HY69/1SA	Sedan 4-Door	$25,707	$28,095
1998	Oldsmobile	Regency	3HC69/1SA	Sedan 4-Door	$25,981	$28,395
1998	Oldsmobile	Silhouette	3UM16/1SA	GL Extended Wheelbase Minivan 4-Door	$21,688	$23,965
1998	Oldsmobile	Silhouette	3UM16/1SB	GS Regular Wheelbase Minivan 4-Door	$22,109	$24,430
1998	Oldsmobile	Silhouette	3UM16/1SC	GLS Extended Wheelbase Minivan 4-Door	$24,584	$27,165
1998	Plymouth	Breeze	JAPH41/21A	Sedan 4-Door	$13,476	$14,675
1998	Plymouth	Neon	PLPL22/23A	Coupe 2-Door Competition	$10,405	$11,000
1998	Plymouth	Neon	PLPL22/21D	Coupe 2-Door Highline	$10,415	$11,255
1998	Plymouth	Neon	PLPL42/25A	Sedan 4-Door Competition	$10,589	$11,200
1998	Plymouth	Neon	PLPL42/21D	Sedan 4-Door Highline	$10,595	$11,455
1998	Plymouth	Prowler	PRPS27	Roadster 2-Door 2-Seater	$35,863	$38,300
1998	Plymouth	Voyager	NSHL52/22S	Standard 2WD Models Base, 112\WB	$15,845	$17,415
1998	Plymouth	Voyager	NSHH52/26A	Standard 2WD Models SE, 112\WB (ex. CA/CT/MA/NY)	$19,255	$21,290
1998	Plymouth	Voyager	NSHH52/28A	Standard 2WD Models SE, 112\WB (CA/CT/MA/NY Only)	$19,425	$21,490
1998	Plymouth	Voyager	NSHL53/24S	Grand 2WD Models Base, 199\WB (ex. CA/CT/MA/NY)	$18,270	$20,125

Year	Mfr.	Make	Code	Model	Invoice Price	Retail Price
1998	Plymouth	Voyager	NSHH53/26A	Grand 2WD Models SE, 199\WB (ex. CA/CT/MA/NY)	$20,171	$22,285
1998	Plymouth	Voyager	NSHL53/28S	Grand 2WD Models Base, 199\WB (CA/CT/MA/NY Only)	$18,653	$20,575
1998	Plymouth	Voyager	NSHH53/28A	Grand 2WD Models SE, 199\WB (CA/CT/MA/NY Only)	$20,341	$22,485
1998	Pontiac	Bonneville	X69/1SA	SE Sedan 4-Door	$20,487	$22,390
1998	Pontiac	Bonneville	Z69/1SA	SSE Sedan 4-Door	$26,892	$29,390
1998	Pontiac	Firebird	S87V/1SA	Coupe 2-Door Base	$16,484	$18,015
1998	Pontiac	Firebird	V87/V1SA	Coupe 2-Door Formula	$20,921	$22,865
1998	Pontiac	Firebird	V87V/1SA	Coupe 2-Door Trans Am	$23,767	$25,975
1998	Pontiac	Firebird	S67V/1SA	Convertible 2-Door Base	$22,239	$24,305
1998	Pontiac	Firebird	V67V/1SA	Convertible 2-Door Trans Am	$27,189	$29,715
1999	Pontiac	Grand Am	2NE37/1SA	Coupe 2-Door SE	$14,521	$15,870
1999	Pontiac	Grand Am	2NE37/1SB	Coupe 2-Door SE1	$15,802	$17,270
1999	Pontiac	Grand Am	2NE37/1SC	Coupe 2-Door SE2	$17,175	$18,770
1999	Pontiac	Grand Am	W37/1SA	Coupe 2-Door GT (1998 Model)	$14,936	$16,324
1999	Pontiac	Grand Am	2NE69/1SA	Sedan 4-Door SE	$14,704	$16,070
1999	Pontiac	Grand Am	2NE69/1SB	Sedan 4-Door SE1	$15,985	$17,470
1999	Pontiac	Grand Am	2NE69/1SC	Sedan 4-Door SE2	$17,358	$18,970
1999	Pontiac	Grand Am	W69/1SA	Sedan 4-Door GT (1998 Model)	$15,074	$16,474
1998	Pontiac	Grand Prix	J69/1SA	SE Sedan 4-Door	$17,197	$18,795

Year	Make	Model	Description	Code	Price 1	Price 2
1998	Pontiac	Grand Prix	GT Sedan 4-Door	P69/1SA	$18,908	$20,665
1998	Pontiac	Grand Prix	GT Coupe 2-Door	P37/1SA	$18,680	$20,415
1998	Pontiac	Sunfire	SE Coupe 2-Door	B37/1SA	$11,558	$12,495
1998	Pontiac	Sunfire	SE Sedan 4-Door	B69/1SA	$11,558	$12,495
1998	Pontiac	Sunfire	SE Convertible 2-Door	B67/1SA	$18,033	$19,485
1998	Pontiac	Sunfire	GT Coupe 2-Door	D37/1SA	$14,333	$15,495
1998	Pontiac	Trans Sport	SE Regular Wheelbase Minivan 3-Door	N06V/1SA	$18,860	$20,840
1998	Pontiac	Trans Sport	SE Regular Wheelbase Minivan 4-Door	N16V/1SB	$20,254	$22,380
1998	Pontiac	Trans Sport	SE Extended Wheelbase Minivan 3-Door	N16V/1SB	$20,896	$23,090
1998	Porche	Boxster	Roadster Convertible 2-Door 2-Seater	968310	$35,895	$41,000
1998	Porche	Carrera	Coupe 2-Door S 2WD	993340	$54,969	$63,750
1998	Porche	Carrera	Coupe 2-Door 4S 4WD	993140	$62,962	$73,000
1998	Porche	Carrera	Targa 2-Door 2WD	993410	$61,001	$70,750
1998	Porche	Carrera	Cabriolet 2-Door 2WD	993630	$62,859	$73,000
1998	Porche	Carrera	Cabriolet 2-Door 4WD	993530	$67,492	$78,350
1998	Saab	900-Series	Coupe 3-Door S Turbo	923M	$23,610	$24,500
1998	Saab	900-Series	Coupe 3-Door SE Turbo	953M	$27,911	$30,995
1998	Saab	900-Series	Hatchback 5-Door S	905M	$24,273	$26,955
1998	Saab	900-Series	Hatchback SE Turbo	955M	$28,811	$31,995
1998	Saab	900-Series	Convertible 2-Door S	902M	$32,665	$36,395
1998	Saab	900-Series	Convertible 2-Door SE Turbo	952M	$37,765	$42,195
1998	Saab	9000-Series	CSE Hatchback 5-Door (5-speed Manual)	055M	$34,441	$38,580

Year	Mfr.	Make	Code	Model	Invoice Price	Retail Price
1998	Saab	9000-Series	055A	CSE Hatchback 5-Door (4-speed ECT Automatic)	$35,374	$39,625
1998	Saturn	Sedan, Coupe & Wagon	ZZF69	Sedan SL 4-Door (5-speed Manual)	$9,218	$10,595
1998	Saturn	Sedan, Coupe & Wagon	ZZG69	Sedan SL1 4-Door (5-speed Manual)	$9,827	$11,295
1998	Saturn	Sedan, Coupe & Wagon	ZZH69	Sedan SL1 4-Door (4-speed Automatic)	$10,575	$12,155
1998	Saturn	Sedan, Coupe & Wagon	ZZJ69	Sedan SL2 4-Door (5-speed Manual)	$11,097	$12,755
1998	Saturn	Sedan, Coupe & Wagon	ZZK69	Sedan SL2 4-Door (4-speed Automatic)	$11,845	$13,615
1998	Saturn	Sedan, Coupe & Wagon	ZZE27	Coupe SC1 2-Door (5-speed Manual)	$10,958	$12,595
1998	Saturn	Sedan, Coupe & Wagon	ZZF27	Coupe SC1 2-Door (4-speed Automatic)	$11,706	$13,455
1998	Saturn	Sedan, Coupe & Wagon	ZZG27	Coupe SC2 2-Door (5-speed Manual)	$12,924	$14,855
1998	Saturn	Sedan, Coupe & Wagon	ZZH27	Coupe SC1 2-Door (4-speed Automatic)	$13,672	$15,715
1998	Saturn	Sedan, Coupe & Wagon	ZZG35	Wagon SW1 4-Door (5-speed Manual)	$10,697	$12,295
1998	Saturn	Sedan, Coupe & Wagon	ZZH35	Wagon SW1 4-Door (4-speed Automatic)	$11,445	$13,155
1998	Saturn	Sedan, Coupe & Wagon	ZZJ35	Wagon SW2 4-Door (5-speed Manual)	$12,402	$14,255
1998	Saturn	Sedan, Coupe & Wagon	ZZK35	Wagon SW2 4-Door (4-speed Automatic)	$13,150	$15,115
1998	Subaru	Forester	WCA	Base, Sport Utility 4-Door 4WD (5-speed Manual)	$17,454	$18,695
1998	Subaru	Forester	WCB	L, Sport Utility 4-Door 4WD (5-speed Manual)	$18,034	$19,995
1998	Subaru	Forester	WCC	L, Sport Utility 4-Door 4WD (4-speed ECT Automatic)	$18,745	$20,795
1998	Subaru	Forester	WCD	S, w/o Cold Package, Sport Utility 4-Door 4WD (5-speed Manual)	$19,925	$22,195

Year	Make	Model	Code	Description		
1998	Subaru	Forester	WCE	S, w/o Cold Package, Sport Utility 4-Door 4WD (4-speed ECT Automatic)	$20,636	$22,995
1998	Subaru	Forester	WCF	S, w/Cold Package, Sport Utility 4-Door 4WD (5-speed Manual)	$20,191	$22,495
1998	Subaru	Forester	WCG	S, w/Cold Package, Sport Utility 4-Door 4WD (4-speed ECT Automatic)	$20,902	$23,295
1998	Subaru	Impreza	WMA	Coupe AWD 2-Door L (5-speed Manual)	$14,445	$15,895
1998	Subaru	Impreza	WMB	Coupe AWD 2-Door L (4-speed ECT Automatic)	$15,162	$16,695
1998	Subaru	Impreza	WMC	Coupe AWD 2-Door 2.5RS (5-speed Manual)	$17,404	$19,195
1998	Subaru	Impreza	WMD	Coupe AWD 2-Door 2.5RS (4-speed ECT Automatic)	$18,121	$19,995
1998	Subaru	Impreza	WJA	Sedan AWD 4-Door L (5-speed Manual)	$14,445	$15,895
1998	Subaru	Impreza	WJB	Sedan AWD 4-Door L (4-speed ECT Automatic)	$15,162	$16,695
1998	Subaru	Impreza	WLA	Sport Wagon AWD 5-Door L (5-speed Manual)	$14,804	$16,295
1998	Subaru	Impreza	WLB	Sport Wagon AWD 5-Door L (4-speed ECT Automatic)	$15,521	$17,095
1998	Subaru	Impreza	WLC	Sport Wagon AWD 5-Door Outback (5-speed Manual)	$16,321	$17,995
1998	Subaru	Impreza	WLD	Sport Wagon AWD 5-Door Outback (4-speed ECT Automatic)	$17,038	$18,795
1998	Subaru	Legacy	WAA	Sedan 4-Door 4WD L (5-speed Manual)	$17,278	$19,195
1998	Subaru	Legacy	WAB	Sedan 4-Door 4WD L (4-speed ECT Automatic)	$17,992	$19,995
1998	Subaru	Legacy	WAD	Sedan 4-Door 4WD GT Base (5-speed Manual)	$20,453	$22,795
1998	Subaru	Legacy	WAE	Sedan 4-Door 4WD GT Base (4-speed ECT Automatic)	$21,167	$23,595

Year	Mfr.	Make	Code	Model	Invoice Price	Retail Price
1998	Subaru	Legacy	WAG	Sedan 4-Door 4WDGT Limited (4-speed ECT Automatic)	$22,314	$24,895
1998	Subaru	Legacy	XAH	Sedan 4-Door 4WD 30th Anniversary Sport Utility Base (4-speed ECT Automatic) (1999 Model)	$20,990	$23,395
1998	Subaru	Legacy	XAI	Sedan 4-Door 4WD 30th Anniversary Sport Utility Limited (4-speed ECT Automatic) (1999 Model)	$22,946	$25,595
1998	Subaru	Legacy	WBA	Wagon 4-Door 4WD Brighton (5-speed Manual)	$15,788	$16,895
1998	Subaru	Legacy	WBB	Wagon 4-Door 4WD Brighton (4-speed ECT Automatic)	$16,502	$17,695
1998	Subaru	Legacy	WBC	Wagon 4-Door 4WD L (5-speed Manual)	$17,898	$19,895
1998	Subaru	Legacy	WBD	Wagon 4-Door 4WD L (4-speed ECT Automatic)	$18,612	$20,695
1998	Subaru	Legacy	WBF	Wagon 4-Door 4WD GT Base (5-speed Manual)	$21,073	$23,495
1998	Subaru	Legacy	WBG	Wagon 4-Door 4WD GT Base (4-speed ECT Automatic)	$21,787	$24,295
1998	Subaru	Legacy	WBT	Wagon 4-Door 4WD Outback Base (5-speed Manual)	$20,183	$22,495
1998	Subaru	Legacy	WBU	Wagon 4-Door 4WD Outback Base (4-speed ECT Automatic)	$20,897	$23,295
1998	Subaru	Legacy	WBV	Wagon 4-Door 4WD Outback w/Cold Package (5-speed Manual)	$20,541	$22,895
1998	Subaru	Legacy	WBW	Wagon 4-Door 4WD Outback w/Cold Package (4-speed ECT Automatic)	$21,255	$23,695
1998	Subaru	Legacy	WBX	Wagon 4-Door 4WD Outback Limited w/o Dual Moonroofs (5-speed Manual)	$22,049	$24,595

Year	Make	Model	Code	Description		
1998	Subaru	Legacy	WBY	Wagon 4-Door 4WD Outback Limited w/o Dual Moonroofs (4-speed ECT Automatic)	$22,763	$25,395
1998	Subaru	Legacy	WBZ	Wagon 4-Door 4WD Outback Limited w/Dual Moonroofs (4-speed ECT Automatic)	$23,822	$26,595
1998	Subaru	Legacy	WDX	Wagon 4-Door 4WD 30th Anniversary Outback Limited w/o Dual Moonroofs (5-speed Manual)	$22,049	$24,595
1998	Subaru	Legacy	WDY	Wagon 4-Door 4WD 30th Anniversary Outback Limited w/o Dual Moonroofs (4-speed ECT Automatic)	$22,763	$25,395
1998	Subaru	Legacy	WDZ	Wagon 4-Door 4WD 30th Anniversary Outback Limited w/Dual Moonroofs(4-speed ECT Automatic)	$23,822	$26,595
1998	Suzuki	Esteem	SGL632W	GL Sedan 4-Door (5-speed Manual)	$11,399	$11,999
1998	Suzuki	Esteem	SGL642W	GL Sedan 4-Door (4-speed Automatic)	$12,349	$12,999
1998	Suzuki	Esteem	SGL635W	GLX Sedan 4-Door (5-speed Manual)	$12,444	$13,099
1998	Suzuki	Esteem	SGL645W	GLX Sedan 4-Door (4-speed Automatic)	$13,394	$14,099
1998	Suzuki	Esteem	SGL64FW	GLX+ Sedan 4-Door (4-speed Automatic)	$14,154	$14,899
1998	Suzuki	Esteem	WGN632W	GL Wagon 4-Door (5-speed Manual)	$11,874	$12,499
1998	Suzuki	Esteem	WGN642W	GL Wagon 4-Door (4-speed Automatic)	$12,824	$13,499
1998	Suzuki	Esteem	WGN63EW	GLX Wagon 4-Door (5-speed Manual)	$12,919	$13,599
1998	Suzuki	Esteem	WGN64EW	GLX Wagon 4-Door (4-speed Automatic)	$13,869	$14,599
1998	Suzuki	Esteem	WGN64FW	GLX+ Wagon 4-Door (4-speed Automatic)	$14,819	$15,599
1998	Suzuki	Sidekick	FCE623W	2-Door JS Soft Top 2WD (5-speed Manual)	$12,444	$13,099
1998	Suzuki	Sidekick	FCE653W	2-Door JS Soft Top 2WD (4-speed Automatic)	$13,014	$13,699
1998	Suzuki	Sidekick	FAE623W	2-Door JX Soft Top 4WD (5-speed Manual)	$13,828	$12,869

Year	Mfr.	Make	Code	Model	Invoice Price	Retail Price
1998	Suzuki	Sidekick	FAE653W	2-Door JX Soft Top 4WD (4-speed Automatic)	$14,386	$15,469
1998	Suzuki	Sidekick	LTL663W	4-Door JS Hard Top 2WD (5-speed Manual)	$13,391	$14,399
1998	Suzuki	Sidekick	LTL693W	4-Door JS Hard Top 2WD (4-speed Automatic)	$14,274	$15,349
1998	Suzuki	Sidekick	LPL663W	4-Door JX Hard Top 2WD (5-speed Manual)	$14,559	$15,999
1998	Suzuki	Sidekick	LPL693W	4-Door JX Hard Top 2WD (4-speed Automatic)	$15,423	$16,949
1998	Suzuki	Sidekick	LSL77CW	4-Door Sport JS Hard Top 2WD (5-speed Manual)	$15,378	$16,899
1998	Suzuki	Sidekick	LSL78CW	4-Door Sport JS Hard Top 2WD (4-speed Automatic)	$16,288	$17,899
1998	Suzuki	Sidekick	LRL77CW	4-Door Sport JX Hard Top 4WD (5-speed Manual)	$16,288	$17,899
1998	Suzuki	Sidekick	LRL78CW	4-Door Sport JX Hard Top 4WD (4-speed Automatic)	$17,198	$18,899
1998	Suzuki	Sidekick	LRL77TW	4-Door Sport JLX Hard Top 4WD (5-speed Manual)	$17,599	$19,399
1998	Suzuki	Sidekick	LRL77TW	4-Door Sport JLX Hard Top 4WD (4-speed Automatic)	$18,563	$20,399
1998	Suzuki	Swift	HES532W	3-Door Hatchback (5-speed Manual)	$8,462	$9,099
1998	Suzuki	Swift	HES552W	3-Door Hatchback (3 Speed Automatic)	$9,066	$9,749
1998	Suzuki	X-90	LCC664W	2WD (5-speed Manual)	$12,595	$13,399
1998	Suzuki	X-90	LCC694W	2WD (4-speed Automatic)	$13,488	$14,349
1998	Suzuki	X-90	LAC664W	4WD (5-speed Manual)	$13,763	$14,799
1998	Suzuki	X-90	LAC694W	4WD (4-speed Automatic)	$14,646	$15,749
1998	Toyota	4Runner	8641	2WD 4-Door Base (5-speed Manual)	$17,997	$20,558
1998	Toyota	4Runner	8640	2WD 4-Door Base (4-speed ECT Automatic)	$18,785	$21,458
1998	Toyota	4Runner	8642	2WD 4-Door SR5 (4-speed ECT Automatic)	$21,990	$25,118

Year	Make	Model	Code	Description		
1998	Toyota	4Runner	8648	2WD 4-Door Limited (4-speed ECT Automatic)	$28,233	$32,248
1998	Toyota	4Runner	8657	4WD On-Demand 4-Door Base, (5-speed Manual)	$19,881	$22,708
1998	Toyota	4Runner	8658	4WD On-Demand 4-Door Base, (4-speed ECT Automatic)	$20,688	$23,608
1998	Toyota	4Runner	8665	4WD On-Demand 4-Door SR5 (5-speed Manual)	$22,997	$26,268
1998	Toyota	4Runner	8664	4WD On-Demand 4-Door SR5 (4-speed ECT Automatic)	$23,784	$27,168
1998	Toyota	4Runner	8668	4WD On-Demand 4-Door Limited (5-speed Manual)	$30,307	$34,618
1998	Toyota	Avalon	3534	XL Sedan 4-Door w/Bucket Seats	$21,254	$24,278
1998	Toyota	Avalon	3536	XL Sedan 4-Door w/Bench Seat	$21,981	$25,108
1998	Toyota	Avalon	3544	XLS Sedan 4-Door w/Bucket Seats	$24,336	$28,128
1998	Toyota	Avalon	3546	XLS Sedan 4-Door w/Bench Seat	$24,336	$28,128
1998	Toyota	Camry	2525	4 Cyl. Sedan 4-Door CE (5-speed Manual)	$15,003	$16,938
1998	Toyota	Camry	2526	4 Cyl. Sedan 4-Door CE (4-speed ECT Automatic)	$15,712	$17,738
1998	Toyota	Camry	2532	4 Cyl. Sedan 4-Door LE (4-speed ECT Automatic)	$17,699	$20,218
1998	Toyota	Camry	2540	4 Cyl. Sedan 4-Door XLE (4-speed ECT Automatic)	$19,810	$22,628
1998	Toyota	Camry	2527	V6 Sedan 4-Door CE (5-speed Manual)	$17,563	$19,828
1998	Toyota	Camry	2534	V6 Sedan 4-Door LE (4-speed ECTi Automatic)	$19,748	$22,558
1998	Toyota	Camry	2544	V6 Sedan 4-Door XLE (4-speed ECTi Automatic)	$21,771	$24,868
1998	Toyota	Celica	2175	Coupe 2-Door GT (5-speed Manual)	$17,780	$20,111
1998	Toyota	Celica	2172	Coupe 2-Door GT (4-speed ECT Automatic)	$18,484	$20,911
1998	Toyota	Celica	2183	Convertible 2-Door GT (5-speed Manual)	$21,759	$24,550
1998	Toyota	Celica	2184	Convertible 2-Door GT (4-speed ECT Automatic)	$22,460	$25,350

Year	Mfr.	Make	Code	Model	Invoice Price	Retail Price
1998	Toyota	Celica	2195	Liftback 3-Door GT (5-speed Manual)	$18,155	$20,536
1998	Toyota	Celica	2192	Liftback 3-Door GT (4-speed ECT Automatic)	$18,860	$21,336
1998	Toyota	Corolla	1714	VE Sedan 4-Door (5-speed Manual)	$10,854	$11,908
1998	Toyota	Corolla	1715	VE Sedan 4-Door (3 Speed Automatic)	$11,309	$12,408
1998	Toyota	Corolla	1721	CE Sedan 4-Door (5-speed Manual)	$12,568	$13,788
1998	Toyota	Corolla	1722	CE Sedan 4-Door (4-speed ECT Automatic)	$13,297	$14,588
1998	Toyota	Corolla	1737	LE Sedan 4-Door (5-speed Manual)	$13,107	$14,798
1998	Toyota	Corolla	1738	LE Sedan 4-Door (4-speed ECT Automatic)	$13,816	$15,598
1998	Toyota	Land Cruiser	6156	Sport Utility 5-Door 4WD	$39,518	$45,950
1998	Toyota	Pickup T100	8711	2WD Regular Cab Base (5-speed Manual)	$13,744	$14,828
1998	Toyota	Pickup T100	8710	2WD Regular Cab Base (4-speed ECT Automatic)	$14,579	$15,728
1998	Toyota	Pickup T100	8723	2WD Xtracab Base (5-speed Manual)	$16,844	$18,798
1998	Toyota	Pickup T100	8722	2WD Xtracab Base (4-speed ECT Automatic)	$17,650	$19,698
1998	Toyota	Pickup T100	8725	2WD Xtracab SR5 (5-speed Manual)	$18,199	$20,428
1998	Toyota	Pickup T100	8724	2WD Xtracab SR5 (4-speed ECT Automatic)	$19,001	$21,328
1998	Toyota	Pickup T100	8823	4WD Xtracab Base (5-speed Manual)	$20,052	$22,638
1998	Toyota	Pickup T100	8822	4WD Xtracab Base (4-speed ECT Automatic)	$20,849	$23,538
1998	Toyota	Pickup T100	8825	4WD Xtracab SR5 (5-speed Manual)	$21,485	$24,398
1998	Toyota	Pickup T100	8824	4WD Xtracab SR5 (4-speed ECT Automatic)	$22,278	$25,298
1998	Toyota	Rav4	4413	2WD Hard Top Sport Utility 2-Door (5-speed Manual)	$14,026	$15,388

1998	Toyota	Rav4	4412	2WD Hard Top Sport Utility 2-Door (4-speed ECT Automatic)	$14,983	$16,438
1998	Toyota	Rav4	4417	2WD Hard Top Sport Utility 4-Door (5-speed Manual)	$14,809	$16,248
1998	Toyota	Rav4	4416	2WD Hard Top Sport Utility 4-Door (4-speed ECT Automatic)	$15,768	$17,298
1998	Toyota	Rav4	4415	2WD Soft Top Sport Utility 2-Door (5-speed Manual)	$14,026	$15,388
1998	Toyota	Rav4	4414	2WD Soft Top Sport Utility 2-Door (4-speed ECT Automatic)	$14,983	$16,438
1998	Toyota	Rav4	4423	4WD Hard Top Sport Utility 2-Door (5-speed Manual)	$15,052	$16,798
1998	Toyota	Rav4	4427	4WD Hard Top Sport Utility 4-Door (5-speed Manual)	$15,822	$17,658
1998	Toyota	Rav4	4426	4WD Hard Top Sport Utility 4-Door (4-speed ECT Automatic)	$16,763	$18,708
1998	Toyota	Rav4	4425	4WD Soft Top Sport Utility 2-Door (5-speed Manual)	$15,052	$16,798
1998	Toyota	Rav4	4424	4WD Soft Top Sport Utility 2-Door (4-speed ECT Automatic)	$15,993	$17,848
1998	Toyota	Sienna	5322	CE Minivan 4-Door	$18,724	$21,140
1998	Toyota	Sienna	5332	LE Minivan 4-Door	$20,573	$23,500
1998	Toyota	Sienna	5334	LE Minivan 5-Door	$20,989	$23,975
1998	Toyota	Sienna	5344	XLE Minivan 5-Door	$23,514	$27,100

Year	Mfr.	Make	Code	Model	Invoice Price	Retail Price
1998	Toyota	Supra	2396	Base w/o Sport Roof Liftback 2-Door (4-speed ECT Automatic)	$28,972	$30,918
1998	Toyota	Supra	2394	Base w/Sport Roof Liftback 2-Door (4-speed ECT Automatic)	$32,677	$35,468
1998	Toyota	Supra	2383	Turbo Liftback 2-Door (6 Speed Manual)	$37,177	$40,308
1998	Toyota	Supra	2387	Turbo Liftback 2-Door (4-speed ECT Automatic)	$35,726	$38,588
1998	Toyota	Tacoma	7103	2WD 4-Cyl. Regular Cab (5-speed Manual)	$11,493	$12,538
1998	Toyota	Tacoma	7104	2WD 4-Cyl. Regular Cab (4-speed ECT Automatic)	$12,154	$13,258
1998	Toyota	Tacoma	7113	2WD 4-Cyl. Base Xtracab (5-speed Manual)	$13,330	$14,708
1998	Toyota	Tacoma	7114	2WD 4-Cyl. Base Xtracab (4-speed ECT Automatic)	$13,983	$15,428
1998	Toyota	Tacoma	7162	2WD 4-Cyl. Prerunner Xtracab (4-speed ECT Automatic)	$15,657	$17,238
1998	Toyota	Tacoma	7153	2WD 6V Base Xtracab (5-speed Manual)	$14,545	$16,048
1998	Toyota	Tacoma	7154	2WD 6V Base Xtracab (4-speed ECT Automatic)	$15,361	$16,948
1998	Toyota	Tacoma	7164	2WD 6V Prerunner Xtracab (4-speed ECT Automatic)	$16,506	$18,168
1998	Toyota	Tacoma	7503	4WD 4-Cyl. Regular Cab (5-speed Manual)	$15,616	$17,428
1998	Toyota	Tacoma	7504	4WD 4-Cyl. Regular Cab (4-speed ECT Automatic)	$16,422	$18,328
1998	Toyota	Tacoma	7513	4WD 4-Cyl. Base Xtracab (5-speed Manual)	$16,916	$18,878
1998	Toyota	Tacoma	7514	4WD 4-Cyl. Base Xtracab (4-speed ECT Automatic)	$17,723	$19,778
1998	Toyota	Tacoma	7553	4WD V6 Base Xtracab (5-speed Manual)	$17,892	$19,968
1998	Toyota	Tacoma	7554	4WD V6 Base Xtracab (4-speed ECT Automatic)	$18,699	$20,868

Year	Make	Model	Description		
1998	Toyota	Tacoma	7557	4WD V6 Limited Xtracab (5-speed Manual)	$21,531	$24,028
1998	Toyota	Tacoma	7558	4WD V6 Limited Xtracab (4-speed ECT Automatic)	$22,336	$24,928
1998	Toyota	Tercel	1307	CE Sedan 2-Door (5-speed Manual)	$11,929	$12,690
1998	Toyota	Tercel	1308	CE Sedan 2-Door (3 Speed Automatic)	$12,400	$13,190
1998	Volkswagon	Cabrio	1V72Q4	GL Convertible 2-Door	$16,289	$17,975
1998	Volkswagon	Cabrio	1V73Q4	GLS Convertible 2-Door	$20,240	$22,290
1998	Volkswagon	Golf	1W13Q4	GL Sedan 4-Door	$12,455	$13,485
1998	Volkswagon	Golf	1W1KQ4	K2 Sedan 4-Door	$13,904	$14,895
1998	Volkswagon	Golf	1W14Q4	GTI Hatchback 2-Door	$15,351	$16,670
1998	Volkswagon	Golf	1W1VT4	GTI-VR6 Hatchback 2-Door	$18,678	$20,235
1998	Volkswagon	Jetta	1W23Q4	GL Sedan 4-Door	$13,242	$14,595
1998	Volkswagon	Jetta	1W2PQ4	GT Sedan 4-Door	$13,651	$14,990
1998	Volkswagon	Jetta	1W2LQ4	K2 Sedan 4-Door	$14,691	$15,995
1998	Volkswagon	Jetta	1W28Q4	GLS Sedan 4-Door	$15,341	$16,945
1998	Volkswagon	Jetta	1W2334	TDI Sedan 4-Door	$14,522	$15,770
1998	Volkswagon	Jetta	1W27T4	GLX Sedan 4-Door	$19,335	$20,955
1998	Volkswagon	New Beetle	1C13L4	Base Coupe 2-Door	$14,336	$15,200
1998	Volkswagon	New Beetle	1C1354	TDI Coupe 2-Door	$15,527	$16,475
1998	Volkswagon	Passat	3B24G5	GLS Sedan 4-Door	$18,676	$20,750
1998	Volkswagon	Passat	3B2445	TDI Sedan 4-Door	$19,078	$21,200
1998	Volkswagon	Passat	3B24S5	GLS V6 Sedan 4-Door	$20,855	$23,190
1998	Volkswagon	Passat	3B55S5	GLX Sedan 4-Door	$23,589	$26,250

Year	Mfr.	Make	Code	Model	Invoice Price	Retail Price
1998	Volvo	70 Series	S70 M	S70 Sedan 4-Door Base (5-speed Manual)	$24,785	$26,985
1998	Volvo	70 Series	S70 A	S70 Sedan 4-Door Base (4-speed Automatic)	$25,760	$27,960
1998	Volvo	70 Series	S70 GTMS	S70 Sedan 4-Door GT (5-speed Manual)	$27,240	$29,540
1998	Volvo	70 Series	S70 GTAS	S70 Sedan 4-Door GT (4-speed Automatic)	$28,215	$30,515
1998	Volvo	70 Series	S70 GLT	S70 Sedan 4-Door GTL (4-speed Automatic)	$30,040	$32,440
1998	Volvo	70 Series	S70 T5M	S70 Sedan 4-Door T5 (5-speed Manual)	$31,060	$34,010
1998	Volvo	70 Series	S70 T5A	S70 Sedan 4-Door T5 (4-speed Automatic)	$32,035	$34,985
1998	Volvo	70 Series	V70 M	V70 2WD Wagon 5-Door Base (5-speed Manual)	$26,085	$28,285
1998	Volvo	70 Series	V70 A	V70 2WD Wagon 5-Door Base (4-speed Automatic)	$27,060	$29,260
1998	Volvo	70 Series	V70 GTMS	V70 2WD Wagon 5-Door GT (5-speed Manual)	$28,540	$30,840
1998	Volvo	70 Series	V70 GTAS	V70 2WD Wagon 5-Door GT (4-speed Automatic)	$29,515	$31,815
1998	Volvo	70 Series	V70 GLT	V70 2WD Wagon 5-Door GLT (4-speed Automatic)	$31,340	$33,740
1998	Volvo	70 Series	V70 T5M	V70 2WD Wagon 5-Door T5 (5-speed Manual)	$32,360	$35,310
1998	Volvo	70 Series	V70 T5A	V70 2WD Wagon 5-Door T5 (4-speed Automatic)	$33,335	$36,285
1998	Volvo	70 Series	V70 AWDN	V70 AWD Wagon 5-Door AWD (w/o Sunroof)	$31,720	$34,420
1998	Volvo	70 Series	V70 AWDA	V70 AWD Wagon 5-Door AWD (w/Sunroof)	$32,920	$35,620
1998	Volvo	70 Series	V70 AWXN	V70 AWD Wagon 5-Door XC Cross Country (w/o Sunroof)	$33,470	$36,420
1998	Volvo	70 Series	V70 AWXC	V70 AWD Wagon 5-Door XC Cross Country (w/Sunroof)	$34,670	$37,620

1998	Volvo	70 Series	V70 RAWD	V70 AWD Wagon 5-Door R	$36,795	$40,995
1998	Volvo	70 Series	C70 M	C70 Coupe 2-Door Base (5-speed Manual)	$34,795	$38,995
1998	Volvo	70 Series	C70 A	C70 Coupe 2-Door Base (4-speed Automatic)	$35,770	$39,970
1998	Volvo	90 Series	S90	Sedan 4-Door	$31,600	$34,300
1998	Volvo	90 Series	V90	Wagon 5-Door	$33,150	$35,850

Glossary

acquisition fee   In leasing, a fee charged at lease inception to cover the lessor's loan-processing costs (a similar charge may be called an "assignment fee" or "initiation fee").

advertising association fee   Regional ad cost spread between area dealers (not all dealers participate); sometimes charged in a lease.

aftersell   Those items that a dealer markets to car shoppers after the car itself, trade-in, and financing issues are handled. Aftersell is usually handled by the F & I (financing and insurance) representative, and may include everything from dealer-sponsored extended warranties to undercoating and other products. A significant portion of dealer profits arise from aftersell, and the consumer is be wise to consider minimizing involvement.

antilock brakes   Brakes designed to prevent wheels from locking and skidding when a driver brakes hard (antilocks pump your brakes automatically, many times a second, and let you retain steering control).

APR (Annual Percentage Rate)   Interest rate used in figuring payments. In leasing, may be called base interest rate.

back end   See "F & I."

Blue Book   In automotive circles, refers to the *Kelley Blue Book* used car pricing guide, a widely used standard.

bodily injury liability insurance   Coverage for injuries you might cause another person.

capitalized cost (gross cap)   The agreed price of the car plus any extras such as service plans, gap insurance, and other fees. Adjusted (net) cap cost is capitalized cost less any reduction in the cost of the vehicle (a rebate, down payment, or the value of your trade-in).

capitalized cost reduction   Down payment on a lease (cash, the value of your trade-in, or a rebate amount you choose to put toward up-front costs).

closed-end lease   Common consumer lease that presupposes the residual value of a vehicle at lease end, in which the lessor bears the risk of any difference between that and the actual value at lease end.

collision insurance   Coverage for damage from a collision that happens to the car of the policyholder.

comprehensive insurance   Coverage for damage to the car of the policyholder when a collision with another car isn't involved (may cover fire, theft, earthquake, floods, falling objects, etc.).

credit rating   A statistical description of your credit habits.

credit report   A detailed credit history, on file with major credit bureaus, which lenders may order to take a look at a consumer's credit habits (consumers may see their own, as well).

daytime running lights Activated by the ignition switch, they are reduced-intensity headlamp lights designed to increase the contrast between vehicles and backgrounds.

dealer cost (aka invoice price) What it costs a dealer to acquire a car, including transportation to get it to the car lot. Part of the dealer cost figure includes the "holdback."

depreciation Reduction of a car's value over time.

disposition fee Fee that a lessor pays at the end of a lease to cover the dealer's cost in reselling it.

early termination penalty Substantial penalty for turning a lease car in early (due partly to the fact that initial depreciation is amortized over the life of a lease in order to provide a standard monthly payment parameter).

excess mileage charge Charge assessed at lease end for exceeding annual mileage allotment (usually 10,000–15,000 miles per year); often 10–25 cents per mile.

excess wear-and-tear charge Charge assessed at lease end for treating the vehicle more roughly than normal.

F & I (Financing & Insurance) Dealer term for the "back end" of a car sale. This department is where financing is arranged, and insurance coverage and other extras are sold. It's the department where aftersell is typically handled.

gap insurance Coverage for the difference between what you've paid on the car and what it's worth.

gap waiver Language included in some leases that protects you from gap charges. See also "gap insurance."

holdback   An amount paid by a manufacturer to a dealer after completion of a sale, often 1–3% of the MSRP.

lease company   Bank or other financial institution that is buying the vehicle from the dealer and leasing it to you. It may be a "captive finance company" that is affiliated with the manufacturer (such as Ford Motor Credit, Toyota Motor Credit, etc.), a bank, a bank-related institution, or an independent financing organization.

lemon laws   State laws designed to help consumers in situations in which their (typically new) cars must repeatedly be serviced for the same problem or need numerous types of repairs.

lessee   The person leasing.

lessor   The company financing a lease.

Manufacturer's Suggested Retail Price (MSRP) Also called "sticker price," what the manufacturer thinks dealers should reasonably charge for a car.

medical or PIP (Personal Injury Protection) insurance   Coverage for injuries that could occur to occupants of the policyholder's vehicle.

money factor   The rate of the financing expense, used to calculate your lease payment. It is equal to $1/24$ of the APR.

net interest rate   Total interest rate for the lease, deduced from the net capitalized cost.

open-end lease   Type of lease typically seen in business leasing arrangements, in which the lessor may bear the risk of any difference between the anticipated resale value of the car, as determined at lease inception, and the actual residual value of the vehicle at lease end.

option discount adjustment Manufacturer purchase discounts on certain options packages, which in leasing are described instead at full retail value for purposes of residual calculation.

option to buy Part of a lease contract outlining whether you can buy a vehicle at the end of its lease term and for how much.

property damage liability insurance Coverage for damage to another person's property.

rebate Incentive offering a flat amount off the purchase price of a new car; often manufacturer-sponsored.

rent charge Also called "lease charge," a leasing term indicating the interest cost of financing.

residual Leasing term used to describe the expected future wholesale value of a vehicle (such as at the end of a lease term), expressed either as a dollar amount or as a percentage of the original price (usually MSRP).

retail price The price of a used car when costs of refurbishment, detailing, and any needed repairs are factored in; plus dealer carrying costs and some profit.

rule of 78 A type of financing arrangement often seen at a dealership. It favors the lender by assigning interest charges so that most of the interest expense is paid off before most of the principal.

salvage title A specific kind of title assigned to vehicles that have been "salvaged," for instance, after being damaged in a natural disaster. Cars holding salvage titles can be difficult to insure and often draw no more than half the usual price on the market.

secret warranty program When a manufacturer routinely performs free repairs on cars with persistent problems outside of the official warranty or after it has expired. Common problems may be identified in a technical service bulletin (TSB) by the manufacturer.

security deposit (refundable) Refundable amount that you pay at the outset of a lease, often close to a month's lease payment. You get it back at the end of the lease unless you're liable for other charges, which could be deducted from the security deposit amount.

simple interest loan Method of calculating interest charges in consumer financing, often found in a bank loan.

subsidized lease Also known as a "subvented" lease, a lease offer with a manufacturer's incentive attached—may include rebate or special interest rate.

Technical Service Bulletin (TSB) Detail of appropriate repair procedures issued by a manufacturer for problems common to a certain vehicle. See also "secret warranty program."

term Number of months a lease or loan is paid back over.

title State document of legal vehicle ownership.

trade-in value What a dealer offers for your used vehicle. It does not include the costs of refurbishment, and may be lower than "wholesale" values in some uses of the term.

total out-of-pocket cost Total of payments, fees, deposits, cap cost reduction from the beginning to the end of the lease; not including tax, license, or registration.

trade-in-allowance The worth you're being allowed for trading in your old vehicle.

uninsured motorist insurance Coverage for treatment of policyholder injuries after a collision with a driver who doesn't have insurance.

up-front costs In a lease, that which is paid at the beginning of a lease (often includes security deposit, down payment, advanced payment, and taxes).

upside down (aka negative equity) Owing more money on a car than it's worth. This happens because of swift depreciation and the way the cost of financing is paid off.

variable rate loan Type of financing arrangement in which the effective interest rate may vary within certain parameters over the life of the loan.

VIN (Vehicle Identification Number) Unique number used to identify each vehicle (often found on the driver's side dash).

wholesale price Value of a used vehicle before dealer profit is figured in. According to some uses of the term, may include the cost of refurbishing cars for resale, and thus exceed "trade-in" values.

Resource Guide

Automobile Manufacturer Phone Numbers

Acura
(800) 382-2238

Audi
(800) 822-2834

BMW
(800) 831-1117

Buick
(800) 521-7300

Cadillac
(800) 458-8006

Chevrolet
(800) 222-1020

Chrysler
(800) 992-1997

Dodge
(800) 992-1997

Eagle
(800) 992-1997

Ford
(800) 392-3673

GMC
(800) 462-8782

Honda
(310) 783-2000

Hyundai
(800) 633-5151

Infiniti
(800) 662-6200

Isuzu
(800) 255-6727

Jaguar
(201) 818-8500

Jeep
(800) 992-1997

Kia
(800) 333-4542

Land Rover
(800) 637-6837

Lexus
(800) 255-3987

Lincoln
(800) 392-3673

Mazda
(800) 222-5500

Mercedes Benz
(800) 222-0100

Mercury
(800) 392-3673

Mitsubishi
(800) 222-0037

Nissan
(800) 647-7261

Oldsmobile
(800) 442-6537

Peugeot
(201) 935-8400

Plymouth
(800) 992-1997

Pontiac
(800) 762-2737

Porsche
(800) 545-8039

Saab
(800) 955-9007

Saturn
(800) 553-6000

Subaru
(800) 782-2783

Suzuki
(800) 934-0934

Toyota
(800) 331-4331

Volkswagen
(800) 822-8987

Volvo
(800) 458-1552

Internet resources

CAR CRITERIA ON THE INTERNET

National Highway Traffic Safety Administration
www.nhtsa.dot.gov

NHTSA Auto Safety Hot Line:
(800) 424-9393

Insurance Institute for Highway Safety
www.highwaysafety.org
(703) 247-1500

Microsoft CarPoint
www.carpoint.com

Bank Rate Monitor (for auto loan rates)
www.bankrate.com

Edmund's
www.edmunds.com

IntelliChoice
www.intellichoice.com

Kelley Blue Book
www.kbb.com

National Automobile Dealers Association
www.nada.com

AUTO PRICING WEB SITES

AutoSite
www.autosite.com

Microsoft CarPoint
www.carpoint.msn.com

Edmund's
www.edmunds.com

IntelliChoice Online
www.intellichoice.com

Kelley Blue Book
www.kbb.com

Recommended Reading List

Center for the Study of Services publications
(800) 475-7283:
  Car Deals (national newsletter)

Insurance Institute for Highway Safety publications
(703) 247-1500:
  "About Your Airbags"
  "Shopping for a Safer Car"
  "Driver Death Rates"

Highway Loss Data Institute publications
(703) 247-1600:
  "Injury Collision & Theft Losses"

Federal Reserve System publications
(202) 452-3244:
  "Keys to Vehicle Leasing" brochure
  Publications Services, MS-127
  Board of Governors of the Federal Reserve
  System, Washington, DC 20551

Important Documents

Auto budgeting

HOW MUCH CAR CAN I AFFORD?

To get the Prudent Cash Price you should pay for a car, use your income and current car expenses as guidelines. First, figure your yearly Fuel & Upkeep Costs.

$_____ Fuel, Maintenance, Repairs, Insurance (per month)

× 12

= $_____ Yearly Fuel & Upkeep

Now decide what portion of your income you will base your car purchase on (seven to 15% is suggested), and subtract Yearly Fuel & Upkeep from that figure to arrive at your Prudent Cash Price.

$_____ Annual Income

× .07

= _____

– $_____ Yearly Fuel & Upkeep

– $_____ Any Additional Amount Insurance Will Cost You

= $_____ Subtotal Prudent Cash Price

And perform a little calculation to cover the cost of sales tax and incidentals at purchase.

$_____ Your state sales tax percentage plus 1% (6% sales tax would be stated as ".07")

Appendix E

Make adjust-
ments if the car
you expect to
get will have
vastly better fuel
economy or
lower upkeep
costs.

× $____ Subtotal Prudent Cash Price

= $____ Sales Tax & Incidentals Allowance

One more step and you're done.

     $____ Subtotal Prudent Cash Price

− $____ Sales Tax & Incidentals Allowance

= $____ Prudent Cash Price

The "How Much Car Can I Afford?" chart shows
how much you can spend on a new auto if you pay
cash and want to stick between the 7% of income
the average American spends on transportation
(remember, that's just an average—many people
spend more) and the 15% cap some consumer credit counselors suggest. Since you're probably not paying cash and you'd doubtless like to unload that old
set of wheels, we've got to do more figuring.

Your Affordable
Car Price takes
financing, sales
tax, and insur-
ance costs into
account, but
remember, it's
just a rule of
thumb.

I HAVEN'T GOT CASH, HOW MUCH CAR CAN I AFFORD?

From the Prudent Cash Price you just determined, subtract both
the expected value of your trade-in and any down payment you
expect to make.

     $____ Prudent Cash Price

− $____ Value of Trade-In

− $____ Down Payment

= $____ Amount to be Financed

Now use the Financing Cost Scale (on the following page) to see
how much interest you'll have to pay on a typical four-year
loan.

     $____ Prudent Cash Price

− $____ Financing Cost (from the Financing Cost Scale)

=   ____

+ $____ Value of Trade-In

= $____

×   ____ Your State's Sales Tax (.05, .07, etc.)

= $____ Your Affordable Car Price

FINANCING COST SCALE

How much will you spend on interest over the life of your loan? This table gives you a good idea of the real cost hidden inside an extra percentage point or two.

Amount to be Financed/Loan Rate (4-year)

	2%	4%	6%	8%	10%	12%	14%	16%
$5,000	200	400	650	850	1,100	1,300	1,550	1,800
$10,000	400	850	1,250	1,700	2,150	2,650	3,100	3,600
$15,000	600	1,250	1,900	2,600	3,250	3,950	4,700	5,400
$20,000	850	1,700	2,550	3,450	4,350	5,300	6,250	7,200
$25,000	1,050	2,100	3,200	4,300	5,450	6,600	7,800	9,000
$30,000	1,250	2,500	3,800	5,150	6,500	7,900	9,350	10,800
$35,000	1,450	2,950	4,450	6,000	7,600	9,250	10,900	12,600
$40,000	1,650	3,350	5,100	6,850	8,700	10,550	12,450	14,400
$50,000	2,050	4,200	6,350	8,600	10,850	13,200	15,600	18,000

(Amounts are rounded to the nearest $50.)

APPROXIMATE MONTHLY CAR PAYMENT AFFORDABILITY RANGE

$_____ (½ Weekly Net Income) to $_____ (Weekly Net Income)

Multiply each number by 48 to find acceptable purchase-price and finance-cost figures (assuming four year financing)

$_____ to $_____

Then to estimate acceptable purchase prices, refer to the Financing Cost Scale above and pick out a likely interest rate. Subtract from each amount the figure from the Financing Cost Scale best representing the total expected cost of interest:

$_____ to $_____ is the range of purchase prices you should not exceed.

Auto pricing

How can you tell the model year of a car from its VIN (Vehicle Identification Number)? The following table can help you decode it.

WHAT YEAR? CHECK THE VIN

The tenth character in a 17-digit Vehicle Identification Number refers to the vehicle year.

1981	B	1991	M
1982	C	1992	N
1983	D	1993	P
1984	E	1994	R
1985	F	1995	S
1986	G	1996	T
1987	H	1997	V
1988	J	1998	W
1989	K	1999	X
1990	L	2000	Y

TARGET BUY PRICE (RULE OF THUMB)

$_____ Dealer Invoice Price + 5% – $_____ Any Dealer Rebate Amount = $_____ Target Buy Price

WHAT DID THE DEALER REALLY PAY FOR THIS CAR?

First, figure the amount of the dealer's built-in profit in dollar terms:

$_____ Manufacturer's Suggested Retail Price (less any destination charges if included in MSRP)

× ._____ Dealer Holdback Percentage (usually 2–3% of MSRP—expressed as .02 or .03)

= $_____ Dealer Holdback Amount in Dollars

Now use that figure to compute the real cost of a car to the dealer—it's less than what's commonly called "dealer cost":

$_____ Dealer Cost

– $_____ Dealer Holdback Amount in Dollars

= $_____

+ $_____ Vehicle Delivery Charges

– $_____ Any Dealer Rebate Amount

= $_____ REAL DEALER COST

DEALER HOLDBACK RATES BY MANUFACTURER

Make	Holdback
Acura	2% of the Base MSRP
Audi	No Holdback
BMW	2% of the Base MSRP
Buick	3% of the Total MSRP
Cadillac	3% of the Total MSRP
Chevrolet	3% of the Total MSRP
Chrysler	3% of the Total MSRP
Dodge	3% of the Total MSRP
Eagle	3% of the Total MSRP
Ford	3% of the Total MSRP
GMC	3% of the Total MSRP
Honda	2% of the Base MSRP (except Prelude, which has no Holdback.)
Hyundai	2% of the Total Invoice
Infiniti	1% of the Total MSRP + 1% of the Total Invoice
Isuzu	3% of the Total MSRP
Jaguar	2% of the Base Invoice
Jeep	3% of the Total MSRP
Kia	No Holdback
Land Rover	No Holdback
Lexus	No Holdback
Lincoln	3% of the Total MSRP
Mazda	2% of the Base MSRP
Mercedes-Benz	3% of the Total MSRP
Mercury	3% of the Total MSRP
Mitsubishi	2% of the Total MSRP
Nissan	2% of the Total Invoice + 1.5% (floor-planning allowance)
Oldsmobile	3% of the Total MSRP
Plymouth	3% of the Total MSRP
Pontiac	3% of the Total MSRP
Porsche	No Holdback
Saab	3% of the Base MSRP

As a rule of thumb, the holdback amount varies from 2% for many imports to 3% for most domestic cars based on the MSRP of the car with desired options. But import car holdbacks may be calculated as a percentage of base MSRP or base Dealer Invoice instead. (Source: *Kelley Blue Book*)

Saturn	One-price sales; customer pays MSRP
Subaru	2% of the Total MSRP
Suzuki	2% of the Base MSRP
Toyota	2% of the Base Invoice (Amount may differ in Southeastern U.S.)
Volkswagen	2% of the Total MSRP
Volvo	$300 Flat Amount

(Source: Edmund's—1998 percentages)

Auto pricing comparisons

Use the Financing Cost Scale, if needed, to figure your approximate financing cost. Other data can be found using the sources mentioned in Chapter 4.

ESTIMATING AND COMPARING TOTAL COST OF OWNERSHIP

New Car Make, Model, Year:	Used Car Make, Model, Year:
1. Add these items:	
$ _____ Expected Purchase Price	$ _____ Expected Purchase Price
+ $_____ Sales Tax	+ $_____ Sales Tax
+ $_____ Total Financing Cost	+ $_____ Total Financing Cost
= $_____ "Buying Cost"	= $_____ "Buying Cost"
2. Then add up these anticipated annual figures:	
$ _____ Insurance	$ _____ Insurance
$ _____ State Property Tax	$ _____ State Property Tax
$ _____ Fuel Costs	$ _____ Fuel Costs
$ _____ Repairs	$ _____ Repairs
= $_____ "Ownership Cost"	= $_____ "Ownership Cost"
And multiply the Ownership Cost by 5:	And multiply the Ownership Cost by 5:
= $_____ "5-Year Ownership Cost"	= $_____ "5-Year Ownership Cost"
3. Add the final results of both:	
$ _____ Buying Cost	$ _____ Buying Cost
+ $_____ 5-Year Ownership Cost	+ $_____ 5-Year Ownership Cost
= $_____ "Buy & Own Subtotal"	= $_____ "Buy & Own Subtotal"

4. Subtract the 5-year resale value (residual):

$ _____ Buy & Own Subtotal	$ _____ Buy & Own Subtotal
– $_____ 5-Year Resale Value	– $_____ 5-Year Resale Value
= $_____ Total Cost of Ownership (5 Years)	= $_____ Total Cost of Ownership (5 Years)

Auto financing

MONTHLY PAYMENT (FOR EVERY $100 FINANCED)

Interest Rate	24 months	36 Months	48 Months	60 Months
4%	$4.34	$2.95	$2.26	$1.84
6%	$4.43	$3.04	$2.35	$1.93
8%	$4.52	$3.13	$2.44	$2.03
10%	$4.61	$3.23	$2.54	$2.12
12%	$4.71	$3.32	$2.63	$2.22
14%	$4.80	$3.42	$2.73	$2.33

COMPARING LOAN TERMS OR INTEREST RATES

1. Divide the amount to be financed by 100, and put the answer here: _____.

2. Multiply that figure by the dollar amount for your interest rate and selected term, shown in the Monthly Payment Table above, and write the result here: _____. This is your monthly payment.

3. Multiply that figure by the number of months in the term, and write that result here: _____.

4. Subtract the amount to be financed (from Step 1) and put the result here: _____. This is your total financing cost over the term.

5. Repeat the steps for a loan term or rate you'd like to compare this one to, and see which has the lower total financing costs.

6. Subtract the lower figure from the higher one. The difference is the amount you'll save, and you can write that here: _____.

If you're caught in a quandary between getting a loan, paying cash, or leasing, you can get some idea how those options compare by using the worksheet below.

COMPARING CASH, LOANS, AND LEASING

Rough estimations are necessary when considering opportunity cost (and expected interest earned on any amount of cash on hand as a result of not paying cash for the vehicle).

Loan:

$_____$ Sales Tax & Down Payment

+ $_____$ (Monthly Payment $\_\_\_\_\_$ × $\_\_\_\_\_$ Term (in months)

= $_____$ Cost of Vehicle

− $_____$ Estimated Resale Value (at end of term)

− $_____$ Expected Earned Interest (on any amount of cash on hand as a result of not paying cash for the vehicle)

= $_____$ Cost of this Option (at end of term)

Cash:

$_____$ Price of Car & Sales Tax

+ $_____$ Opportunity Cost (amount you would otherwise expect to earn on the money if invested or saved) Price of Car & Sales Tax $_____$ × expected interest rate to be earned $\_\_\_\_$% × (term of loan option in months) $_____$

= $_____$ Cost of Vehicle

− $_____$ Estimated Resale Value (at end of loan option term)

= $_____$ Cost of this Option (at same time as end of loan term)

Lease:

$_____$ Leasing Fees and Up-Front Payments

+ $_____$ Total of Monthly Payments (monthly payment $\_\_\_\_\_$ × lease term in months $\_\_\_\_\_$)

= $_____$ Cost of Vehicle

− $_____$ Expected Earned Interest (on any amount of cash on hand as a result of not paying cash for the vehicle)

= $_____$ Cost of this Option (at end of lease term)

Do your calculations with equivalent loan and lease terms.

Credit

CREDIT REPORTING BUREAUS

Equifax
P.O. Box 105783
Atlanta, GA 30348
(800) 685-1111
www.equifax.com

Experian (formerly TRW)
P.O. Box 2104
Allen, TX 75013-2104
(888) 397-3742
www.experian.com

TransUnion Corp.
P.O. Box 390
Springfield, PA 19064-0390
(312) 408-1400
www.transunion.com

Jane Consumer
1234 Pleasant Street
Lovely, RI 12345
(123) 456-7890

Equifax
P.O. Box 105783
Atlanta, GA 30348

July 1, 1998

Dear Equifax:

Please send me a copy of my credit report on file with your agency. I am including a check for $8 made out to Equifax, and pertinent information is as follows:

Name: Jane Lorraine Consumer
Social Security Number: 123-45-6789
Date of Birth: 1/1/70
Current Address: 1234 Pleasant Street; Lovely, RI 12345
Current Phone: (123) 456-7890
Previous Addresses (last 2 years): 12 Sunny Lane; Near Lovely, RI 12345
Current Employer: Jane Lorraine Interiors

Thank you. I'll expect this report, sent to my address on the letterhead, in a timely fashion as required by law.

Sincerely,

Jane Lorraine Consumer

Sample Credit
Report Request
Letter.

Your Rights Under the Fair Credit Reporting Act (source: Federal Trade Commission):

1. **You must be told if information in your file has been used against you.** Anyone who uses information from a CRA to take action against you—such as denying an application for credit, insurance, or employment—must tell you, and give you the name, address, and phone number of the CRA that provided the consumer report.

2. **You can find out what is in your file.** At your request, a CRA must give you the information in your file, and a list of everyone who has requested it recently. There is no charge for the report if a person has taken action against you because of information supplied by the CRA, if you request the report within 60 days of receiving notice of the action. You also are entitled to one free report every twelve months if you certify that: (1) you are unemployed and plan to seek employment within 60 days, (2) you are on welfare, or (3) your report is inaccurate due to fraud. Otherwise, a CRA may charge you up to eight dollars.

3. **You can dispute inaccurate information with the CRA.** If you tell a CRA that your file contains inaccurate information, the CRA must investigate the items (usually within 30 days) by presenting all relevant evidence you submit to its information source, unless your dispute is frivolous. The source must review your evidence and report its finding to the CRA. (The source also must advise national CRAs—to whom it has provided data—of any error.) The CRA must give you a written report of the investigation and a copy of your report if the investigation results

in any change. If the CRA's investigation does not resolve the dispute, you may add a brief statement to your file. The CRA must normally include a summary of your statement in future reports. If an item is deleted or a dispute statement is filed, you may ask that anyone who has recently received your report be notified of the change.

4. **Inaccurate information must be corrected or deleted.** A CRA must remove or correct inaccurate or unverified information for its files, usually within 30 days after you dispute it. However, the CRA is not required to remove accurate data from your file unless it is outdated (as described following) or cannot be verified. If your dispute results in any change to your report, the CRA cannot reinsert a disputed item into your file unless the information source verifies its accuracy and completeness. In addition, the CRA must give you a written notice, telling you it has reinserted the item. The notice must include the name, address, and phone number of the information source.

5. **You can dispute inaccurate items with the source of the information.** If you tell anyone, such as a creditor who reports to a CRA, that you dispute an item, they cannot then report the information to a CRA without including a notice of your dispute. In addition, once you've notified the source of the error in writing, it cannot continue to report the information if it is, in fact, an error.

6. **Outdated information cannot be reported.** In most cases, a CRA cannot report negative information that is more than seven years old; ten years old for bankruptcies.

7. **Access to your file is limited.** A CRA may provide information about you only to people with a need recognized by the FCRA—usually to consider an application with a creditor, insurer, employer, landlord, or other business entity.

8. **Your consent is required for reports that are provided to employers, or reports that contain medical information.** A CRA cannot give out information about you to your employer or prospective employer without your written consent. A CRA cannot report medical information about you to creditors, insurers, or employers without your permission.

9. **You may choose to exclude your name from CRA lists for unsolicited credit and insurance offers.** Creditors and insurers may use file information as the basis for sending you unsolicited offers of credit or insurance. Such offers must include a toll-free phone number for you to call if you want your name and address removed from future lists. If you call, you must be kept off the lists for two years. If you request, complete, and return the CRA form provided for this purpose, you must be taken off the lists indefinitely.

10. **You may seek damages from violators.** If a CRA, a user, or (in some cases) a provider of CRA data violates the FCRA, you may sue them in state or federal court.

YOUR LEASE CALCULATOR

Fill in the appropriate information:

	Sample	Your Figures
Term	36 months	_____ months
MSRP	$20,000	$_____
Cap Cost (sell price)	$19,000	$_____
Residual	$10,000 (50%)	$_____ (_____%)
State Sales Tax Percentage	.06 (6%)	_____ (_____%)
Money Factor (from Table 11.3)	.00400	_____

Then figure your lease costs:

	Sample	Your Figures
Total Depreciation (cap cost – residual)	$9,000	$_____
Monthly Depreciation (total dep. ÷ term)	$250	$_____
Monthly Lease Fee [money factor × (cap cost + residual)]	$116	$_____
Monthly Rent (monthly depreciation + monthly lease fee)	$366	$_____

And arrive at a final figure:

	Sample	Your Figures
Total Monthly Payment (monthly rent × sales tax percentage)	$387.96	$_____

(Source: *Automotive Lease Guide*)

Use the information in the table below with the worksheet above. It shows the monthly interest dollars needed to keep the yield indicated.

MONEY, MONEY, MONEY FACTORS

	Money Factor	Yield*
(Cap Cost + Residual) ×	.00325	7.8%
(Cap Cost + Residual) ×	.00350	8.4%

(Cap Cost + Residual) ×	.00375	9.0%
(Cap Cost + Residual) ×	.00400	9.6%
(Cap Cost + Residual) ×	.00425	10.2%
(Cap Cost + Residual) ×	.00450	10.8%
(Cap Cost + Residual) ×	.00475	11.4%
(Cap Cost + Residual) ×	.00500	12.0%
(Cap Cost + Residual) ×	.00525	12.6%

(Source: Automotive Lease Guide)
*Yield will vary slightly with length of lease

Deal papers

Sample Dealer
Bill of Sale
(page 1).

PRE-COMPUTED INTEREST
MOTOR VEHICLE CONTRACT AND SECURITY AGREEMENT

Buyer's Name Joe Carbuyer

Buyer's Residence or Business Address

1234 Shady Lane
Carcity, CA 12345

Co-Buyer's Name and Address

Date of Contract July 2, 1998

Agreement No. 12345678

Stock No. 12345

Sales Agent John Q. Salesman

Date 7/2/98

Source LOCAL

Home Phone (123) 456-7890
Business Phone

Contract language: The words 'we', 'us' and 'our' refer to the creditor (seller) named below or, upon assignment, its assignee. The words "you" and "your" refer to the buyer and co-buyer if any named herein. We sell you the vehicle described below on credit. The credit price is listed as the "Total Sale Price". The "Cash Price" is also listed. By signing this contract you choose to buy the "vehicle" on credit and agree to pay Total Sale Price, according to schedules, terms and agreements on the front and back of this contract. If this contract is signed by a buyer and co-buyer, each person is individually and jointly responsible for all contract agreements.

SEE OTHER SIDE OF THIS CONTRACT FOR ADDITIONAL TERMS AND AGREEMENTS:

NEW/USED	YEAR	MAKE	CYL	DIESEL/ GAS/OTHER	BODY STYLE	MODEL	ODOMETER READING
new	1998	BigM	6	gas	coupe	BigM Mobile	25
VIN	COLOR	TRIM	TIRES	TRANS	KEY	LIC NO	ROS NO.
0BHBM01A2BC012345	russet red	beige cloth			no	new	1234567

APR (Credit Cost as Annual Rate)	Finance Charge (Amount credit will cost)	Amount Financed (Amount of credit provided to you)	Total of Payments (Amount you will have paid after completing all scheduled payments)	Total Sale Price (Total cost of purchase on credit, including down payment of $3,371.00)
9.50%	34,902.29	018,847.51	023,769.98	027,120.98

Payment Schedule		
Number of Payments	Amount of Payments	When Payments Are Due
One Payment of	None	
One Payment of	None	
59 Payments	395.83	Monthly, beginning July 2, 1998
One Final Payment	395.83	June 2, 2003

Security: You are giving a security interest in goods purchased.
Late Charges: For payments more than 10 days late you may be charged 5% of the late amount.
Prepayment: If you pay early, you may be entitled to a refund of a portion of the finance charge.
See contract documents for additional information regarding nonpayment, default, any required prepayment in full before the scheduled date and prepayment refunds.

Notices: Names and addresses of all persons to whom notices required or permitted by law to be sent are at top of this form. If you are buying a used vehicle with this contract, as indicated in the description of the vehicle above, federal regulation may require a special buyers guide to be displayed on the window.
(THE INFORMATION ON THE WINDOW FORM FOR THIS VEHICLE IS PART OF THIS CONTRACT. INFORMATION ON THE WINDOW FORM OVERIDES ANY CONTRARY PROVISIONS IN THE CONTRACT.)

Sample Dealer Bill of Sale (page 2).

STATEMENT OF INSURANCE

NOTICE: No person is required as a condition of financing the purchase of a motor vehicle to purchase, or negotiate, any insurance through a particular insurance company, agent or broker.

You have requested Seller to include in the balance due under this agreement the following insurance. Insurance is to expire: WITH__ BEFORE__ AFTER__ the due date of the final installment. Buyer requests seller to procure insurance upon the described property against fire, theft, and collision for the term of this agreement. Any insurance will not be in force until accepted by the insurance carrier.

$ none ded. comp., fire & theft ____ mos. $ none
$ none deductible collision ____ mos. $ none
Bodily injury $____ limits ____mos. $ none
Property damage $____ limits ____mos. $ none
Medical ____ mos. $ none
TOTAL VEHICLE INSURANCE PREMIUMS $ none

The foregoing declarations are hereby acknowledged.
Date 7/2/98 Seller _____
Buyer _____

Broker Fee Disclosure

If this Contract reflects the retail sale of a new motor vehicle the sale is not subject to a fee received by an autobroker unless the following is checked:
____ Name of Autobroker receiving fee, if applicable:
_____
_____

NOTICE OF RESCISSION RIGHTS

If buyer signs here, the provisions of paragraph "K" on the reverse side shall be applicable to this contract.
Buyer's Signature _____
Co-Buyer's Signature _____

CREDIT INSURANCE AUTHORIZATION AND APPLICATION

You voluntarily request the credit insurance checked below, if any, and understand that such insurance is not required. You acknowledge disclosure of the cost of such insurance and authorize it to be included in the balance payable under the security agreement. Any returned or refunded credit insurance premiums shall be applied to sums due under this contract. Only the persons whose names are signed below are insured.

Credit Life_____ Mos. Premium $ none
Joint Life_____ Mos Premium $ none
Credit Disability_____ Mos. Premium $ none
Total Credit Insurance Premiums $ none (b)

__ You want Credit Life Insurance
X You do not want Credit Life Insurance
__ You want Credit Disability Insurance (Primary Buyer Only)
X You do not want Credit Disability Insurance
__ You want Joint Credit Life Insurance

You are applying for the credit insurance noted above. Your signature means you agree that: (1) You are not eligible for insurance if you have reached your 65th birthday. (2) You are eligible for disability insurance only if working for wages or profit 30 hours a week or more on the Effective Date. (3) Only Primary Buyer is eligible for disability insurance.

DISABILITY INSURANCE MAY NOT COVER CONDITIONS FOR WHICH YOU HAVE SEEN A PHYSICIAN IN THE LAST 6 MONTHS (see "Total Disabilities Not Covered" in your policy or certificate).

Date 7/2/98 Primary Buyer _____
Age 29
Date____ Co-Buyer _____
Age____

Itemization of Amount Financed				3 INSURANCE AMOUNTS	
1	A. Cash Price Motor Vehicle and Accessories (A)	$19,160.00		Total premiums per Statement of Insurance (a + b)* (3)	none
	1. Cash Price Vehicle	$16,680.00	4	STATE SMOG CERT. FEE (4)	none
	2. Cash Price Accessories	$2,480.00	5	TOTAL (1 to 4) (5)	$22,218.59
	B. Document Preparation Charge (B) (not a governmental fee)	$35.00	6	A. Trade-In	
	C. Smog Fee Paid to Seller (c)	none		Yr: 91 Make: Jeep	
	D. Sales Tax (on A+B+C)	$1,538.59		Model: Wrangler (A)	$3,000.00
	E. Luxury Tax	none		VIN: 0BMBH01A2BC012345	
	F. Service Contract (optional)*	$1,020		Odometer: 83,853	
	G. Other	none		B. Less Pay Off (B)	$4,628.92
	To whom paid_____			C. TRADE-IN (A less B) (C)	-$1,628.92
	TOTAL CASH PRICE (A to G) (1)	$21,798.59		D. Deferred downpayment due before 2nd installment (D)	none
	*We may retain, or receive, a portion of amount.			E. Manufacturer's Rebate (E)	none
2	PUBLIC FEE AMOUNTS			F. Remaining cash downpmt. (F)	$5,000
	A. License (A)	$420.00		TOTAL DOWNPAYMENT (6C+D+E+F) (6)	$3,371.08
	B. Registration (B)	incl	7	AMOUNT FINANCED (5 less 6) (7)	$18,847.51
	C. Smog Impact Fee (C)	none			
	TOTAL OFFICIAL FEES (A+B+C)(2)	$420.00			

Sample Dealer
Bill of Sale
(page 3).

PREPAYMENT REFUND: Any refund for prepayment in full will be calculated as follows:
___ according to the Actuarial Method ___ according to the Sum of the Periodic Time Balances X according to the Rule of 78s
(If no selection is checked calculation method for prepayment refund will be the Sum of the Periodic Time Balances)

VEHICLE USE: X Personal, Family or Household ___ Commercial or Agricultural

OFFICIAL FEES (Not Financed): The Buyer will pay estimated fee(s) of $10.00 to appropriate public authority to transfer registration after full payment.

OPTION: ___ You pay no finance charge if the amount financed, item 7, is paid in full on or before _____.
19_____. SELLER'S INITIALS:_____

SELLER ASSISTED LOAN: FOR THIS LOAN, BUYER MAY BE REQUIRED TO PLEDGE SECURITY AND WILL BE
OBLIGATED FOR THE INSTALLMENT PAYMENTS ON SECURITY AGREEMENT AND LOAN.
Proceeds of Loan - From N/A   Amount $ none Finance Charge $ none Total $ none
Payable none installments of $ none $ none from this loan is described in (6D) above.

SERVICE CONTRACT (Optional) You request a service contract with the following company for the term indicated. Cost is
shown in item (1F) above.
Company BigManufacturer AllProtect Term 100,000 miles or 84 Months
Buyer Joe Carbuyer (X) *Joe Carbuyer*

If you have a complaint regarding this sale, try to resolve it with the seller. Complaints regarding unfair or deceptive practices or
methods by the seller may be referred to the city attorney, the district attorney, or the Department of Motor Vehicles, Division of
Investigations and Occupational Licensing for your state. After this contract is signed, seller may not alter financing or payment
terms unless you agree in writing to the change. You do not have to agree to any change, and it is an unfair or deceptive
practice for the seller to make unilateral changes.

Buyer's Signature (X) *Joe Carbuyer*   X_____

The minimum public liability insurance limits provided in law must be met by everyone purchasing a vehicle. If you
are uncertain whether your insurance policy will cover your newly bought vehicle in an accident, contact your
insurance agent.

*Warning: Your present policy may not cover collision damage or may not provide for full replacement costs for the
vehicle being bought. If you do not have full insurance coverage, supplemental coverage for collision damage may
be available through your insurer or through selling dealer. Unless otherwise noted, coverage you obtain through
dealer protects only the dealer, usually up to amount of unpaid balance after vehicle repossession and resale. For
advice on full coverage to protect you in event of loss or damage to vehicle, contact your insurer or its agent. The
buyer shall sign to acknowledge that buyer understanding these public liability terms and conditions.*

s/s   (X) *Joe Carbuyer*   X_____

NO COOL-OFF PERIOD
This state's law does not provide for a cancellation period for vehicle sales. You cannot later cancel this contract simply for
change of mind, belief the vehicle costs too much, or desire to acquire a different vehicle. After you sign below, you may only
cancel this contract with the seller's agreement or for a legal cause, such as fraud or misrepresentation.

Buyer acknowledges (1) before signing agreement buyer read both sides of agreement and received a legible copy, completely
filled-in, and that (2) buyer received a copy of all other documents buyer signed during negotiations pertaining to contract.

Buyer's Signature (X) *Joe Carbuyer*   **Co-Buyer's Signature** X_____
Seller BigManufacturer   Address 123 AUTOMALL WAY
          By *Jan* (Jan Salesmanager) Title Mgr.

Truth In Lending Copy
1. This document is to be provided to BUYER prior to signing 2. Both buyer and seller sign this copy after contract is signed.

BigMCredit

Vehicle Lease Agreement

Approval #1234567

Lease Date: 7/1/98

Lessor Name & Address	Lessee Name & Address
BigDeal BigM Motors 1234 AutoMall Way Cartown, CA 12345	Owen Forlong 123 Payment Street Cartown, CA 12345
Dealer Number: (123) 456-7890	County: Car County

Garaging Address, if different: _____

"You", (the "Lessee" and "Co-Lessee", if applicable) agree to lease from Lessor the following Vehicle. If more than one Lessee executes this Lease, each Lessee will be individually liable for the entire amount owing under this Lease. Lessor will assign this Lease and leased Vehicle to BigManufacturer Credit, a division of MegaManufacturer Credit, Inc., or its assignee (the "Holder").

Lease Vehicle Description

Year: 1998
Make: BigM
Model: BigMMobile

Gross Trade-in Allowance: $2,471.02
Amount Owed on Trade-in: $.
Net Trade-in Allowance: $2,471.02

Payment Calculations

1. Amount Due at Lease Signing or Delivery:
$2,471.02

3. Other Charges (not part of monthly payment)

A. Turn-in Fee $250.00
B. _____ $_____
C. **TOTAL** $250.00

2. Monthly Payments

A. Your first monthly payment in the amount of $326.77 is due July 1, 1998, followed by monthly payments in the amount of $326.77 due on the 1st of every month, beginning August 1, 1998.
B. The total of your monthly payments: $11,763.72

4. Total of Payments (amount paid by lease end):

$14,157.97

(Section 1 plus Section 2(B) plus Section 3(C) less Section 5(A)(3) less Section 5(A)(4))

2. Amount Due at Lease Signing or Delivery Itemization

A. Amount Due at Lease Signing or Delivery:

1. Capitalized Cost Reduction:	$1,578.98
2. Taxes on Cap Cost Reduction:	$130.27
3. First monthly payment:	$326.77
4. Refundable Security Deposit:	$none
5. Title Fees:	$none
6. Registration Fees:	$435.00
7. License Fees:	$none
8. Sales Tax:	$none
9. _____ : $	
10. _____ : $	
11. **TOTAL:**	$2,471.02

B. How the Amount Due at Lease Signing or Delivery is Paid:

1. Net Trade-in Allowance:	$2,471.02
2. Rebates, Non-Cash Credits:	$none
3. Cash Amount:	$none
4. Credit Card Amount:	$none
5. **TOTAL :**	$2,471.02

6. How Your Monthly Payment is Determined:

A. Gross Capitalized Cost. Agreed Vehicle value $19,800 and any other items you pay for over the term of the lease (including fees, taxes, insurance, outstanding prior balance, service agreements etc.)	$20,250
B. Capitalized Cost Reduction. The total of any cash, noncash credit, rebate or net trade allowance you pay in order to reduce Gross Capitalized Cost	$1,578.98
C. Adjusted Capitalized Cost. Used to calculate your Base Monthly Payment	$18,671.02
D. Residual Value. Vehicle value at lease end	$11,871.90
E. Depreciation and Amortized Amounts. Amount charged for value decline in vehicle during normal usage, and other items paid over term of lease	$6,799.12
F. Rent Charge. Amount charged beyond amortized amounts and depreciation	$4,068.20
G. Base Monthly Payment Total. Depreciation + Amortized Amounts + Rent Charge	$10,867.32
H. Lease Term. Number of months of your lease	36
I. Base Monthly Payment	$301.87
J. Sales Tax	$24.90
K. Total Monthly Payment	$326.77

Early Termination: You may face a sizable charge for ending this lease before the expiration of its term, up to several thousand dollars, depending on when the lease is terminated. The earlier the lease is ended, the greater this charge will probably be.

7. Excessive wear charges may apply based on standards of normal use and excess miles beyond 45,000 allowed lease term miles with maximum odometer reading of 45,002 at a charged rate of 50.12 per mile.

YES ___ NO _X_ Mileage allowed includes 0 over the lease term purchased at $0.12 per mile, included in your payment.

8. Lease-End Purchase Option. You have the option to purchase this vehicle at the end of the lease term for the purchase price of $11,871.90 and a fee of none and all amounts owed under this lease, plus any official fees and taxes due in connection with vehicle purchase.

9. Other Important Terms. See the front and back of this lease for additional information on early termination, your options in purchasing the vehicle, maintenance responsibilities, warranties, insurance, security interests if applicable, and late and default charges.

Typical Title
Information.

STATE NAME
CERTIFICATE OF TITLE
(MOCKUP ONLY - NOT A REAL TITLE)

12345678901

AUTOMOBILE
VEHICLE ID NUMBER   YR / MODEL / MAKE   PLATE NUMBER
1ABCD23E4CT567890   93 BIGM   123456
BODY TYPE MODEL   AX   UNLADEN WEIGHT   FUEL
UT   G
TRANSFER DATE   FEES PAID   REGISTRATION EXP.   ISSUE DATE
                                  $371   10/8/98   11/3/97
YR FIRST SOLD / CLASS / YR   MO   EQUIPMT/TRUST NO.
                                  BK   93   BY
MOTORCYCLE ENGINE NO.   ODOMETER DATE   ODOMETER READING
                                                            10/07/1997   51324 MI
                                                            ACTUAL MILEAGE

REGISTERED OWNER(S)
TOM CAROWNER
1234 TOM'S DRIVE
CARCITY, STATE 12345

I certify under penalty of perjury under the laws of This State, that the signature(s) below releases interest
in the vehicle.

1a._____   X_____
          DATE   SIGNATURE OF REGISTERED OWNER
1a._____   X_____
          DATE   SIGNATURE OF REGISTERED OWNER

Federal and State law requires you state mileage upon transfer of ownership. Failure to complete or
providing a false statement may result in fines and/or imprisonment.
Odeometer now reads _____ miles and to the best of my knowledge reflects the actual mileage
unless one of the following statements is checked.
WARNING: ___ Odometer reading not actual mileage
                          ___ Mileage exceeds odometer's mechanical limits
I certify under penalty of perjury under the laws of This State the foregoing is true and correct.

DATE	TRANSFEROR/SELLER SIGNATURE(S) X	DATE	TRANSFEREE/BUYER SIGNATURE(S) X
PRINTED NAME OF AGENT SIGNING FOR A COMPANY		PRINTED NAME OF AGENT SIGNING FOR A COMPANY	

IMPORTANT
READ CAREFULLY
Any change of Lienholder (security interest holder) must be reported to the Department of Motor Vehicles
within 10 days.
LIENHOLDER(S)

                                                            2. X_____
                                                            Signature releases interest in vehicle.
                                                            Date of release_____

                                                                                      TS 12345678

                              123456

The Bank

Name and Address of Borrower(s)	Officer Initials	Loan No.	Date
John Carshopper 123 ABC St. Carcity STATE 12345			7/1/98

PROMISSORY NOTE, DISCLOSURE STATEMENT AND SECURITY AGREEMENT

In this Promissory Note, Disclosure Statement and Security Agreement the words Borrower, you, your and yours mean each and every person signing this document. The words Bank, We, Us, Our and Ours refer to The Bank.
(Office)___Carcity____
For value received, the undersigned Borrower, if more than one jointly and severally promise to pay to the order of The Bank at its office at ___Carcity_____ the sum of _Five Thousand Eight Hundred Thirty Three and 80/100_____ Dollars ($_5,833.80___) payable according to the payment schedule and subject to terms and conditions set forth in this document.

ANNUAL PERCENTAGE RATE	FINANCE CHARGE	FINANCED AMOUNT	PAYMENTS TOTAL
13.085%	$1,049.31	$4,784.49	$5,833.80

Your payment schedule:

Number of Payments	Amount of Payments	Due Dates
36	$162.05	monthly beginning 7/1/98

INSURANCE: Credit life insurance and credit disability insurance is not required to obtain credit and won't be provided unless you sign and agree to the terms. By signing this document you acknowledge you have the option of assigning any other policies you own or may procure for the purpose of covering this loan.

Type	Premium	Signature
Credit / Single / Life / Joint	N/A	I want credit life insurance_____
Credit Life & Disability Insurance	N/A	I want credit life and disability insurance_____

Security: You're giving a security interest in:
_x_ Goods purchased
___ Funds on deposit with us
___ Your principal place of residence
_x_ Other _1993 Ford Escort_____
___ This is an unsecured loan
Filing Fee $ _____
Late Charge: If required payment is not made within 10 days of the due date, the charge will be 5% of the late payment.
Prepayment: If you pay off your loan before it is due you may receive a refund of part of the finance charge.
SECURITY: Borrower grants The Bank a security interest in the property described below, and any proceeds coming into your possession by virtue of insurance. Such property is subject to all terms, provisions and conditions set forth on the reverse side. Borrower warrants that the property is owned by them and is free of all other liens and security interests except_____.
Property (collateral): _____1993 Ford Escort #1ABCD23D4ST567890

Itemization of amount financed (TOTAL FINANCED$ 4,784.49)

$ 4,777.29	Amount given to borrower directly	$	Amount paid on your account		
Amounts paid on your behalf:					
$ 7.20	State documentary stamps	$	State Intangible Tax	$	Filing and recording fees
$	Insurers	$	Credit Bureaus	$	Prepaid Finance Charge

The finance charge is interest calculated over the term of the loan at the rate of 12.5% per annum plus a fee of $50.00 as reimbursement for costs of loan origination.

Borrowers make the agreements set forth in all sections of this document and acknowledge they received a fully completed copy prior to signing.

EXECUTED under seal on the date first written above

_____ Witness   _____Borrower's Signature (SEAL)
_____ Witness   _____Borrower's Signature (SEAL)

Lemon laws

LEMON LAWS

Who do lemon laws apply to?	Generally speaking, those whose (typically new) cars have repeatedly been in for service, yet remain essentially unfixable or have numerous needed repairs off the bat.
What if I have a used car or I'm leasing?	Some states have lemon laws that pertain to lessees and used car buyers.
When do lemon laws kick in?	This varies state by state. In California, for example, lemon law presumption requires:
	1. The manufacturer or its agents to have made four or more attempts to repair the same problem (or the vehicle's been out of service more than 30 days, all totaled, while being repaired for any number of problems).
	2. The four repair attempts or 30 days out of service have occurred within 12 months of the vehicle's delivery to the consumer or 12,000 miles on the odometer, whichever occurs first.
	3. The problems are covered by the warranty; substantially reduce the vehicle's use, value, or safety to the consumer; and are not caused by abuse of the vehicle.
	4. If required by the warranty materials or by the owner's manual, the consumer has directly notified the manufacturer about the problem(s).
What might be my next step, after efforts with the manufacturer?	An arbitration board can force the manufacturer into action—but look for a state-sponsored arbitration board over an industry-sponsored one.
Where can I find out more information?	Try your state attorney general's office or consumer affairs division.

Insurance

AutoCity Consumer Insurance
1234 Consumer Pkwy.
Auto City, CA 12345
(123) 456-7890

```
            AUTOMOBILE INSURANCE RATE QUOTATION

                                           Page 1 of 1
                                           July 1, 1998

JOE CARBUYER

The following annual premiums are subject to any changes
that might arise from a revision of rate schedule.

AUTO                     USE                 MILEAGE
1 1993 BigM Bigmobile    Pleasure            7,000

COVERAGES                LIMIT OF LIABILITY   PREMIUMS
----------------------------------------------------AUTO 1--
LIABILITY                $300,000 each accident  $692.80
MEDICAL PAYMENTS         $5,000                  $ 58.40
UNINSURED MOTORISTS      $300,000 each accident  $238.40
DAMAGE TO YOUR AUTO      Actual Cash Value less
                          a deductible of:
                         AUTO 1
1. Collision             $500                   *$387.40
2. Other than
   Collision Loss        $500                    $215.20
TOWING AND LABOR         $   75 each disablement $  6.40
----------------------------------------------------------
*WAIVER OF COLLISION DEDUCTIBLE                  INCLUDED
INCREASED TRANS EXPENSES $30 DAY/$900 MAXIMUM    $ 20.00
----------------------------------------------------------
                 TOTAL PREMIUM THIS AUTO    $1,618.40

TOTAL ANNUAL PREMIUM          $1618.40

Up to ten installments are permitted under the installment
plan. Details will be included with your policy.
```

TYPICAL COVERAGE CATEGORIES

1. Bodily injury liability	For injuries that you might cause to another person
2. Medical or PIP (Personal Injury Protection)	For injuries that can occur to occupants of the policyholder's vehicle (PIP can sometimes cover medical payments, loss of wages, and the expense of replacing services usually performed by a person who can't perform them due to an accident.)
3. Property damage liability	For damage you do to another person's property
4. Collision	For damage that happens to the car of the policyholder from a collision

5. Comprehensive	For damage to the car of the policyholder when a collision with another car isn't involved (may cover fire, theft, earthquake, floods, falling objects, etc.)
6. Uninsured motorist coverage	For treatment of policyholder injuries after a collision with a driver who doesn't have insurance

A

Abuse to car, 188
Acquisition fees, 119, 120,
    210, 212, 224, 314, 431
Add-ons, 46, 96, 98, 100, 224,
    252, 295–301
Advertising association fees,
    212, 431
Affordability, 13–18, 289–90.
    See also Budgeting
    compromising and, 21
    wants versus needs,
        13–15
    worksheets, 15–17
        monthly payment, 60,
        447
Aftersell, 96, 98, 100, 295–301,
    431
Airbags, 38–39
Air conditioning, 299–300
Annuals, 26, 45, 49, 73
Antilock brakes, 40, 45, 431
APR (annual percentage
    rate), 154, 212, 215,
    432
"As is" sales, 170, 280, 283,
    344
Auctions, used car, 111–12,
    167, 168, 175–80
    buying tips, 176–79
    clear titles, 115, 178, 183,
        435
    process at, 179–80
    pros and cons of buying at,
        177
    sample prices, 176
Auto-By-Tel, 92–93, 147
Automatic transmission, 47
Automotive News, 73, 85
AutoSite, 74, 76, 441
AutoVantage, 92

B

Back end fees, 96, 98, 100,
    295–301, 433
Bank auto loans, 141–44,
    150–52, 260. *See also*
    Loans
    sample, 318, 463
Bank Rate Monitor, 27, 124,
    148, 440
Best-selling cars, 19–20
Better Business Bureau, 89,
    95, 346–47
Bill of Sale, 280, 305–8,
    458–60
Blue Book. *See Kelley Blue Book*
Bodily injury liability
    insurance, 351, 353,
    432, 465
Brakes, 45, 190
    antilock, 40, 45, 431
Brokers, 93–94
Budgeting, 14–15, 53–68
    financing cost scale,
        18, 447
    major cost areas, 57
    payment methods,
        54–57
    setting budget, 15–18
    software, 15
    spending limits,
        289–90
    techniques for, 59–60
    timetable for, 58–59
    what to avoid, 21–22
    worksheets, 15–17, 60,
        445–47
Buyers Guide, 171
Buyer's remorse, 332–33
Buying a car, process of
    22–24
Buying services, 92–93, 100

467

The *Unofficial Guide*™ Reader Questionnaire

If you would like to express your opinion about buying or leasing a car or this guide, please complete this questionnaire and mail it to:

The *Unofficial Guide*™ Reader Questionnaire
Macmillan Lifestyle Group
1633 Broadway, floor 7
New York, NY 10019-6785

Gender: ___ M ___ F

Age: ___ Under 30 ___ 31–40 ___ 41–50 ___ Over 50

Education: ___ High school ___ College ___ Graduate/Professional

What is your occupation?

_____

How did you hear about this guide?
___ Friend or relative
___ Newspaper, magazine, or Internet
___ Radio or TV
___ Recommended at bookstore
___ Recommended by librarian
___ Picked it up on my own
___ Familiar with the *Unofficial Guide*™ travel series

Did you go to the bookstore specifically for a book on buying or leasing a car? Yes ___ No ___

Have you used any other *Unofficial Guides*™?
Yes ___ No ___

If Yes, which ones?

_____
_____
_____

What other book(s) on buying or leasing a car have you purchased?

_____

_____

_____

Was this book:
___ more helpful than other(s)
___ less helpful than other(s)

Do you think this book was worth its price?
Yes ___   No ___

Did this book cover all topics related to buying or leasing a car adequately?   Yes ___   No ___

Please explain your answer:

_____

_____

_____

Were there any specific sections in this book that were of particular help to you?   Yes ___   No ___

Please explain your answer:

_____

_____

_____

On a scale of 1 to 10, with 10 being the best rating, how would you rate this guide? ___

What other titles would you like to see published in the *Unofficial Guide*™ series?

_____

_____

Are *Unofficial Guides*™ readily available in your area?   Yes ___   No ___

Other comments:

_____

_____

_____

_____

Get the inside scoop...with the
Unofficial Guides™!

The Unofficial Guide to Alternative Medicine
   ISBN: 0-02-862526-9   Price: $15.95
The Unofficial Guide to Buying a Home
   ISBN: 0-02-862461-0   Price: $15.95
The Unofficial Guide to Buying or Leasing a Car
   ISBN: 0-02-862524-2   Price: $15.95
The Unofficial Guide to Childcare
   ISBN: 0-02-862457-2   Price: $15.95
The Unofficial Guide to Cosmetic Surgery
   ISBN: 0-02-862522-6   Price: $15.95
The Unofficial Guide to Dieting Safely
   ISBN: 0-02-862521-8   Price: $15.95
The Unofficial Guide to Eldercare
   ISBN: 0-02-862456-4   Price: $15.95
The Unofficial Guide to Hiring Contractors
   ISBN: 0-02-862460-2   Price: $15.95
The Unofficial Guide to Investing
   ISBN: 0-02-862458-0   Price: $15.95
The Unofficial Guide to Planning Your Wedding
   ISBN: 0-02-862459-9   Price: $15.95

All books in the *Unofficial Guide*™ series are available at your local bookseller, or by calling 1-800-428-5331.

About the Author

Donna Howell can tell you everything you need to know about buying or leasing a car. Donna is a consumer journalist based in Los Angeles who recently survived her own car-shopping adventure. Donna has been a television news reporter and a producer at *Inside Edition* and *American Journal*. She holds a Master's degree from Columbia University's Graduate School of Journalism, where she was a duPont Fellow and Pulitzer Traveling Fellow. Donna loves to take road trips in her car; her favorite drives include Malibu and Decker canyons.